THEODORE ROOSEVELT'S HIST★RY OF THE ✦ UNITED STATES

THEODORE ROOSEVELT'S
HIST★RY
OF THE UNITED STATES

HIS OWN WORDS,
Selected and Arranged by

Daniel Ruddy

Smithsonian Books

HARPER
An Imprint of HarperCollins*Publishers*
www.harpercollins.com

THEODORE ROOSEVELT'S HISTORY OF THE UNITED STATES. Copyright © 2010 by
Daniel Ruddy. Foreword copyright © 2010 by Edmund Morris. All rights
reserved. Printed in the United States of America. No part of this book may
be used or reproduced in any manner whatsoever without written permission
except in the case of brief quotations embodied in critical articles and reviews.
For information, address HarperCollins Publishers, 10 East 53rd Street, New
York, NY 10022.

HarperCollins books may be purchased for educational, business, or
sales promotional use. For information, please write: Special Markets
Department, HarperCollins Publishers, 10 East 53rd Street, New York, NY
10022.

Designed by Mary Austin Speaker

Library of Congress Cataloging-in-Publication Data
Roosevelt, Theodore, 1858–1919.
    Theodore Roosevelt's history of the United States : his own words /
selected and arranged by Daniel Ruddy.—1st ed.
        p.   cm.
Includes bibliographical references and index.
    ISBN 978-0-06-183432-5
        1. United States—History. 2. United States—Politics and government.
3. Roosevelt, Theodore, 1858–1919—Political and social views. I. Ruddy,
Daniel. II. Title.
    E178.R786   2010
    973.91'1092—dc22   2009034370

10 11 12 13 14   OV/RRD   10 9 8 7 6 5 4 3

To my father and mother

The other day [Senator Cushman K. Davis] remarked, anent an investigating committee on which he and Cabot were both serving, that it reminded him of Byron's description of Mitford: "He had every qualification of a historian: extreme partiality and abundant wrath."

—Theodore Roosevelt,
letter to his sister Anna, May 27, 1894

Impartiality does not mean neutrality. The best historian must of necessity take sides.

—Theodore Roosevelt,
letter to George Otto Trevelyan,
January 25, 1904

The greatest historian should also be a great moralist. It is no proof of impartiality to treat wickedness and goodness on the same level.

—Theodore Roosevelt,
"History as Literature," address
delivered to the American Historical
Association in Boston, December 27, 1912

CONTENTS

FOREWORD

by Edmund Morris

HISTORIOGRAPHY—THE REVIEW OF CHANGING FASHIONS IN historical thought over the decades—has much in common with keeping tabs on the stock market. In the 1970s, when guilt about the Vietnam era was causing an epidemic of antiwar, anticapitalist, and even Marxist revisionism in the writing and teaching of American history, some of the more savvy professors on campus were said to be exchanging a hot investment tip: "Sell Woodrow Wilson and buy Theodore Roosevelt."

Immediately after his death in 1919 at the age of sixty, TR (the first of our chief executives to be known by his initials) was generally considered to be the greatest American president since Lincoln and Washington. If his stature was slightly less than theirs, that was because they were both identified with nation-changing wars. But TR's presidency (1901–1909) was entirely peaceful, once he had suppressed a nasty insurrection in the Philippines, bequeathed to him by his predecessor William McKinley. In 1906, he became the first American to win the Nobel Peace Prize. It was awarded to him for his masterly mediation of the Russo-Japanese War and his behind-the-scenes diplomacy defusing the Morocco crisis, which nearly accelerated the advent of World War I.

However admirable these achievements, and however selfless he was in declining a third term (which he could have had on a silver platter in 1908), Theodore Roosevelt did not strike the historians of the 1920s as a heroic or tragic figure. Then as now, heroism and tragedy were essential for sentimental veneration. He was seen rather as a popular and courageous reformer who had revived the power of government to prosecute abusive corporations, made the conservation of national resources a top administrative priority, fomented a progressive revolution within the Republican Party, and, in countless arm-waving homilies, preached the gospel of good citizenship. (If you visit Theodore Roosevelt Island, his densely forested memorial in the Potomac River between Washington and Rosslyn, Virginia, you will come upon him standing white and colossal, his fist forever aloft, haranguing the birds and mosquitoes.)

He was also remembered as the impatient man of action who cut the Panama Canal after "centuries of conversation" by other nations, who ushered the United States onto the world stage as an industrial and naval power, and who, in his postpresidential years, became a passionate crusader for early American involvement in World War I.

For these and many other positive reasons—including his sheer personal lovability, which even Woodrow Wilson acknowledged was hard to resist—Theodore Roosevelt was posthumously considered worthy of a place on Mount Rushmore, alongside the Emancipator and the Father of the Nation. But in 1931, Henry F. Pringle published a witty, well-researched, and devastatingly iconoclastic biography that almost overnight sent TR's reputation among historians plummeting. At that time, with fascism and Nazism rising in Europe, pacific isolationism crudescent at home, and a new, Democratic Roosevelt emerging as a contender for the presidency, TR's rhetoric—with its glorification of armed strength, its Golden Rule morality, and its Darwinian disdain for the viability of lesser, weaker nations—began to sound dated.

Not until 1958, the centennial of his birth, did a new generation of biographers show that he had been a much more substantial statesman than was commonly supposed. Edward Wagenknecht's *The Seven Worlds of Theodore Roosevelt* (recently reissued) put him on a par with

Thomas Jefferson as a multicultural Renaissance man. Carleton Putnam's sober, scholarly *Theodore Roosevelt: The Formative Years, 1858–1886* portrayed a born leader rising through sheer personal and intellectual force. Howard K. Beale's massive *Theodore Roosevelt and the Rise of America to World Power* demolished Pringle's argument that TR was an impulsive, flag-waving jingoist in foreign affairs. William Harbaugh's *Power and Responsibility* (1961), while not uncritical of some aspects of TR's "big stick" diplomacy, recognized the greatness of his achievement in domestic policy.

A stream of books and monographs in the last quarter of the twentieth century confirmed the upward trend in TR's historical stature. The trend has continued ever since, and today, his stock is once again high, while that of the vainglorious Woodrow Wilson finds fewer and fewer buyers.

This is not to say that TR doesn't still have his fierce detractors. One amateur historian has even tried to blame him for Pearl Harbor. Critics of what is perceived, in our current gender-obsessed historiography, as the Rough Riders' "masculinity" are especially shrill. They are unlikely to be quieted anytime soon by his lusty indictments of the "sublimated sweetbreads" and "logical vegetarians" who choose the sanctity of academe, rather than the open arena of political life, to pipe their soprano criticism.

It is to the credit of Daniel Ruddy, the coauthor in this book, that he has courageously ignored his partner's stern advice: "Impartiality does not mean neutrality. The best historian must of necessity take sides." Mr. Ruddy recognizes that when a man as articulate as Theodore Roosevelt is expressing opinions, intrusive comment is superfluous. We have become so inured, in recent decades, to the decline in the ability of our leaders to say what they think in clear, strong, unambiguous language (Barack Obama being the exception that proves the rule) that TR's amazing force of utterance, and the virtuosity of his written prose style, almost make one recoil. Here is a bona fide intellectual, diplomat, and politician without peer coming at us like a great roaring steam train from the past. Daniel Ruddy has nimbly leaped aboard, and managed, without TR's noticing, to control the locomotive's speed and itinerary. But at no point does he "take sides," in the manner of so many smug scholars who impose their presentism on those who lived in other times, and often as not understood life better.

Daniel Ruddy is modest in calling this book *Theodore Roosevelt's History of the United States*, since his own scholarship in assembling the text is formidable. As somebody who has spent the better part of thirty years studying TR's gigantic output of prose and speech, I have nothing but admiration for a young historian's ingenuity in putting together what is, in a sense, a Rooseveltian *apologia pro vita sua*, with not one word of other argument interpolated.

The most he has permitted himself to do, as editor and compiler, is what every serious historian since Plutarch has done to improve expression: group sentences and paragraphs and thought sequences that naturally belong together. Although TR may have said or written a thing one day and developed it further a year later, or ten years later, he was a remarkably consistent man. This text not only sounds like him, it is him.

Ladies and gentlemen—the twenty-sixth president of the United States.

Edmund Morris is the fauthor of The Rise of Theodore Roosevelt; Theodore Rex; Dutch: A Memoir of Ronald Reagan; *and* Beethoven: The Universal Composer. *He will shortly publish the third volume of his life of Theodore Roosevelt.*

INTRODUCTION

The Historian on Mount Rushmore

Theodore Roosevelt's History of the United States was compiled and arranged to provide readers with a unique account of American history from 1776 to 1918. Roosevelt's ideas about our nation's past can be found sprinkled throughout his voluminous writings, but these "pearls of thought" (as the reviewer of one of his books described them in 1888[1]) have never before been pulled together in one place. This book gathers them together into a coherent whole, enabling the reader to understand Roosevelt's historical perspective in its entirety, and revealing, as a by-product, the patterns of his thought.

Roosevelt, as an observer of history, was a hanging judge who did not hesitate to deliver unambiguous verdicts on the leaders and events of our nation's past. Adding needed flavor to a subject that is too often discussed in bland academic language, he keeps us awake with bold, colorful, and sometimes controversial opinions that cut to the core, capturing the essence of obscure and prominent historic figures alike: Thomas Paine was a "filthy little atheist"; Andrew Jackson "not more than half civilized"; John Tyler "a politician of monumental littleness"; Winfield Scott "a good general, but otherwise a wholly absurd and flatulent personage"; Millard Fillmore "a pompous old non-entity." William McKinley had "no more backbone than a chocolate éclair." William Jennings Bryan was "a professional yodeler, a human trombone"; William Howard Taft a "flubdub with a streak of the common and the second rate in him"; and Woodrow Wilson "a true logothete."

After reading this sample of Roosevelt's verbal bombs we may admit that his opinions are interesting and entertaining. Nonetheless, it is fair to ask why they should matter to us more than anyone else's opinions. There are a few reasons they should.

President John F. Kennedy once told the historian David Herbert Donald that "no one has a right to grade a president—not even poor James Buchanan—who has not sat in his chair."[2] With membership in the exclusive club that includes all living and dead American presidents, Roosevelt meets President Kennedy's high standard and, in fact, exceeds it. Of the forty-three men who have served as president, only two could legitimately claim to be professional historians: Theodore Roosevelt and Woodrow Wilson.

Both men wrote extensively about American history before becoming president, but Wilson's historical works are remembered most for their "incompleteness," "superficiality," and "antique, affected style."[3] Roosevelt's works, in contrast, withstand the test of time. Two of them—*The Naval War of 1812* and *The Winning of the West*—are classics that enjoy the respect of scholars even today, more than a century after they were written. Roosevelt's qualifications to make historical judgments are undoubtedly strong, yet there remains an understandable concern: Theodore Roosevelt was a political partisan, and therefore his historical views are biased and questionable.

It is true that Roosevelt was a staunch Republican for nearly his entire public career, and yes, he detested the Democratic Party *as a whole*, but he did *not* hate all individual Democrats. His admiration for Andrew Jackson and Thomas Hart Benton clearly shows this distinction, and highlights an important fact: Roosevelt judged men mainly by their actions. "Like all men of good sense," said Roosevelt, "I judge men by the aggregate of their deeds." As one might expect, the actions he favored tended to occur more often in the Republican Party than in the party he opposed. Put another way, party affiliation was more *effect* than cause as a factor in his historical judgments.

Because Roosevelt judged leaders against their actual performance in the public arena, it was not inconsistent for him to embrace one pillar of the Democratic Party (Andrew Jackson) and simultaneously reject the other (Thomas Jefferson). Roosevelt admired Jackson for his bold sincerity, valiant prowess on the field of battle, and staunch devotion to the Union. But when he measured Jefferson's record against this standard of Jacksonian strength, he recoiled in disgust at what he saw: duplicitous intrigues for personal gain, cowardly avoidance of the battlefield, and wrongheaded hostility toward the concentration of government power needed to advance national interests. Roosevelt despised Jefferson as an undesirable anti-Jacksonian—a "scholarly, timid, and shifty doctrinaire" whose influence on the United States was, on the whole, "very distinctly evil."

Party affiliation influenced Roosevelt's historical judgments at the margins, but it never guaranteed either his praise or his condemnation; other yardsticks mattered much more. His own loyalty to the Grand Old Party (this was not assured after he left the presidency in 1909) certainly did not stop him from criticizing fellow Republicans and their antecedents among the extinct Federalists and Whigs. Even his hero Abraham Lincoln came up short in certain areas, notably for negligence in allowing "great corruptionist" army contractors to thrive during the Civil War. This was no small criticism, since Lincoln's acceptance of wartime corruption as a price to be paid for defeating the South helped sow the seeds for many of the ugly weeds of public corruption that sprang up after the war, creating a defining problem for Roosevelt's generation to solve. Ironically, Roosevelt's political career as an energetic reformer was built on his participation in cleaning up the mess that, by implication, he criticized Lincoln for helping to create.

Bearing in mind that Roosevelt had the biases any historian will have—we each naturally see American history from our own perspective—his opinions are nonetheless credible and arguably of some importance because he is, if nothing else, the only historian on Mount Rushmore. As someone who actually shaped history himself, and did so favorably enough to reach this lofty perch, he speaks to us with a unique authority[4] that even fellow "statesman-historians" such as Woodrow Wilson and Henry Cabot Lodge do not possess.

When we climb up to the summit of Mount Rushmore to see American history from the height Roosevelt occupies, we also step back in time. Today, the United States bestrides the world as a superpower, and that fact shapes—and distorts—our perspective on American history. In Roosevelt's youth America's position in the world was different. Although the nation had undergone rapid industrialization after the Civil War, it still lacked a modern navy and army, and it could not yet match the military power of the major European nations. Roosevelt saw American history through the lens of that weakness. He could not forget the profound national humiliation that occurred during the War of 1812 when a few thousand British troops burned the United States' weakly defended capital.

Nowadays, this almost forgotten event from the distant past seems of minor importance, but for Roosevelt, who defined his love of country as "the pride of personal possession," it cut deeply into his hypersensitive, patriotic soul. The lesson to be learned from this perception gap—the different perspectives of different generations—is that while the facts of history are fairly constant, we as observers are not. We inevitably judge the past through the prism of our own time and our own society, emphasizing what is important to us at the expense of what was important to the generations that came before us, forgetting that our generation does not have a monopoly on historical truth.

The value of viewing American history through Theodore Roosevelt's eyes comes from the freshness that this view provides. It is an old view, but it is new to us. By stepping back in time to his generation to see the past through his eyes, we can look anew at George Washington, Thomas Jefferson, Abraham Lincoln, and others, and cast aside the limitations of our more distant modern observation point. Roosevelt's life spanned the years 1858 to 1919. As a consequence, he was roughly 100 years closer to the events of our early history than we are today. That proximity has advantages. A closer object is usually more easily seen, as long as there is also enough room for perspective.

What did Roosevelt see when he looked back in time? He saw a great nation that had struggled mightily to be born and to grow in strength, held down by leaders like Thomas Jefferson, John C. Calhoun, and Jefferson Davis—men he believed were narrow-minded, shortsighted, intriguing politicians who put their own interests above those of the nation, forming the ideological core of "a party that tried to destroy the Union."[5] Opposing them, he saw broad-minded, farsighted, constructive statesmen (men like George Washington, Alexander Hamilton, and Abraham Lincoln) dragging a reluctant nation into the future against a strong, persistent, and irresponsible antinational tide.

As Theodore Roosevelt discusses these and other leaders—who run the gamut from traitor to hero—he also indirectly tells us something about himself and his deepest values. Although this book is not a biography, we get to see a side of Roosevelt that cannot be fully revealed in the published narratives of his life. By focusing on Roosevelt the historian, we see how deeply he thought about America's past and the important influence it had upon his worldview and decision making. Feeling the emotion that informs each of his historical judgments, we also discover the deep, personal connection he had with those who occupied the White House before him.

Above all else, his reverence for Abraham Lincoln shines through. "I thought of Lincoln, shambling, homely, with his strong, sad, deeply furrowed face, all the time," said Roosevelt about his own time in the White House. "I saw him in the different rooms and in the halls. For some reason or other he was to me infinitely the most real of the dead Presidents." Roosevelt worshipped Lincoln, not just for his commitment to a lofty ideal and the political skill he demonstrated in attaining it, but most of all for Lincoln's courage in sacrificing his life for that ideal. Roosevelt wanted to be his generation's Lincoln, to achieve, if circumstances permitted, something as significant and noble. To that end, he built his own political career on Lincoln's spirit and principles.

When we explore Roosevelt's connections to the past, we begin to see that he was not an isolated figure in American history, but rather an important link in a continuum reaching back to the birth of the United States. He understood this and knew that the chain of history extending behind him could be used to advantage if the lessons it held were unlocked and acted upon. Analytical in his thinking, Roosevelt observed, "We can never learn how to produce a certain effect unless we know rightly what the causes were that produced a similar effect in the past." Seen in this light, his political calculations and policy initiatives were not merely random choices or momentary whims, but rather well-thought-out actions that he carefully weighed against benchmarks from the past—benchmarks he had created for himself through inductive analysis of the constants and variables that had produced particular historical outcomes.

The key to understanding Roosevelt the historian and statesman is to remember that, deep down, he was also a scientist, at least in how his mind worked, in its analytical tendencies, in the way it habitually classified people and events as though they were birds, butterflies, or some other species. As a young man at Harvard he had wanted to pursue a career in natural science, but had put that desire aside to become a man of letters and politics. Nonetheless, his highly disciplined, scientific mind remained fully charged when he turned his full attention to study the history of mankind, which was a laboratory as fascinating and vast as the natural world. But unlike a scientist, Roosevelt was concerned with more than observing what he called "the mere operation of nature's laws"; he wanted to activate what he learned for his own advantage and that of the United States.

We can see Roosevelt's practical use of historical knowledge[6] plainly enough in his landmark Northern Securities antitrust suit of 1902, whereby he intentionally picked a fight with the plutocratic financiers of the day. Seventy years before TR wrapped himself in this warm cloak of "trust busting," Old Hickory had won reelection in 1832, when he started a popular political war against the Bank of the United States, which, like the "trusts" of TR's time, was the stranglehold of "money power." Roosevelt was not blind to the forces that had fueled Jackson's electoral victory. He knew that he would increase his own chances of political success if he followed Jackson's example and pulled down on the powerful lever of economic populism. Striking out at the "trusts" instead of the Bank of the United States, Roosevelt substituted a new "malefactor of great wealth" for an old one, and so easily won the White House in 1904, using a campaign formula that Jackson had tested and proved.[7]

"Trust busting" helped Roosevelt secure another term in the White House, but he pressed forward with this well-thought-out activism for reasons that went beyond self-interest. He was sincerely worried about the "ugly forces" he felt seething "beneath the social crust." The deadly labor riots that had flared up regularly during his life gave him reason to be concerned, but the volcanic eruption of widespread popular enthusiasm in the summer of 1896 for William Jennings Bryan ("the cheapest faker we have ever had proposed for President") confirmed his fears that the riots were not isolated events.

In these ominous, dark clouds of brewing unrest he saw a storm as violent and destructive as the French Revolution forming on the horizon. As a responsible statesman, as a historian who understood that wise leadership could have prevented revolutions in the past, as someone who always tried to be "farsighted" (this was one of his favorite expressions), he acted to remove—or at least suppress—the conditions that might trigger a similar revolution on American soil.

In this sense, Roosevelt's "trust busting" was a public declaration that the United States would learn from history. A loud reform agenda, spearheaded by his antitrust actions, would show the discontented masses that he was on their side. Instead of showing them "let them eat cake" indifference of the French noblesse prior to 1789, he would punish "malefactors of great wealth" on their behalf. He knew this approach was a departure from the Grover Cleveland and William McKinley model of presidential leadership, which sought to maintain an uneasy status quo when confronted by societal turbulence, but that is what he wanted: to increase the public perception[8] that he, unlike his immediate predecessors in the White House, was truly independent of Wall Street power brokers. If he succeeded (and we can see now that he did succeed), he would not only enhance his own political fortunes, but also stabilize and strengthen the nation as it made the transition into a new century of "boundless possibilities" (this expression reflecting TR's optimism about the nation's future is imprinted inside every new passport issued today to American citizens[9]).

Roosevelt's thoughts on his presidency and on the entire period of his adult life appear in Chapters 5 and 6, along with some of his uncanny predictions about the future. These interesting observations reveal his disdain for Winston Churchill ("a dreadful cad"); his contempt for Woodrow Wilson ("his soul is rotten through and through"); his fear of William Randolph Hearst ("the most potent single influence for evil we have in our life"); his disappointment in Oliver Wendell Holmes ("I could carve out of a banana a judge with more backbone"); his belief that an armed conflict with Japan was inevitable ("it will be rapine on their part, not war"); and his warning of a coming revolution in Russia ("a red terror which will make the French Revolution pale").

Roosevelt's insights into men and events were not always original,[10] but in all cases he drew the picture of the nation's past in bold, vivid colors, painting characters as shrewdly as a novelist. He deplored the "dry-as-dust" historians of his day who mindlessly compiled facts into unreadable books. In his own work he tried, as he put it, "to make dead men living before our eyes," to breathe life into American history. Honoring Roosevelt's desire that books about history be made interesting and readable, this book uses his own entertaining, thought-provoking opinions to jolt us awake to our nation's past.

Once we are awakened, it is also instructive to pay attention to what Roosevelt *did not say* about America's past. We expect the outspoken Roosevelt to have something to say about every important person and event since the birth of the republic, but this was not the case. There are gaps of silence in the historical record that cry out for explanation. The Explanatory Notes attempt to account for the most notable of these gaps and answer, for example, why Roosevelt has left us no judgments about the career of John Adams or the presidency of Ulysses Grant. While the gaps themselves are open to interpretation, the process of thinking through why they exist can be revealing.

It is noteworthy, for instance, that in all the praise Roosevelt showers on Alexander Hamilton he says nothing of substance about Hamilton's financial genius or his impact on the American economy. This, and other evidence,[11] suggests that Roosevelt (like Andrew Jackson) possessed only a rudimentary understanding of finance and economics. His failure to elaborate on Hamilton's financial genius supports the notion that Roosevelt's economic policies and "trust busting" sprang not from expert knowledge but rather from political, moral, and historical considerations. Implicit insights such as this, coupled with those that spring explicitly from Roosevelt's own words, help make this book the vehicle for a multidimensional interpretation of Roosevelt as both historian and political actor.

An analysis of Roosevelt's perspective on America's past reveals much about the man and the nation he led, and it also shows us something else. History is not merely the road behind us that led us to where we are today. It is an active force that lives in the present when it is brought to life and used by an influential leader to help steer the nation on its journey forward. Many presidents have looked to American history for navigational guidance to determine the best road ahead for the United States, but none have relied on it more[12] than Theodore Roosevelt, the historian who studied history to make history.

A Note on the Text and Format

This book grew out of a simple what-if question: "If you could talk with any living or dead person about American history, who would it be?" My answer was Theodore Roosevelt. I had come across a handful of his biting historical observations and was intrigued enough to think to myself how interesting it would be to talk with him about the nation's past, to hear more of his opinions and to understand why he thought the way he did. Knowing I could not resurrect the dead, I decided to do the next best thing and create Roosevelt's part of the conversation. The result is this book, which is based exclusively on Roosevelt's own words, as documented in the Source Notes. I have not added a single word of my own to the main text, reserving my comments for the Explanatory Notes.

To create this book, I first went through the historical record in order to identify and extract all relevant material—Roosevelt's own words, which he either spoke or wrote about American history. Direct quotes were taken from his letters (he is estimated to have written roughly 150,000), his books (there are twenty volumes in the National Edition of his collected works), his speeches, newspaper articles about him, and the individual accounts of those who recorded what they heard Roosevelt say in their presence. After this mass of material was gathered, it was sorted according to subject (for example, all of Roosevelt's comments about Thomas Jefferson were gathered together for use as potential building blocks to construct the section on Jefferson). Individual paragraphs within specific sections were then created, stitching together Roosevelt's own words to create a readable fabric that captured, as well as possible, the most important and interesting elements of Roosevelt's point of view.

As part of this stitching process, I have had in some cases to alter the original punctuation by, for example, combining fragments of different sentences. I have retained every instance where Roosevelt used an exclamation point (!) or *italics*, however, because these stylistic elements represent emphasis he wanted to communicate to the reader. In most cases I have also retained Roosevelt's original usage choices: for example, keeping "especial" instead of replacing it with "special." But in order to be consistent throughout the text, I have fully spelled out words that he sometimes abbreviated, for example, choosing to use "though" in every relevant instance instead of "tho" here and there. For consistency's sake, I have also standardized the spelling, capitalization, and usage of a few other words.

Moreover, I have made every effort to avoid any distortion (an obvious danger, given the method I used to create this book) and give the best possible representation of Roosevelt's beliefs, *as I saw those beliefs*. The words used in the body of this book all belong to Roosevelt, but the selection and arrangement of his words are mine. Another person given the same task that I took on would inevitably have made different choices. He or she would have emphasized things that I downplayed and downplayed things that I emphasized. In that sense, no book like this can be a truly pure representation of Roosevelt's historical perspective.

Keeping all this in mind, consider this book a time machine of sorts. By reading it you can transport yourself back in time to a pleasant summer evening in the year 1918, to Roosevelt's home Sagamore Hill, high on a hill in Oyster Bay, New York. Pull up a rocking chair and join TR on the veranda, with its fine view of Long Island Sound. After you settle in you can engage him in the topic that interests you most—American history. It is a good topic to bring up because it interests him, too; in fact, it is one of his passions. You will not be able to say much as he rambles on about Thomas Jefferson, "that slippery demagogue," and Abraham Lincoln, "my great hero," and other notable people and events, but that is OK. You came to listen, not to talk.

DANIEL RUDDY
SAN FRANCISCO,
CALIFORNIA

PART I
On Writing History

History as Literature

Our People Have Filled a Vacant Continent

How completely the old life of fifty years ago has vanished! It is melancholy to read of the great mountain forests now growing bare of life, in the very places where as late as 1891 I saw the elk in herds of thousands, where in 1889 I killed eight different kinds of game on a single trip. How the antelope have gone! I remember that on the Little Missouri they were as numerous as ever they had been. On the prairie flats I saw them in bands. It was a pretty wild country at the time, the buffalo not yet gone, and an occasional scrap with Indians, of a mild sort.

For a number of years I spent most of my time on the frontier, and lived and worked like any frontiersman. The wild country in which we dwelt and across which we wandered was in the far West. My ranch was in North Dakota, close to the eastern edge of Montana, and I could not begin to put on the map all my travels around there. I was just in time to see the last of the real wilderness life and real wilderness hunting. We guarded our herds of branded cattle and shaggy horses; hunted bear, bison, elk, and deer; and established civil government, and put down evil-doers, white and red, on the banks of the Little Missouri, and among the wooded, precipitous foothills of the Bighorn, exactly as did the pioneers who a hundred years previously built their log cabins in the valley of the Great Smokies.

I think of it all as I pass down the river.[1] It is my first trip on the Mississippi. After speaking at Keokuk this morning, we got aboard this brand-new stern-wheel of the regular Mississippi type and started downstream. I, of course, felt an almost irresistible desire to ask the pilot about Mark Twain. There is no hold to the boat, just a flat bottom with a deck, and on this deck a foot or so above the water stands the engine room, completely open at the sides and all the machinery visible as you come up to the boat. It is pleasant going down the Mississippi. The river is beautiful, at least in my eyes—the forests and the corn fields, the islands, the shifting muddy currents, and just at this moment a glorious sunset.

How wonderful in its rapidity of movement has been the history of our country, compared with the history of the Old World. For untold ages this river had been flowing through the lonely continent, not yet very greatly changed since the close of the Pleistocene. During all these myriads of years the prairie and the forest came down to its banks. The immense herds of the buffalo and the elk wandered along them season after season, and the Indian hunters on foot or in canoes trudged along the banks or skimmed the water. Probably a thousand years saw no change that would have been noticeable to our eyes. Then three centuries ago began the work of change.

For a century its effects were not perceptible. Just nothing but an occasional French fleet or wild half-savage French Canadian explorer passing up or down the river or one of its branches in an Indian canoe, then the first faint changes, the building of one or two little French fur traders' hamlets. Then the change came with a rush. Our settlers reached the headwaters of the Ohio, and flatboats and keelboats began to go down to the mouth of the Mississippi, and the Indians and the game they followed began their last great march to the west. For ages they had marched back and forth, but from this march there was never to be a return.

Of course, our whole national history has been one of expansion.[2] This expansion is not a matter of regret, but of pride. Under Washington and Adams we expanded westward to the Mississippi. Under Jefferson we expanded across the continent to the mouth of the Columbia. Under Monroe we expanded into Florida, Andrew Jackson being the most prominent figure in the acquisition, and then into Texas and California, and finally, largely through the instrumentality of Seward, into Alaska. We have a magnificent empire west of the Mississippi, and it is being developed by Americans of the very best stamp. I only wish one of my forefathers had been a trapper and crossed the continent in 1808!

Gouverneur Morris thoroughly appreciated the marvelous future that lay before the United States. Writing in 1801, he says: "As yet we crawl along the outer shell of our country. The interior excels the part we inhabit in soil, in climate, in everything. The proudest empire in Europe is but a bauble compared to what America *will* be, *must* be, in the course of two centuries, perhaps one!" In all the history of mankind there is nothing that quite parallels the way in which our people have filled a vacant continent with self-governing commonwealths, knit into one nation. Save only the preservation of the Union itself, no other task has been so important as the conquest and settlement of the West. Our greatest statesmen have always been those who believed in the nation—who had faith in the power of our people to spread until they should become the mightiest among the people of the world.

The Barbarian Virtues

I have been part of all that I describe. I have seen the things and done them. I have herded my own cattle. I have killed my own food. I have shot bears, captured horse thieves, and "stood off" Indians. The descriptions are literally exact. Few eastern men have seen the wild life for themselves. I heartily enjoy this life, with its perfect freedom, for I am very fond of hunting, and there are few sensations I prefer to that of galloping over limitless prairies, rifle in hand, or winding my way among the barren, fantastic, and grimly picturesque deserts of the so-called Bad Lands. You would be amused to see me, in my broad sombrero hat, fringed and beaded buckskin shirt, horsehide chaparajos or riding trousers, and cowhide boots, with braided bridle and silver spurs.

Every now and then I meet friends of my youth who incline to praise me for having gone into politics, or for living in the country in very simple manner with a fair-sized family of small children, instead of whirling about in that social life of New York which in recent years has had its summer center at Newport. I always explain to these good people that they might just as well praise me for having cared to ride horseback and go hunting in the Rocky Mountains, instead of sitting in a corner and knitting. Personally, the life of the Four Hundred, in its typical form, strikes me as being as flat as stale champagne.

I used to hunt at Hempstead. The members of the Four Hundred who were out there rode hard and well, and I enjoyed riding to hounds with them. But their companionship before and afterward grew so intolerable that toward the end I would take a polo pony and ride him fourteen miles over before the hunt and fourteen miles back after the hunt, rather than stay overnight at the club.

Glory and honor give what riches can never give. The architects of a nation's material prosperity do much, but they can never do as much as the men who build up the structure of glorious memories and traditions which forms the rare inheritance of a mighty and masterful people. The victories of peace are great, but the victories of war are greater. No merchant, no banker, no railroad magnate, no inventor of improved industrial processes, can do for any nation what can be done for it by its fighting men.[3] It is better for a nation to produce one Grant or one Farragut than a thousand shrewd manufacturers or successful speculators.

One of the prime dangers of civilization has always been its tendency to cause the loss of virile fighting virtues, of the fighting edge. When men get too comfortable and lead too luxurious lives, there is always a danger lest the softness eat like an acid into their manliness of fiber. The barbarian, because of the very conditions of his life, is forced to keep and develop certain hardy qualities which the man of civilization tends to lose. Unless we keep the barbarian virtues, gaining the civilized ones will be of little avail.[4] Oversentimentality, oversoftness, washiness, and mushiness are the great dangers of this age and of this people.

We believe in waging relentless war on rank-growing evils of all kinds. The man who does nothing cuts the same sordid figure in the pages of history, whether he be cynic, or fop, or voluptuary. There is little use for the being whose tepid soul knows nothing of the great and generous emotion, of the high pride, the stern belief, the lofty enthusiasm, of the men who quell the storm and ride the thunder. It is war-worn Hotspur, spent with hard fighting, he of the many errors and the valiant end, over whose memory we love to linger, not over the memory of the young lord who "but for the vile guns would have been a soldier." Every public servant, no matter how valuable—and not omitting Washington or Lincoln or Marshall—at times makes mistakes.

Peace is not the end. Righteousness is the end. When the Savior saw the money-changers in the Temple he broke the peace by driving them out. At that moment peace could have been obtained readily enough by the simple process of keeping quiet in the presence of wrong. But instead of preserving the peace at the expense of righteousness, the Savior armed himself with a scourge of chords and drove the money changers from the Temple.

I do not want to see Christianity professed only by weaklings. I want to see it a moving spirit among men of strength. The non-resistance of the Christians in *Quo Vadis* made me so angry! The non-resistance of good people always does. Christianity was saved in Europe solely because the peoples of Europe fought. If the peoples of Europe in the seventh and eighth centuries, and on up to and including the seventeenth century, had not possessed a military equality with, and gradually a growing superiority over, the Mohammedans who invaded Europe, Europe would at this moment be Mohammedan, and the Christian religion would be exterminated. From the hammer of Charles Martel to the sword of Sobieski, Christianity owed its safety in Europe to the fact that it was able to show that it could and would fight as well as the Mohammedan aggressor.

A politician who really serves his country well, and deserves his country's gratitude, must usually possess some of the hardy virtues which we admire in the soldier who serves his country well in the field. Far better it is to dare mighty things, to win glorious triumphs, even though checkered by failure, than to take rank with those poor spirits who neither enjoy much nor suffer much, because they live in the gray twilight that knows not victory nor defeat. I feel we cannot too strongly insist upon the need of the rough, manly virtues. A nation that cannot fight is not worth its salt, no matter how cultivated and refined it may be. Peace is a goddess only when she comes with sword girt on thigh.

I Claim to Be a Historian

I do wish people would learn history. They won't learn, or at any rate only a little, partly because they do not care to read history that is not pleasant. A number of women teachers in Chicago are credited with having proposed, in view of war, hereafter to prohibit in the teaching of history any reference to war and battles. Intellectually, of course, such persons show themselves unfit to be retained as teachers a single day, and indeed unfit to be pupils in any school more advanced than a kindergarten. Any teachers, in school or college, who occupied the position these foolish, foolish teachers have sought to take, would be forever stopped from so much as mentioning Washington and Lincoln because their lives are forever associated with great wars of righteousness.

True teachers of history must tell the facts of history. To learn anything from the past it is necessary to know, as near as may be, the exact truth. It is an absolute disqualification for a historian when it is once settled beyond doubt that he deliberately perverts the truth. Next to truth-telling, the essential attribute of a book is that one shall be able to read it.[5] Otherwise, it might as well be written in cuneiform. Many learned people seem to feel that the quality of readableness in a book is one which warrants suspicion. Indeed, not a few learned people seem to feel that the fact that a book is interesting is proof that it is shallow.

In a very small way I have been waging war with their kind on this side of the water for a number of years. We have a preposterous little organization called I think the *American Historical Association,* which, when I was just out of Harvard and very ignorant, I joined. Fortunately I had enough good sense, or obstinacy, or something, to retain a subconscious belief that, inasmuch as books were meant to be read, good books ought to be interesting, and the best books capable in addition to giving one a lift upward in some direction. After a while it dawned on me that all of the conscientious, industrious, painstaking little pedants, who would have been useful people in a rather small way if they had understood their own limitations, had become because of their conceit distinctly noxious. They solemnly believed that if there were only enough of them, and that if they only collected enough facts of all kinds and sorts, there would cease to be any need hereafter for great writers, great thinkers.

The great historian has vision and imagination, the power to grasp what is essential and to reject the infinitely more numerous non-essentials, the power to embody ghosts, to put flesh and blood on dry bones, to make dead men living before our eyes. In short, he must have the power to take the science of history and turn it into literature,[6] not merely a huge string of erudite treatises on minute points of inter-est only to specialists. In any great work of literature the first element is great imaginative power. No quantity of photographs will ever be equivalent to one Rembrandt.

If great events lack a great historian, and a great poet writes about them, it is the poet who fixes them in the mind of mankind, so that in after-time importance the real has become the shadow and the shadow the reality. Shakespeare has definitely fixed the character of the Rich-ard III of whom ordinary men think and speak. Keats forgot even the right name of the man who first saw the Pacific Ocean, yet it is his lines which leap to our minds when we think of the "wild surmise" felt by the indomitable explorer-conqueror from Spain when the vast new sea burst on his vision.

History is not a panegyric. There are always men who consider it unpatriotic to tell the truth, if the truth is not very flattering. But aside from the morality of the case, we can never learn how to produce a cer-tain effect unless we know rightly what the causes were that produced a similar effect in times past. The greatest historian should also be a great moralist. It is no proof of impartiality to treat wickedness and goodness as on the same level. It is a wicked thing to be neutral between right and wrong. The best historian must of necessity take sides. All that is necessary is that the faults and merits of each party should be set forth clearly and fairly. I do not think partisanship should ever obscure the truth.

It is sometimes the habit to speak of America as a nation with a future only, not with a past. No matter who makes this assertion it is a falsehood. Since I have been a boy and first studied the history of this country my veins have thrilled and tingled as I read of the conquest of this continent by the white race, the establishment of national independence, the building of the National Government, the long contest over slavery, the war for the preservation of the Union—these are the really great matters with which American history deals. To me, the history of the United States in all its phases and periods has been so absorbingly interesting that I am unable to understand what people mean when they say that they find it uninteresting.

It is an excellent thing to study the history of the great deeds of the past, and of the great men who did them, with an earnest desire to profit thereby so as to render better service in the present. There are few things more important than that the American of today should preserve a sense of the unbroken continuity of the nation's history.[7] History, taught for a directly and immediately useful purpose to pupils and teachers of pupils, is one of the necessary features of a sound education in democratic citizenship.

I have now been in politics for a long time, and I know political history fairly well. I have had on occasion to fight bosses and rings and machines, and have had to get along as best I could with bosses and rings and machines when the conditions were different. I have seen reform movements that failed and reform movements that succeeded and have taken part in both. In particular, I have been so placed as to see very much of the inside of the administrations of three presidents in addition to my own—that is, of Harrison, Cleveland, and McKinley.

I claim to be a historian,[8] and I speak simply in the spirit of one. My literary work occupies a good deal of my time, and I have on the whole done fairly well at it. My books so far published are *The Winning of the West, The Naval History of the War of 1812, The History of New York City, The Life of Gouverneur Morris*, and *The Life of Thomas Hart Benton*. Rather a formidable list, are they not? If I had time for literary work I would write, write, write.

Do you know what I should really like to do? I should like to get some position in a college where I could give lectures on United States history to graduates, and at the same time start to write a history of the United States. Although a Republican politician, I think I have learned to be able to do justice to men, that is, to state facts accurately no matter how much I may differ from them on questions of opinion. As regards most historical questions there is always room for a difference of opinion.

When I think of the kind of life I have led, the marvel is that I have gotten as far as I have. I have always expressed my opinions with great freedom,[9] and though I think I have grown fairly judicious now, this was certainly not the case years ago. There are plenty of printed statements I have made, some of them absolutely true, some of them true from my standpoint, but expressed in such a shape as legitimately to give offense. As I grow older and less hotheaded, I grow better able to take a fair view of men with whose political opinions I do not agree. I wish I could persuade the general public to take a broader view of me as a historian!

The Party That Tried to Destroy the Union

I am by inheritance and by education a Republican. A gentleman told me recently that he doubted if I would vote for the Angel Gabriel if found at the head of the Democratic Party, to which I responded that the Angel Gabriel would never be found in such company. Speaking quite dispassionately, and simply as a historian, the Democrats can be trusted to invariably walk in the darkness even when to walk in the light would be manifestly to their advantage. I do congratulate myself that my father was a Republican and that I am a Republican. It seems to me it would be a dreadful thing to have to live down being descended from Vallandigham, and I should mortally hate to have had men like Seymour and McClellan for ancestors.

Certainly, I would prefer to go with a party that has a record of which it is proud rather than to act with a party which has a record of which all honest men must be ashamed. We know that it is the party that tried to destroy the Union, that supported slavery, that favored greenbackism, that opposed putting the finances of the country on a sound basis, that has committed about every sin it was capable of committing.

As long as the history of our nation has lasted, the Democrats have been one and the same, from Jefferson, miscalled the Great; from Polk, the mendacious; through Pierce, the Copperhead; to Buchanan, who faced both ways. You can follow the record of their party from its inception down to this time. We have always had to thank Heaven that our opponent was the Democracy, for whenever we have committed a blunder they have capped it by committing two.

I do not propose to apologize for all that my party has done in time past. I say and I believe that my party, the Republican Party, has the grandest record of any that was ever on this continent; that it has been the salvation of this country; that its leaders, from Lincoln down, will rank on par with those of the Revolution. We are the party of moral ideas. I think we can say this much, Republicans have not always done well, but it will be an evil day when they do as badly as the Democrats. It is the party that had in it Alexander Hamilton, of the older days, that had Webster and Clay, the great party which has produced a Lincoln, the party of Seward and Chase. The Republican Party stands for the national idea.

A Notch Higher in the Scale

In speaking to my own countrymen there is one point upon which I wish to lay especial stress, that is, the necessity for a feeling of broad, radical, and intense Americanism. I believe, and I feel most people who live here do and ought to believe, that America is, on the whole, a notch higher in the scale than any other country, and an infinite number of notches higher than most other countries. The man in whom intense love of country is wanting is a very despicable creature, no matter how well equipped with all the minor virtues and graces, literary, artistic, and social.

The men who actually do the things best worth doing in American life are, as they always have been, purely, and usually quite unconsciously, American. The paths in which we have done the best work are precisely those where our work has been most original and our workers least hampered by Old World conventions and ideas. Yet there are small groups to whom all this does not apply. The vulgar rich who lack refinement naturally turn to countries where wealth, whether inherited or acquired, can buy them certain kinds of recognition which it cannot here, and so do their anti-types, the refined, fastidious people of weak fiber, the artists and literary men of more cultivation than intellect, and more intellect than character.

We produce some educated men who lack the virile qualities that he must needs possess who would swim in the bracing turbulent tide of democracy. Thus it comes about that the brainless woman of fashion or of would-be fashion flees to London or Paris as naturally as the émigré novelist himself. Thank Heaven Henry James is now an avowedly British novelist—the little emasculated mass of inanity. The Americans who make their home abroad are men too weak to make their way at home. The acquisition of a species of flaccid cosmopolitanism is one of the surest signs of a feeble nature.

The man who becomes Europeanized,[10] who loses his power of doing good work on this side of the water, and who loses his love of his native land, is not a traitor, but he is a silly and undesirable citizen. He is as emphatically a noxious element in our body politic as is the man who comes here from abroad and remains a foreigner. These permanent exiles are too feeble a folk to deserve more than an allusion. Besides, if they live abroad permanently, they simplify the solution of our difficult national problem by eliminating therefrom certain unimportant but objectionable factors.

I am constitutionally incapable of spending six month anywhere in Europe without becoming exceedingly homesick for America. Being a healthy man with a brain and tastes that any manly man should have, I of course would not wish to stay in Europe too long.

I Am Forever Reading

Books are the greatest of all companions. Ah, I like books—like to look at them, like to see them standing there so learnedly on the shelves, like to read them, review them, and would, if I had time, like to write them. I like to read better than anything else. I am forever reading. It is history, in great part, history with action to it, that most attracts me. I admit a liking for novels where something happens. I want ghosts who do things. I don't care for the Henry James "The Turn of the Screw" kind of ghosts. I want real sepulchral ghosts, the kind that knock you over and eat fire, ghosts which are ghosts and none of your weak shallow apparitions.

I am old-fashioned, or sentimental, or something, about books! Whenever I read one I want, in the first place, to enjoy myself, and, in the next place, to feel that I am a little better and not a little worse for having read it. It is only the very exceptional novel which I will read if He does not marry Her, and even in exceptional novels I much prefer this consummation. I am not defending my attitude. I am merely stating it. Of course, I know that the best critics scorn the demand among novels readers for "the happy ending."

Have you seen that London *Yellow Book*?[11] I think it represents the last stage of degradation. What a miserable little snob Henry James is. His polished, pointless, uninteresting stories about the upper social classes of England make one blush to think that he was an American. The book is simply diseased.

There is a good deal of Browning which I am wholly unable to read. I don't care a rap what the inner meaning of "Childe Roland" is. What I care for is the lift, the thrill the poem gives, the look of the desolate country, the dauntless bearing of the Knight, and the strange thoughts and sights and the squat blind tower itself. I used to ranch in the Bad Lands, and I always thought of the hills which lay like giants at a hunting when I saw the great buttes grow shadowy and awful in the dusk. I am very fond of "Prospice"—what can a poet do better than sound the praises of a good fighter and a good lover? "Love Among the Ruins," that has always been one of my favorites.

The two great fiction writers of today with a serious purpose are Tolstoy and Kipling, and each stands as typical for something in his own race and nationality. There are parts of Tolstoy I do like and there are parts of Kipling I do not. But after all it is the Slav, not the Englishman, who shows decadence. A sexual degenerate, the man has a diseased mind. He is not wholesome. He is not sane. *Kreutzer Sonata* is a fit supplement to his *My Religion*, for erotic perversion very frequently goes hand in hand with a wild and fantastic mysticism. When he again and again spends pages in descanting on the wickedness and folly of war, and passes over other vices without a word of reproach, he certainly in so far acts as the apologist for the latter.

Rudyard Kipling is a pleasant little man, bright, nervous, voluble, an underbred little fellow, with a tendency to criticize America to which I put a stop by giving him a very rough handling, since which he has not repeated the offense. But he is a genius, and is very entertaining. His wife is fearful, however. I hope it is true that Kipling is not to be admitted to the Players. There is no earthly reason that he should not call New York a pig trough,[12] but there is also no reason why he should be allowed to associate with the pigs. I fear he is at bottom a cad.

It always interests me about Dickens to think how much first-class work he did and how almost all of it was mixed up with every form of cheap, second-rate matters. I am very fond of him. There are innumerable characters that he has created to symbolize vices, virtues, follies, and the like almost as well as the characters in Bunyan, and therefore I think the wise thing to do is simply to skip the bosh and twaddle and vulgarity and untruth and get the benefit out of the rest. Of course, one fundamental difference between Thackeray and Dickens is that Thackeray was a gentleman and Dickens was not.

Dickens was an ill-natured selfish cad and boor who had no understanding of what the word "gentleman" meant and no appreciation of hospitality or good treatment. He was utterly incapable of seeing the high purpose and the real greatness which would have been visible all around him here in America to any man whose vision was both keen and lofty. He could not see the qualities of the young men growing up here, though it was these qualities that enabled these men to conquer the West and to fight to a finish the great Civil War.

I commend a careful reading of *Martin Chuzzlewit* to the pessimists of today.[13] Dickens remarked, with hearty geniality, great good taste, and careful abstention from exaggerated statement, that the republic was "so maimed and lame, so full of sores and ulcers, foul to the eye and almost hopeless to the sense, that her best friends turned from the loathsome creature with disgust." You will find it a real comfort to see what a well-meaning pessimist of the past thought of our people sixty-five years ago, and then think of the extraordinary achievement, the extraordinary gain, morally no less than materially, of those sixty-five years. Dickens can be read now with profit. Elijah Pogram, Hannibal Chollop, Jefferson Brick, and Scadder have their representative today, plenty of them. But it is rank folly to regard these as the only, or the chief, types in our national life.

We Must Strike Out for Ourselves

Unquestionably, and very naturally, we have not produced writers that stand relatively as high as our statesmen and soldiers. We have done a great deal more than we have written. After all, taming a continent is nobler work than studying *belles lettres*. Edgar Allan Poe is our one supereminent genius. In spite of the persistent effort to belittle him, and I must say it has come largely from New England, he still remains the most eminent literary character we have produced. Even as sane a man as Holmes declared Poe to be one-fifth genius and four-fifths guff. If any man was ever about five-fifths genius, that man is Poe. The next most eminent literary man I think we have produced is

Hawthorne, in spite of the fact that I do not care for him and seldom read him.

I have steadfastly endeavored to have employed the very best American artists where I have authority in the matter. When I was president, I cheerfully outraged the feelings of the ultra–Civil Service reformers by fishing a poet, Arlington Robinson, out of a Boston millinery store,[14] where he was writing metrical advertisements for spring hats, and put him in the Customs House. This got him a start, and he has done well ever since, although it is perhaps needless to say that Taft promptly turned him out. It was my son Kermit who first called my attention to Robinson's poems. He took a great fancy to them and gave a copy to his mother and another copy to me. I hunted him up, found he was having a very hard time, and put him in the Treasury Department. I am free to say that he was put in less with a view to the good of the government service than with a view of helping American letters, just as Walt Whitman and John Burroughs were given government positions. A poet may do far more for a country than the owner of a nail factory.

It is a very great disadvantage to any literature if it is modeled on foreign lines. Just as long as we were strictly colonial and strove to be mere parts of Britain we failed to produce anything which ranked as literature. It was only when, with Benjamin Franklin, we started to develop on our own lines that our literature began to be worth taking into account. Tolstoy wrote for mankind, but he wrote as a Russian about Russians, and if he had not done so he would have accomplished nothing. Our American writers, artists, dramatists, must all learn the same lesson until it becomes instinctive with them, and with the American public.

It is always better to be an original than an imitation. We must strike out for ourselves. We must work according to our own ideas, and must free ourselves from the shackles of conventionality, before we can do anything. When that day comes, we shall understand why a huge ornate Italian villa or French château or make-believe castle, or, in short, any mere inappropriate copy of some building somewhere else, is a ridiculous feature in an American landscape. We shall use statues of such a typical American beast as the bison—which peculiarly lends itself to the purpose—to flank the approach to a building like the New York Library, instead of placing there, in the worst possible taste, a couple of lions which suggest a caricature of Trafalgar Square.

The answer the neo-Greek or Roman purists make, when they say, "We can't build better, nor as well. All we can do is copy," is slanderous to the times and, at most, is a personal confession of their own incompetency. Native creative ability has been given no fair opportunity in America.

The names of many of our cities, towns, and villages are not only hideous but ludicrous. Such names as Memphis in Tennessee; Paris and Versailles in Kentucky; Syracuse, Elmira, and Utica in New York stand as high-water marks of hedge-school pedantry, utter poverty of imagination, and absurd, uneasy pretentiousness. They, and the men who tolerate them, cannot be sufficiently ridiculed.

As is natural, we have won our greatest success in the field of an abounding material achievement. We have conquered a continent. We have laced it with railways. We have dotted it with cities. Quite unconsciously, and as a mere incident to this industrial growth, we have produced some really marvelous artistic effects. Take, for instance, the sight offered the man who travels on the railroad from Pittsburgh through the line of iron and steel towns which stretch along the Monongahela. I shall never forget a journey I thus made a year or so ago. The morning was misty, with showers of rain. The flames from the pipes and doors of the blast furnaces flickered red through the haze. The huge chimneys and machinery were of strange and monstrous shapes. From the funnels the smoke came saffron, orange, green, and blue, like a landscape of Turner's. What a chance for an artist of real genius!

I know nothing at all, in reality, of art, I regret to say, but I do know what pictures I like. I am not at all fond of Rubens. He is eminently a fleshly, sensuous painter, and yet his most famous pictures are those relating to the Divinity. Above all, he fails in his female figures. Ruben's women are handsome animals, excellent as pictures of rich Flemish housewifes, but they are either ludicrous or revolting when meant to represent either the Virgin or a saint. I think they are not much better as heathen goddesses. I don't like a chubby Minerva, a corpulent Venus, and a Diana who is so fat that I know she could never overtake a cow, let alone a deer.

Perhaps the pictures I really get most enjoyment out of are the landscapes. They interest me far more than pictures of saints and madonnas. I suppose this sounds heretical, but it is true. I have really tried to like the holy pictures, but I can't. Rembrandt is by all odds my favorite. I am very much attracted by his strongly contrasting coloring, and I could sit for hours examining his heads—they are so lifelike and expressive.

Here Lies Wolfe Victorious

Life is a long campaign where every victory merely leaves the ground free for another battle, and sooner or later defeat comes to every man, unless death forestalls it. For the last six years I have worked very hard, but it has all been sedentary. I have grown both fat and stiff. I am feeling like a worn-out and crippled old man! Cabot, thank Heaven, is getting very gray about the hair and beard, and still continues to be a fit associate for me.

I am not in the least concerned as to whether I will have any place in history, and, indeed, I do not remember ever thinking about it. Without being able clearly to formulate the reasons for my philosophy, I am perfectly clear as to the philosophy itself: I want to be a straight and decent man and do good service. The life that is worth living, and the only life that is worth living, is the life of effort, the life of effort to attain what is worth striving for.

What does the fact amount to that here and there a man escapes oblivion longer than his fellows? Ozymandias in the desert—when a like interval has gone by who will know more of any man of the present day than Shelley knew of him? That queer creature Eugene Ware, my pension commissioner, once wrote the following verses on this very question:

History

Over the infinite prairie of level eternity,
Flying as flies the deer,
Time is pursued by a pitiless, cruel oblivion,
Following fast and near.
Ever and ever the famished coyote is following
Patiently in the rear;
Trifling the interval, yet we are calling it "History"
—Distance from wolf to deer.

Whether the distance between the wolf and the deer is a couple of inches or a quarter of a mile is not really of much consequence in the end. Be this as it may, our duty is the same: to strive toward the light as it is given to us to see the right, and take with iron front whatever fate befalls.

It is a good thing to die in the harness at the zenith of one's fame, with the consciousness of having lived a long, honorable, and useful life. After we are dead it will make not the slightest difference whether men speak well or ill of us. But in the days or hours before dying it must be pleasant to feel that you have done your part as a man and have not yet been thrown aside as useless, and that your children and children's children, in short all those that are dearest to you, have just cause for pride in your actions. When it comes our turn to go out into the blackness, I only hope the circumstances will be as favorable. There are many worse ways of ending than in battle. Of course, the finest of all epitaphs is "Here Lies Wolfe Victorious."[15]

PART II
Revolutionary Era
(1776-1824)

PART IX

Rochester Life

(1834–1841)

The Revolutionary War

One of the Great Historic Events

I do not want to be misled by national feeling, and yet I cannot help believing that the American Revolution was one of the great historic events which will always stand forth in the story of mankind.

The American colonies revolted from England because England declined to treat them as freemen with equal rights, but insisted that the American was subject to the Englishman. The European theory of a colony was that it was planted by the home government for the benefit of the home government and home people, not for the benefit of the colonists themselves. The colony was held to be the property of the mother country—property to be protected and well treated as a whole, but property nonetheless. The English and the Americans were not the subjects of a common sovereign, for the English themselves were the sovereigns, the Americans were the subjects. Whether their yoke bore heavily or bore lightly, whether it galled or not, mattered little. It was enough that it was a yoke to warrant a proud, free people in throwing it off.

England's treatment of her American subjects was thoroughly selfish, but that her conduct toward them was a wonder of tyranny will not now be seriously asserted. On the contrary, she stood decidedly above the general European standard in such matters, and certainly treated her colonies far better than France and Spain did, and she herself had undoubted grounds for complaint in, for example, the readiness of the Americans to claim military help in time of danger, together with their frank reluctance to pay for it.

However, admitting all that can be urged against them does not alter the fact—by none more freely conceded than by English historians nowadays—that on the main question the mutinous provinces were in the right. They were in many ways well treated, but they were never treated as equals, and they were sometimes treated badly. Yet, for all this, the feeling of loyalty was strong and hard to overcome. It is perfectly possible that if British statesmen had shown less crass and brutal stupidity, if they had shown even the wise negligence of Walpole,[1] this feeling of loyalty would have been enough to keep England and America united.

But the chance was lost when once a prince like George the Third came to the throne. It has been the fashion to represent this king as a well-meaning though dull person, whose good morals and excellent intentions partially atoned for his mistakes of judgment. But such a view is curiously false. His private life, it is true, showed very admirable but commonplace virtues, as well as the appalling littleness, barrenness, and stagnation, of the average British greengrocer. But in his public career he fairly rivaled the Stuarts in his perfidy, wrongheadedness, political debauchery, and attempts to destroy free government, and to replace it by a system of personal despotism.

Had England's king and Parliament been guided by the most far-seeing statesmen, and had causes of irritation been avoided, and a constantly increasing measure of liberty[2] and participation in the government allowed the colonists, it may have been that the empire would have been kept together. The revolt of America was not one of those historic events which are inevitable and foreordained. Wise statesmanship, and a temper in the British people willing to correspond, might have prevented it.

English writers are fond of insisting upon the alleged fact that America only won her freedom by the help of foreign nations. Such help was certainly most important, but, on the other hand, it must be remembered that during the first and vital years of the contest the Revolutionary colonists had to struggle unaided against the British. When the French court declared in our favor the worst was already over: Trenton had been won, Burgoyne had been captured, and Valley Forge was a memory of the past.

I have studied history a good deal, and it is a matter of rather grim amusement to me to listen to the praise bestowed on our national past at the expense of our national present. Beyond all question we ought to have fought that war, and it was very creditable to Washington and some of his followers and to a goodly portion of the Continental troops, but I cannot say that it was very creditable to the nation as a whole. There were two and a half millions of us then, just ten times as many as there were of the Boers in South Africa, and Great Britain was not a fourth as strong as she was in the Boer War, and yet on the whole I think the Boers made a good deal better showing than we did.

My forefathers, northerners and southerners alike, fought in the Revolutionary army, so I am not prejudiced against our Revolutionary people. But while they had many excellent qualities I think they were lacking as a whole in just the traits in which we are lacking today, and I do not think they were as fine, on the whole, as we are now. The second greatest Revolutionary figure, Franklin, to my mind embodied just precisely the faults which are most distrusted in the average American of the North today.

The Revolutionary leaders can never be too highly praised, but taken in bulk the Americans of the last quarter of the eighteenth century do not compare to advantage with the Americans of the third quarter of the nineteenth century. In our Civil War it was the people who pressed on the leaders, and won almost as much in spite of as because of them. But the leaders of the Revolution had to goad the rank and file into line. In the Civil War our people—a mere democracy—were better than in the Revolution, when they formed in part a provincial aristocracy.

If the Americans of the Revolution were not perfect, how their faults dwindle when we stand them side by side with their European compeers! What European nation then brought forth rulers as wise and pure as our statesmen, or masses as free and self-respecting as our people? There was far more swindling, jobbing, cheating, and stealing in the English army than in ours, and the outcome of the war proves that their nation as a whole was less resolute than our own. As for the other European powers, the faults of our leaders sink out of sight when matched against the ferocious frivolity of the French noblesse, or the ignoble, sordid, bloody baseness of those swinish German kinglets who let out their subjects to do hired murder.

The War Brought Forth Many Hard Fighters

It has been so habitual among American writers to praise all the deeds, good, bad, and indifferent, of our Revolutionary ancestors, and to belittle and make light of what we have recently done, that most men seem not to know that the Union and Confederate troops of the Civil War fought far more stubbornly and skillfully than did their forefathers at the time of the Revolution.

We certainly have overestimated the actual fighting qualities of the Revolutionary troops, and have never laid enough stress on the folly and jealousy with which the States behaved during the contest. A very slight comparison of the losses suffered in the battles of the Revolution with those suffered in the battles of the Civil War is sufficient to show the superiority of the soldiers who fought in the latter. No Revolutionary regiment or brigade suffered such a loss as befell the First Minnesota at Gettysburg, where it lost 215 out of 263 men, 82 percent. None of the European contests since the close of the Napoleonic struggles can be compared to it. The Light Brigade at Balaclava lost only 34 percent, or 247 men out of 673.

Had the Americans of 1776 been united, and had they possessed the stubborn, unyielding tenacity and high devotion to an ideal shown by the North, or the heroic constancy and matchless valor shown by the South, in the Civil War, the British would have been driven off the continent before three years were over. The truth is that in 1776 our main task was to shape new political conditions, and then to reconcile our people to them, whereas in 1860 we had merely to fight fiercely for the preservation of what was already ours. In the first emergency we needed statesmen, and in the second warriors, and statesmen and warriors were forthcoming.

The war brought forth many hard fighters, but only one great commander—Washington.[5] For the rest, on land, Cornwallis, Greene, Rawdon, and possibly Lafayette and Rochambeau, might all rank as fairly good generals, probably in the order named, although many excellent critics place Greene first. I have never felt that Cornwallis received justice, or that minor men like Tarleton and Grey received justice. (I am putting them all together from a military standpoint and without any intention at the moment of alluding to any possible differences in character among them.) It was not possible that Cornwallis should win, as events actually were, yet he defeated army after army, battling always against superior numbers, conquered the Southern States—though no man with his resources could have held them down—and succumbed only when neither he nor anyone else could have altered the final outcome by further resistance. His being hemmed in and forced to surrender to greatly superior forces at Yorktown was entirely Clinton's fault, and not at all his own.

Tarleton was a most dashing leader of dragoons in partisan warfare, and if he was often ruthlessly unsparing, so were many of his opponents. My admiration for that somewhat ruthless cavalryman has grown steadily. In my library his volume stands side by side with the memoirs of "Light-Horse Harry" Lee—where it belongs. Men are apt to consider as cruel any form of killing to which they are unaccustomed. The British thought the sharpshooters who picked off their officers were nothing short of murderers, and the Americans stigmatized any fight that was won by unsparing use of saber or bayonet, whether under Tarleton or Grey.

He Was at Heart a Lucifer

If a man is not decent, then the abler he is the more dangerous he is to the community. In the Revolutionary War one of the bravest and most brilliant soldiers during the early years of the contest was the man who has left his name as a byword of infamy to the nations for all time, the man who fought with distinguished gallantry in Canada, the man who led all the American forces in the great battle of Saratoga and left his leg on the field of victory. That man, with all his courage, all his daring, all his superb military genius, turned because the root of righteousness was not in him, sought to betray his comrades for money, and left the name of Benedict Arnold as a hissing forevermore.

What a base web was shot through the woof of his wild daring! He was at heart a Lucifer, that child of thunder and lover of the battle's hottest heat, and dreadful it is to think that when he fell his fall should have been, not that of the lightning-blasted Son of the Morning, but that of a mere Mammon or Belial.

We Have Bunker Hill

Now, about these Bunker Hill cannon. We have Bunker Hill, and I am not much concerned about who may own the cannon that were on top of it. Certainly nothing could induce me to ask for them, and I should be exceedingly sorry to see any American ask for them. To ask outright for the restoration of a trophy (not in the way of exchange) to my mind puts the man asking, and his nation, in a rather humiliating and unworthy position.

I had not the least sympathy with the people who wanted to purchase for America the flag of the *Chesapeake*, and I was glad a British subject purchased it and gave it to a British society. I did not want to regain that flag by gold. It was lost by blood. So with these cannon.

I suppose somewhere we have the cannon captured at Saratoga and Yorktown, and I would not want to get back the cannon captured from us unless it was in the way of an exchange. I should think that all soldiers would feel as I do, that the value of a trophy consists in the fact that it is a trophy, that it represents superior prowess, and that there is no point in getting back in peace something that we lost in war.

The Treaty of Peace

A Place in the Political Firmament

Great Britain had begun the struggle with everything—allies, numbers, wealth—in her favor. Toward the close, the odds were all the other way. In America, the day had gone conclusively against the island folk. We had waged war against Britain, with France and Spain as allies. But in making peace we had to strive for our rights against our friends almost as much as against our enemies. To conduct the negotiations for our side we chose three of our greatest statesmen—Franklin, Adams, and Jay.

Congress, in appointing our commissioners, had, with little regard for the national dignity, given them instructions which, if obeyed, would have rendered them completely subservient to France, for they were directed to undertake nothing in the negotiations without the knowledge and concurrence of the French cabinet. Jay promptly persuaded his colleagues to unite with him in disregarding the instructions of Congress on this point. Had he not done so, the dignity of our government would "have been in the dust." Franklin was at first desirous of yielding obedience to the command, but Adams immediately joined Jay in repudiating it.

There was much generous and disinterested enthusiasm for America among Frenchmen individually, but the French government, with which alone we were to deal in making peace, had acted throughout from purely selfish motives, and in reality did not care an atom for American rights. We owed France no more gratitude for taking our part than she owed us for giving her an opportunity of advancing her own interests, and striking a severe blow at an old-time enemy and rival. The peace negotiations brought all this out very clearly. The great French minister, Vergennes, who dictated the policy of his court all through the contest, cared nothing for the Revolutionary colonists themselves, but he was bent upon securing them their independence, so as to weaken England, and he was also bent upon keeping them from gaining too much strength, so that they might always remain dependent allies of France.

He wished to establish the "balance of power" system in America. The American commissioners he at first despised for their blunt, truthful straightforwardness, which he, trained in the school of deceit, and a thorough believer in every kind of finesse and double-dealing, mistook for boorishness. Later on, he learned to his chagrin that they were able as well as honest, and that their resolution, skill, and farsightedness made them, where their own deepest interests were concerned, overmatches for the subtle diplomats of Europe.

America, then, was determined to secure not only independence, but also a chance to grow into a great continental nation. She wished her boundaries fixed at the Great Lakes and the Mississippi. She also asked for the free navigation of the latter to the Gulf, and for a share of the fisheries. Our true policy was admirably summed up by Jay in his letter to Livingston, where he says: "Let us be honest and grateful to France, but let us think for ourselves . . . Since we have assumed a place in the political firmament, let us move like a primary and not secondary planet." Fortunately, England's own self-interest made her play into our hands. As Fox put it, it was necessary for her to "insist in the strongest manner that, if America is independent, she must be so of the whole world. No secret, tacit, or ostensible connection with France."

Our statesmen won. We got all we asked, as much to the astonishment of France as of England. We proved even more successful in diplomacy than in arms. As Fox had hoped, we became independent not only of England, but of all the world. We were not entangled as a dependent subordinate in the policy of France, nor did we sacrifice our western boundary to Spain. It was a great triumph—greater than any that had been won by our soldiers. Franklin had a comparatively small share in gaining it. The glory of carrying through successfully the most important treaty we ever negotiated belongs to Jay and Adams, and especially to Jay. The chief credit for the resulting diplomatic triumph, almost as essential as the victory at Yorktown itself to our national well-being, belongs to him.[1]

Wherein the Philosopher Fell Short

Mr. Brander Matthews's volume on American literature[2] is a piece of work as good of its kind as any American scholar has ever had in his hands. No better little sketch of Benjamin Franklin has ever appeared than that which he gives. He is profoundly impressed by Franklin's greatness, and yet he shows, in a sentence in which he contrasts him with Abraham Lincoln, his appreciation of Franklin's character wherein the philosopher fell short.[3] He wrote:

> *Humor, indeed, he had so abundantly it was almost a failing. Like Abraham Lincoln, another typical American, he never shrank from a jest. Like Lincoln, he knew the world well and accepted it for what it was, and made the best of it, expecting no more. But Franklin lacked the spirituality, the faith in the ideal, which was at the core of Lincoln's character. And here was Franklin's limitation: what lay outside the bounds of common sense he did not see— probably he did not greatly care to see; but common sense he had in a most uncommon degree.*

Thomas Paine

The Filthy Little Atheist

I have written various historical books and I have expressed the reasons for my judgment on various public men. What I wrote of Tom Paine in the book the *Life of Gouverneur Morris* over thirty years ago contains the substantial truth and whether I would now tell it in quite the same language does not matter. I certainly would not alter the essential matter.

I was a very young man when I wrote the book in question, and if I had understood the curiously superstitious feeling that so many people seem to have about Thomas Paine, and inasmuch as I do not regard his career as of any consequence now, I would not have made any allusion to him—be it understood not because my allusion was not essentially true, but because I always wish to avoid hurting people's feelings if I can legitimately avoid doing so. I wrote:

> One man had a very narrow escape. This was Thomas
> Paine, the Englishman, who had at one period rendered
> such a striking service to the cause of American indepen-
> dence, while the rest of his life had been as ignoble as it was

varied. He had been elected to the Convention, and, having sided with the Gironde, was thrown into prison by the Jacobins. He at once asked Morris to demand him as an American citizen, a title to which he of course had no claim. Morris refused to interfere too actively, judging rightly that Paine would be saved by his own insignificance and would serve his own interests best by keeping still. So the filthy little atheist had to stay in prison, "where he amused himself with publishing a pamphlet against Jesus Christ." There are infidels and infidels. Paine belongs to the variety— whereof America possesses at present one or two shining examples—that apparently esteems a bladder of dirty water as the proper weapon with which to assail Christianity. It is not a type that appeals to the sympathy of an onlooker, be said onlooker religious or otherwise.

Permit me to say that the word "atheist" was used in the sense of denial of the existence of the God of the Christians. The only alteration I would make, in the interest of a rather meticulous correctness of terminology, would be in the use of the world "deist" instead of atheist. "Atheist" would have been the proper term if I had been dealing with the thirteenth century, for example. But in the eighteenth century the word "deist" had come into use to describe the men who denied the existence of the God of revealed religion, whereas atheist was a man who denied the existence of any God. Even in the sixteenth and seventeenth centuries the terms were sometimes used interchangeably.

I think the kind of language that Paine used about Christianity and the Bible improper and unworthy, when compared with the language which Huxley, for example, used. From the standpoint of men who do not accept the Orthodox view of revealed religion, Huxley was right and Paine was wrong in the method of treatment of the subject. I should myself, of course, describe Huxley as an agnostic rather than either an atheist or a deist.[1]

I have no patience with those who attack, who would destroy, a man's belief in religion—no patience with those who would convert the Jew *en masse*, or the Catholic. More likely than not, where they succeed at all they succeed only in destroying something—they take something real away and give nothing in return, leaving the victim bankrupt. I am always sorry for the faithless man, just as I am sorry for the woman without virtue. I have found, though, that however they may appear outwardly, most men at bottom are religious, just as the preponderating majority of men are honest and of women virtuous. Otherwise civilization would end overnight.

I am mighty weak on the Lutheran and Calvinistic doctrines of salvation by faith, myself, and though I have no patience with much of the Roman Catholic theory of church government, including the infallibility of the pope, the confessional, and a celibate clergy, I do believe in the gospel of works as put down in the Epistle of James.

I wonder if you recall one verse of Micah that I am very fond of— "to do justly and to love mercy and to walk humbly with thy God"— that to me is the essence of religion. To be just with all men, to be merciful to those to whom mercy should be shown, to realize that there are some things that must always remain a mystery to us, and when the time comes for us to enter the great blackness, to go smiling and unafraid. That is my religion, my faith.[2] To me it sums up all religion; it is all the creed I need. It seems simple and easy, but there is more in that verse than in the involved rituals and confessions of faith of many creeds we know.

The word "filthy" described with scientific accuracy Paine's bodily habits and condition at the time alluded to. The expression referred to a visit Gouverneur Morris reports having paid to Paine, when Paine had been lying in bed for some days. The language of Morris, while truthful, was made when he was disgusted. The quotation appears in Spark's life and writings of Gouverneur Morris. If you will turn to Volume I, pages 416–418, you will see the following statements: "He had become disgusting in his person and deportment . . . for several months he lived in Mr. Monroe's house, but so intemperate were his habits and so disagreeable his person that it was necessary to exclude him from the family and send his meals to his own apartments." The statements quoted, the words "disgusting" and "so disagreeable his person," mean "filthy" and nothing but filthy. A swine in a sty was physically clean by comparison.

I haven't the time to write volumes on every point where I differ from friends or from strangers concerning historical figures. My own view is that sound students of history and politics must come to the conclusion that Washington was immensely right and Paine immensely wrong during the decade which included Paine's residence as a Revolutionary in Paris. I think Paine was a man who rendered very great service at one period of his career, and very much the reverse at subsequent periods.

George Washington

The Greatest American

As a nation we have had our full share of great men, but the two men of pre-eminent greatness who, as the centuries go on, will surely loom above all others are Washington and Lincoln. Washington, alike statesman, soldier, and patriot, stands alone. He was not only the greatest American; he was also one of the greatest men the world has ever known. Few centuries and few countries have ever seen his like. Of Americans, Lincoln alone is worthy to stand even second.

I think you will find that the fundamental difference between our two great national heroes and almost any other men of equal note in the world's history is that when you think of our two men you think inevitably not of glory, but of duty, not of what the man did for himself in achieving name, or fame, or position, but of what he did for his fellows. Washington created the republic, rose by statecraft to the highest position, and used that position only for the welfare of his fellows and for so long as his fellows wished him to keep it.

Washington was the Revolution. Without Washington we should probably never have won our independence of the British crown, and we should almost certainly have failed to become a great nation, remaining instead a cluster of jangling little communities, drifting toward the type of government prevalent in Spanish America. After the American Revolution Washington's greatness of character, sound common sense, and entirely disinterested patriotism made him a bulwark both against anarchy and against despotism coming in the name of a safeguard against anarchy.

If, when that most imbecile of Congresses, the Continental Congress headed by Horatio Gates and his crowd, was hounding him, and when it drove the army into practical mutiny by cutting down their pay to starvation, and when that army called to Washington to lead it where he might, if then he had had the passions of Cromwell or his lack of judgment, he would have dissolved the Congress and trod the path of Cromwell.

Judgment Which Never Seemed to Be at Fault

I should like to have continued as president,[1] if I had felt it right, and in accordance with the best spirit of our traditions, so to do, and, had I wished it, I think I could have continued. In my own case, I could so easily have persuaded myself that I was really needed to carry out my own policies. I sometimes felt that it was weakness which made me adhere to my resolution. Nine-tenths of my reasoning bade me accept another term, and only one-tenth, but that one-tenth was the still small voice, kept me firm. But how much harder it must have been for Washington, with no precedents to follow, with a united army and people back of him!

There was every justification for him, apparently, to have accepted another term and to continue on in power. But he was always sane, always poised, always patriotic. It is so easy for a man to deceive himself into doing what others want him to do when it coincides with his own wishes. Of course, there are those who believe that he declined a renomination for fear that he would be defeated, or that it was due to momentary irritation, but I find nothing to bear out either of these theories. I believe he was actuated purely by patriotism, his far-reaching vision which pierced the future, and saw the danger to our republic if such a precedent were not established. It was his judgment—that judgment which never seemed to be at fault.

Washington Was Not a Genius

Only a very limited amount of the success of life comes to persons possessing genius. The average man who is successful—the average statesman, the average public servant, the average soldier, who wins what we call great success—is not a genius. He is a man who has merely the ordinary qualities that he shares with his fellows, but who has developed those ordinary qualities to a more than ordinary degree.

Washington was not a genius. I could not find anything about him that smacked of anything more than talent. I regard him as the greatest man in our history and one of the very greatest men in the world. Certainly he possessed something which pitched him on a different plane from other men of his time and on a plane which I do not find any other American occupying since then. He was just the average man of his day, the very best type of his day with indomitable will, unbounded courage, and no end of faith, and no end of patience. It isn't genius that does big things. Washington was courage, determination, and patience raised to the nth power. That's why he is generally held to be the greatest of Americans.

A Great General of the Fabian Order

Washington was, not even excepting Lincoln, the very greatest man of modern times, and a great general, of the Fabian order,[2] too, but on the battlefield I doubt if he equaled any one of half a dozen of the Union and Rebel chiefs who fought in the great Civil War.

Many of us read with a good deal of interest Lord Wolseley's article in *Macmillan's Magazine* for March 1886. Lord Wolseley speaks a good deal of General Washington,[3] evincing a desire to place General

Lee "on the same pedestal" with him. But he says nothing that warrants us in thinking that he knows more than the simple facts that there was a man named Washington, and that he was a general. As a mere military man, Washington himself cannot rank with the wonderful war chief who for four years led the army of northern Virginia.

It may interest his lordship to learn that Washington was not only a general, but a great constructive statesman. The salient difference between Washington and Lee ought to be apparent to even the dimmest vision. The one succeeded in building up the mighty structure which the other failed in trying to tear down. To compare Lee to Washington—who was as pure a patriot as Hampden, a greater statesman than Pitt, and almost as great a general as Wellington—is absurd.

Washington's main difficulties were, not with the foe in front, but with the politicians and people behind, with the shortsighted and sour jealousies of the different States, the mixed impotence and intrigue of Congress, the poverty of the people, the bankruptcy of the government, the lukewarm timidity of many, the open disaffection of not a few, and the jobbery of speculators who were sometimes to be found high in the ranks of the army itself. Moreover, he had to contend with the general dislike of discipline and sustained exertion natural to the race of shrewd, brave, hardy farmers whom he led—unused as they were to all restraint, and unable to fully appreciate the necessity of making sacrifices in the present for the sake of the future. But his soul rose above disaster, misfortune, and suffering. If Washington had been backed up as Lee was, the Revolutionary War would have been over in three years, instead of lasting nearly eight.

A Strong Nation Can Only Be Saved by Itself

Washington would not let his officers try to make him dictator, nor allow the Continental Army to march against the weak Congress which distrusted it, was ungrateful to it, and refused to provide for it. Unlike Cromwell, he saw that the safety of the people lay in working out their own salvation, even though they showed much wrongheadedness and blindness, not merely to morality, but to their own interests. And, in the long run, the people justified this trust.

A strong nation can only be saved by itself, and not by a strong man, though it can be greatly aided and guided by a strong man. A weak nation may be doomed anyhow, or it may find its sole refuge in a despot. A nation struggling out of darkness may be able to take its first steps only by the help of a master hand, as was true of Russia under Peter the Great. And if a nation, whether free or unfree, loses the capacity for self-government, loses the spirit of sobriety and of orderly liberty, then it has no cause to complain of tyranny. But a really great people, a people really capable of freedom and of doing mighty deeds in the world, must work out its own destiny, and must find men who will be its leaders—not its masters.

Liberty and Religion Are Natural Allies

Washington's Farewell Address contains advice which is permanently applicable. No American should ever forget Washington's insistence upon the absolute necessity of preserving the Union, his appeals to our people that they should cherish the American nationality as something indestructible from within and as separating us in clear-cut manner from all other nations, his stern refusal to yield to the tyranny of either an individual or a mob, and his demand that we seek both liberty and order as indispensable to the life of a democratic republic.

In this fortunate country of ours liberty and religion are natural allies and go forward hand in hand. Washington demanded a national morality based on religious principles. In his Farewell Address to his countrymen, Washington said: "Morality is a necessary spring of popular government . . . and let us with caution indulge the supposition that morality can be maintained without religion. Whatever may be conceded to the influence of refined education on minds of peculiar structure, reason and experience both forbid us to expect that national morality can prevail in exclusion of religious principle."

Washington lacked Lincoln's gift of words, but not Lincoln himself possessed more robust common sense in the thought that lies back of words. In this case the thought is not new. Only a few good thoughts are new, but it was given expression at a time when the European movement with which the American people were in most complete sympathy—the French Revolution—had endeavored to destroy the abuses of priestcraft and bigotry by abolishing not only Christianity but religion, in the sense in which religion is properly understood. The result was a cynical disregard of morality and a carnival of cruelty and bigotry, committed in the names of reason and liberty, which equaled anything ever done by Torquemada and the fanatics of the Inquisition in the names of religion and order. Washington wished his fellow countrymen to walk clear of such folly and iniquity.

It is impossible to estimate too highly the devoted patriotism and statesmanship of the founders of our national life, and however high we rank Washington, I am confident that we err, if anything, in not ranking him high enough, for on the whole the world has never seen a man deserving to be placed above him.

Alexander Hamilton

The Most Brilliant American Statesmen Who Ever Lived

Alexander Hamilton stands in the very first class of American statesmen. Hamilton's extraordinary career of usefulness was crowded into the half dozen years following the Constitutional Convention—a short period, but one during which his services were as signal as any ever rendered a nation in time of peace, while in intellect he showed a combination of brilliancy and solidity literally unparalleled in political annals.

I have recently been reading a book—the best life of Alexander Hamilton that has ever been written—by an Englishman named Oliver. He shows how, in Hamilton's few years of public life, which ended by his seeing the actual triumph of the men and the seeming triumph of the principles to which he was most opposed, he nevertheless accomplished an amount of work which has remained vital and effective until the present day. It is little short of a scandal that there should be no monument to Alexander Hamilton in Washington, the man of most brilliant mind[1] whom we have ever developed in this country, as great a cabinet officer as we have ever had.

Hamilton had about him that "touch of the purple" which is always so strongly attractive, the touch of the heroic, the touch of the gallant, the dashing, the picturesque,[2] which ranks the possessors among those historical characters about whom one really cares to read. That mighty leader of thought, that great constructive statesman, that master of finance, was not even born in this country. His father was a Scotchman, his mother a Frenchwoman, but he had not one thought or one feeling in his heart that was not American. He was an American in every instinct. All of his plans were for the greatness of this country, and there are but two or three names in all our history which will stand above his.

Do you know how the Constitution was formed? Have you ever read *The Federalist*? If so, you know that the Constitution could not have been formed at all if the questions of expediency had not been given full weight no less than questions of principle. You also know that Alexander Hamilton, the chief champion in securing the adoption of the Constitution, was entirely opposed to most of the provisions incorporated in it. Had he refused to support the best of the only two practicable courses, he would have been a mere curse to the country.

The biggest and most beneficial "deal" in our history was when Alexander Hamilton made a deal with Jefferson by which he allowed that slippery demagogue to have the national capital put in the South, on the Potomac, in consideration of the nation cementing the Union by assuming the debts of the States. It was a simple deal, and an unworthy deal on Jefferson's part, but a great act of patriotic statesmanship on Hamilton's.

Hamilton was a struggling man of moderate means, like his great fellow Federalist Marshall. Neither had in him one touch of the demagogue or the insincere rhetorician. Each regarded with scorn the mob spirit, especially when manifested in ferocious lawbreaking envy of upright men of means. But each also sincerely endeavored to judge every man of his worth as a man and to shape the institutions and policy of his country with an eye single to the large national interests of the people as a whole.

Hamilton embodied what was best in the Federalist Party, excepting of course in so far as you can say that Washington was a Federalist. Hamilton, the most brilliant American statesmen who ever lived, possessing the loftiest and keenest intellect of his time, was of course the foremost champion in the ranks of the New York Federalists. Second to him came Jay, pure, strong, and healthy in heart, body, and mind. They were men of singularly noble and lofty character. Hamilton, born out of New York, was in some ways a more characteristic New Yorker than Jay, for New York, like the French Revolution, has always been pre-eminently a career open to talents. Jay lacked Hamilton's brilliant audacity and genius, but he possessed an austere purity and poise of character[3] which his greater companion did not.

Wonderful Genius to Force a Ratification

As soon as the project for a closer union of the States was broached, Hamilton and Jay took it up with ardor. New York followed their lead, but the State as a whole was against them. The most popular man within its bounds was stout old George Clinton and he led the opposition to the proposed Union. Clinton was a man of great strength of character, a good soldier and staunch patriot of the Revolutionary War. He was the greatest man in New York, but he could not hope ever to be one of the greatest in the Union. The cold, suspicious temper of the small country freeholders, and the narrow jealousy they felt for their neighbors, gave him excellent material on which to work.

Nevertheless, Hamilton won, thanks to the loyalty with which New York City stood by him. By untiring effort and masterful oratory he persuaded the State to send three delegates to the federal Constitutional Convention. He himself went as one, and bore a prominent part in the debates, his two colleagues, a couple of anti-Federalist nobodies, early leaving him. He then came back to the city, where he wrote and published, jointly with Madison and Jay, a series of letters, afterward gathered into a volume called *The Federalist*—a book which ranks among the ablest and best which have ever been written on politics and government. These articles had a profound effect on the public mind.

Finally, he crowned his labors by going as a representative from the city to the State convention and winning from a hostile body a reluctant ratification of the federal Constitution. It needed all of Hamilton's wonderful genius to force a ratification of the Constitution in spite of the stupid selfishness of the Clintonian faction. As it was, he was only barely successful, although backed by all the best and ablest leaders in the community.

Hamilton's Distrust of Democracy

After Washington, the greatest and best of the Federalist leaders, died, and after the Jeffersonian Democrats came into power, the two parties throughout the country began to divide on a very humiliating line. They fought each other largely on questions of foreign policy. Hamilton, of course, was the leader of his party. But his qualities, admirably though they fitted him for the giant tasks of constructive statesmanship with which he successfully grappled, did not qualify him for party leadership. He was too impatient and dictatorial, too heedless of the small arts and unwearied, intelligent industry of the party manager.

Four-fifths of the talent and ability and good sense of the country were to be found in the Federalist ranks. For the Federalists had held their own so far, by sheer force of courage and intellectual vigor, over foes in reality more numerous. Their great prop had been Washington. His colossal influence was to the end decisive in party contests, and he had in fact, although hardly in name, almost entirely abandoned his early attempts at non-partisanship, had grown to distrust Madison as he long before had distrusted Jefferson, and had come into constantly closer relations with their enemies. His death greatly diminished the chances of Federalist success.

The Federalists upheld the honor and interest of the country, and, on the whole, represented what was highest and best in the American character. But their leading statesmen were riven by jealousies, and they developed very little of the not very high, but in popularly governed communities absolutely necessary, ability for political manipulation. The Federalists were split into two factions, one following the president, Adams, in his efforts to keep peace with France,[4] if it could be done with honor, while the others, under Hamilton's lead, wished war at once.

In spite of the jarring between the leaders, the Federalists nominated Adams and Pinckney. In the ensuing presidential election many of the party chiefs, notably Marshall of Virginia, already a strong Adams man, faithfully stood by the ticket in its entirety, but Hamilton, Morris, and many others at the North probably hoped in their hearts that, by the aid of the curious electoral system which then existed, some chance would put the great Carolinian in the first place and make him president.

It was in New York that the decisive struggle took place, for that was the pivotal State, and there the Democrats, under the lead of the Livingstons and Clintons, but above all by the masterly political maneuvers of Aaron Burr, gained a crushing victory. Hamilton, stung to madness by the defeat, and sincerely believing that the success of his opponents would be fatal to the Republic, actually proposed to Jay,[5] the governor, to nullify the action of the people by the aid of the old legislature, a Federalist body, which was still holding over, although the members of its successor had been chosen. Jay, as pure as he was brave, refused to sanction any such scheme of unworthy partisanship.

In the electoral college, Jefferson and Burr, the Democratic-Republican candidates for president and vice president, had a tie vote under the curious system then prevailing, and this left the House of Representatives to decide which should be given the presidency. The Federalists, as a whole, from hatred to Jefferson, supported Burr. But Hamilton, to his honor, opposed this move with all his might, and from thenceforth was regarded by Burr with peculiar and sinister hostility. Jefferson was finally chosen.

In a government such as ours it was a foregone conclusion that a party which did not believe in the people would sooner or later be thrown from power unless there was an armed breakup of the system.

The distrust was felt, and of course excited corresponding and intense hostility. Had the Federalists been united, and had they freely trusted in the people, the latter would have shown that the trust was well founded. But there was no hope for leaders who suspected each other and feared their followers. The great Federalist Party fell from power,[6] not to regain it, save in local spasms here and there. It was a party of many faults—above all the unforgivable fault of distrusting the people—but it was the party which founded our government, and ever most jealously cherished the national honor and integrity.

I have not much sympathy with Hamilton's distrust of democracy. Nobody knows better than I that a democracy may go very wrong indeed, and I loathe the kind of demagogy which finds expression in such statements as "The voice of the people is the voice of God," but in my own experience it has certainly been true that the highly cultivated classes, and the moneyed classes, especially those of large fortune, whose ideal tends to be mere money, are not fitted for any predominant guidance in a really great nation. I do not dislike, but I certainly have no especial respect or admiration for and no trust in, the typical big moneyed man of my country.

A Statesman Rather Than a Politician

Hamilton was a statesman rather than a politician. He had quarreled uselessly with some of the greatest men in his own party, and he could not devote his mind to the mastery of the petty political detail and intrigue in which Burr reveled. Hamilton's admirers are apt to speak as if this was really to his credit, but such a position is all nonsense. A politician may be and often is a very base creature, and if he cares only for party success, if he panders to what is evil in the people, and still more if he cares only for his own success, his special abilities merely render him a curse. But among free peoples, and especially among the free peoples who speak English, it is only in very exceptional circumstances that a statesman can be efficient, can be of use to the country, unless he is also (not as a substitute, but in addition) a politician.

This is a very rough-and-tumble, workaday world, and the persons, such as our "anti-imperialist" critics over here who sit in comfortable libraries and construct theories, or even the people who like to do splendid and spectacular feats in public office without undergoing all the necessary preliminary outside drudgery, are and deserve to be at a disadvantage compared to the man who takes the trouble, who takes the pains, to organize victory. Lincoln unconsciously carried out the Hamiltonian tradition—was superior to Hamilton just because he was a politician and was a genuine democrat and therefore suited to lead a genuine democracy.

Over a century ago, in the days of Hamilton and Jefferson, there was a divorce between the national and the democratic ideas here in the United States, divorce which in our case was healed by Abraham Lincoln. We never have accomplished anything save under the lead of some man like Lincoln who did combine the Hamiltonian and Jeffersonian spirit.

Northwest Ordinance of 1787

The Blow Was Dealt by Southern Men

The far Northwest was won by the arms and diplomacy of the United States, by the victory of Wayne and the Treaty of Jay. The lands became part of the Federal domain, and were nationalized so far as they could be under the Confederation. It remained for Congress to determine the conditions under which the settlers could enter the new land, and under which new States should spring up therein. These conditions were fixed by the famous Ordinance of 1787, one of the two or three most important acts every passed by an American legislative body, for it determined that the new Northwestern States—the children, and ultimate leaders, of the Union—should get their growth as free commonwealths, untainted by the horrible curse of Negro slavery.

The Ordinance of 1787 was so wide-reaching in its effects, was drawn in accordance with so lofty a morality and such far-seeing statesmanship, and was fraught with such weal for the nation, that it will ever rank among the foremost of American State papers,[1] coming in that little group which includes the Declaration of Independence, the Constitution, Washington's Farewell Address, and Lincoln's Emancipation

Proclamation and Second Inaugural. It marked out a definite line of orderly freedom along which the new States were to advance.

The sixth and most important article declared that there should never be slavery or involuntary servitude in the Northwest, otherwise than for the punishment of convicted criminals, provided, however, that fugitive slaves from the older States might lawfully be reclaimed by their owners. This was the greatest blow struck for freedom and against slavery in all our history, save only Lincoln's Emancipation Proclamation, for it determined that in the final struggle the mighty West should side with the right against the wrong. It was in its results a deadly stroke against the traffic in, and ownership of, human beings, and the blow was dealt by Southern men, to whom all honor should be given.

Like so many other great political triumphs, the passage of the Ordinance of 1787 was a compromise. Slavery was prohibited on the one hand, and on the other, that the Territory might not become a refuge for runaway Negroes, provision was made for the return of such fugitives. The popular conscience was yet too dull about slavery to be stirred by the thought of returning fugitive slaves into bondage. The slave question was not at the time a burning issue between North and South, for no northerner thought of crusading to destroy the evil, while most enlightened southerners were fond of planning how to do away with it.

The Constitution

Rarely in the World's History

The national convention to form a Constitution met in May 1787, and rarely in the world's history has there been a deliberative body which contained so many remarkable men, or produced results so lasting and far-reaching. The Congress whose members signed the Declaration of Independence had but cleared the ground on which the framers of the Constitution were to build.

Among the delegates in attendance, easily first stood Washington and Franklin—two of that great American trio in which Lincoln stood third. Next came Hamilton from New York, having as colleagues a couple of mere obstructionists sent by the Clintonians to handicap him. From Pennsylvania came Robert Morris and Gouverneur Morris; from Virginia, Madison; from South Carolina, Rutledge and the Pinckneys; and so on through the other States. Adams and Jefferson were abroad. Jay was acting as secretary for foreign affairs, in which capacity, by the way, he had shown most unlooked-for weakness in yielding to Spanish demands about the Mississippi.

The statesmen who met in 1787 were earnestly patriotic. They unselfishly desired the welfare of their countrymen. They were cool, resolute men, of strong convictions, with clear insight into the future. They were thoroughly acquainted with the needs of the community for which they were to act. Above all, they possessed that inestimable quality, so characteristic of their race, hardheaded common sense. Their theory of government was a very high one, but they understood perfectly that it had to be accommodated to the shortcomings of the average citizen. They were emphatically good men. They were not less emphatically practical men.

They were resolute to free themselves from the tyranny of man, but they had not unlearned the reverence felt by their fathers for their fathers' God. They were sincerely religious. The advanced friends of freedom abroad scoffed at religion, and would have laughed outright at a proposition to gain help for their cause by prayers, but to the founders of our Constitution, when matters were at a deadlock, and the outcome looked almost hopeless, it seemed a most fit and proper thing that one of the chief of their number should propose to invoke to aid them a wisdom greater than the wisdom of human beings.

All our great men saw the absolute need of establishing a National Union—not a league or a confederation—if the country was to be saved. It was all-important that there should be a Union, but it had to result from the voluntary action of all the States, and each State had a perfect right to demand just whatever it chose. The really wise and high-minded statesmen demanded for themselves nothing save justice.

The Revolution had left behind it among many men love of liberty, mingled with lofty national feeling and broad patriotism. But to other men it seemed that the chief lessons taught had been successful resistance to authority, jealousy of the Central Government, and intolerance of all restraint. Accordingly as one or the other of these mutually hostile sets of sentiments prevailed, the acts of the Revolutionary leaders were to stand justified or condemned in the light of coming years. As yet the success had only been in tearing down. There remained the harder and all-important task of building up.

The task of building up was accomplished, and the acts of the men of the Revolution were thus justified. It was the after-result of the Revolution, not the Revolution itself, which gave to the governmental experiment inaugurated by the Second Continental Congress its unique and lasting value. It was this result which marks most clearly the difference between the careers of the English-speaking and Spanish-speaking peoples on this continent. The wise statesmanship typified by men such as Washington and Marshall, Hamilton, Jay, John Adams, and Charles Cotesworth Pinckney prevailed over the spirit of separatism and anarchy. Seven years after the war ended, the Constitution went into effect, and the United States became in truth a nation.

The Hard Logic of Disaster

Long before the Revolutionary War had closed, the old government of the confederation had demonstrated its almost utter impotence, and things grew worse after the peace. The people at large were slow to accept the idea that a new and stronger government was necessary. The struggle they had just passed through was one for liberty, against power, and they did not realize that license and anarchy are liberty's worst enemies. The best and wisest men in the land saw from the first the need of a real and strong Union, but the mass of the people came to this idea with the utmost reluctance. It was beaten into their minds by the hard logic of disaster.

The outbreak of armed rebellion in Massachusetts and North Carolina, the general lawlessness, the low tone of commercial honor, the bankruptcy of the States and their loss of credit at home and abroad, the contempt with which the confederation was treated by European nations, and the jarring interests of the different commonwealths themselves, which threatened at any moment to break out in actual civil war—all these combined with the wisdom and eloquence of the ablest statesmen in the land, and the vast weight of Washington's character, were needed to convince an obstinate, suspicious, and narrow-minded, though essentially brave, intelligent, and patriotic people, that they must cast aside their prejudices and jealousies and unite to form a stable and powerful government. Had they not thus united, their triumph in the Revolutionary War would have been a calamity for America instead of a blessing.

No sooner was peace declared, and the immediate and pressing danger removed, than the confederation relapsed into a loose knot of communities, as quarrelsome as they were contemptible. The States'-rights men for the moment had things all their own way, and speedily reduced us to the level afterward reached by the South American republics. Their leaders were designing politicians who feared that their importance would be lost if their sphere of action should be enlarged. Among these leaders the three most important were, in New York, George Clinton, and, in Massachusetts and Virginia, two much greater men—Samuel Adams and Patrick Henry. All three had done excellent service at the beginning of the Revolutionary troubles. Patrick Henry lived to redeem himself, almost in his last hour, by the noble stand he took in aid of Washington against the Democratic nullification agitation of Jefferson and Madison. Henry himself made one slip when he opposed the adoption of the federal Constitution, but this does not at all offset the services he rendered our common country both before and afterward. But the usefulness of each of the other two was limited to the early portion of his career.

A Bundle of Compromises

The difficulties for the convention to surmount seemed insuperable. On almost every question that came up, there were clashing interests. Strong government and weak government, pure democracy or a modified aristocracy, small States and large States, North and South, slavery and freedom, agricultural sections as against commercial sections—on each of twenty points the delegates split into hostile camps that could only be reconciled by concessions from both sides. The Constitution was not one compromise. It was a bundle of compromises, all needful.

Morris believed in letting the United States interfere to put down a rebellion in a State, even though the executive of the State himself should be at the head of it, and he was supported in his views by Pinckney, the ablest member of the brilliant and useful but unfortunately short-lived school of South Carolina Federalists. Pinckney was a thoroughgoing nationalist.[1] He wished to go a good deal further than the convention actually went in giving the central government complete control. Thus he proposed that Congress should have power to negative by a two-thirds vote all State laws inconsistent with the harmony of the Union. Madison also wished to give Congress a veto over State legislation.

The fierce little Palmetto State has always been a freelance among her Southern sisters. For instance, though usually ultra-democratic, she was hostile to the two great Democratic chiefs, Jefferson and Jackson, though both were from the South. The brilliant little group of Federalist leaders within her bounds, headed by men of national renown like Pinckney and Harper, kept her true to Federalism by downright force of intellect and integrity, for they were among the purest as well as the ablest statesmen of the day.

Serious struggle took place over the matter of slavery, quite as important then as ever, for at that time the Negroes were a fifth of our population, instead of, as now, an eighth. The question, as it came before the convention, had several sides to it, the especial difficulty rising over the representation of the slave States in Congress, and the importation of additional slaves from Africa. No one proposed to abolish slavery offhand, but an influential though small number of delegates recognized it as a terrible evil, and were very loath either to allow the South additional representation for the slaves, or to permit the foreign trade in them to go on.

Some of the high-minded Virginian statesmen were quite vigorous in their denunciation of the system. One of them, George Mason, portrayed the effects of slavery upon the people at large with bitter emphasis, and denounced the slave traffic as "infernal," and slavery as a national sin that would be punished by a national calamity—stating therein the exact and terrible truth. In shameful contrast, many of the Northerners championed the institution. In particular, Oliver Ellsworth, of Connecticut, whose name should be branded with infamy because of the words he then uttered.[2] He actually advocated the free importation of Negroes into the South Atlantic States, because the slaves "died so fast in the sickly rice-swamps" that it was necessary ever to bring fresh ones to labor and perish in the places of their predecessors.

The Virginians were opposed to the slave trade, but South Carolina and Georgia made it a condition of their coming into the Union. It was accordingly agreed that it should be allowed for a limited time— twelve years, and this was afterward extended to twenty. It was better to limit the duration of the slave trade to twenty years than to allow it to be continued indefinitely, as would have been the case had the South Atlantic States remained by themselves. The three-fifths representation of the slaves was an evil anomaly, but it was no worse than allowing the small States equal representation in the Senate.

No man who supported slavery can ever have a clear and flawless title to our regard, and those who opposed it merit, in so far, the highest honor. But the opposition to it sometimes took forms that can be considered only as the vagaries of lunacy. The only hope of abolishing it lay first in the establishment and then in the preservation of the Union. The crazy talk about the iniquity of consenting to any recognition of slavery whatever in the Constitution is quite beside the mark.

Had the slavery interest been in the least dissatisfied, or had the plan of government been a shade less democratic, or had the smaller States not been propitiated, the Constitution would have been rejected offhand, and the country would have had before it decades, perhaps centuries, of misrule, violence, and disorder. If the Constitution of 1789 had declared for the abolition of slavery in all the States, it would never have been adopted, and the English-speaking people of North America would have plunged into a condition of anarchy like that of the after-time South American republics.

The fierceness of the opposition to the adoption of the Constitution, and the narrowness of the majority by which Virginia and New York decided in its favor, while North Carolina and Rhode Island did not come in at all until absolutely forced, showed that the refusal to compromise on any one of the points at issue would have jeopardized everything.

The men who opposed the adoption of the present Constitution of the United States committed an error to the full as great as that of the

Tories themselves, and they strove quite as unsuccessfully, to damage their country. The adoption of the Constitution was the completion of the work begun by the War of Independence. This work had two stages, each essential, and those who opposed it during the second stage, like those who opposed it in the first, however honest of intent, did all they could to injure America. The Tory and the disunionist, or non-unionist, were equally dangerous enemies of the national growth and well-being.

Recollect that the strongest opponent of the adoption of the Constitution—that is, the man who most strenuously opposed and doubted its wisdom—was Thomas Jefferson.[5] We got our Constitution, not because of, but in spite of Jefferson and his followers. The Jeffersonian or antinational opponents of the adoption of the Constitution soon after turned round and simulated excessive zeal for the letter of the Constitution in order to destroy its spirit.

The doctrinaires to the contrary notwithstanding, we proved that a strong central government was perfectly compatible with absolute democracy. Indeed, the separatist spirit does not lead to true democratic freedom. Anarchy is the handmaiden of tyranny. Hamilton said: "A government ought to contain in itself every power requisite to the full accomplishment of the objects committed to its care, and the complete execution of the trust for which it is responsible, free from every other control but a regard to the public good and *to serve the people*." (The italics are my own.) There never existed a public man who was less of a demagogue than Hamilton, and yet he thus explicitly recognizes the need of law being in harmony with public opinion.

Gouverneur Morris

The Open Champion of Treason

Gouverneur Morris was too unstable and erratic to leave a profound mark upon our political development,[1] but he performed two or three conspicuous feats, he rendered several marked services to the country, and he embodied to a peculiar degree both the qualities which made the Federalist Party so brilliant and useful, and those qualities which finally brought about its downfall.

Imperious, lighthearted, good-looking, well-dressed, he ranked as a wit among men, as a beau among women. He was equally sought for dances and dinners. He was a fine scholar and a polished gentleman, a capital storyteller, and had just a touch of erratic levity that served to render him still more charming. Occasionally he showed whimsical peculiarities, usually about very small things, that brought him into trouble, and one such freak cost him a serious injury. In his capacity of young man of fashion, he used to drive about town in a phaeton with a pair of small, spirited horses, and because of some whim, he would not allow the groom to stand at their heads. So one day they took fright, ran, threw him out, and broke his leg. The leg had to be amputated and he was ever afterward forced to wear a wooden one.

It is a painful thing to have to record that the closing act in a great statesman's career not only compares ill with what went before, but is actually to the last degree a discreditable and unworthy performance. In fact, throughout the War of 1812 he appeared as the open champion of treason to the nation, of dishonesty to the nation's creditors, and of cringing subservience to a foreign power. It is impossible to reconcile his course with his previous career. The men who opposed the War of 1812, and preferred to have the nation humiliated by unresented insult from a foreign power rather than see her suffer the losses of an honorable conflict, occupied a position little short of contemptible.

The utter weakness and folly of Jefferson's second term, and the pitiable incompetence shown both by him, by his successor, and by their party associates in dealing with affairs, so inflamed and exasperated Morris as to make him completely lose his head, and hurried him into an opposition so violent that his follies surpassed the worst of the follies he condemned. He gradually lost faith in our republican system, and in the Union itself. Though one of the founders of the Constitution, though formerly one of the chief exponents of the national idea, and though once a main upholder of the Union, he abandoned every patriotic principle and became an ardent advocate of northern secession. He sneered at the words "Union" and "Constitution" as being meaningless.

Morris's opposition to the war led him to the most extravagant lengths. In his hatred of the opposite party he lost all loyalty to the nation. He championed the British view of their right to impress seamen from our ships. He approved of peace on terms they offered, which included the curtailment of our western frontier. Singularly forgetful of his speeches in the Senate ten years before, he declared that he wished that a foreign power might occupy and people the West. He found space in his letters to exult over the defeats of Bonaparte, but could spare no word of praise for our own victories.

He actually advocated repudiating our war debt, on the ground that it was void, being founded on a moral wrong. He thus advanced the theory that in a government run by parties, which came into power alternately, any debt could be repudiated, at any time, if the party in power happened to disapprove of its originally being incurred. No greenback demagogue of the lowest type ever advocated a proposition more dishonest and more contemptible.

He was an exceptionally able man, and a wealthy one. But he went farther wrong at this period than the majority of our people—the "mob" as he would have contemptuously called them—have ever gone at any time.

His Feat Stands by Itself in Diplomatic History

We have never had a foreign minister who deserved more honor than Morris. As minister to France he successfully performed the most difficult task ever allotted to an American representative at a foreign capital. His two years' history as minister forms one of the most brilliant chapters in our diplomatic history. Morris was the only foreign minister who remained in Paris during the Terror.

He stayed at risk of his life, and yet, while fully aware of his danger, he carried himself as coolly as if in a time of profound peace, and never flinched for a moment when he was obliged for his country's sake to call to account the rulers of France for the time being—men whose power was as absolute as it was ephemeral and bloody, who had indulged their desire for slaughter with the unchecked ferocity of madmen, and who could by a word have had him slain as thousands had been slain before him. Once or twice, in the popular tumults, even his life was in danger. On one occasion it is said that it was only saved by the fact of his having a wooden leg, which made him known to the mob as "a cripple of the American war for freedom."

Few foreign ministers have faced such difficulties, and not one has ever come near to facing such dangers as Morris did during his two years' term of service. His feat stands by itself in diplomatic history, and, as a minor incident, the letters and dispatches he sent home give a very striking view of the French Revolution.

Writing to a friend who was especially hostile to Romanism, Morris once remarked, with the humor that tinged even his most serious thoughts, "Every day of my life gives me reason to question my own infallibility, and of course leads me farther from confiding in that of the Pope. But I have lived to see a new religion arise. It consists in a denial of all religion, and its votaries have the superstition of not being superstitious. They have this with as much zeal as any other sect, and are as ready to lay waste the world in order to make proselytes."

His horror of the base mob, composed of people whose kind was absolutely unknown in America, increased continually, as he saw them going on from crimes that were great to crimes that were greater, incited by demagogues who flattered them and roused their passions and appetites, and blindly raging because they were of necessity disappointed in the golden prospects held out to them. He scorned the folly of the enthusiasts and doctrinaires who had made a constitution all sail and no ballast, that overset at the first gust, who had freed from all restraint a mass of men as savage and licentious as they were wayward.

The shelter of Morris's house and flag was sought from early morning till past midnight by people who had nowhere else to go, and who felt that within his wall they were sure of at least a brief safety from the maddening savages in the streets. As far as possible they were sent off to places of greater security, but some had to stay with him till the storm lulled.

An American gentleman who was in Paris on that memorable day, after viewing the sack of the Tuileries, thought it right to go to the house of the American minister. He found him surrounded by a score of people, of both sexes, among them the old Count d'Estaing, and other men of note, who had fought side by side with us in our war of independence, and whom now our flag protected in their hour of direst need. Silence reigned, only broken occasionally by the weeping of the women and children.

As his visitor was leaving, Morris took him to one side, and told him, "Whether my house will be a protection to them or to me, God only knows, but I will not turn them out of it, let what will happen to me. You see, sir, they are all persons to whom our country is more or less indebted, and, had they no such claim upon me, it would be inhuman to force them into the hands of the assassins." No one of Morris's countrymen can read his words even now without feeling a throb of pride in the dead statesman who, a century ago, held up so high the honor of his nation's name in the times when the souls of all but the very bravest were tried and found wanting.

A Penetrating Observer

As an American statesman he has many rivals, and not a few superiors, but as a penetrating observer and recorder of contemporary events, he stands alone among the men of his time. He kept a full diary during his stay abroad, and was a most voluminous correspondent, and his capacity for keen, shrewd observation, his truthfulness, his wonderful insight into character, his sense of humor, and his power of graphic description all combine to make his comments on the chief men and events of the day a unique record of the inside history of western Europe during the tremendous convulsions of the French Revolution. No other American of note has left us writings half so humorous and amusing, filled, too, with information of the greatest value.

Like most men of strong character, he had no taste for the "cosmopolitanism" that so generally indicates a weak moral and mental makeup. He enjoyed his stay in Europe to the utmost, and was intimate with the most influential men and charming women of the time, but he was heartily glad to get back to America, refused to leave it again, and always insisted that it was the most pleasant of all places in which to live.

He enjoyed the life of the salon very much, but it did not in the least awe or impress him, and he was of too virile fiber, too essentially a man, to be long contented with it alone. He likewise appreciated the fashionable men, and especially the fashionable women, whom he met there. But his amusing comments on them, as shrewd as they are humorous, prove how little he respected their philosophy, and how completely indifferent he was to their claims to social pre-eminence. The authors, philosophers, and statesmen of the salon were rarely, almost never, men of real greatness. Their metal did not ring true. They were shams, and the life of which they were a part was a sham. Not only was the existence hollow, unwholesome, effeminate, but also in the end tedious.

The French Revolution

They Did Not Believe in Anything

The French Revolution[1] was in its essence a struggle for the abolition of privilege, and for equality in civil rights. In all really free countries, the best friends of freedom regarded the revolutionists, when they had fairly begun their bloody career, with horror and anger. It was only to oppressed, debased, and priest-ridden peoples that the French Revolution could come as the embodiment of liberty. Compared to the freedom already enjoyed by Americans, it was sheer tyranny of the most dreadful kind. The then existing generation of Frenchmen were not, and never would be, fitted to use liberty aright. With a people who made up in fickle ferocity what they lacked in self-restraint, and a king too timid and shortsighted to turn any crisis to advantage, the French statesmen, even had they been as wise as they were foolish, would hardly have been able to arrest or alter the march of events.

There was never another great struggle, in the end productive of good to mankind, where the tools and methods by which that end was won were so wholly vile as in the French Revolution. Alone among movements of the kind, it brought forth no leaders entitled to our respect, none who were both great and good, none even who were very great, save, at its beginning, strange, strong, crooked Mirabeau, and at its close the towering world-genius who sprang to power by its means, wielded it for his own selfish purposes, and dazzled all nations over the wide earth by the glory of his strength and splendor.

The days of Danton and Robespierre are not days to which a French patriot cares to look back, but at any rate he can regard them without the shame he must feel when he thinks of the times of Louis Quinze. Danton and his like, at least, were men, and stood far, far above the palsied coward—a eunuch in his lack of all virile virtues— who misruled France for half a century, who, with his followers, indulged in every crime and selfish vice known, save one such as needed a particle of strength, or the least courage, in the committing.

Before the Bastille fell the people who had most at stake were incapable not only of serious action to ward off their fate, but even of serious thought as to what their fate would be. The men—the nobles, the clerical dignitaries, and the princes of the blood—chose the church as a place wherein to cut antics that would have better befitted a pack of monkeys, while the women, their wives and mistresses, exchanged with them impure jests at their own expense, relished because of the truth on which they rested. Brutes might still have held sway at least for a time, but these were merely vicious triflers. They did not believe in their religion. They did not believe in anything.

In writing to Washington, Gouverneur Morris painted the outlook in colors that, though black indeed, were not a shade too dark: "Everybody agrees that there is an utter prostration of morals, but this general proposition can never convey to an American mind the degree of depravity. It is not by any figure of rhetoric or force of language that the idea can be communicated. A hundred anecdotes and a hundred thousand examples are required to show the extreme rottenness of every member . . . It is however from such crumbling matter that the great edifice of freedom is to be erected here . . . The great mass of the common people have no religion but their priests, no law but their superiors, no morals but their interest."

Looking at the maddening mob, the American minister thanked God from his heart that in his own country there was no such populace, and prayed with unwonted earnestness that our education and morality should forever stave off such an evil. Said Morris: "Since I have been in this country I have seen the worship of many idols, and but little of the true God."

The people who five years before had fallen down in the dirt as the consecrated matter passed by now danced the carmagnole in holy vestments, and took part in some other mummeries a great deal more blasphemous. At the famous Feast of Reason, a kind of opera performed in Notre Dame, the president of the Convention, and other public characters, adored on bended knees a girl who stood in the place *ci-devant* most holy to personate reason herself. This girl, Saunier by name, followed the trades of an opera dancer and harlot. She was "very beautiful and next door to an idiot as to her intellectual gifts." Among her feats was having appeared in a ballet in a dress especially designed, by the painter David, at her bidding, to be more indecent than nakedness. Altogether, she was admirably fitted, both morally and mentally, to personify the kind of reason shown and admired by the French revolutionists. Those individuals of arrested mental development who now make pilgrimages to Our Lady of Lourdes had plenty of prototypes, even in the atheistical France of the revolution.

The popular party in France, composed in part of amiable visionaries, theoretic philanthropists, and closet constitution-mongers, and in part of a brutal, sodden populace, maddened by the grinding wrongs of ages, knew not whither its own steps tended. The sentimental humanitarians—who always form a most pernicious body, with an influence for bad hardly surpassed by that of the professionally criminal class—of course throve vigorously in an atmosphere where theories of mawkish benevolence went hand in hand with the habitual practice of vices too gross to name.

The wild friends of the French Revolution, especially in America, supported it blindly, with but a very slight notion of what it really signified. The scenes that passed were literally beyond the imagination of the American mind. The most hideous and nameless atrocities were so common as to be only alluded to incidentally, and to be recited in the most matter-of-fact way in connection with other events. For instance, a man applied to the Convention for a recompense for damage done to his quarry, a pit dug deep through the surface of the earth into the stone bed beneath. The damage consisted in such a number of dead bodies having been thrown into the pit as to choke it up so that he could no longer get men to work it. Hundreds, who had been the first in the land, were thus destroyed without form or trial, and their bodies thrown like dead dogs into the first hole offered.

A Danger That We Shall Embark on That Evil Course

Most of the men of our little world do not see beyond their own circle. They know nothing of the lives and desires of their fellow country-men. They do not realize the fervor of intensity with which these countrymen are demanding a change in the old order of things in politics and in the world of great business. The evils against which they rise in revolt are very real, and moreover are very base, and if the men in revolt are not well led, and if a substantial measure of victory is not achieved under sane and moderate leadership, there is a danger that we shall embark on that evil course of oscillation between ex-tremes that permanently lowered the French character during the years between 1789 and 1871.

The abuses of the old regime, the folly of the reactionaries, and the folly of the demagogues combined to bring about the Red Terror. The reaction against the Red Terror brought about Napoleonism. Then came the White Terror, and the reaction against this also found vent in revolution. The Second Republic came in under the nominal lead of the moderates, but the extreme radicals, the men who would correspond to some of the Bryanites and some of the Debsites of today, got control and adopted every kind of impossible policy, including the famous na-tional workshops for the unemployed. In the end Louis Napoleon's pinchbeck empire of intrigue was the inevitable result. When it fell, the Red Commune rose on its ruins.

If we put in power mere visionaries, or else crooks like Hearst, on a wave of unthinking or class feeling, it will provoke a reaction, and then the ultraconservatives and Bourbons who think they can stop this movement will have their inning, and we shall be very apt to see the victory of some man or organization, which deliberately intends to let wealthy men and wealthy corporations do whatever they want uncontrolled. In the revolt against Hearstism such a movement might very well be triumphant, and then the Bourbons and tricksters and conscienceless speculators and exploiters who organized it would plume themselves on their successful cunning, whereas they would be merely paving the way for another violent reaction against themselves.

There are plenty of very wealthy men who think that if they can get rid of me and of my ideas, their troubles in this country are over. Some of them would now welcome hard times or a panic. It is well for the men who believe this to realize that they would run the risk, in such event, of so violent a counterreaction as to sweep in a man of the real radical type—a man who would pursue legislation in a vindictive spirit.

John Marshall

Distinctly among the Greatest of the Great

The three men to whom throughout our national history we as a people owe most are two presidents, Washington and Lincoln; and one chief justice, John Marshall. Marshall is the one man whose services to the nation entitle him to be grouped with the two great Presidents. He is distinctly among the greatest of the great, and no man, save Washington and Lincoln, alone, deserves heartier homage from us. Marshall's permanent greatness was not due so much to his legal ability as to the fact that he was a great constructive statesman who understood that the Constitution needed to be so interpreted as to aid a vigorous and growing nation in its development.

Marshall was in a real sense one of the founders of our Constitution. He deserves a place beside the greatest of the men who wrought out the Constitution and secured its adoption. I should put the name of Marshall second only to the names of Washington and Hamilton in point of effectiveness in building up our present Constitution. Marshall's career of greatness and usefulness really began only after Hamilton's had come to an end. It was less showy than Hamilton's, but much more long-continued, and the resulting benefit was as substantial.

The office of chief justice is, under some circumstances, as great an office as that of president, and at all times comes second only to it in importance. Under Marshall, the Supreme Court of the United States worked a tremendous revolution, not merely in ordinary law, but in the fundamental constitutional law of the land. The Court in his time, and while it responded to his teaching, was the most vital governmental element in our national growth. Marshall performed a great and needed service, one of the greatest services any statesman ever performed, when in a period of national weakness he put the Supreme Court behind the national ideal.

There is no need of discussing the question whether or not judges have a right to make law. The simple fact is that by their interpretation they inevitably do make the law in a great number of cases. Therefore it is vital that they should make it aright. The American judges who have left their mark deepest on history did so while acting, not really as judges at all, but as lawgivers, for, although nominally they only interpreted, in reality they made the law. In consequence, a judge like Marshall occupies in history a place such as no European judge could possibly have occupied.

When Marshall was appointed it was usually assumed, when the subject was discussed at all, that Congress, like the English House of Commons, could pass upon the validity of its own acts. When the adherents of Jefferson and Madison opposed this proposition, as they did in the Kentucky and Virginia Resolutions, the position they took was that the legislature of each State was a judge of constitutional matters at issue between the States and the nation, and that the States could declare void an act of Congress.

No one at the time thought of turning to the Supreme Court as the arbiter in such a matter. For the first fourteen years of its existence it occupied a position of no importance in the national government. Jay had resigned the chief justiceship, and declined reappointment, because he felt that the judiciary was not clothed with any real authority. But Marshall, in his first constitutional opinion, held that the Supreme Court possessed in itself the ultimate power to declare whether or not an act of Congress was void. No such power was expressly prescribed by the Constitution, and not only Jefferson but Jackson, with an emphasis amounting to violence, denounced Marshall's position and asserted that no such power existed.

It was not the adoption of the Constitution nor its administration by some of its founders during the first dozen years of its life which put the Supreme Court in its present position under the Constitution. The Supreme Court itself, for the great benefit of the nation, read its own place into the Constitution, after the lapse of years during which no one, not even of the founders of the Constitution, had dreamed of giving it such a place. It was the appointment of Marshall and the exercise by that great man of his extraordinary personal influence which gave the Supreme Court its great power in our government, and which thereby also gave an enormous impetus to the growth among us of that spirit which made and kept us a nation: a great, free, united people.

The reason why Marshall was so great a chief justice, the reason why he was a public servant whose services were of such incalculable value to our people, is to be found in the very fact that he thus read into the Constitution what was necessary in order to make the Constitution march. He stands among the men who actually did the constructive work of building a coherent national fabric out of the loose jumble of exhausted and squabbling little commonwealths left on the Atlantic coast by the ebb of the Revolutionary War.

The Leader in Giving a Broad Construction

Marshall, the champion of the Constitution when its adoption was in question and its greatest expounder after its adoption, was, of course, the leader in giving a broad construction,[1] in reading into it whatever was necessary in order to make it fulfill its purpose of securing justice for the people as a whole, in their national capacity. He was utterly incapable of treating it as a fetish or as a straitjacket.

A wise court will recognize that the Constitution cannot be made a straitjacket, that the process of formal amendment can very rarely be resorted to, and that there must be a process of growth and adjustment by the decisions of the court itself. If we interpret the Constitution in narrow instead of broad fashion, if we forsake the principles of Washington, Marshall, and Hamilton, we as a people will render ourselves impotent to deal with any abuses which may be committed by the men who have accumulated the enormous fortunes of today. Both law and life are to be considered in order that the law and the Constitution shall become, in John Marshall's words, "a living instrument and not a dead letter."

We are now entering on a period when the vast and complex growth of modern industrialism renders it of vital interest to our people that the court should apply the old essential underlying principles of our government to the new and totally different conditions in such fashion that the spirit of the Constitution shall in very fact be preserved and not sacrificed to a narrow construction of the letter. Much of the future of this country depends upon the direction from which the judges of the Supreme Court approach the great constitutional questions that they will have to decide.

Not a Particle of Arrogance

John Marshall came of the ordinary, plain, colonial stock. Marshall himself was in the best sense of the term a self-made man. As a very young man he served in the Continental Army under Washington, honorably but without special distinction. The majority of the men who had done the real fighting in our own Revolutionary War became staunch nationalists, and saw so much of the evil that springs from weak government and from lawlessness and disorder that they were among the strongest upholders of a strong government and of the efficient military forces without which there can be no strength.

Marshall was an entirely democratic man in every sense of the word which makes it a word of praise. He had not a particle of arrogance in dealing with others, was simple, straightforward, and unaffected, being at ease in the courtroom or in any public gathering, with any neighbor of no matter what social standing. There was about him none of that starched self-consciousness which men who are more anxious to seem great than to be great are so apt to mistake for dignity. Indeed, it is apparent that in dress and in manner he was rather easygoing. During the years before he became chief justice the Jeffersonians complained bitterly that his specious aspect of democracy misled the people into believing that he was not at heart an aristocrat. As a matter of fact, it was his democracy which was real and theirs which was spurious. He despised and detested shams.

He earned his living as a hardworking Virginia lawyer. As a lawyer he showed marked ability, and he relied on his own reasoning and paid comparatively scant attention to precedents. This is an admirable quality in a profession like the law, which always tends to become formalized or fossilized, and it is not merely an admirable, but an indispensable, quality in a great judge of the American type.

Marshall practiced law at intervals, served a term in Congress, served a few months in President John Adams's cabinet, and was appointed chief justice by Adams just before the latter left the presidency. He was a strong Federalist, but, unlike the dominant men of the party after they lost their leader, Washington, he never lost his head, and declined to go with his party when it unwisely defied popular feeling (in the case of the Alien and Sedition laws) by enacting legislation which the people ought to have approved, but which, as a matter of fact, they did not.

Marshall's Stand on Privilege

With most of our great statesmen whom I especially admire there will be one side which I emphatically do not admire. For instance, I cannot too strongly express my esteem for Marshall because of the way he acted nationally—and without nationality our democracy would have been an utter failure and worse than a failure. But I have not the slightest sympathy with Marshall's stand on privilege or vested rights as against popular rights—as witness the Dartmouth College case.[2] I feel toward Hamilton in just the same way. Marshall did not work for the great democratic principle of sanely, though cautiously and resolutely, endeavoring to make each of us, so far as may be, "his brother's keeper."

Thomas Jefferson

I Distrust Him and His Influence

Thank Heaven I have never hesitated to criticize Jefferson. He was infinitely below Hamilton. I think the worship of Jefferson a discredit to my country. I feel that while one should be sober in judgment, one should avoid above all things being colorless in dealing with matters of right and wrong. In my estimation Jefferson's influence upon the United States as a whole was very distinctly evil.[1]

I am a strong anti-Jeffersonian. The more I study Jefferson, the more profoundly I distrust him and his influence, taken as a whole. Many who get discouraged by the attitude of latter-day politicians may draw some hope and comfort from the reflection that the nation actually lived through the experiment of trying Jefferson's ideas. Nevertheless, the trial of this same experiment caused bitter loss and mortification. Of course, I am simply unable to understand how the American people tolerated Jefferson and Madison at the beginning of the nineteenth century.

I think Thomas Jefferson's election meant that the American people were not developed to the standard necessary for the appreciation of

Washington, Marshall, and Hamilton—a standard which they did not reach until Lincoln came to the front sixty years later, for Lincoln had, in addition to the good qualities of Hamilton and Marshall, also those good qualities which they lacked and which Jefferson possessed. The country suffered for at least two generations because of its folly in following Jefferson's lead.

The people that do harm in the end are not the wrongdoers whom all execrate. They are the men who do not do quite as much wrong, but who are applauded instead of being execrated. The career of Benedict Arnold has done us no harm as a nation, because of the universal horror it inspired. The men who have done us harm are those who have advocated disunion, but have done it so that they have been enabled to keep their political position. We are naturally prone to treat words as substitutes for deeds and refuse to prepare, to refuse to organize in advance to meet crises, to refuse to look facts in the face if they are unpleasant facts. Jefferson has been the apologist for and has given impetus to our very worst tendencies.

I think Jefferson on the whole did harm in public life. At the same time, there are two points Jefferson stood at advantage compared to his Federalist opponents (always excepting Washington). He did thoroughly believe in the people, just as Abraham Lincoln did. In the second place, Jefferson believed in the West and in the expansion of our people westward, whereas the northeastern Federalists allowed themselves to get into a position of utter hostility to western expansion. In 1803, under President Jefferson, the greatest single stride in expansion that we ever took was taken by the purchase of the Louisiana territory.

While I am a Jeffersonian in my genuine faith in democracy and popular government, I am a Hamiltonian in my governmental views, especially with reference to the need of the exercise of broad powers by the National Government. Naturally you will understand that I am speaking with no pretense at exactness in thus using the names of Jefferson and Hamilton.

Jefferson Was Not a Fighting Man

What I chiefly object to in Jefferson is his utter inefficiency as an executive officer in the face of a foreign foe. I feel that he and Madison had a good deal to their discredit in connection with the War of 1812.

History has not yet done justice to the ludicrous and painful folly and stupidity of which the government founded by Jefferson, and carried on by Madison, was guilty, both in its preparation for, and in its way of carrying on, this war. Nor is it yet realized that the men just mentioned, and their associates, are primarily responsible for the loss we suffered in it and the bitter humiliation some of its incidents caused us. We suffered disgrace after disgrace, while the losses we inflicted, in turn, on Great Britain were so slight as hardly to attract her attention.

Jomini has left on record[2] the contemptuous surprise felt by all European military men when a State, with a population of eight million souls, allowed a handful of British soldiers to penetrate unchecked to its capital, and there destroy the public buildings. The small British army marched at will through Virginia and Maryland, burned Washington, and finally retreated from before Baltimore.

American historians usually condemn without stint the army of Ross and Cockburn. But by right they should keep all their condemnation for their own country, so far as the taking of Washington is concerned. For the sin of burning a few public buildings is as nothing compared with the cowardly infamy of which the politicians of the stripe of Jefferson and Madison, and the people whom they represented, were guilty in not making ready, by sea and land, to protect their capital and in not exacting full revenge for its destruction. We dislike, reprobate, and, if possible, punish the man who strikes another unprovoked. But, after all, in our hearts, we despise him less than we do the timid being who submits to the blow without retaliation.

Ever since the Federalist Party had gone out of power in 1800, the nation's ability to maintain order at home and enforce respect abroad had steadily dwindled, and the twelve years' nerveless reign of the "Doctrinaire Democracy" had left us impotent for attack and almost as feeble for defense. Jefferson, who never understood anything about warfare, being a timid man, belonged to the visionary school which always denounced the army and navy.

Jefferson, though a man whose views and theories had a profound influence upon our national life, was perhaps the most incapable executive that ever filled the presidential chair. Being almost purely a visionary, he was utterly unable to grapple with the slightest actual danger, and, not even excepting his successor, Madison, it would be difficult to imagine a man less fit to guide the State with honor and safety through the stormy times that marked the opening of the present century.

Without the prudence to avoid war or the forethought to prepare for it, the administration drifted helplessly into a conflict in which only the navy prepared by the Federalists twelve years before, and weakened rather than strengthened during the intervening time, saved us from complete and shameful defeat. True to its theories, the House of Virginia made no preparations, and thought the war could be fought by "the nation in arms." The exponents of this particular idea, the militiamen, a partially armed mob, ran like sheep whenever brought into the field.

A class of professional noncombatants is as hurtful to the real, healthy growth of a nation as is a class of fire-eaters. In the long run, a Quaker may be quite as undesirable a citizen as is a duelist. No man who is not willing to bear arms and to fight for his rights can give a good reason why he should be entitled to the privilege of living in a free community. Jefferson was not a fighting man.[3] But unfortunately the nation lacked the wisdom to see this, and it chose and re-chose for the presidency Thomas Jefferson, who avowed that his "passion was peace," and whose timidity surpassed even his philanthropy.

Had Jefferson and the other leaders of popular opinion been wiser and firmer men, they could have led the people to make better preparation, but the people themselves did not desire wiser or better leadership. Though he led the people wrong, it must be remembered that they were more than willing to follow his lead. The president, the Congress, and the people as a whole all showed an unworthy dread of the appeal to arms.

The wrongs inflicted on our seafaring countrymen by their impressment into foreign ships formed the main cause of the war. Any innocent merchant vessel was liable to seizure at any moment, and when overhauled by a British cruiser short of men was sure to be stripped of most of her crew. The British were themselves the judges as to whether a seaman should be pronounced a native of America or of Britain. If a captain lacked his full complement there was little doubt as to the view he would take of any man's nationality.

Instead of declaring war, Jefferson put in practice one of his favorite schemes, that of commercial war, as he called it. In other words, he declared an embargo on all American shipping, refusing to allow any of it to leave American ports, and hoping thus so to injure the interests of England and France as to force them to refrain from injuring America. A futile hope, rightly destined to meet with the failure that should attend the efforts of men and nations that lack the most elementary and needful of all virtues, the orderly courage of the soldier.

Jefferson could not make his embargo work. It did some damage to Great Britain and France, but by no means enough to force either to yield, while it wrought such ruin in America as very nearly to bring about a civil war. It was a mean and ignoble effort to avoid war, and it spoke ill for its promoters that they should prefer it to the manlier course which would have appealed to all really brave and generous natures. At the very end of his administration Jefferson was forced to submit to the repeal of his pet measure.

The temper of Jefferson's mind, and the extraordinary military foolishness of the American people as a whole, may be gathered from the fact that, in preparing for war, all he could suggest was that the ships of war should be laid up so as not to tempt the enemy to capture them, and that the United States should rely upon the worthless militia on shore, and a preposterous system of what may be called horse-gunboats, that is, gunboats which could be drawn ashore and carried on wheeled vehicles to any point menaced by a hostile fleet.

For a variety of reasons they failed utterly in every serious attack that they made on a man-of-war. They were utterly useless except in perfectly calm weather, for in any wind the heavy guns caused them to career over so as to make it difficult to keep them right side up, and impossible to fire. Even in smooth water they could not be fought at anchor, requiring to be kept in position by means of sweeps, and they were very unstable, the recoil of guns causing them to roll so as to make it difficult to aim with any accuracy after the first discharge.

It does not seem that they were very well managed, but they were such ill-conditioned craft that the best officers might be pardoned for feeling uncomfortable in them. Their operations throughout the war offer a painfully ludicrous commentary on Jefferson's remarkable project of having our navy composed exclusively of such craft. The failure of the gunboats ought to have taught the lesson (though it did not) that too great an economy in providing the means of defense may prove very expensive in the end, and that good officers and men are powerless when embarked in worthless vessels.

Father of Nullification and Therefore Secession

The separatist feeling has at times been strong in almost every section of the Union. Calhoun and Pickering, Jefferson and Gouverneur Morris, Wendell Phillips and William Taney, Aaron Burr and Jefferson Davis—these and many others of thought and action, East and West, North and South, at different periods of the nation's growth, and at different stages of their own careers, have, for various reasons, and with widely varying purity of motive, headed or joined in separatist movements. Nevertheless, they warred against the right, and strove mightily to bring about the downfall and undoing of the nation.

Even when their motives were disinterested and their purposes pure, and even when they received much provocation, they must be adjudged as lacking the wisdom, the foresight, and the broad devotion to all the land over which the flag floats, without which no statesman can rank as really great. The enemies of the Union were the enemies of America and of mankind, whose success would have plunged their country into an abyss of shame and misery. It is well indeed for our land that we of this generation have at last learned to think nationally, and, no matter in what State we live, to view our whole country with the pride of personal possession.

Virginia stands easily first among all our commonwealths for the statesmen and warriors she has brought forth, and it is noteworthy that during the long contest between the nationalists and separatists, which forms the central fact of our history in the first three-quarters of a century of our national life, she gave leaders to both sides, Washington and Marshall to the one, and Jefferson to the other, when the question was one of opinion as to whether the Union should be built up.

When in 1798 Virginia was preparing to take part in the abortive secession agitation of that year, Patrick Henry warned her truthfully that if there was a rising, she would find her levies opposed to troops led by her own great war chief. The famous Alien and Sedition laws were exciting great disgust, and in Virginia and Kentucky, Jefferson was using them as handles wherewith to guide seditious agitation—not that he believed in sedition, but because he considered it good party policy, for the moment, to excite it. The parties hated each other with rancorous virulence. The newspapers teemed with the foulest abuse of public men; accusations of financial dishonesty were rife. Washington himself was not spared.

Patrick Henry opposed the motion in Virginia and threatened its adherents with being brought face-to-face with the armed men of the nation under Washington. The State's greatest orator, Henry, halted beside the grave to denounce the seditious schemes of the disunion agitators with the same burning, thrilling eloquence that, thirty years before, had stirred to their depths the hearts of his hearers when he bade defiance to the tyrannous might of the British king.

A generation later, during Jackson's presidential terms, Old Hickory and his adherents were engaged in struggles with the Nullifiers. At this time it is not necessary to discuss nullification as a constitutional dogma. It is an absurdity too great to demand serious refutation. The United States has the same right to protect itself from death by nullification, secession, or rebellion that a man has to protect himself from death by assassination.

The nullification movement in South Carolina had nothing to do, except in the most distant way, with slavery. Its immediate cause was the high tariff. Remotely, it sprang from the same feelings which produced the Virginia and Kentucky Resolutions of 1798. The South Carolinian statesmen proclaimed the doctrine of nullification—that is, proclaimed that if any State deemed a federal law improper, it could proceed to declare that law null and void so far as its own territory was concerned. Jefferson was quoted as the father of the idea, and the Kentucky Resolutions of 1798–1799, which he drew, were cited as the precedent for the South Carolinian action. The Nullifiers were correct. Jefferson was the father of nullification, and therefore of secession.[4]

He used the word "nullify" in the original draft which he supplied to the Kentucky legislature, and though the body struck it out of the resolutions which they passed in 1798, they inserted it in those of the following year. This was done mainly as an unscrupulous party move on Jefferson's part, and when his side came into power he became a firm upholder of the Union. And, being constitutionally unable to put a proper value on truthfulness, he even denied that his resolutions could be construed to favor nullification—though they could by no possibility be construed to mean anything else. The authors of the Kentucky and Virginia Resolutions of 1798 and of the resolutions of the Hartford Convention in 1814 tried in later years to show that these also were not disunion movements. The effort is as vain in one case as is the other.

That Slippery Demagogue

Heaven knows how cordially I despise Jefferson, but he did have one great virtue which his Federalist opponents lacked—he stood for the plain people, for the same people whom Abraham Lincoln afterward represented. Hamilton and the Federalists fell from power because they could not learn the one great truth taught by Jefferson—that in America a statesman should trust the people, and should endeavor to secure to each man all possible individual liberty, confident that he will use it aright.

I have always regarded Jefferson, in spite of his having rendered great services to the people, as also having been one of the most mischievous enemies of democracy, one of the very weakest whom we have ever had in public life. The extreme doctrinaires, who are fiercest in declaiming in favor of freedom, are in reality its worst foes, far more dangerous than any absolute monarch ever can be. When liberty becomes license, some form of one-man power is not far distant.

It is a mistake to suppose that there was a general monarchial tendency in his time. There was not. The tendency was overwhelmingly against monarchy, and the revival of the monarchic idea was due partly to the silly inefficiency of men like Jefferson when they actually tried to administer or help administer the government, and partly to the violent excesses of the men such as the French revolutionists. I believe that the French revolutionists, when, not content with what they had gained in 1789, they pushed forward into the four years of red anarchy that culminated in the terror, did more to damage democracy, more to put back the cause of popular government, than any despot or oligarchy from that time to this. Remember that these were the men who made a "religion" of democracy, who typified "liberty" as a goddess, and who prattled words like these while their hearts were black with murder committed in such names.

We are naturally democratic as a people, naturally individualistic. Where Jefferson did good, he did good merely by upholding and justifying our doing what we should have done in any event. The one great reason for our having succeeded as no other people ever has, is to be found in that common sense which has enabled us to preserve the largest possible individual freedom on the one hand, while showing an equally remarkable capacity for combination on the other.

The absolute terror with which even moderate Federalists had viewed the victory of the Democrats was in a certain sense justifiable, for the leaders who led the Democrats to triumph were the very men who had fought tooth and nail against every measure necessary to make us a free, orderly, and powerful nation. The Jeffersonians, with all their unwisdom and demagogy, had embodied principles so wholly absurd in practice that it was out of the question to apply them at all to the actual running of the government. Jefferson could write or speak—and could feel too—the most high-sounding sentiments, but once it came to actions he was absolutely at sea, and on almost every matter—especially where he did well—he had to fall back on the Federalist theories. Almost the only important point on which he allowed himself free scope was that of the national defenses. And here, particularly as regards the navy, he worked very serious harm to the country. Otherwise, he generally adopted and acted on the views of his predecessors.

I have no use for the Hamiltonian who is aristocratic, or for the Jeffersonian who is a demagogue. Let us trust the people as Jefferson did, but not flatter them. I have never cared in the least for the kind of popularity which Lafayette so thoroughly enjoyed, and which Jefferson enjoyed, popularity which the popular man basks in for and of itself, without reference to transmuting it into any positive achievement. That slippery demagogue, that popular idol, Jefferson, had behind him the mass of the people as the rank and file of his party, yet was less fit to conduct the country in troublous times than any president we have ever had. The scholarly, timid, and shifty doctrinaire who supplanted the elder Adams was politically very successful, but this will not alter my opinion.

Tortuous Intrigues against Washington

The twelve years' history of Washington's and Adams's administrations is the history of a nearly balanced struggle between the Federalists and the anti-Federalists, who gradually adopted the name first of Republicans and then of Democrats. The men who favored the adoption of the Constitution grew into the Federal party. The great opponent of Washington's ideals, Thomas Jefferson, opposed it, and wished to construe it as narrowly as possible and to restrict the powers of the central government even to the point of impotence. The Jeffersonians believed in a government so weak as to be ineffective.

The various bodies of men who afterward coalesced into the Republican Party were frantically in favor of the French Revolution, regarding it with a fatuous admiration quite as foolish as the horror with which it affected most of the Federalists. They were already looking to Jefferson as their leader, and Jefferson, though at the time secretary of state under Washington, was secretly encouraging them, and was playing a very discreditable part toward his chief.

At this period Genet was in the midst of his preposterous career as minister from the French Republic to the United States. The ultra-admirers of the French Revolution not only lost their heads, but turned Genet's as well, and persuaded him that the people were with him and were ready to oppose Washington and the Central Government in the interests of revolutionary France. Genet wished to embroil America with England, and sought to fit out American privateers on the seacoast towns to prey on English commerce, and to organize on the Ohio River an armed expedition to conquer Louisiana, as Spain was then an ally of England and at war with France.

Kentucky was ripe for Genet's intrigues, and he found the available leader for the movement in the person of George Rogers Clark. Genet immediately commissioned Clark as a major-general in the service of the French Republic, and sent out various Frenchmen—Michaux, La Chaise, and others—with civil and military titles, to coöperate with him, to fit out his force as well as possible, and to promise him pay for his expenses. They got some supplies, but found they would have to get most from Philadelphia.

Jefferson's course in the matter was characteristic.[5] Openly, he was endeavoring in a perfunctory manner to carry out Washington's policy of strict neutrality in the contest between France and England, but secretly he was engaged in tortuous intrigues against Washington and was thwarting his wishes, so far as he dared, in regard to Genet. It is impossible that he could have been really misled as to Michaux's character and the object of his visits. Nevertheless, he actually gave him a letter of introduction to the Kentucky governor, Isaac Shelby.

I cannot imagine it possible for Jefferson to have been ignorant of the real desires of Michaux; and his absolutely tortuous dealings with Genet at the same time show the lengths to which he was willing to go in deceiving Washington and supporting France. The mass of the Jeffersonians put the interests of France above the interest and honor of America.

Jefferson was the underhanded but malignantly bitter leader of the antinational forces which gradually rallied against the Washington policies. The campaign he carried on against Washington and then against the Federal Party was as unscrupulous as anything Hearst, Pulitzer, or the *Evening Post* do nowadays. Partly owing to the adroit and successful demagogy of Jefferson, Virginia finally became so estranged from Washington that when his administration was closing, the legislature actually refused to pass a formal resolution approving the wisdom of his course as president.

Isn't it humiliating to realize that Jefferson—who I think was, not even excepting Buchanan, the most incompetent chief executive we ever had—should have been, as president, rather more popular than Washington himself at the very close of his administration, and that almost all of the State legislatures should have petitioned him to serve for another term and should have sent him formal messages of grateful thanks for his services after his term was over?

Jefferson led the people wrong, and followed them when they went wrong. And though he had plenty of imagination and of sentimental aspiration, he had neither courage nor farsighted common sense, where the interests of the nation were at stake. It was the work of Washington and Hamilton, accomplished in the teeth of the Jeffersonian resistance after the Revolutionary War, which of course rendered it possible for Lincoln and Grant and the men who upheld the one or followed the other to keep this country a nation.

We Were Bound to Have Louisiana

The Jeffersonian Republican Party did very much that was evil, but on the vital question of the West and its territorial expansion the Jeffersonian Party was, on the whole, emphatically right, and its opponents, the Federalists, emphatically wrong. The Jeffersonians believed in the acquisition of territory in the West, and the Federalists did not. The Jeffersonians believed that the westerners should be allowed to govern themselves precisely as other citizens of the United States did, and should be given their full share in the management of national affairs.

So it was with the acquisition of Louisiana. This purchase was the greatest instance of expansion in our history. It definitely decided that we were to become a great continental republic, by far the foremost power in the western hemisphere. It is one of three or four great landmarks in our history—the great turning points in our development.

Jefferson, Livingston, and their fellow statesmen and diplomats concluded the treaty which determined the manner in which it came into our possession. But they did not really have much to do with fixing the terms even of this treaty, and the part which they played in the acquisition of Louisiana in no way resembles, even remotely, the part which was played by Seward, for instance, in acquiring Alaska. If it had not been for Seward, and the political leaders who thought as he did, Alaska might never have been acquired at all. But the Americans would have won Louisiana in any event, even if the treaty of Livingston and Monroe had not been signed. The real history of the acquisition must tell of the great westward movement begun in 1769, and not merely of the feeble diplomacy of Jefferson's administration.

No American settlers were thronging into Alaska. The desire to acquire it among the people at large was vague, and was fanned into sluggish activity only by the genius of the far-seeing statesmen who purchased it. The credit of such an acquisition really does belong to the men who secured the adoption of the treaty by which it was acquired. The honor of adding Alaska to the nation domain belongs to the statesmen who at the time controlled the Washington government. They were not figureheads in the transaction. They were the vital, moving forces.

The winning of Louisiana was due to no one man, and least of all to any statesman or set of statesmen. It followed inevitably upon the great westward thrust of the settler folk—a thrust which was delivered blindly, but which no rival race could parry until it was stopped by the ocean itself. We were bound to have Louisiana, if not by bargain and sale then by fair shock of arms.

The vast region that was then known as upper Louisiana—the territory stretching from the Mississippi to the Pacific—was owned by the Spaniards, but only in shadowy fashion, and could not have been held by any European power against the sturdy westward pressure of the rifle-bearing settlers. The Spanish rulers realized fully that they were too weak effectively to cope with the Americans. It was at this time that the French influence over Spain was most complete. The need of the Spaniards seemed to Napoleon his opportunity. By the bribe of a petty Italian principality he persuaded the Bourbon king of Spain to cede Louisiana to the French.

Jefferson was president, and Madison secretary of state. Both were men of high and fine qualities who rendered, at one time or another, real and great service to the country. Jefferson in particular played in our political life a part of immense importance. But the country has never had two statesmen less capable of upholding the honor and dignity of the nation, or even of preserving its material well-being when menaced by foreign foes. They were peaceful men, quite unfitted to grapple with an enemy who expressed himself through deeds rather than words. When stunned by the din of arms they showed themselves utterly inefficient rulers.

It was these two timid, well-meaning statesmen who now found themselves pitted against Napoleon and Napoleon's minister, Talleyrand— against the greatest warrior and lawgiver and against one of the greatest diplomats of modern times. Against two men, moreover, whose sodden lack of conscience was but heightened by the contrast of their brilliant genius and lofty force of character—two men who were unable to so much as appreciate that there was shame in the practice of venality, dishonesty, mendacity, cruelty, and treachery.

Jefferson was the least warlike of presidents, and he loved the French with a servile devotion. But his party was strongest in precisely those parts of the country where the mouth of the Mississippi was held to be of right the property of the United States, and the pressure of public opinion was too strong for Jefferson to think of resisting it. Jefferson was forced to tell his French friends that if their nation persisted in its purpose, America would be obliged to marry itself to the navy and army of England. Even he could see that for the French to take Louisiana meant war with the United States sooner or later. And as above all things he wished peace, he made every effort to secure the coveted territory by purchase.

Jefferson took various means, official and unofficial, of impressing upon Napoleon the strength of feeling in the United States over the matter, and the utterances came as near menace as his pacific nature would permit. To the great French conqueror, however, accustomed to violence and to the strife of giants, Jefferson's somewhat vacillating attitude did not seem impressive, and the one course which would have impressed Napoleon was not followed by the American president. Jefferson refused to countenance any proposal to take prompt possession of Louisiana by force or to assemble an army which could act with immediate vigor in time of need.

It was no argument of Jefferson's or of the American diplomats, but the inevitable trend of events, that finally brought about the change in Napoleon's mind. The army he sent to Haiti wasted away by disease and in combat with the blacks. Napoleon could not afford to hamper himself with the difficult defense of a distant province, and to incur the hostility of a new foe, at the very moment when he was entering on another struggle with his old European enemies. Moreover, he needed money in order to carry on the struggle.

The ratification of the treaty brought on sharp debates in Congress. Jefferson had led his party into power as the special champion of States' rights and the special opponent of National Sovereignty. He and they rendered a very great service to the nation by acquiring Louisiana, but it was at the cost of violating every precept which they had professed to hold dear, and of showing that their warfare on the Federalists had been waged on behalf of principles which they were obliged to confess were shams the moment they were put to the test.

This First Exploring Expedition

The earliest and most important expeditions of the Americans into the unknown country which the nation had just purchased were led by young officers of the regular army. The first of these expeditions was planned by Jefferson himself and authorized by Congress. The explorers were carefully instructed to report upon the geography, physical characteristics, and zoology of the region traversed, as well as upon its wild human denizens. Jefferson was fond of science, and in appreciation of the desirability of non-remunerative scientific observation and investigation he stood honorably distinguished among the public men of the day. To him justly belongs the credit of originating this first exploring expedition[6] ever undertaken by the United States government.

Beyond the Mississippi all that was really known was the territory in the immediate neighborhood of the little French villages near the mouth of the Missouri. The headwaters of the Missouri were absolutely unknown. What lay beyond them, and between them and the Pacific, was not even guessed at. The Rocky Mountains were not known to exist, so far as the territory newly acquired by the United States was concerned.

The two officers chosen to carry through the work belonged to families already honorably distinguished for service on the western border. One was Captain Meriwether Lewis, representatives of whose family had served so prominently in Dunmore's War. The other was Lieutenant (by courtesy Captain) William Clark, a younger brother of George Rogers Clark. These two hardy and daring adventurers opened the door to the heart of the far West—a great deed. No man had ever crossed or explored that part of the continent which the United States had just acquired. They pointed the way to the tens of thousands of settlers who were to come after them, and who were to build thriving commonwealths in the lonely wilderness which they had traversed.

Later on, Lewis was made governor of Louisiana Territory, and a couple of years afterward died, as was supposed, by his own hand in a squalid log cabin on the Chickasaw trace, though it was never certain that he had not been murdered. Clark was afterward governor of the territory, when its name had been changed to Missouri, and he also served honorably as Indian agent. But neither of them did anything further of note, nor indeed was it necessary, for they had performed a feat which will always give them a place on the honor roll of American worthies.

Jefferson stood for many ideas which, in their actual working, have proved pernicious to our country, but he deserves well of all Americans, in the first place because of his services to science, and, in the next place, what was of far more importance, because of his steadfast friendship for the great West, and his appreciation of its magnificent future.

Aaron Burr

A Man Who Is Morally Capable of Any Iniquity

We have never had in the presidential chair any man who did not sincerely desire to benefit the people and whose own personal ambition were not entirely honorable, although as much cannot be said of certain aspirants for the place, such as Aaron Burr. Have you ever read Burr's journal, which he kept for his daughter? It is the journal of a man who is morally capable of any iniquity.

In New York, Aaron Burr led a political career as stormy and checkered as the careers of New York politicians have generally been. His career had been striking. As friend or as enemy he had been thrown intimately and on equal terms with the greatest political leaders of the day. He had supplied almost the only feeling which Jefferson, the chief of the Democratic Party, and Hamilton, the greatest Federalist, ever possessed in common. For bitterly though Hamilton and Jefferson had hated each other, there was one man whom each of them had hated more, and that was Aaron Burr. There was not a man in the country who did not know about the brilliant and unscrupulous party leader who had killed Hamilton in the most famous duel that ever took place on American soil, and who, by a nearly successful intrigue, had come within one vote of supplanting Jefferson in the presidency.

He had shown himself as adroit as he was unscrupulous in the use of all arts of the machine manager. The fitful and gusty breath of popular favor made him at one time the most prominent and successful politician in the State, and one of the two or three most prominent and successful in the nation. Then his open enemies and secret rivals all combined against him. The Clintonians and Livingstons reduced Burr's influence in the Democratic Party to a nullity, and finally drove him out, receiving the hearty support of Jefferson, who always strove to break down any possible rival in his party.

He was not renominated for vice president, George Clinton being put in his place. In the State election about the same time Morgan Lewis was nominated for governor. Burr ran for the office as an Independent, hoping to carry not only his own faction of the Democracy, but also the entire Federalist vote. The majority of the Federalists did support him, but a large number, under Hamilton's lead, refused to do so, and though he carried the city, he was beaten overwhelmingly in the State at large. Hamilton grew to regard him with especial dislike and distrust, because of his soaring ambition, his cunning, and his lack of conscience.

Burr was now a ruined man, hated by all factions and parties. Nevertheless, he played out the losing game to the last with unmoved force and unflinching resolution. And he took cool and ferocious vengeance on his greatest and most formidable foe, Hamilton. The duel was then a recognized feature of society and politics, and had become a characteristic adjunct of the savage party contests in New York. One of Burr's followers had killed Hamilton's eldest son in a duel.

In 1804, after his defeat for the governorship, Burr forced a duel on Hamilton, and mortally wounded him in a meeting with pistols at Weehawken, then a favorite resort for duelists. Hamilton's death caused the utmost horror and anger. The whole city mourned him, even his political opponents forgetting all save his generous and noble qualities, and the renown of his brilliant statesmanship. Burr was thenceforth an ostracized man, and dueling in New York received its deathblow.

One of the Worst of All Possible Crimes

Shifty and fertile in expedients, his local prestige ruined, Aaron Burr turned his restless eyes toward the West. He had already been obscurely connected with separatist intrigues in the Northeast, and he determined to embark in similar intrigues on an infinitely grander scale in the West and Southwest. A particularly spectacular adventurer, Burr was ready to go into either the conquest of Mexico, or a part of it, or else into a scheme to separate the West, according as circumstances might turn out.

Such events as Burr's conspiracy cannot be properly understood if we fail to remember that they were but the most spectacular or most important manifestations of what occurred many times. There have always been plenty who took part in or directed them for their own selfish ends, or whose minds were so warped and their sense of political morality so crooked as to make them originate schemes that would have reduced us to the impotent level of the Spanish-American republics. Burr had been vice president of the United States, and was a brilliant and able man, of imposing personality, whose intrigues in the West attracted an attention altogether disproportionate to their real weight. His conspiracy was merely one, and by no means the most dangerous, of the various conspiracies in which men like Wilkinson, Sebastian, and many of the members of the early Democratic societies in Kentucky bore a part.

In 1803, Aaron Burr of New York was undoubtedly anxious to bring about in the Northeast what sixty years later Jefferson Davis of Mississippi so nearly succeeded in doing in the South. And the attempt of the South to make a hero of the one is as foolish as it would be to make a hero of the other in the North. There are very few of our statesmen whose characters can be painted in simple, uniform colors, like Washington and Lincoln on the one hand, or Burr and Davis on the other. The moral difference between Benedict Arnold on the one hand, and Aaron Burr or Jefferson Davis on the other, is precisely the difference that obtains between a politician who sells his vote for money and one who supports a bad measure in consideration of being given some high political position. At present, treason, like adultery, ranks as one of the worst of all possible crimes.

In spite of Burr's personal courage he lacked entirely the great military qualities necessary to successful revolutionary leadership of the kind to which he aspired. Though in some ways the most practical of politicians, he had a strong element of the visionary in his character. It was perhaps this, joined to his striking moral defects, which brought about and made complete his downfall in New York. His wild schemes had in them too strong an element of the unreal and the grotesque to be in very fact dangerous.

Burr was put on trial for high treason with Wilkinson as State's evidence. Jefferson made himself the especial champion of Wilkinson. Nevertheless, the general cut a contemptible figure at the trial, for no explanation could make his course square with honorable dealing. Burr was acquitted on a technicality. In the matter of treason I do not think him worse than some of the men who at the same time loudly condemned him. Wilkinson, the double traitor, the bribe taker, the corrupt servant of a foreign government, remained at the head of the American army.[1] Thus ended ingloriously the wildest, most spectacular, and least dangerous of all the intrigues for western disunion.

The War of 1812

In the Teeth of the Mightiest Naval Power

My criticism of the United States in 1812 is heavy but it is not because she went to war with England. It is because she did not prepare effectively in advance for the war and wage it effectively, and indeed, as far as I am concerned, I think she ought to have declared war on both France and England.

There was but one possible way by which to gain and keep the respect of either France or Britain: that was by the possession of power, and the readiness to use it if necessary, and power in this case meant a formidable fighting navy. Had America possessed a fleet of twenty ships of the line, her sailors could have plied their trade unmolested, and the three years of war, with its loss of blood and money, would have been avoided. From the merely monetary standpoint such a navy would have been the cheapest kind of insurance, and morally its advantages would have been incalculable, for every American worth the name would have lifted his head higher because of its existence.

During the early years of this century England's naval power stood at a height never reached before or since by that of any other nation. On every sea her navies rode, not only triumphant, but with none to dispute their sway. Since the year 1792 each European nation, in turn, had learned to feel bitter dread of the weight of England's hand. In the Baltic the descendents of the Vikings had seen their whole navy destroyed at Copenhagen. A few years before 1812, the greatest sea fighter of all time had died at Trafalgar Bay, and in dying had crumbled to pieces the navies of France and of Spain.

Such was Great Britain's naval power when the Congress of the United States declared war upon her. While she could number her thousand sail, the American navy included but half a dozen frigates, and six or eight sloops and brigs. And it is small surprise that the British officers should have regarded their new foe with contemptuous indifference. It must be but a poor-spirited American whose veins do not tingle with pride when he reads of the cruises and fights of the sea captains, and their grim prowess, which kept the old Yankee flag floating over the waters of the Atlantic for three years, in the teeth of the mightiest naval power the world has ever seen.

On land and water the contest took the form of a succession of petty actions, in which the glory acquired by the victor seldom eclipsed the disgrace incurred by the vanquished. Americans declared that Canada must and should be conquered, but the conquering came quite as near being the other way. British writers insisted that the American navy should be swept from the sea, and during the sweeping process it increased fourfold.

In June 1812, Madison sent in his declaration of war, the two chief grievances alleged being the right of search and the impressment of seamen. War was declared, and as a contest for the rights of seamen, it was largely waged on the ocean. We also had not a little fighting to do on land, in which, as a rule, we came out second best. Few or no preparations for the war had been made, and the result was such as might have been anticipated. After dragging on through three dreary and uneventful years it came to an end in 1815, by a peace which left matters in almost precisely the state in which the war had found them.

The material results were not very great, at least in their effect on Great Britain, whose enormous navy did not feel in the slightest degree the loss of a few frigates and sloops. But morally the result was of inestimable benefit to the United States. The victories kept up the spirits of the people, cast down by the defeats on land; practically decided in favor of the Americans the chief question in dispute, Great Britain's right of search and impressments; and gave the navy, and thereby the country, a worldwide reputation. I doubt if ever before a nation gained so much honor by a few single-ship duels. For there can be no question which side came out of the war with the greatest credit. Our victorious sea fights were magnified absurdly by most of our writers at the time, but they do not need to be magnified, for as they are any American can look back upon them with the keenest national pride.

The British navy, numbering at the outset a thousand cruisers, had accomplished less than the American, which numbered but a dozen. Of the twelve single-ship actions, two undoubtedly redounded most to the credit of the British, in two the honors were nearly even, and in the other eight the superiority of the Americans was very manifest. For a hundred and thirty years England had no equal on the sea, and now she suddenly found one in the untried navy of an almost unknown power.

Incompetent Commanders and Untrained Troops

The events of the war on land teach very little to the statesman who studies history in order to avoid in the present the mistakes of the past, but besides this, the battles and campaigns are of very little interest to the student of military matters. While our navy had been successful, the war on land had been for us full of humiliation.

The battles, though marked by as bloody and obstinate fighting as ever took place, were waged between small bodies of men, and were not distinguished by any feats of generalship, so that they are not of any special interest to the historian. In fact, the only really noteworthy feat of arms of the war took place at New Orleans, and the only military genius that the struggle developed was Andrew Jackson. His deeds are worthy of all praise, and the battle he won was in many ways so peculiar as to make it well worth a closer study than it has yet received.

Our defeats were exactly such as any man might have foreseen, and there is nothing to be learned from the follies committed by incompetent commanders and untrained troops when in the presence of skilled officers having under them disciplined soldiers. After two years of warfare, Scott records in his autobiography[1] that there were but two books of tactics (one written in French) in the entire army on the Niagara frontier. British troops, trained in many wars, thrashed the raw troops opposed to them whenever they had anything like a fair chance.

All through the war the seacoasts of the United States had been harried by small predatory excursions. A part of what is now the State of Maine was conquered with little resistance, and kept until the close of hostilities. In August 1814, a more serious invasion was planned, and some 5,000 regular troops—regulars, sailors, and marines—were landed, under the command of General Ross. So utterly helpless was the Democratic administration at Washington, that during the two years of warfare hardly any steps had been taken to protect the Capitol or the country round about. What little was done was done entirely too late and bungled badly in addition.

Ross and Cockburn moved against Washington and encountered a huddle of seven thousand American militia at Bladensburg. It would not be called an army. A few companies were in uniform. The rest were clad as they would have been clad in the fields, except that they had muskets. They were under two or three worthless generals, one named Winder being in supreme command, and various members of the cabinet, notably Monroe, accompanied by President Madison in riding or driving aimlessly about among the troops. As Ross and Cockburn led their troops into Washington they were fired on from a house, Ross's horse being killed. They then proceeded to burn the Capitol and the White House, together with various other public buildings. Having completed their work, Ross and Cockburn marched back to the coast.

That Hundred Years of Peace Committee

The War of 1812 was a thoroughly discreditable war from the stand-point of our people as a whole, and yet in 1912 the British and American peace enthusiasts were filled with a plan, in the first place, to get a monument to George Washington at Westminster Abbey, where I would regard it as preposterous to put him, and in the next place, to erect a statue to Queen Victoria in Central Park, thereby furnishing a steady occupation for the police force in protecting it from Celtic enthusiasts whose life ambition it would be to blow it up. John Paul Jones in front of the Admiralty office, and Ross and Cockburn in Washington, preferably one in front of the White House and the other of the Capitol, would, I have not a doubt, be accepted with rapture by that delegation. A more preposterous body than the American and British members of that "Hundred Years of Peace" committee you could not well imagine.

Thomas Macdonough

A Higher Fame Than Any Other Commander

The victory of Lake Erie was most important, but the "glory" acquired by it most certainly has been estimated at more than its worth. Most Americans, even the well educated, if asked which was the most glorious victory of the war, would point to this battle. Captain Perry's name is more widely known than that of any other commander. Every schoolboy reads about him, if of no other sea captain, yet he certainly stands on a lower grade than either Hull or Macdonough, and not a bit higher than a dozen others.

When Great Britain seriously turned her attention to her transatlantic foe, and assembled in Canada an army of 14,000 men at the head of Lake Champlain, congressional forethought enabled it to be opposed by soldiers who, it is true, were as well disciplined, as hardy, and as well commanded as any in the world, but who were only a few hundred strong, backed by more or less incompetent militia. Only Macdonough's skill and Sir George Prevost's incapacity saved us from a serious disaster. The sea fight reflected high honor on our seamen.

Sir George Prevost, with an army of veteran troops, marched south along the shores of Lake Champlain to Plattsburg, which was held by General Macomb with 2,000 regulars and perhaps double that number of nearly worthless militia—a force that the British could have scattered to the winds. But the British fleet was captured by Commodore Macdonough in the fight on the lake. The effects of the victory were immediate and of the highest importance. Sir George Prevost and his army fled in great haste and confusion back to Canada, leaving our northern frontier clear for the remainder of the war, while the victory had a very great effect on the negotiations for peace.

It will always be a source of surprise that the American public should have so glorified Perry's victory over an inferior force, and have paid comparatively little attention to Macdonough's victory, which really was won against decided odds in ships, men, and metal. Lake Erie teaches us the advantage of having the odds on our side; Lake Champlain, that, even if they are not, skill can counteract them. The British sailors on the lakes were as good as our own, but no better. None of their commanders compares with Macdonough.

Macdonough in this battle won a higher fame than any other commander of the war, British or American. He had a decidedly superior force to contend against. It was solely owing to his foresight and resource that we won the victory. His skill, seamanship, quick eye, readiness of resource, and indomitable pluck are beyond all praise. Down to the time of the Civil War he is the greatest figure in our naval history. A thoroughly religious man, he was as generous and humane as he was skillful and brave. One of the bravest of our sea captains, he has left a stainless name behind him.

The Feats of That Greatest of All Soldiers

I do not mean in any way or shape to compare Macdonough to Nelson, the greatest sea fighter of all time. Trafalgar and the Nile were great victories, but in according to the great sea captain who won them all the praise to which he is entitled, it yet remains true that his opponents were of so poor an order as to offer him every possible advantage and to make his victory as nearly certain as such a thing can be. The

English navy at that great culminating period of its achievement and glory won its tremendous victories against foes of utter military inefficiency. At Copenhagen the Danes had only hulks. The Spanish warships were such in name only. It was physically impossible for them to win against an antagonist who could fight at all. The Dutch navy suffered from precisely the trouble of the French, as it was a revolutionary navy, disorganized by a revolution. The French navy, the chief foe, was manned in a fashion which made it ludicrous to think of its opposing any respectable opponent.

Contrast all this with the feats of that greatest of all soldiers, Hannibal, who led a mercenary army upon an expedition as daring as that of Alexander, into the heart of the most formidable fighting nation of antiquity, and with his sepoys again and again defeated the superior numbers of the most formidable troops that the world then held. Nelson won crushing and decisive victories over a foe whom all his fellow admirals also invariably, though much less decisively, beat. But Hannibal defeated a foe against whom no army not commanded by himself could make head, and for a space nearly equally a lifetime of half a generation, marched to and fro at will through that foe's own country.

James Madison

A Mere Pale Shadow of Jefferson

In the Constitutional Convention Madison, a moderate Federalist, was the man who, of all who were there, saw things most clearly as they were, and whose theories most closely corresponded with the principles finally adopted. And although even he was at first dissatisfied with the result, and both by word and by action interpreted the Constitution in widely different ways at different times, still this was Madison's time of glory.

He was one of the statesmen who do extremely useful work, but only at a single given crisis. While the Constitution was being formed and adopted, he stood at the very front. But in his later career he sunk his own individuality, and became a mere pale shadow of Jefferson, showing sheeplike submission to the abler, more crafty, and more unscrupulous man at the time of the nullification of the Virginia and Kentucky Resolutions, which Madison fathered jointly with Jefferson. Men like Madison, Samuel Adams, and Patrick Henry did the nation great service at times, but each at some one or two critical junctures ranged himself with the forces of disorder.

He did not believe that the ignorant and dependent could be trusted to vote, thinking the freeholders the safest guardians of our rights. On the suffrage his views are perfectly defensible. It is simply idle folly to talk of suffrage as being an "inborn" or "natural" right. There are enormous communities totally unfit for its exercise, while true universal suffrage has never been, and never will be, seriously advocated by anyone. There must always be an age limit, and such a limit must necessarily be purely arbitrary. The wildest Democrat of Revolutionary times did not dream of doing away with the restrictions of race and sex which kept most Americans from the ballot box.

A Ridiculously Incompetent Leader for a War

Excepting Jefferson, we have never produced an executive more helpless than Madison, when it came to grappling with real dangers and difficulties. Like his predecessor, he was only fit to be president in a time of profound peace. He was utterly out of place the instant matters grew turbulent, or difficult problems arose to be solved, and he was a ridiculously incompetent leader for a war with Great Britain.[1] The nerveless administration at Washington did not even take steps to defend the capital city.

He was entirely too timid to have embarked on such a venture of his own accord, and was simply forced into it by the threat of losing his second term. The fiery young Democrats of the South and West, and their brothers in the Middle States, were the authors of the war. They themselves, for all their bluster, were but one shade less incompetent than their nominal chief, when it came to actual work, and were shamefully unable to make their words good by deeds. The South and West brought on the War of 1812, wherein the East was the chief sufferer.

The bulk of our people, and the politicians, from the president down, who represented our people, made a wretched showing in that war, and because of this showing the Union came very near splitting up. If history were rightly taught, this fact would be brought out clearly in our schools. The blame that attaches to Madison and the elder Democratic-Republican leaders, as well as to their younger associates,

Clay, Calhoun, and the rest, who fairly flogged them into action, relates to their failure to make any preparations for the contest, to their helpless inability to carry it on, and to the extraordinary weakness and indecision of their policy throughout, and on all these points it is hardly possible to visit them with too unsparing censure.

The administration drifted into a war which it had neither the wisdom to avoid nor the forethought to prepare. During the first year the monotonous record of humiliations and defeats was only relieved by the splendid victories of the navy which the Federalists had created twelve years previously. It must be remembered that Jackson won his fights absolutely unhelped by the administration. In fact, the government at Washington does not deserve one shred of credit for any of the victories we won, although to it we directly owe the greater number of our defeats. The federal government, throughout the campaign, did absolutely nothing for the defense of Louisiana; neither provisions nor munitions of war of any sort were sent to it, nor were any measures taken for its aid.

The administration of the War Department continued to be a triumph of imbecility to the very last. Monroe's biographer (see *James Monroe*, by Daniel C. Gilman, Boston, 1883, p. 123) thinks he made a good secretary of war. I think he was as much a failure as his predecessors, and a harsher criticism could not be passed on him. Like the other statesmen of his school, he was mighty in word and weak in action, bold to plan but weak to perform. As an instance, contrast his fiery letters to Jackson with the fact that he never gave him a particle of practical help.

Although nominally the peace left things as they had been, practically we gained our point, and we certainly came out of the contest with a greatly increased reputation abroad. In spite of the ludicrous series of failures which began with our first attempt to invade Canada, and culminated at Bladensburg, yet in a succession of contests on the ocean and lakes, we shattered the charmed shield of British naval invincibility. Above all, the contest gave an immense impetus to our national feeling, and freed our politics forever from any dependence on those of a foreign power.

James Monroe

Those Whose Greatness Is Thrust upon Them

James Monroe, the last president of the great House of Virginia, was a courteous, high-bred gentleman, of no especial ability, but well-fitted to act as presidential figurehead during the politically quiet years of that era of good feeling which lasted from 1816 to 1824. He was a very amiable gentleman, but distinctly one who comes in the category of those whose greatness is thrust upon them.[1]

As minister to France, Monroe stayed long enough to get our affairs into a snarl, and was later recalled by Washington, receiving from the latter more than one scathing rebuke. His appointment was an excellent example of the folly of trying to carry on a government on a "nonpartisan" basis. Washington was only gradually weaned from this theory by bitter experience. Both Jefferson and Monroe helped to teach him the lesson.

The United States having requested the French government to withdraw Genet, a harlequin rather than a diplomat, it was done at once, and in return a request was forwarded that the United States would reciprocate by relieving Morris, which of course had to be done also. Monroe, as Morris's successor, entered upon his new duties with an immense flourish, and rapidly gave a succession of startling proofs that he was a minister altogether too much to the taste of the frenzied Jacobinical republicans to whom he was accredited. Indeed, his capers were almost as extraordinary as their own, and seem rather like the antics of some of the early French commanders in Canada, in their efforts to ingratiate themselves with their Indian allies, than like the performance we should expect from a sober Virginian gentleman on a mission to a civilized nation.

However, the fault was really less with him than with his party and with those who sent him. Monroe was an honorable man with a very unoriginal mind, and he simply reflected the wild, foolish views held by all his fellows of the Jeffersonian Democratic-Republican school concerning France. To appoint Monroe, an extreme Democrat, to France, while at the same time appointing Jay, a strong Federalist, to England, was not only an absurdity which did nothing toward reconciling the Federalists and Democrats, but, bearing in mind how these parties stood respective toward England and France, it made also an actual wrong, for it made our foreign policy seem double-faced and deceitful.

While one minister was formally embracing such of the Parisian statesmen as had hitherto escaped the guillotine, and was going through various other theatrical performances that do not appeal to any but a Gallic mind, his fellow was engaged in negotiating a treaty with England that was so obnoxious to France as almost to bring us to a rupture with her. The Jay Treaty was not altogether a good one, and a better might perhaps have been secured. Still, it was better than nothing, and Washington was right in urging its adoption, even while admitting that it was not entirely satisfactory. But certainly, if we intended to enter into such engagements with Great Britain, it was rank injustice to both Monroe and France to send such a man as the former to such a country as the latter.

PART III
Jacksonian Era
(1825-1850)

John Quincy Adams

The Blackleg and the Puritan

The year 1824 saw the complete break-up of the Jeffersonian democracy, which had taken office in 1801. With the close of Monroe's second term the "era of good feeling" came to an end, and the great Democratic-Republican Party split up into several fragments, which gradually crystallized round two centers. But in 1824 this process was still incomplete, and the presidential election of that year was a simple scramble between four candidates—Jackson, Adams, Clay, and Crawford. Jackson had the greatest number of votes, but as no one had a majority, the election was thrown into the House of Representatives, where the Clay men, inasmuch as their candidate was out of the race, went over to Adams and elected him.

Adams, after his election, which was owing to Clay's support, gave Clay the position of secretary of state in his cabinet. Their affair unquestionably had an unfortunate look, and Jackson furiously denounced this as a corrupt bargain, with, so far as appears, little or no justification. The assault was directed with especial bitterness toward Clay, whom Jackson ever afterward included in the very large list of individuals whom he hated with the most rancorous and unreasoning virulence.

Randolph of Roanoke, the privileged eccentric of the Senate, in one of those long harangues in which he touched upon everybody and everything, except possibly the point at issue, made a rabid onslaught upon the Clay-Adams coalition as an alliance of "the Blackleg and the Puritan."[1] Clay, who was susceptible enough to the charge of loose living, but who was a man of rigid honor and rather fond than otherwise of fighting, promptly challenged him, and a harmless interchange of shots took place.

Two tolerably well-defined parties now emerged from the chaos of contending politicians: one was the party of the administration, whose members called themselves National Republicans, and later on Whigs. The other was the Jacksonian Democracy.

Paying Too Little Heed to Party

Adams's inaugural address and first message outlined the Whig policy as favoring a protective tariff, internal improvements, and a free construction of the Constitution generally. The Jacksonians accordingly took the opposite side on all these points, partly from principle and partly from perversity. In the Senate they assailed with turgid eloquence every administration measure, whether it was good or bad, very much of their opposition being purely factious in character. There has never been a time when there was more rabid, objectless, and unscrupulous display of partisanship.

Adams certainly went too far in his nonpartisanship when it came to appointing cabinet and other high officers, his views on such points being not only fantastic, but absolutely wrong. The colorless character of his administration was largely due to his having, in his anxiety to avoid blind and unreasoning adherence to party, committed the only less serious fault of paying too little heed to party, for a healthy party spirit is prerequisite to the performance of effective work in American political life. Adams was not elected purely for himself, but also on account of the men and the principles that he was supposed to represent, and when he partly surrounded himself with men of opposite principles, he just so far, though from the best of motives, betrayed his supporters, and rightfully forfeited much of their confidence.

Adams Rendered a Real Service

John Quincy Adams, after leaving the presidency, again entered public life as a congressman, and achieved conspicuous success in the lower house. Adams rendered a real service when he went to Congress after being president: that is, he showed more regard for the work to be done than for the titular position. Adams did much to earn the gratitude of all Americans. Not the least of his services was his positive refusal to side with the majority of the cultivated people of New England and the Northeast in the period just before the War of 1812, when these cultivated people advised spiritless submission to improper English demands.

In 1812–1814 the Federalist Party, when it declared itself to be the ally of a foreign foe and opposed the national interest at home, became hopelessly discredited when it was abandoned by the best Federalists, or men of the John Quincy Adams type. There were many other Federalist leaders in the same position as himself, especially in the three southern New England States, where the whole Federalist Party laid itself open to the gravest charges of disloyalty.

I Believe with All My Heart in the Monroe Doctrine

The Monroe Doctrine may be briefly defined as forbidding European encroachment on American soil. I believe with all my heart in the Monroe Doctrine. If the Monroe Doctrine did not already exist it would be necessary forthwith to create it. An American may, of course, announce his opposition to the Monroe Doctrine, although by so doing he forfeits all title to far-seeing and patriotic devotion to the interests of his country.

The Monroe Doctrine had for its first exponent Washington. In its present shape it was in reality formulated by John Quincy Adams, who, during the presidency of Monroe, first clearly enunciated the doctrine which bears his chief's name, asserting it against both Spain and Russia. In the clearest and most emphatic terms he stated that the United States could not acquiesce in the acquisition of new territory within the limits of any independent American State, whether in the Northern or Southern Hemisphere, by any European power. He took the position against Russia when Russia threatened to take possession of what is now Oregon. He took this position against Spain when, backed by other powers of Continental Europe, she threatened to reconquer certain of the Spanish-American States.

The Monroe Doctrine is not international law, but there is no necessity that it should be. All that is needful is that it should continue to be a cardinal feature of American policy on this continent. Lawyers, as lawyers, have absolutely nothing whatever to say about it. To argue that it cannot be recognized as a principle of international law is a mere waste of breath. Nobody cares whether it is or is not so recognized, any more than any one cares whether the Declaration of Independence and Washington's Farewell Address are so recognized.

We speak of international law, but international law is something wholly different from private or municipal law, and the capital difference is that there is a sanction for the one and no sanction for the other, that there is an outside force which compels individuals to obey the one, while there is no such outside force to compel obedience as regards the other. International law will, I believe, as the generations pass, grow stronger and stronger until in some way or other there develops the power to make it respected. But as yet it is only in the first formative period. As yet, as a rule, each nation is of necessity obliged to judge for itself in matters of vital importance between it and its neighbors.

The Monroe Doctrine was in danger of falling not merely into disuse, but into contempt, until we began to build up our navy. The Monroe Doctrine won't be observed by foreign nations with sufficient strength to disregard it when once it becomes their interest to disregard it, unless we have a navy sufficient to make our assertion of the doctrine good. The Monroe Doctrine, unbacked by a navy, is an empty boast.

A good many of you are probably acquainted with the old proverb: "Speak softly and carry a big stick—you will go far." If a man continually blusters, if he lacks civility, a big stick will not save him from trouble, and neither will speaking softly avail, if back of the softness there does not lie strength, power. As regards the Monroe Doctrine, there is not the least need of blustering about it. The Monroe Doctrine is as strong as the United States Navy, and no stronger.

Andrew Jackson

My Admiration Has Grown Steadily

Andrew Jackson did some awful things and in many respects he was
not more than half civilized, but he was a great deal of a man for all
that, and I have always had a certain sneaking admiration for him.
There has never been a more genuine and rugged American than Old
Hickory. There was one point where Jackson did so well that a lover of
the nation must needs forgive him much for its sake. At this time South
Carolina had entered on a career of nullification and incipient secession. Jackson had many faults, but he was devotedly attached to the
Union, and he had no thought of fear when it came to defending his
country. By his resolute and defiant bearing and his fervent champion-
ship of the federal government he overawed the disunionist party and
staved off for thirty years the attempt at secession.

I was very deeply pleased to have Buell's *Life of Andrew Jackson*
dedicated to me.[1] I am pleased when I have my name coupled with
Andrew Jackson's. You must not think that I put him up with Abraham Lincoln. I do not put anybody up with Abraham Lincoln, but I
have great admiration for Andrew Jackson, and my admiration has
grown steadily since I have been president.[2] Jackson was an American,

and one of the three or four greatest presidents that this nation ever had, one of the three or four greatest public men that any nation has developed in the same length of time—a man who made mistakes, but a man of iron will and incorruptible integrity, fearless, upright, devoted to the welfare of his countrymen, bone of our bone and flesh of our flesh, a typical American if ever there was one.

I draw a sharp distinction between Old Hickory and a great many other presidents. Different presidents have construed and have been able to exercise in widely differing manners the powers conferred upon them. The power wielded by Andrew Jackson was out of all proportion to that wielded by Buchanan, although in theory each was alike. So a strong president may exert infinitely more influence. This is merely stating that in any office the personal equation is always of vital consequence. The Jacksonian Democracy, nominally the party of the multitude, was in reality the nearest approach the United States has ever seen to the "one-man power," and to break with Jackson was to break with the Democratic Party.

After leaving the presidency, in 1837, he retired to The Hermitage, where he lived peacefully and happily until 1845, dying on June 8th of that year. With the exception of Washington and Lincoln, no man has left a deeper mark on American history, and though there is much in his career to condemn, yet all true lovers of America can unite in paying hearty respect to the memory of a man who was emphatically a true American, who served his country valiantly on the field of battle against a foreign foe, and who upheld with the most staunch devotion the cause of the great federal Union.

An Indelible Mark on American History

Andrew Jackson, one of the men whose good fortune it has been to leave an indelible mark on American history, was born on March 15, 1767, almost on the dividing line separating the western portions of what were then the English colonies of North and South Carolina. Jackson himself was too young to take any part in the Revolution as a soldier, but his kin-people and their friends fought and suffered for the American cause, and young Andrew helped them as well as a resolute, hardy boy might.

Young Andrew was struck by a British officer, with a sword, for refusing to pull off his boots, when made captive with other American militia after an unsuccessful fight. The sword scarred both his head and the hand with which he sought to ward the blow, and Jackson, as implacable in enmity as he was persistent in friendship, never forgot or forgave the injury, and never cherished any save feelings of hostility toward the nation of the officer who inflicted it.

When twenty-one years old he made up his mind to better his fortune by removing to what was then the Far West, and accordingly he journeyed through the wilderness to Nashville, Tennessee. Nashville was at that time a straggling village of rude log huts planted down in the midst of the beautiful forest country of middle Tennessee. When Tennessee was made a State, in 1796, Jackson was elected as its first congressman, and shortly afterward as one of its senators.

In the backwoods, love of freedom tended to confound itself with lawlessness, and the Federalist Party had comparatively few supporters. Jackson himself was a radical Democrat in his feelings at this time, and he carried his party spirit so far as to refuse to take part in any measure designed to recognize the wisdom and beneficence of Washington's administration. In after-years it is not likely that even Jackson, little prone though he was to feel regret for anything he had done, cared to remember his attitude of sullen hostility to the founder of the federal government.

When Andrew Jackson was in Congress he voted for the first warships we ever built as part of our regular navy, and he voted against the grant of money to pay our humiliating tribute to the pirates of the Barbary States. Old Hickory was a patriot through and through, and there was not an ounce of timidity in his nature, and of course he felt only indignant contempt for a policy which purchased an ignoble peace by cowardice instead of exacting a just peace by showing we were as little willing to submit to as to inflict aggression. Had a majority of Jackson's colleagues and successors felt as he did about the navy, had it been built up instead of being brought to a standstill, it would probably never have been necessary to fight the War of 1812.

A Real Military Genius

Andrew Jackson, a real military genius, stands out in history as the ablest general the United States produced, from the outbreak of the Revolution to the beginning of the Great Rebellion.[3] No true American can think of his deeds at New Orleans without profound and unmixed thankfulness. Jackson showed military talent of a very high order.

A very charming English historian of our day has compared Wellington with Washington. It would have been far juster to have compared him with Andrew Jackson. Both were men of strong, narrow minds, and bitter prejudices, with few statesmanlike qualities, who, for brilliant military services, were raised to the highest civil positions in the gift of the State. Wellington's military successes were far greater, for he had more chances, but no single feat of his surpassed the remarkable victory won against his ablest lieutenant and choicest troops by a much smaller number of backwoods riflemen under Andrew Jackson. As a statesman Wellington may have done less harm than Jackson, for he had less influence, but he has no such great mark to his credit as the old Tennesseean's attitude toward the Nullifiers.

Andrew Jackson had the "instinct for the jugular." He would recognize his real foe and strike savagely at the point where the danger threatened. The War of 1812 brought him at once into national prominence. He went heartily into the war from the first, was commissioned as a general, and took the field with a column of raw militia. The crowning event of the war was the Battle of New Orleans, remarkable in its military aspect and a source of pride to every American. It was a perfectly useless shedding of blood, since peace had already been declared. Nevertheless, it was not only glorious but profitable to the United States. Louisiana was saved from being severely ravaged, and New Orleans from possible destruction, and after our humiliating defeats in trying to repel the invasions of Virginia and Maryland, the signal victory of New Orleans was really almost a necessity for the preservation of the national honor.

Jackson is certainly by all odds the most prominent figure that appeared during this war, and stands head and shoulders above any other commander, American or British, that it produced. It will be difficult, in all history, to show a parallel to the feat that he performed. In three weeks' fighting, with a force largely composed of militia, he utterly defeated and drove away an army twice the size of his own, composed of veteran troops, and led by one of the ablest of European generals. There is hardly a contest of modern times where the defeated side suffered such frightful carnage, while the victors came off almost scathless. According to their official returns the British loss was 2,036. The Americans lost but 70 men.

Jackson's success was achieved against the best troops of all Europe, while his own soldiers were militia or raw regulars whom he himself had trained. He was almost the only commander who ever succeeded in making the backwoodsmen amenable to discipline, but they loved and admired him extremely, and feared him not a little—a fear by no means without foundation, as he, and he alone among backwoods commanders, summarily punished in various ways, even by death, those of his men who were guilty of any flagrant disobedience of orders.

The Tennessee backwoodsmen and Louisiana volunteers, when mastered and controlled by the iron will and warlike genius of Andrew Jackson, performed at New Orleans a really great feat. The Battle of New Orleans at once made Jackson one of the heroes of the country. Jackson even thus early loomed up as the greatest and arch-typical representative of his people and his section.

A Great Hold on the People at Large

In the presidential election of 1828, Jackson and Adams were pitted against each other as the only candidates before the people, and Jackson won an overwhelming victory. The followers of the two were fast developing respectively into Democrats and Whigs, and the parties were hardening and taking shape, while the dividing lines were being drawn more clearly and distinctly. But the contest was largely a personal one, and Jackson's success was due to his own immense popularity more than to any party principle which he was supposed to represent.

Until 1828 all the presidents, and indeed almost all the men who took the lead in public life, alike in national and in State affairs, had been drawn from what in Europe would have been called the "upper classes." They were mainly college-bred men of high social standing, as well educated as any in the community, usually rich or at least well-to-do. The Jacksonian Democracy stood for the revolt against these rulers. Its leaders, as well as their followers, all came from the mass of the people. The majority of the voters supported Jackson because they felt he was one of themselves, and because they understood that his election would mean the complete overthrow of the classes in power.

The change was a great one. It was not a change in the policy under which the government was managed, as in Jefferson's triumph, but of the men who controlled it. The two great Democratic victories had little in common, almost as little as had the two great leaders under whose auspices they were respectively won—and few men were ever more unlike than the scholarly, timid, and shifty doctrinaire, who supplanted the elder Adams, and the ignorant, headstrong, and straightforward soldier, who was victor over the younger. That the change was the deliberate choice of the great mass of the people, and that it was for the worse, was then, and has been ever since, the opinion of most thinking men.

The Jacksonian Democracy was already completely ruled by a machine, of which the most important cogs were the countless office-holders, whom the spoils system had already converted into a band of well-drilled political mercenaries. A political machine can only be brought to a state of high perfection in a party containing very many ignorant and uneducated voters, and the Jacksonian Democracy held in its ranks the mass of the ignorance of the country. Besides this such an organization requires, in order that it may do its most effective work, to have as its leader and figurehead a man who really has a great hold on the people at large, and who yet can be managed by such politicians as possess the requisite adroitness, and Jackson fulfilled both these conditions.

A Perfect Curse in Our Politics

The two great reasons for Jackson's success throughout his political career were to be found in the strength of the feeling in his favor among the poorer and least educated classes of voters, and in the ardent support given him by the low politicians, who, by playing on his prejudices and passions, molded him to their wishes, and who organized and perfected in their own and his interests a great political machine, founded on the "spoils system."

Jackson's administration derives a most unenviable notoriety as being the one under which the spoils system became, for the first time, grafted on the civil service of the nation, appointments and removals in the public service being made dependent upon political qualifications, and not, as hitherto, upon merit or capacity. The old spoils system was (and is) a perfect curse in our politics, and there is nothing more important in American life than to drive it out, and that is what we are gradually doing.

Like the Utterance of Some Great Federalist

It was during Monroe's last term that Henry Clay brought in the first protective tariff bill, as distinguished from tariff bills to raise revenue with protection as an incident only. It was passed by a curiously mixed vote, which hardly indicated anyone's future position on the tariff excepting that of Clay himself. Slavery was doubtless remotely one of the irritating causes that combined to work South Carolina up to a fever heat of insanity over the nullification excitement, but in its immediate origin nullification arose from the outcry against the protective tariff.

In Washington, the current at first seemed to be all setting in favor of the Nullifiers. They even counted on Jackson's support, as he was a southerner and a States'-rights man. But he was also a strong Unionist, and, moreover, at this time, felt very bitterly toward Calhoun, with whom he had just had a split, and had in consequence remodeled his cabinet, thrusting out all Calhoun's supporters, and adopting Van Buren as his political heir—the position which it was hitherto supposed the great Carolina separatist occupied.

He declared himself in unmistakable terms. It was on the occasion of the Jefferson birthday banquet, April 13, 1830. An effort was then being made to have Jefferson's birthday celebrated annually, and the Nullifiers, rightly claiming him as their first and chief apostle, attempted to turn this particular feast into a demonstration of nullification. When it came to Jackson's turn he electrified the audience by proposing: "Our federal Union: it must be preserved." Calhoun at once answered with: "The Union, next to our liberty the most dear."

The issue between the president and the vice president was now complete, and the Jacksonian Democracy was squarely committed against nullification. Jackson had risen to the occasion as only a strong and a great man could rise, and his few, telling words rang throughout the whole country, and will last as long as our government. One result, at least, the Nullifiers accomplished—they completely put an end to the Jefferson birthday celebrations.

Jackson promptly issued a proclamation against nullification, composed jointly by himself and the great Louisiana jurist and statesman, Livingston. It is one of the ablest, as well as one of the most important, of all American State papers. It is hard to see how any American can read it now without feeling his veins thrill. Some claim it as being mainly the work of Jackson, others as that of Livingston.[4] It is great honor for either to have had a hand in its production. The intensely national and anti-separatist tone of Jackson's declaration—a document that might have come from Washington or Lincoln, and that would have reflected high honor on either—was very repugnant to many of the southern Democrats, and was too much even for certain of the Whigs. In fact, it reads like the utterance of some great Federalist or Republican leader.

He had openly avowed his intention, if matters went too far, of hanging Calhoun "higher than Haman." Some historians have treated this as if it were an idle threat, but such it certainly was not. Jackson undoubtedly fully meant what he said, and would have acted promptly had the provocation occurred, and moreover, he would have been sustained by the country. He was not the man to weigh minutely what would and what would not fall just on one side or the other of the line defining treason. Had a collision occurred, neither Calhoun nor his colleague would ever have been permitted to leave Washington, and brave though they were, the fact unquestionably had much influence with them.

The feeling in Congress, as a whole, was as strong against the tariff as it was against nullification, and Jackson had to take this into account. His signing the compromise bill was a piece of weakness out of keeping with his whole character, and especially out of keeping with his previous course toward the Nullifiers. The position assumed by Benton and Webster, that South Carolina should be made to submit first and should have the justice of her claims examined into afterward, was unquestionably the only proper attitude.

Benton wrote: "A compromise made with a state in arms is capitulation to that state. . . . The injury was great then, and a permanent evil example. It remitted the government to the condition of the old confederation, acting upon sovereignties instead of individuals." His criticisms on the wisdom of the compromise bill were perfectly just. Had the anti-Nullifiers stood firm, the Nullifiers would probably have given way, and if not, would certainly have been crushed. Against a solid North and West, with a divided South, even her own people not being unanimous, and with Jackson as chief executive, South Carolina could not have made even a respectable resistance. A salutary lesson then might very possibly have saved infinite trouble and bloodshed thereafter.

In Jackson's case it must be remembered that, so far as his acts depended purely on his own will and judgment, no fault can be found with him. He erred only in ratifying a compromise agreed to by the vast majority of the representatives of the people in both houses of Congress.

He Created a Worse Evil Than He Destroyed

During both Jackson's presidential terms he and his adherents were engaged in two great struggles: that with the Nullifiers, and that with the Bank. Jackson's attack upon the Bank was a move undertaken mainly on his own responsibility, and one which, at first, most of his prominent friends were alarmed to see him undertake. He was ultimately successful.

He had much justice on his side in this contest, and the destruction of the Bank was by no means altogether to be regretted, but he created a worse evil than he destroyed when he undertook to meddle in the finances and help out divers wildcat State banks. The tremendous commercial panic in 1837 was due in part to Jackson's ruinous policy of making deposits in numerous State banks, and thereby encouraging wild inflation of credit.

An assault upon "the money power" is apt to be popular in a Democratic republic,[5] partly on account of the vague fear with which poorer and more ignorant voters regard a powerful institution whose workings they do not understand and partly on account of the jealousy they feel toward those who are better off than themselves. When these feelings are appealed to by men who are intensely in earnest, and who are themselves convinced of the justice and wisdom of their course, they become very formidable factors in any political contest.

The Bank itself, beyond doubt, possessed enormous power, too much power for its own or outsiders' good. Its president, Biddle, was a man of some ability, but conceited to the last degree, untruthful, and to a certain extent unscrupulous in the use he made of the political influence of the great moneyed institution over which he presided. Some of the financial theories on which he managed the Bank were wrong, yet on the whole, it was well conducted, and under its care the monetary condition of the country was quiet and good, infinitely better than it had been before, or than, under the auspices of the Jacksonian Democracy, it afterward became.

A Central Bank Would Be a Very Good Thing

Today, our fiscal system is not good from the purely fiscal side. I am inclined to think that from this side, a central bank would be a very good thing.[6] Certainly, I believe that at least a central bank, with branch banks, in each of the States (I mean national banks, of course) would be good, and I doubt whether our people would support either scheme at present. And there is this grave objection that the inevitable popular distrust of big financial men might result very dangerously if it were concentrated upon the officials of one huge bank.

Sooner or later there would be in that bank some insolent man whose head would be turned by his own power and ability, who would fail to realize other types of ability and the limitations upon his power, and would by his actions awaken the slumbering popular distrust and cause a storm in which he would be as helpless as a child, and which would overwhelm not only him but other men and other things of far more importance. That sentence is as long and involved as if I were a populist senator, but I hope it conveys my idea. As yet our people do not fully realize the modern interdependence in financial and business relations. I believe that there will be an awakening, but it will be gradual.

Dealings with the Indians

Indelible Blots on Our Fair Fame

I took peculiar pride in the fact that so many men of Indian blood, especially of Cherokee blood, were in my regiment during the war with Spain, and that they did so well. It made me feel more than ever that it was indeed a typical American regiment. It is greatly to be wished that some competent person would write a full and true history of our national dealings with the Indians. Undoubtedly the latter have often suffered terrible injustice at our hands. A number of instances, such as the conduct of the Georgians to the Cherokees in the early part of the present century, or the whole treatment of Chief Joseph and his Nez Perces, might be mentioned, which are indelible blots on our fair fame.

I saw recently in one of our prominent magazines a reference to what the writer was pleased to call the "murder" of Sitting Bull, the great Sioux medicine chief, who was for so many years the mainspring of hostility to the United States among the Dakota tribes, being even a greater bane to his own people than to ours. Of course to speak of Sitting Bull's killing as "murder" is a piece of simple hysterics. Sitting Bull had always been an arch-plotter and stirrer-up of mischief. Sitting

Bull was shot while resisting arrest. The killing was not only a most righteous deed, but was absolutely inevitable, and very beneficial in its results.

Hideous, Unnamable, Unthinkable Tortures

The most righteous of all wars is a war with savages, though it is apt to be also the most terrible and inhuman. It is primeval warfare, and it is waged as war was waged in the ages of bronze and iron. All the merciful humanity that even war has gained during the last two thousand years is lost. A sad and evil feature of such warfare is that the whites, the representatives of civilization, speedily sink almost to the level of their barbarous foes, in point of hideous brutality. Odd things happen in a battle, and the human heart has strange and gruesome depths and the human brain still stranger shallows.

The excesses so often committed by the whites, when, after many checks and failures, they at last grasped victory, are causes for shame and regret, yet it is only fair to keep in mind the terrible provocations they had endured. One attack, simple enough in its incidents, deserves notice. In 1784, a family of "poor white" immigrants who had just settled in Kentucky were attacked in the daytime, while in the immediate neighborhood of their squalid cabin. The father was shot, and one Indian was in the act of tomahawking the six-year-old son, when an elder brother, from the doorway of the cabin, shot the savage. The Indians then fled. The boy thus rescued grew up to become the father of Abraham Lincoln.

The hideous, unnamable, unthinkable tortures practiced by the red men on their captured foes, and on their foes' tender women and helpless children, were such as we read of in no other struggle, hardly even in the revolting pages that tell the deeds of the Holy Inquisition. It was inevitable—indeed it was in many respects proper—that such deeds should awake in the breasts of the whites the grimmest, wildest spirit of revenge and hatred.

Anyone who has ever been in an encampment of wild Indians, and has had the misfortune to witness the delight the children take in torturing little animals, will admit that the Indian's love of cruelty for cruelty's sake cannot possibly be exaggerated. The young are so trained that when old they shall find their keenest pleasure in inflicting pain in its most appalling form. Among the most brutal white borderers a man would be instantly lynched if he practiced on any creature the fiendish torture which in an Indian camp either attracts no notice at all, or else merely laughter. The expression "too horrible to mention" is to be taken literally, not figuratively. Impalement on charred sticks, fingernails split off backward, finger joints chewed off, eyes burnt out—these tortures can be mentioned, but there are others equally normal and customary which cannot even be hinted at, especially when women are the victims.

They Did Not Own the Land

Much maudlin nonsense has been written about the governmental treatment of the Indians, especially as regards taking their land. The simple truth is that they had no possible title to most of the lands we took, not even that of occupancy, and at the most were in possession merely by virtue of having butchered the previous inhabitants. It cannot be too often insisted that they did not own the land. To recognize the Indian ownership of the limitless prairies and forests of this continent—that is, to consider the dozen squalid savages who hunted at long intervals over a territory of a thousand square miles as owning it outright—necessarily implies a similar recognition of the claims of every white hunter, squatter, horse thief, or wandering cattleman.

From the very nature of things, it was wholly impossible that there should not be much mutual wrongdoing and injury in the intercourse between the Indians and ourselves. It was equally out of the question to let them remain as they were, and to bring the bulk of their number up to our standard of civilization with sufficient speed to enable them to accommodate themselves to the changed conditions of their surroundings.

The dealings of the government with the Indian have often been unwise, and sometimes unjust, but they are very far indeed from being so black as is commonly represented, especially when the tremendous difficulties of the case are taken into account. The Cherokees had advanced far on the road to civilization, and it was undoubtedly a cruel grief and wrong to take them away from their homes, but the only alternative would have been to deprive them of much of their land, and to provide for their gradually becoming citizens of the States in which they were. For a movement of this sort the times were not, and, unfortunately, are not yet, ripe.

Martin Van Buren

His Own Dexterous Political Manipulations

Van Buren faithfully served the mammon of unrighteousness, both in his own State and, later on, at Washington, and he had his reward, for he was advanced to the highest offices in the gift of the nation. Jackson liked Van Buren because the latter had served him both personally and politically—indeed Jackson was incapable of distinguishing between a political and personal service. This liking, however, would not alone have advanced Van Buren's interests, if the latter, who was himself a master in the New York State machine, had not also succeeded in enlisting the goodwill and self-interest of the members of the Kitchen Cabinet.

Van Buren was the first product of what are now called "machine politics" that was put into the presidential chair. He owed his elevation solely to his own dexterous political manipulations, and to the fact that, for his own selfish ends, and knowing perfectly well their folly, he had yet favored or connived at all the actions into which the administration had been led either through Jackson's ignorance and violence, or by the crafty unscrupulousness of the Kitchen Cabinet. The people at large would never have thought of him for president of their own accord, but he had become Jackson's political legatee, partly because he had personally endeared himself to the latter, and partly because the politicians felt that he was a man whom they could trust.

The Last True Jacksonian Democrat

Van Buren was the last true Jacksonian Democrat—Union Democrat—who became president. The South Carolina separatists and many of their fellows refused to vote for him. Until Van Buren's overthrow the nationalists had held the upper hand in shaping Democratic policy, but after that even the leadership of the party passed completely into the hands of the separatists. As far as slavery was concerned, however, the southerners had hitherto had nothing whatever to complain of in Van Buren's attitude. He was careful to inform them in his inaugural address that he would not sanction any attempt to interfere with the institution.

Previous Financial Misdeeds

The withdrawals of the United States deposits from one responsible bank and their distribution among scores of others, many of which were in the most rickety condition, was a step better calculated than any other to bring about a financial crash. It gave a stimulus to extravagance, and evoked the wildest spirit of speculation that the country had ever seen.

The Jacksonians during the period of Van Buren's presidency rightfully suffered for their previous financial misdeeds. Van Buren, cool, skillful, and farsighted politician though he was, on this occasion showed that he was infected with the common delusion as to the solidity of the country's business prosperity. No effort was made to stave off even so much of the impending disaster as was at that late date preventable.

A few days after Van Buren's inauguration the country was in the throes of the worst and most widespread financial panic it has ever seen. The distress was fairly appalling both in its intensity and in its universal distribution. All the banks stopped payment, and bankruptcy was universal. Bank paper depreciated with frightful rapidity, especially in the West. Specie increased in value so that all the coin in the country, down to the lowest denomination, was almost immediately taken out of circulation, being either hoarded or gathered for shipment abroad in bullion.

He had no reason to blame his own conduct for his final downfall. He got just as far along as he could possibly get. He succeeded because of, and not in spite of, his moral shortcomings. If he had always governed his actions by a high moral standard he would probably never have been heard of. Still, there is some comfort in reflecting that, exactly as he was made president for no virtue of his own, but simply on account of being Jackson's heir, so he was turned out of office, not for personal failure, but because he was taken as a scapegoat, and had the sins of the political fathers visited on his own head.

The Election of 1840

The Old Indian Fighter Harrison

The defeat of Van Buren marks an era in more ways than one. During his administration slavery played a less prominent part in politics than did many other matters. This was never so again. The presidential election of 1840 was the last into which slavery did not enter as a most important, and in fact as the vital and determining, factor. In the contest between Van Buren and Harrison it did not have the least influence upon the results.

There was much poetic justice in the fact that the presidential election which decided their fate was conducted on as purely irrational principles, and was as merely one of sound and fury, as had been the case in the election twelve years previously, when they came into power. The Whigs, having exhausted their language in denouncing their opponents for nominating a man like Andrew Jackson, proceeded to look about in their own party to find one who should come as near him as possible in all the attributes that had given him so deep a hold on the people, and they succeeded perfectly when they pitched on the old Indian fighter, Harrison.

The principles of the Whigs were hazily outlined at the best, and the party was never a very creditable organization. Indeed, throughout its career, it could be most easily defined as the opposition to the Democracy. It was a free constructionist party, believing in giving a liberal interpretation to the doctrines of the Constitution. Otherwise, its principles were purely economic, as it favored a high tariff, internal improvements, a bank, and kindred schemes. Its leaders, however they might quarrel among themselves, agreed thoroughly in their devout hatred of Jackson and all his works.

Harrison was a true Whig. He was, when nominated, a prominent member of the Whig Party, although of course not to be compared with its great leader, Henry Clay, or with its most mighty intellectual chief, Daniel Webster, whose mutual rivalry had done much to make his nomination possible. General Harrison had already shown himself to be a good soldier, and a loyal and honest public servant, although by no means standing in the first rank as regards warcraft or statecraft, but the mass of his supporters apparently considered the facts, or supposed facts, that he lived in a log cabin the walls of which were decorated with coonskins, and that he drank hard cider from a gourd, as being more important than his capacity as a statesmen or his past services to the nation.

"Tippecanoe" proved quite as effective a war cry in bringing about the downfall of the Jacksonians as "Old Hickory" had shown itself to be a dozen years previously in raising them up. The Whigs in 1840 completely overthrew the Democrats, and for the first time elected a President and held the majority of both houses of Congress. Yet, as it turned out, all that they really accomplished was to elect a president without a party, for Harrison died when he had hardly more than sat in the presidential chair, and was succeeded by the vice president, Tyler, of Virginia.

John Tyler

A Politician of Monumental Littleness

A chance stroke of death put the presidency in the hands of one who represented the smallest element in the coalition that overthrew Van Buren. Tyler was properly nothing but a dissatisfied Democrat, who hated the Jacksonians, and had been nominated only because the Whig politicians wished to strengthen their ticket and ensure its election by bidding for the votes of the discontented in the ranks of their foes. Tyler could hardly be called a Whig at all. On the contrary, he belonged rightfully in the ranks of those extreme Democrats who were farthest removed from the Whig standard, and who were as much displeased with the Union sentiments of the Jacksonians as they were with the personal tyranny of Jackson himself.

Tyler of Virginia, whose disunion attitude was almost as clearly marked as that of Calhoun himself, went into opposition to his original party for reasons akin to those that influenced Calhoun. Tyler, however, had little else in common with Calhoun, and least of all his intellect. He has been called a mediocre man, but this is unwarranted flattery. He was a politician of monumental littleness. His chief mental and moral attributes were peevishness, fretful obstinacy, inconsistency, incapacity to make up his own mind, and the ability to quibble indefinitely over the most microscopic and hairsplitting plays upon words, together with an inordinate vanity that so blinded him to all outside feeling as to make him really think that he stood a chance to be renominated for the presidency.

His Mind Oscillated Like a Pendulum

Tyler's first message to Congress read like a pretty good Whig document, outlining what legislation he deemed proper, he being by virtue of his position the nominal and titular leader of the Whigs. However, the ink with which the message was written could hardly have been dry before the president's mind began to change. The leaven had already begun working in his mind, and, not having much to work on, soon changed it so completely that he was willing practically to eat his own words.

The Whigs, especially in the Senate, under Henry Clay, prepared at once to push through various measures that should undo the work of the Jacksonians. Clay, who was their real and very positive chief, and who was, moreover, determined to assert his chieftainship, in his turn laid down a program for his party to follow. Among the political theories to which Clay clung most closely, only the belief in a bank ranked higher in his estimation than his devotion to a protective tariff. The establishment of a national bank seemed to him to be the chief object of a Whig success. At last he stood at the head of the party controlling both branches of the legislative body, and devoted to his behests, and, if a little doubtful about the president, he still believed he could frighten him into doing as he was bid.

Tyler could not at first make up his mind what to do, or rather, he made it up in half a dozen different ways every day. His peevishness, vacillation, ambitious vanity, and sheer puzzleheadedness made him incline first to the side of his new friends and present supporters, the Whigs, and then to that of his old Democratic allies. But though his mind oscillated like a pendulum, yet each time it swung farther and farther over to the side of the Democracy, and it began to look as if he would certainly in the end come to a halt in the camp of the enemies of the Whigs. His approach to his destination was merely hastened by Clay's overbearing violence and injudicious taunts.

He said that his conscience would not permit him to sign a bill to establish a bank that was called a bank. He objected to the name "bank" and proposed to style it "Fiscal Institute," and afterward the "Fiscal Agent," and finally the "Fiscal Corporation." Such preposterous folly on the president's part was more than the hot-blooded and overbearing Kentuckian could stand. Clay could not bring himself to adopt such a ludicrous title. After a while, however, a compromise title was agreed on, but only a shadow less imbecile than the original one proposed by the president, and it was agreed to call the measure the "Fiscal Bank" bill.

The president vetoed it. An intrigue was going on among a few unimportant congressmen and obscure officeholders to form a new party with Tyler at its head, and the latter willingly entered into the plan, his mind, which was not robust at best, being completely dazzled by his sudden elevation and his wild hopes that he could continue to keep the place which he had reached.

He had given the Whigs reason to expect he would sign the bill. So, when his veto came in, it raised a perfect whirlwind of wrath and bitter disappointment. His cabinet all resigned, except Webster, who stayed to finish the treaty with Great Britain, and the Whigs formally read him out of the party. Clay could not resist reading Tyler a lecture on his misconduct during the course of a speech in the Senate. The Democrats looked on with huge enjoyment, and patted Tyler on the back, but nevertheless they despised him heartily, and abandoned him wholly when he had served their turn.

Left without any support among the regulars of either side, and his own proposed third party turning out a stillborn abortion, he simply played out his puny part until his term ended, and then dropped noiselessly out of sight. It is only the position he filled, and not in the least his ability, for either good or bad, in filling it, that prevents his name from sinking into merciful oblivion.

James Polk

Backed by Rabid Southern Fire-Eaters

In 1844 the Whig candidate for the presidency, Henry Clay, was defeated by Mr. Polk, the nominee of the Democracy. The majorities in several of the States were very small. This was the case, for example, in New York, the change in whose electoral vote would have also changed the entire result. From this time the slavery question dwarfed all others.

Van Buren was the last Democratic president who ruled over a Union of States. All his successors, up to the time of Lincoln's election, merely held sway over a Union of sections. The spirit of separation had identified itself with the maintenance of slavery, and the South was rapidly uniting into a compact array of States with interests that were hostile to the North. With the defeat of Van Buren the Jacksonian Democracy, as such, lost forever its grip on the direction of national affairs. When, under Polk, the Democrats came back, they came under the lead of the very men whom the original Jacksonians had opposed and kept down.

The separatist and annexationist Democrats, the extreme slavery wing of the party, rejected Van Buren and nominated Polk, who was their man. The Whigs nominated Clay, who was heartily opposed to all the schemes of the disunion and extreme slavery men, and who, if elected, while he might very properly have consented to the admission of Texas with its old boundaries, would never have brought on a war nor have attempted to add a vast extent of new slave territory to the Union.

Hardly was Polk elected before it became evident that the separatist and disunion elements within the party had obtained the upper hand. The first sign of the new order of things was the displacement of Blair, editor of *The Globe*, the Democratic newspaper organ. Blair was a strong Unionist, and had been bitterly hostile to Calhoun and the Nullifiers. Polk's chances of election were so precarious that he was most anxious to conciliate the separatists—besides which he at heart sympathized with their views, and had himself been brought forward in the Democratic convention to beat the national candidate, Van Buren. Moreover, Tyler withdrew from the contest in his favor, in part payment for which help, soon after the election, Blair was turned out.

Almost every good element in the country stood behind Clay. The vast majority of intelligent, high-minded, upright men supported him. Polk was backed by rabid Southern fire-eaters and slavery extensionists, who had deified Negro bondage and exalted it beyond the Union, the Constitution, and everything else; by the almost solid foreign vote, still unfit for the duties of American citizenship; by the vicious and criminal classes in all the great cities of the North and in New Orleans; by the corrupt politicians, who found ignorance and viciousness tools ready forged to their hands, wherewith to perpetuate the gigantic frauds without which the election would have been lost. And lastly, he was also backed indirectly but most powerfully by the political Abolitionists.

These Abolitionists had formed themselves into the Liberty Party, and ran Birney for president, and though they polled but little over sixty thousand votes, yet as these were drawn almost entirely from the ranks of Clay's supporters, they were primarily responsible for his defeat, for the defections were sufficiently large to turn the scale in certain pivotal and closely contested States, notably New York.

Birney Simply Committed a Political Crime

Owing to a variety of causes, the Abolitionists have received an immense amount of hysterical praise, which they do not deserve, and have been credited with deeds done by other men, whom they in reality hampered and opposed rather than aided. The Liberty Party, in running Birney, simply committed a political crime, evil in almost all its consequences.[1] They in no sense paved the way for the Republican Party, or helped forward the anti-slavery cause.

With the purpose of advancing the cause of abstract right, but with the result of sacrificing all that was best, most honest, and most high-principled in national politics, the Abolitionists joined hands with the Northern roughs and Southern slavocrats to elect the man who was, excepting Tyler, the very smallest of the line of small presidents who came in between Jackson and Lincoln. These three men—Calhoun, Birney, and Isaiah Rynders—may be taken as types of the classes that were chiefly instrumental in the election of Polk,[2] and that must, therefore, bear the responsibility for all the evils attendant thereon, including among them the bloody and unrighteous war with Mexico.[3]

Innocent Blood Is Crying from Heaven against Him

Abraham Lincoln was in Congress while Polk was president during the Mexican War. On pages 100 to 146 of Volume I of *Lincoln's Complete Works*, by Nicolay and Hay, Lincoln justifies himself in voting in favor of a resolution censuring the president for his action prior to and during the war (which was still going on). He examines the president's official message of justification and says that part of the message "is from beginning to end the sheerest deception." He continues that he "more than suspects" that the president "is deeply conscious of being in the wrong, that he feels that innocent blood is crying from heaven against him," that one of the best generals had "been driven into disfavor, if not disgrace, by the President" for speaking unpalatable truths about the length of time the war would take, and ends by saying that the president has bungled his work and "knows not where he is. He is bewildered, confounded, and a miserably perplexed man."

Remember that this is Lincoln speaking, in wartime, of the president. The general verdict of history has justified him. Patriotism means to stand by the country. It does not mean to stand by the president. It is patriotic to support him in so far as he efficiently serves the country. Lincoln had to deal with various critics of the "stand by the president" type. To one he answers that "the only alternative is to tell the truth or to lie," and that he would not "skulk" on such a question.

The Oregon Settlement

We Ought to Have Taken It All

It is difficult to exaggerate the importance of the treaties and wars by means of which we finally gave definite bounds to our territory beyond the Mississippi. Throughout a large part of our national career our history has been one of expansion, the expansion being of different kinds at different times. This expansion is not a matter of regret, but of pride. It is vain to tell a people as masterful as ours that the spirit of enterprise is not safe. The true American has never feared to run risks when the prize to be won was of sufficient value.

No foot of soil to which we had any title in the Northwest should have been given up. We were the people who could use it best, and we ought to have taken it all. The prize was well worth winning, and would warrant a good deal of risk being run. We had even then grown to be so strong that we were almost sure eventually to win in any American contest for continental supremacy. We were nearby, our foes far away.

Not only the Columbia but also the Red River of the North—and the Saskatchewan and Frazer as well—should lie wholly within our limit, less for our own sake than for the sake of the men who dwell along their banks. Columbia, Saskatchewan, and Manitoba would, as States of the American Union, hold positions incomparably more important, grander, and more dignified than they can ever hope to reach either as independent communities or as provincial dependencies of a foreign power. As long as the Canadian remains a colonist, he remains in a position which is distinctly inferior to that of his cousins, both in England and in the United States. The Englishman at bottom looks down on the Canadian, as he does on anyone who admits his inferiority, and quite properly, too. The American, on the other hand, with equal propriety, regards the Canadian with the good-natured condescension always felt by the freeman for the man who is not free.

The territory along the Pacific coast lying between California on the south and Alaska on the north—"Oregon," as it was comprehensively called—had been a source of dispute for some time between the United States and Great Britain. After some negotiations both had agreed with Russia to recognize the line of 54°40' as the southern boundary of the latter's possession, and Mexico's undisputed possession of California gave an equally well-marked southern limit, at the forty-second parallel. All between was in dispute.

The whole region was still entirely unsettled and as a matter of fact our British rivals were the only parties in actual occupation. The title to the territory was doubtful, as must always be the case when it rests upon the inaccurate maps of foreign explorers, or upon the chance landings of stray sailors and traders, especially if the land in dispute is unoccupied and of vast but uncertain extent, of little present value, and far distant from the powers claiming it. The real truth is that such titles are of very little practical value, and are rightly enough disregarded by any nations strong enough to do so.

The British had trading posts at the mouth of the Columbia, which they emphatically asserted to be theirs. We, on the other hand, claimed an absolutely clear title up to the forty-ninth parallel, a couple of hundred miles north of the mouth of the Columbia, and asserted that for all the balance of territory up to the Russian possessions our title was at any rate better than that of the British. In 1818 a treaty had been made providing for the joint occupation of the territory by the two powers, as neither was willing to give up its claim to the whole.

A Policy by "Masterly Inactivity"

This treaty of joint occupation had remained in force ever since. Under it the British had built great trading stations, and used the whole country in the interests of certain fur trading companies. The aspect of affairs was totally changed when in 1842 a huge caravan of over a thousand Americans made the journey overland from the frontiers of the Missouri, taking with them their wives and their children.

When American settlers were once in actual possession of the disputed territory, it became evident that the period of Great Britain's undisputed sway was over. Calhoun advocated a policy by "masterly inactivity," foreseeing that time was everything to us, inasmuch as the land was sure in the end to belong to that nation whose people had settled in it, and we alone were able to furnish a constantly increasing stream of immigrants. We should have allowed the question to remain unsettled as long as was possible, because every year saw an increasing American population in the coveted lands, and rendered the ultimate decision surer to be for us. When it was impossible to postpone the question longer, we should have insisted upon its being settled entirely in our favor, no matter at what cost.

In 1844 the Democrats made their campaign upon the issue of "fifty-four-forty or fight," and Polk, when elected, felt obliged to insist upon this campaign boundary. To this, however, Great Britain naturally would not consent. Polk's administration was neither capable nor warlike, however well disposed to bluster, and the secretary of state, the timid, shifty, and selfish politician, Buchanan, naturally fond of facing both ways, was the last man to wish to force a quarrel on a high-spirited and determined antagonist like England. Accordingly, he made up his mind to back down and try for the line of forty-nine, as proposed by Calhoun, when in Tyler's cabinet. The English accepted the offer of compromise.

In its immediate effects the adoption of the forty-ninth parallel as the dividing line between the two countries was excellent, and entailed no loss of dignity on either. Yet, as there was no particular reason why we should show any generosity in our diplomatic dealings with England, it may well be questioned whether it would not have been better to have left things as they were until we could have taken all. Wars are, of course, as a rule to be avoided, but they are far better than certain kinds of peace. Every war in which we have been engaged, except the one in Mexico, has been justifiable in its origin, and each one, without any exception whatever, has left us better off, taking both moral and material considerations into account, than we should have been if we had not waged it.

The Annexation of Texas

Conquests Like Those of the Norse Sea Rovers

My admiration of Texas and Texans is no new thing. Since I have been a boy and first studied the history of this country my veins have thrilled and tingled as I read of the mighty deeds of Houston, of Bowie, of Crockett, of Travis; of the men who were victorious at the fight at San Jacinto; of the even more glorious men who fell in the fight of the Alamo, of which it was said: "Thermopylae had its messengers of death, but the Alamo had none."

The conquest of Texas should properly be classed with conquests like those of the Norse sea rovers. The virtues and faults alike of the Texans were those of a barbaric age. They were restless, brave, and eager for adventure, excitement, and plunder. They were warlike, resolute, and enterprising. They had all the marks of a young and hardy race, flushed with the pride of strength and self-confidence. The great Texan hero, Houston, who drank hard and fought hard, who was mighty in battle and crafty in council, and his queerly blended impulses for good and evil, might, with very superficial alternations of character, stand as the type of an Old World Viking. Houston was thoroughly

Jacksonian in type. He was rough, honest, and fearless, a devoted friend and a vengeful enemy.

The Texan struggle for independence stirred up the greatest sympathy and enthusiasm in the United States. The Jackson administration remained nominally neutral, but obviously sympathized with the Texans, permitting arms and men to be sent to their help, without hindrance, and indeed doing not a little discreditable bullying in the diplomatic dealings with Mexico. The victory of San Jacinto, in which Houston literally annihilated a Mexican force twice the strength of his own, virtually decided the contest, and the Senate at once passed a resolution recognizing the independence of Texas.

The Americans at last succeeded in wresting Texas from the Mexicans and making it an independent republic. This republic tried to conquer New Mexico but failed. Then we annexed it, made its quarrels our own, and did conquer both New Mexico and California. From the standpoint of technical right and wrong, it is impossible to justify the American action in these cases, and in the case of Texas there was the dark blot of slavery which rested upon the victors, for they turned Texas from a free province into a slave republic. Nevertheless, it was of course ultimately to the great advantage of civilization that the Anglo-American should supplant the Indo-Spaniard.

Increasing the Slave Domain

The Southerners, desirous of increasing the slave domain, and always in a state of fierce alarm over the proximity of any free State that might excite a servile insurrection, were impatient to add the Lone Star Republic of the Rio Grande to the number of their States. The intrigue for the annexation of Texas, and for thereby extending the slave territory of the Union, had taken shape toward the close of Tyler's term in office, while Calhoun was secretary of state.

The separatist chiefs were intriguing for the presidency, and were using annexation as a cry that would help them, and, failing in this attempt, many of the leaders were willing to break up the Union, and turn the Southern States, together with Texas, into a slaveholding confederacy. Jackson himself, whose name was still a mighty power among the masses, was induced to write a letter favoring instant and prompt annexation. The letter was really procured for political purposes.

The great champion of the old-style Union Democrats was Van Buren, who was opposed to annexation, sharing the feeling that prevailed throughout the Northeast generally. Jackson, though a Southerner, warmly favored Van Buren, and was bitterly opposed to separatists. But the latter, by cunningly working on his feelings, without showing their own hands, persuaded him to write the letter mentioned, and promptly used it to destroy the chances of Van Buren, who was the man they chiefly feared.

Polk's election gave an enormous impulse to the annexation movement, and made it doubly and trebly difficult for anyone to withstand it. Texas was admitted, and the foundation for our war with Mexico was laid. Calhoun, under whom this was done, nevertheless sincerely regretted the war itself, and freely condemned Polk's administration for bringing it on.

Recent historians always speak as if our grasping after territory in the Southwest was due solely to the desire of the Southerners to acquire lands out of which to carve new slaveholding States, and as if it was merely a move in the interests of the slave power. This is true enough so far as the motives of Calhoun, Tyler, and the other public leaders of the Gulf and Southern seaboard States were concerned. But the hearty support given to the movement was due to entirely different causes, the chief among them being the fact that the westerners honestly believed themselves to be indeed created the heirs of the earth, or at least of so much of it as was known by the name of North America.

The western people grew up with warlike traditions and habits of thought, accustomed to give free rein to their passions, and to take into their own hands the avenging of real or supposed wrongs. The pioneer stood where he was because he was a conqueror. He had wrested his land by force from its rightful Indian lords. He fully intended to repeat the same feat as soon as he should reach the Spanish lands lying to the west and southwest. This belligerent, or, more properly speaking, piratical, way of looking at neighboring territory was very characteristic of the West, and was at the root of the doctrine of "Manifest Destiny," which, reduced to its simplest terms, was that it was our manifest destiny to swallow up the land of all adjoining nations who were too weak to withstand us, a theory that forthwith obtained immense popularity among all statesmen of easy international morality.

Henry Clay

Traveling Along a Ridge Crest

Henry Clay was a first-class man, and I think I ought perhaps to say that, looking back now, I probably failed to do justice to the fact that compromises were probably necessary, and that he did do a great deal to preserve the Union. At times a man must cut loose from his associates, and stand alone for a great cause. But the necessity for such action is almost as rare as the necessity for a revolution, and to take such ground continually, in season and out of season, is the sign of an unhealthy nature. It is not possible to lay down an inflexible rule as to when compromise is right and when wrong, when it is a sign of the highest statesmanship to temporize, and when it is merely a proof of weakness. Now and then one can stand uncompromisingly for a naked principle and force people up to it. This is always the attractive course, but in certain great crises it may be a very wrong course.

People are apt to speak as if in political life, public life, it ought to be a mere case of striving upward—striving toward a high peak. The simile is inexact. Every man who is striving to do good public work is traveling along a ridge crest, with the gulf of failure on each side—the gulf of inefficiency on the one side, the gulf of unrighteousness on the other. All kinds of forces are continually playing on him, to shove him first into one gulf and then into the other. These two attitudes—the attitude of deifying mere efficiency, mere success, without regard to the moral qualities lying behind it; and the attitude of disregarding efficiency, disregarding practical results—are the Scylla and Charybdis between which every earnest reformer, every politician who desires to make the name of his profession a term of honor instead of shame, must steer.

Naturally, there are certain subjects on which no man can compromise. No decent politician need compromise in any way save as Washington and Lincoln did. He need not go nearly as far as Hamilton, Jefferson, and Jackson went, but some distance he must go if he expects to accomplish anything. Occasionally one hears some well-meaning person say of another, apparently in praise, that he is "never willing to compromise." It is a mere truism to say that, in politics, there has to be one continual compromise. Of course now and then questions arise upon which a compromise is inadmissible. There could be no compromise with secession, and there was none. There should be no avoidable compromise about any great moral question. But only a very few great reforms or great measures of any kind can be carried through without concession. When we cannot do the best, then, as Abraham Lincoln said, "We have to do the best possible."

South Carolina Gained Most

During the nullification movement in South Carolina, Clay was prepared to shift his stand somewhat from that of abstract moral right to that of expediency. Benton and Webster were too resolute and determined in their hostility to any form of yielding to South Carolina's insolent defiance to admit any hope of getting them to compromise, but the majority of the members were known to be only too ready to jump at any halfway measure which would patch up the affair for the present, no matter what the sacrifice of principle or how great the risk incurred in the future. A compromise which results in a half step toward evil is all wrong.

Accordingly, Clay and Calhoun met and agreed on a curious bill, in reality recognizing the protective system, but making a great although gradual reduction of duties, and Clay introduced this as a "compromise measure." It gave South Carolina much, but not all that she demanded. Her representatives announced themselves satisfied, and supported it, together with all their Southern sympathizers. Webster and Benton fought it stoutly to the last. Unfortunately Congress, as a whole, was by no means so stiff-kneed. It was passed by a great majority.

A certain number of Whigs followed Webster, and a certain number of Democrats clung to Benton, but most Southerners were very reluctant to allow pressure to be brought to bear on South Carolina, and many Northerners were as willing to compromise as Henry Clay himself. Silas Wright, of New York, a typical Northern "doughface" politician, gave exact expression to the "doughface" sentiment which induced Northern members to vote for the compromise, when he stated that he was unalterably opposed to the principle of the bill, but that on account of the extreme desire which he had to remove all cause of discontent in that State, he would vote for what was satisfactory to her, although repugnant to himself. Wright, Marcy, and their successors in New York politics, almost up to the present day, certainly carried cringing subserviency to the South to a pitch that was fairly sublime.

The battle did not result in a decisive victory for either side. This was shown by the very fact that each party insisted that it had won a signal triumph. Calhoun and Clay afterward quarreled in the Senate chamber as to which had given up more in the compromise. South Carolina gained most of that for which she contended, and the victory, as a whole, rested with her. Without doubt, the honors of the nullification dispute were borne off by Benton and Webster. The latter's reply to Hayne, is, perhaps, the greatest single speech of the nineteenth century, and he deserves the highest credit for the stubbornness with which he stood by his colors to the last.

Always Much Bolder in Opening a Campaign

Henry Clay was always much bolder in opening a campaign than in carrying it through. During the War of 1812 the younger Democratic-Republican leaders, men like Clay and Calhoun, were unlike their elders in being willing to fight, but they had not the slightest conception what war meant, or how to meet the formidable foe to whom they had thrown down the glove. Instead of keeping quiet and making preparations, they made no preparations, and indulged in vainglorious boasting, Clay asserting that the militia of Kentucky alone would conquer Canada, and Calhoun, that the conquest would be made almost without effort. The memory of these boasts must have cost bitter mortification to the authors a couple of years later.

John C. Calhoun

Few Criminals Have Worked as Much Harm

John C. Calhoun played a large part in the leadership of this country. Few men who have ever sat in the United States Senate have had such cleverness of intellectual power or such facility of clear expression, and succeeded in clothing wrong conclusions in such effective form that they passed for truths. Few criminals have worked as much harm to their country as he did. The plea of good intentions is not one that can be allowed to have much weight in passing historical judgment upon a man whose wrongheadedness and distorted way of looking at things produced, or helped to produce, such incalculable evil.

Doubtless in private life, or as regards any financial matters, Calhoun's conduct was always blameless, but it may well be that he has received far more credit for purity of motive in his public conduct than his actions fairly entitle him to. Some of Calhoun's recent biographers have credited him with being really a Union man at heart. It seems absolutely impossible that this could have been the case.

Calhoun's hairsplitting and metaphysical disquisitions on the constitutionality of nullification have now little more practical interest than have the extraordinary arguments and discussions of the schoolmen of the Middle Ages. But at the time they were of vital interest, for they were words which it was known South Carolina was prepared to back up by deeds. Calhoun was vice president, the second leader in the federal government, and yet also the avowed leader of the most bitter disunionists. His State supported him by an overwhelming majority.

Much of the opposition he was continually making to supposititious federal and Northern encroachments on the rights of the South must have been merely factious, and it seems likely that, partly from a feeling of revenge and partly with the hope of gratifying his ambition, he was anxious to do all he could to work the South up to the highest pitch of irritation, and keep her there until there was a dissolution of the Union. Thomas Hart Benton evidently thought that this was the case, and in reading the constant threats of nullification and secession which run through all Calhoun's speeches, and the innumerable references he makes to the alleged fact that he had come off victorious in his treasonable struggle over the tariff in 1833, it is difficult not to accept Benton's view of the matter.

Sore with Disappointed Ambition

Certain Southern extremists, under the lead of Calhoun, were anxious to refuse to receive a perfectly proper and respectful petition sent to the Senate by a society of Pennsylvania Quakers praying for the abolition of slavery in the District of Columbia. The District was solely under the control of Congress, and was the property of the nation at large. If the right of petition meant anything, it certainly meant that the people, or any portion thereof, should have the right to petition their representatives in regard to their own affairs.

Calhoun wished to refuse to receive the petitions, on the ground that they touched a subject that ought not even to be discussed, yet he must have known well that he was acting in the very way most fitted to give rise to discussion. He was still smarting from the nullification controversy. He had seceded from his party, and was sore with disappointed ambition, and it seems very improbable that he was honest in his professions of regret at seeing questions come up which would disturb the Union. Benton characterizes his system of slavery agitation, very truthfully, as being one "to force issues upon the North under the pretext of self-defense, and to sectionalize the South, preparatory to disunion."

Calhoun was also greatly exercised over the circulation of abolition documents in the South. At his request a committee of five was appointed to draft a bill on the subject. The bill subjected to penalties any postmaster who should knowingly receive and put into the mail any publication touching on slavery, to go into any State which had forbidden by law the circulation of such a publication. A dozen Southern senators joined with the bulk of the Northerners in defeating the bill, which was lost by a vote of twenty-five to nineteen. A few of the Northern "doughfaces" voted with Calhoun.

They Drank and Dueled and Made Speeches

South Carolina and Mississippi were very much alike. Their two great men of the deified past were Calhoun and Jefferson Davis, and I confess I am unable to see wherein any conscienceless financier of the present day is worse than these two slave owners who spent their years in trying to feed their thirst for personal power by leading their followers to the destruction of the Union.

The Charleston aristocrats offer as melancholy an example as I know of people whose whole life for generations has been warped by their own willful perversity. In the early part of South Carolina's history there was a small Federalist Party and later a small and dwindling Union party within the State, of which I cannot speak too highly. But the South Carolina aristocrats, the Charleston aristocrats and their kinsfolk in the up-country, have never made good their pretensions.

They were no more to blame than the rest of the country for the slave trade of colonial days, but when the rest of the country woke up they shut their eyes tight to the horrors; they insisted that the slave trade should be kept, and succeeded in keeping it for a quarter of a century after the Revolutionary War closed; they went into secession partly to reopen it. They drank and dueled and made speeches, but they contributed very, very little toward anything of which we as Americans are now proud. In the Revolutionary War the South Carolinians made as against the British a fight which can only be called respectable. There was little heroism, and Marion and Sumter, in their fight against Tarleton and the other British commanders, show at a striking disadvantage when compared with De Wet and De la Rey and the other Boer leaders. In the War of 1812 South Carolina did nothing. She reserved her strength until she could strike for slavery and against the Union.

Zachary Taylor

Taylor's Backbone

In 1848 the Democrats nominated Cass, a Northern pro-slavery politician of moderate abilities, and the Whigs put up and elected old Zachary Taylor, the rough frontier soldier and Louisiana slaveholder. Webster's famous sneer at Taylor was aimed at him as a "frontier colonel." In other words, though Taylor had a large plantation in Louisiana, Webster, and many others besides, looked upon him as the champion of the rough democracy of the West rather than as the representative of the polished slaveholders of the South.

The Whigs carried the election and once more held the reins of government. When a Louisiana slaveholder was thus installed in the White House, the extreme Southern men may have thought that they were sure of him as an ally in their fight against freedom. But, if so, they soon found they had reckoned without their host, for the election of Taylor affords a curious, though not solitary, instance in which the American people builded better than they knew in choosing a chief executive. Nothing whatever was known of his political theories, and the Whigs nominated him simply because he was a successful soldier, likely to take the popular fancy. But once elected he turned out to have the very qualities we then most needed in a president—a stout heart, shrewd common sense, and thoroughgoing devotion to the Union.

In his first and only annual message Taylor declared the Union to be the greatest of blessings, which he would maintain in every way against whatever dangers might threaten it. He advised the admission of California, which wished to come in as a free State. He thought the territories of Utah and New Mexico should be left as they were, and he warned the Texans, who were blustering about certain alleged rights to New Mexican soil, and threatening to take them by force of arms, that this could not be permitted.

Naturally, it was bitterly assailed by the disunionists under Calhoun, and even Clay, who entirely lacked Taylor's backbone, was dissatisfied with it as being too extreme in tone, and conflicting with his proposed compromise measure. This is not the place to discuss Clay's proposed compromise. It consisted of five different parts, relating to the recovery of fugitive slaves, the suppression of the slave trade in the District of Columbia, the admission of California as a State, and the territorial condition of Utah and New Mexico.

Benton opposed it as being a concession or capitulation to the spirit of disunion and secession, and therefore a repetition of the error of 1833. Benton always desired to meet and check any disunion movement at the very outset, and, if he had had his way, would have carried matters with a high hand whenever it came to dealing with threats of such a proceeding, and therein he was perfectly right.

Before California was admitted into the Union old Zachary Taylor had died, leaving behind him a name that will always be remembered among our people. He was neither a great statesman nor yet a great commander, but he was an able and gallant soldier, a loyal and upright public servant, and a most kindly, honest, and truthful man. His death was a greater loss to the country than perhaps the people ever knew. Taylor turned out admirably.

One of the Great Presidents

I don't believe in judging people by the way the White House looks and has looked, or even will look. What a poor showing old Zack Taylor would have made measured by this standard! When he died the Fillmores had to have the White House disinfected in order to make it habitable, and yet, Taylor stands out to me as one of the great presidents[1] and Fillmore a pompous old nonentity. I can understand Taylor, when he came to the White House, spreading matting over all the carpets so that he could spit where he chose without hunting for cuspidors. That had been his habit, and he did not like to change and thereby divert his thoughts from the real things in life. I can imagine nothing more diverting or disconcerting than to have to look for cuspidors if one has the habit of spitting.

Thomas Hart Benton

The Tenacity of a Snapping Turtle

Thomas Hart Benton had all the tenacity of a snapping turtle, and was as firm a believer in the policy of "continuous hammering" as Grant himself. It would have been fortunate indeed if Clay and Webster had possessed the fearless, aggressive courage and iron will of the rugged Missourian, who was so often pitted against them in the political arena. In point of moral character I always felt that Benton was far ahead of either of his great Whig rivals.

It has always seemed to me that we never did justice to that fine old fellow. I always felt it was a privilege to have been allowed to say what I thought of the fine old boy in my *Life of Thomas Hart Benton*. In 1832 Benton threw himself in, heart and soul, with the Union party, acting as Jackson's right-hand man throughout the contest with South Carolina, and showing an even more resolute and unflinching front than Old Hickory himself. No better or trustier ally than the Missouri statesman, in a hard fight for a principle, could be desired. He was intensely national in all his habits of thought. He took deep, personal pride in all his country—North, South, East, and West.

During his career, the United States Senate was perhaps the most influential, and certainly the ablest, legislative body in the world. And after Jackson's presidency came to an end the really great statesmen and political leaders of the country were to be found in it, and not in the executive chair. Such senators as Benton, Webster, Clay, and Calhoun, and later on Douglas, Seward, and Sumner, fairly towered above presidents like the obscure Southerners Tyler and Polk, or the truckling, time-serving Northern politicians Pierce and Buchanan.

Benton's long political career can never be thoroughly understood unless it is kept in mind that he was primarily a Western and not a Southern statesman. Like every other hot spirit of the West—and the West was full of little but hot spirits—Benton heartily favored the War of 1812. He served as a colonel of volunteers under Jackson, but never saw actual fighting. Like Jackson, Benton killed his man in a duel.

Benton had his faults and lots of them, but he was a dead game man, he was an entirely disinterested patriot, and he stood by the right when his friends and his constituents went wrong and in spite of the greatest pressure. I really doubt there can be a much severer test of character. The contrast between the conduct toward slavery disunionists of this Democrat from a slaveholding State, with a hostile majority at home against him, and the conduct of Webster, a Whig, enthusiastically backed by his own free State, in the same issue, is a painful one for the latter. Compare his stand against the slavery extremists and disunionists, such as Calhoun, with the position of Webster at the time of his famous 7th of March speech.[1]

The Nickname of "Old Bullion"

Both he and Jackson deserve great credit for having done much to impress the popular mind with the benefit of hard, that is to say honest, money. Benton was such a firm believer in hard money, and a currency of gold and silver, as to have received the nickname of "Old Bullion," and his followers were called "hards." His opponents were soft-money men, in addition to being secessionists and pro-slavery fanatics, and took the name of "softs." The principles of the Bentonians were right, and those of their opponents wrong. To be sure, Benton's knowledge of financial economics was not always profound, but, on the other hand, a thorough mastery of the laws of finance would have been a very serious disadvantage to any champion of Jackson.

A metallic currency is always surer and safer than a paper currency. Where it exists, a laboring man dependent on his wages need fear less than any other member of the community the evils of bad banking. A craze for "soft," or dishonest, money—a greenback movement, or one for short-weight silver dollars—works more to the disadvantage of the whole mass of people than even to that of the capitalists.

Calhoun Alone He Would Never Forgive

Benton was one of those who were present and escaped death at the time of the terrible accident on board the *Princeton*, during Tyler's administration, when the bursting of her great gun killed so many prominent men. Benton was saved owing to the fact that, characteristically enough, he had stepped to one side the better to note the marksmanship of the gunner. Ex-governor Gilmer, of Virginia, who had taken his place, was instantly killed.

Tyler, who was also on board, was likewise saved in consequence of the exhibition of a characteristic trait, for, just as the gun was about to be fired, something occurred in another part of the ship which distracted the attention of the fussy, fidgety president, who accordingly ran off to see what it was, and thus escaped the fatal explosion. The tragic nature of the accident and his own narrow escape made a deep impression upon Benton, and it was noticed that ever afterward he was far more forbearing and forgiving than of old. He became good friends with Webster and other political opponents, with whom he had formerly hardly been on speaking terms. Calhoun alone he would never forgive.

PART IV

Civil War Era
(1851-1876)

Franklin Pierce

The Servile Tool of Men Worse Than Himself

In 1852, the Whig candidate for the presidency, Winfield Scott, a good general, but otherwise a wholly absurd and flatulent personage, was defeated by Franklin Pierce, the nominee of the Democracy, one of the most subservient allies the South ever had in the Northern States. Pierce, the Copperhead, was completely under the control of the secession wing of the party.

We cannot but admire at least the courage and gallant soldiers of the South, who, from a terribly mistaken sense of duty, fought us so grimly and so stubbornly for four long years, but we have nothing but contempt for their cowardly allies of the North, the doughface and the Copperhead, who had all the will, but who fortunately utterly lacked the courage, to be traitors. I can respect an ex-Confederate who fought us openly. I have nothing but contempt for a Northern Copperhead who tried to stab us in safety to himself.

Thomas Hart Benton treated Franklin Pierce with contemptuous hostility, despising him, and seeing him exactly as he was—a small politician, of low capacity and mean surroundings, proud to act as the servile tool of men worse than himself but also stronger and abler. He was ever ready to do any work the slavery leaders set him, and to act as their attorney in arguing in its favor—to quote Benton's phrase, with "undaunted mendacity, moral callosity and mental obliquity." His last message to Congress in the slavery interest Benton spoke of as characteristic, and exemplifying "all the modes of conveying untruths which long ages have invented—direct assertion, fallacious inference, equivocal phrase, and false innuendo."

On the history of the pro-slavery agitation, Benton wrote: "Up to Mr. Pierce's administration the plan had been defensive, that is to say, to make the secession of the South a measure of self-defense against the abolition encroachment and crusades of the North. In the time of Mr. Pierce the plan became offensive, that is to say, to commence the expansion of slavery, and the acquisition of territory to spread it over, so as to overpower the North with new Slave States, and drive them out of the Union . . . The rising of the Free States, in consequence of the abrogation of the Missouri Compromise, checked these schemes . . . The death of Harrison, and the accession of Tyler, was their first great lift; the election of Mr. Pierce their culminating point."

The Missouri Compromise of 1820 had expressly abolished slavery in the territory out of which Kansas and Nebraska were carved. This compromise was to be repealed, and the famous doctrine of nonintervention, or "squatter sovereignty," was to take its place, the people of each Territory being allowed to choose for themselves whether they did or did not wish slavery. It was an outrage to propose to extend its domain by repealing all that part of a compromise measure which worked against it. The "squatter sovereignty" theories of Douglas deserved ridicule.

The Gadsden Treaty was also opposed and condemned by Benton, who considered it to be part of a great scheme or movement in the interests of the slavery disunionists, of which he also believed the Kansas-Nebraska bill to be the first development—the "thin end of the wedge." He opposed the acquirement even of the small piece of territory we were actually able to purchase from Mexico, and showed good grounds for his belief that the administration, acting as usual only in the inter-

est of the secessionists, had tried to get enough north Mexican territory to form several new States, and had also attempted to purchase
Cuba, both efforts being for the purpose of enabling the South either
to become again dominant in the Union or else to set up a separate
confederacy of her own.

The Disunion Abolitionists

A Queer Kind of Immorality

After 1840 the professed Abolitionists formed but a small and comparatively unimportant portion of the forces that were working toward the restriction and elimination of slavery, and much of what they did was positively harmful to the cause for which they were fighting. Those of their number who considered the Constitution as a league with death and hell, and who therefore advocated a dissolution of the Union, acted as rationally as would anti-polygamists nowadays if, to show their disapproval of Mormonism, they should advocate that Utah should be allowed to form a separate nation.

The anti-slavery cause was eminently just, but the more one reads of these professional Abolitionists, the more one feels that they were about as undesirable a class of people as the country ever saw. I do not mean men like Birney, but the men who advocated disunion or anarchy and who betrayed a foolish and feeble violence in dealing with all practical questions. The disunion movement among the Northern Abolitionists, headed by Garrison, was absolutely senseless, for its success meant the immediate abandonment of every hope of abolition.

The only hope of ultimately suppressing slavery lay in the preservation of the Union, and every Abolitionist who argued or signed a petition for its dissolution was doing as much to perpetuate the evil he complained of as if he had been a slaveholder. The men who took a great and effective part in the fight against slavery were the men who remained within their respective parties, like the Democrats Benton and Wilmot, or the Whigs Seward and Stevens.

The cause of the Abolitionists has had such a halo shed round it by the after-course of events, which they themselves in reality did very little to shape, that it has been usual to speak of them with absurdly exaggerated praise. Their courage, and for the most part their sincerity, cannot be too highly spoken of, but their share in abolishing slavery was far less than has commonly been represented. Any single non-Abolitionist politician, like Lincoln or Seward, did more than all the professional Abolitionists combined really to bring about its destruction. Their tendency toward impracticable methods was well shown in the position they assumed toward him who was not only the greatest American, but also the greatest man, of the nineteenth century. For during all the terrible four years that sad, strong, patient Lincoln worked and suffered for the people, he had to dread the influence of the extreme Abolitionists only less than that of the Copperheads.

The plea that slavery was a question of principle, on which no compromise could be accepted, might have been made and could still be made on twenty other points—woman's suffrage, for instance. There are now laws on the statute books in reference to women that are in principle as unjust, and that are quite as much the remnants of archaic barbarism, as was the old slave code. The same laws that in one Southern State gave a master a right to whip a slave also allowed him to whip his wife, provided he used a stick no thicker than his little finger.

Many of their leaders possessed no good qualities beyond their fearlessness and truth—qualities that were also possessed by the Southern fire-eaters. They belonged to that class of men that is always engaged in some agitation or other, only it happened that in this particular agitation they were right. The extreme advocates of any cause always include fanatics, and often fools, and they generally number a considerable proportion of those people whose mind is warped as to make them combine in a very curious degree a queer kind of disinterested zeal with a queer kind of immorality.

Wendell Phillips may be taken as a very good type of the whole. His services against slavery prior to the war should always be remembered with gratitude, but after the war, and until the day of his death, his position on almost every public question was either mischievous or ridiculous, and usually both. When Wendell Phillips denounced Abraham Lincoln as "the slave hound of Illinois," he did not show himself more virtuous than Lincoln, but more foolish. Neither did he advance the cause of human freedom.

Many people in speaking of the Abolitionists apparently forget that the national government, even under Republican rule, would never have meddled with slavery in the various States unless as a war measure, made necessary by the rebellion into which the South was led by a variety of causes, of which slavery was the chief, but among which there were others that were also prominent, such as the separatist spirit of certain of the communities and the unscrupulous, treacherous ambition of such men as Davis, Floyd, and the rest.

The Dred Scott Decision

A Conspiracy against Liberty

Abraham Lincoln said that he believed the Dred Scott decision represented a conspiracy against liberty between the then Supreme Court and the leading officers of the reactionary party to which the Supreme Court belonged. Justice Taney and the majority of the Supreme Court of the nation in 1857 played into the hands of presidents Pierce and Buchanan and the reactionary organization of which he and they were parts. Chief Justice Taney belonged to those who were the "strict constructionists," so called. His decisions, if followed out, would have changed us from a mighty and prosperous nation into a confederation of petty and wrangling republics. He was the judge who announced from the bench that the black man had no rights that the white man was bound to respect.

I do not believe we have ever had a corrupt judge on the Supreme Court, but a chief justice like Taney is a far worse influence on the country than a president like Pierce or Buchanan, and there should be some possibility of removing him. Taney was a curse to our national life because he belonged to the wrong party and faithfully carried out the criminal and foolish views of the party which stood for such a construction of the Constitution as would have rendered it impossible even to preserve the national life.

It was the decision of the court at this time in the Dred Scott case which marked the climax of the then governmental attitude toward slavery, and which gave Abraham Lincoln his opportunity to rise into national prominence by the vigor of his opposition thereto and of his assault upon the court for what it had done. It was Buchanan who treated the courts as a fetish, who protested against and condemned all criticisms of the judges for unjust and unrighteous decisions. It was Lincoln who appealed to the people against the judges when the judges went wrong, who advocated and secured what was practically the re-call of the Dred Scott decision, and who treated the Constitution as a living force for righteousness. Lincoln, mind you, and not Buchanan, was the real upholder and preserver of the Constitution.

Lincoln was always against slavery, but until the upholders of slavery, in 1854, became violently aggressive, he stood by Clay and Webster and against the Abolitionists, and at first he remained a Whig, not becoming a Republican for several months after the formation of the party. He upheld Clay's compromise measures. He took Webster's position on the Fugitive Slave Law. It is one of the melancholy ironies of history that the very men who abandoned and frantically denounced Webster for taking this position later turned ardently to Lincoln, who had also taken it and who did not change from his position until the Civil War had begun.

The Civil War

A Great War for Righteousness

The Civil War was a great war for righteousness. I most earnestly believe in peace, and not in war; but after the firing on Fort Sumter, my voice would have been for war, and for the continuance of war, under no matter what discouragements, until the great object was achieved. Of course, had I been old enough, I would have served on the Northern side. The rebellion was a crime against the Nation. My own belief is that there never was a war in which the right was so wholly on one side, and yet that there never yet was a war in which the wrong side believed so absolutely that it was fighting for righteousness and justice. In the end the slave was freed, the Union restored, and the mighty American republic placed once more as a helmeted queen among nations.

Half a century before the "stars and bars" waved over Lee's last entrenchments, perfervid New England patriots were fond of flaunting "the flag with five stripes," and drinking to the health of the— fortunately stillborn—new nation. The truth is that it is nonsense to reproach any one section with being especially disloyal to the Union. At one time or another almost every State has shown strong particularistic leanings. Connecticut and Pennsylvania, for example, quite as much as Virginia or Kentucky. The separatist feeling is ingrained in the fiber of our race, and though in itself a most dangerous failing and weakness, is yet merely a perversion and distortion of the defiant and self-reliant independence of spirit which is one of the chief of the race virtues.

Slavery was partly the cause and partly merely the occasion of the abnormal growth of the separatist movement in the South. Its growth was furthered and hastened by the actions of the more ambitious and unscrupulous of the Southern politicians, who saw that it offered a chance for them to push themselves forward, and who were perfectly willing to wreak almost irreparable harm to the nation if by so doing they could advance their own selfish interests. In 1860, a majority of Southerners were opposed to secession, but the disloyal element was active and resolute, and hoped to force the remainder into its own way of thinking.

The secession movement of 1860 was pushed to extremities, instead of being merely planned and threatened, and the revolt was peculiarly abhorrent, because of the intention to make slavery the "cornerstone" of the new nation, and to reintroduce the slave trade, to the certain ultimate ruin of the Southern whites, but at least it was entirely free from the meanness of being made in the midst of a doubtful struggle with a foreign foe.

Sold into Slavery by Their Own Fathers

I am half a Southerner myself. I am as proud of the South as I am of the North. The South has retained some barbaric virtues which we have tended to lose in the North, partly owing to a mistaken pseudo-humanitarianism among our ethical creatures. The decline in the militant spirit in the Northeast during the first half of this century was much to be regretted. To it is due, more than to any other cause, the undoubted average individual inferiority of the Northern compared to the Southern troops, at any rate at the beginning of the great war of the Rebellion.

The Southerners, by their whole mode of living, their habits, and their love of outdoor sports, kept up their warlike spirit, while in the North the so-called upper classes developed along the lines of a wealthy and timid bourgeoisie type, measuring everything by a mercantile standard (a peculiarly debasing one if taken purely by itself), and submitting to be ruled in local affairs by low foreign mobs, and in national matters by their arrogant Southern kinsmen. The militant spirit of these last certainly stood them in good stead in the Civil War.

My mother was a Georgian. One of my uncles built the *Alabama* and another fired the last gun from her before she went down, and I am yet supporting one or two venerable black imposters who were slaves in the family before the war. I know what a good side there was to slavery, but I know also what a hideous side there was to it, and this was the important side. *Uncle Tom's Cabin* I think was essentially true so far as the whites were concerned. As for the blacks described, they were true also, but they were the exceptions and not the rule. One of the revolting features of slavery to me was the fact that the large class of mulatto slaves were practically sold into slavery by their own fathers. I have myself known of a white brother selling his half sisters. Slavery is ethically abhorrent to all right-minded men, and it is to be condemned without stint on this ground alone.

The Towering Greatness of Lincoln

The more I study the Civil War and the time following it, the more I feel (as of course everyone feels) the towering greatness of Lincoln, which puts him before all other men of our time. While, on the other hand, I very strongly feel that Chase, Seward, Sumner, and Stanton by no means come up to, say, Hay, Root, Knox, and Taft.

Franklin, Hamilton, Jefferson, Adams, and their fellows most surely stand far above Seward, Sumner, Chase, Stanton, and Stevens, great as were the services which these, and those like them, rendered. But when we come to the fighting men, all this is reversed. As a mere military man, Washington himself cannot rank with the wonderful war chief who for four years led the army of northern Virginia, and the names of Washington and Greene fill up the short list of really good Revolutionary generals. Against these the Civil War shows a roll that contains not only Lee, but also Grant and Sherman, Jackson and Johnston, Thomas, Sheridan, and Farragut.

John Brown Gave the North the Martyr

My view of John Brown is that he was substantially like the fifth monarchy men of Cromwell's time. He was one of those stern, high-minded, and also bloody-minded fanatics, apt to be produced in such a crisis as a civil war. It is almost accidental whether such a man does good or harm to his country. By his death John Brown gave the North the martyr which it needed, but his invasion of Virginia was of course an act of mere criminal folly, and though on the whole his service in Kansas was of very high value to humanity, yet it was stained by at least one shameful deed.

Abraham Lincoln

Perhaps the Only Genius in Our Political History

I do not have to tell you that my great hero is Abraham Lincoln, and I have wanted while president to be the representative of the "plain people" in the sense that he was—not, of course, with the genius and power that he was, but, according to my lights, along the same lines. Lincoln has always meant more to me than any other of our public men, even Washington. Lincoln was an average man, but Lincoln was a genius besides—perhaps the only genius in our political history. They say that Lincoln followed, that he even didn't lead the country in the emancipation of the slaves, in the unyielding demand for the preservation of the Union. That is absurd. He furnished the arguments, put profound truths simply, prepared the sentiment, and then he led.

The old-school Jeffersonian theorists believed in "a strong people and a weak government." Lincoln was the first who showed how a strong people might have a strong government and yet remain the freest on earth. He seized—half unwittingly—all that was best and wisest in the traditions of Federalism. He was the true successor of the Federalist leaders, but he grafted on their system a profound belief that the great heart of the nation beat for truth, honor, and liberty. Lincoln had an almost miraculous understanding of the people.

One of the greatest men in the world's history, one of the two or three greatest men of the nineteenth century, Lincoln saw into the future with the prophetic imagination usually vouchsafed only to the poet and the seer. He had to him all the lift toward greatness of the visionary without any of the visionary's fanaticism or egotism. Lincoln, the uncouth farmer's boy, reared in the grinding toil and poverty of a small cabin on the frontier, the man who worked with his hands, the man who never knew what it was to walk in the soft places of the earth, made his way upward until in our pantheon his figure stands beside that of the dead hero of Mount Vernon.

Lincoln's name will always stand, coupled with the name of Washington, as representing what is highest and best in our American life, as the ideal toward which all public men should strive. While I do not believe in comparisons among great men as a rule, yet if I should have to say who is the first American, I should say Washington. He was both soldier and statesman as well as far-seeing and lofty-minded patriot. Lincoln was not the soldier.

Mr. Matthew Arnold grants us that Washington is distinguished, but says that Lincoln is not.[1] I cannot help thinking the difference Mr. Arnold makes between Washington and Lincoln is due to the fact that one lived a century ago, and the other in our own time. A hundred years ago Englishmen would have laughed at the praise he gives Washington. Fifty years ago they would have still considered it extravagant. Today, they think it just. So it will be with Lincoln. Compare what was said of him in his lifetime with what is said of him even now, and we can form some idea of the verdict of the future.

The Most Real of the Dead Presidents

I think of Lincoln, shambling, homely, with his strong, sad, and, deeply furrowed face, all the time. I see him in the different rooms and in the halls. For some reason or other he is to me infinitely the most real of the dead presidents. So far as one who is not a great man can model himself upon one who was, I try to follow out the general lines of policy which Lincoln laid down. I wish to Heaven I had his invariable equanimity. I try my best not to give any expression to irritation, but sometimes I do get deeply irritated.

In my office in the White House there was a splendid portrait of Lincoln. It is a reproduction of the photograph of him which, to me personally, appeals most. As I understand, it represents him as he was at the time of the Lincoln-Douglas debates. How I wish Lincoln had shaved his face during the presidency as he did during the time of the Lincoln and Douglas debates! But the Homeric heroes also, in reality, wore "chin whiskers"! Oftentimes, when I had some matter to decide, something involved and difficult to dispose of, where there were conflicting rights and all that sort of thing, I would look up at that splendid face and try to imagine him in my place and try to figure out what he would do in the circumstances. It may sound odd to you, but, frankly, it seemed to make my troubles easier of solution.

Yes, to me, Lincoln has ever been a living person, an inspiration, and a help. If I ever envied any man, it was John Hay, who had the wonderful privilege of knowing Lincoln so intimately. John Hay's house was almost the only house in Washington where I continually stopped. Every Sunday on the way back from church I would stop and have an hour's talk with Hay. We would go over foreign affairs and public business generally, and then I would usually get him to talk to me about Lincoln. Hay was Lincoln's private secretary, and the night before the inauguration he gave me a ring containing some of Lincoln's hair, cut from his head just after he was assassinated, and I wore the ring when I took my oath of office. Surely no other president, on the eve of his inauguration, has ever received such a gift. Have you ever read Hay and Nicolay's *Lincoln*? I studied it not merely with pleasure but with profit this summer. How he does loom up as one studies and reads him!

Lincoln's Wonderful Gift of Expression

Abraham Lincoln was a genius, who wrote only as one of the world's rare geniuses do write. Washington, though in some ways an even greater man than Lincoln, did not have Lincoln's wonderful gift of expression, that gift which makes certain speeches of the rail-splitter from Illinois read like the inspired utterances of great Hebrew seers and prophets. (Parenthetically, I would say that aside from being prophets, what magnificent poets Ezekiel, Isaiah, and Jeremiah were!) In all history I do not believe there is to be found an orator whose speeches will last as enduringly as certain of the speeches of Lincoln.

He possessed that marvelous gift of expression which enabled him quite unconsciously to choose the very words best fit to commemorate each deed. His Gettysburg speech and his Second Inaugural are two of the half dozen greatest speeches ever made—I am tempted to call them the greatest ever made. They are great in their wisdom and dignity, and earnestness and loftiness of thought and expression. There is nothing in Demosthenes or Cicero which comes up to Lincoln's Gettysburg speech and Second Inaugural. There is one of his letters which has always appealed to me particularly. It is the one running as follows:

> Executive Mansion
> Washington, Nov. 21, 1864
> To Mrs. Bixby, Boston, Mass.

Dear Madam:

I have been shown in the files of the War Department a statement of the Adjutant General of Massachusetts that you are the mother of five sons who have died gloriously on the field of battle. I feel how weak and fruitless must be any word of mine which should attempt to beguile you from the grief of a loss so overwhelming. But I cannot refrain from tendering you the consolation that may be found in the thanks of the republic they died to save. I pray that our Heavenly Father may assuage the anguish of your bereavement, and leave you only the cherished memory of the loved and lost, and the solemn pride that must be yours to have laid so costly a sacrifice upon the alter of freedom.

Yours very sincerely and respectfully,
A. Lincoln

No president who has ever sat in the White House has borne the burden that Lincoln bore, or been under the ceaseless strain which he endured. It did not let up day or night. Ever he had to consider problems of the widest importance, ever to run risks of the greatest magnitude. It is a touching thing that the great leader, while thus driven and absorbed, could yet so often turn aside for the moment to do some deed of personal kindness. Nobody but one of the world's rare geniuses could have met as Lincoln met the awful crises of the Civil War.

All Personal Bitterness Seemed to Die out of Him

In reading his works and addresses, one is struck by the fact that as he went higher and higher all personal bitterness seemed to die out of him. In the Lincoln-Douglas debates one can still catch now and then a note of personal antagonism. The man was in the arena, and as the blows were given and taken you can see that now and then he had a feeling against his antagonist. When he became president and faced the crisis that he had to face, from that time on I do not think that you can find an expression, a speech, a word of Lincoln's, written or spoken, in which bitterness is shown to any man. His devotion to the cause was so great that he neither could nor would have feeling against any individual.

I remember John Hay telling me that Lincoln throughout his term of service grew constantly more and more sad because he found that his old friends fell off from him and he could make no new friends from the fact that almost everyone honestly thought that he could do the government service in some particular post in which Lincoln rarely saw his way to put the man. It is impossible to conceive of a man farther removed from baseness, farther removed from corruption, from mere self-seeking, but it is also impossible to conceive of a man of more sane and healthy mind—a man less under the influence of that fantastic and diseased morality which makes a man in this workaday world refuse to do what is possible because he cannot accomplish the impossible.

Contrast Cromwell's conduct with that of Lincoln, just before his second election as president. There was a time in the summer of 1864 when it looked as if the Democrats would win, and elect McClellan. At that time it was infinitely more essential to the salvation of the Union that Lincoln should be continued in power than it was to the salvation of the Commonwealth, in 1654, that Cromwell should be continued in power. Lincoln would have been far more excusable than Cromwell if he had insisted upon keeping control. Yet such a thought never entered Lincoln's head. He prepared to abide in good faith the decision of the people, and one of the most touching incidents of his life is the quiet and noble sincerity with which he made preparations, if McClellan was elected, to advise with him and help him in every way, and to use his own power, during the interval between McClellan's election and inauguration, in such a manner as would redound most to the advantage of the latter, and would increase, as far as possible, the chance for the preservation of the Union.

Sane and Tempered Radicalism

Abraham Lincoln, the rail-splitter, the western country lawyer, was one of the shrewdest and most enlightened men of the world, and he had all the practical qualities which enable such a man to guide his countrymen, and yet he was also a genius of the heroic type. Every great and wise statesman has been now radical, now conservative, and has been right in both positions. Washington led the radicals in 1776 and the conservatives in 1789, and he was right in both cases. Lincoln stood with the radicals to abolish slavery and with the conservatives to save the Union, and he was right in both cases. Lincoln was radical compared to Buchanan and Fillmore, and conservative compared to Wendell Phillips and John Brown. Let anybody study Lincoln's history during the Civil War. He is the great example of sane and tempered radicalism.

Such a study of Lincoln's life will enable us to avoid the twin gulfs of immorality and inefficiency—the gulfs which always lie one on each side of the careers alike of man and of nation. The fanatic, the well-meaning moralist of unbalanced mind, the parlor critic who condemns others but has no power himself to do good and but little power to do ill—all these were as alien to Lincoln as the vicious and unpatriotic themselves. I believe his success was due to the fact that he refused to be swerved out of the path of cautious and moderate advance by the denunciations of the fiery and sincere enthusiasts like Wendell Phillips, who, as you will remember, denounced him as "the slave hound of Illinois." I do not think that these extremists were purer and better men than Lincoln, the head of the moderates, was. I think they were merely more foolish men. Lincoln was not halfhearted. His zeal was just as intense, his purpose as inflexible, as the zeal and the purpose of the extremists who denounced him. And his policy of moderation did not mean weakness. On the contrary, when the time was ripe he struck with iron determination, and he saw the time when compromise would be fatal just as he saw the time when insistence upon no compromise would be fatal.

When a very young man in the Illinois legislature, Lincoln fearlessly put himself on record as against slavery, but he resolutely declined to join the antislavery parties in '44 and '48 on the ground that the movements were so inexpedient that they did harm and not good to the cause. And in '56, '58, '60, and even well into '62, he also resolutely declined to join the Abolitionists, and to head a crusade for the total destruction of slavery, confining himself to opposition to the extension of slavery into new territory, until the time was ripe to move for its total abolition.

Lincoln had tremendous influence with the American people, but if he had tried to abolish slavery in 1861, or if he had been against its abolition in 1864, he would have utterly lost all hold upon the people. He would only work within the limits allotted. He had continually to check those who wished to go forward too fast, at the very time that he overrode the opposition of those who wished not to go forward at all. The goal was never dim before his vision, but he picked his way cautiously, without either halt or hurry. His great effort was to prevent the extension of slavery, not to abolish it. Now, it seems to me that Lincoln in these matters showed not abandonment of a high ideal, but great common sense. I do not think he was less moral than Wendell Phillips or Garrison. I believe he was more practical.

His Relations with Simon Cameron

Lincoln lived in such times that it was his duty to compromise a hundredfold more than I have ever found it necessary to, and he did. The whole history of his relations with Simon Cameron, for instance, implies a greater amount of compromise on his part than all the compromises that I have ever had to make or shall have to make put together. This was because the terrible situation he faced demanded it, and of course it is absurd to compare anything I have had to face with even an ordinary everyday tribulation of Lincoln's, so that it is small credit indeed to say, what I believe is the absolute truth, that I have been able to shape my course far more nearly in accordance with the idealistic view than he was able to shape his. I did not think it necessary to go as far as Lincoln did with Simon Cameron.

There were undoubtedly corrupt contractors who backed Lincoln for improper reasons and backed the war against slavery and for the Union for improper reasons. The only weakness in the great war president[2] was his failure to catch up with the great corruptionists connected with the army as contractors.[3] It would have been difficult to conceive of greater errors than the appointment of Simon Cameron in the War Department. It certainly was a mistake against the light.

He Was No Clown

I do not understand why some persons like to portray Lincoln as rude and uncouth,[4] to suggest that he was a lineal descendent of the Pithecanthropus, always telling funny stories. It is as bad as the refining process Washington has gone through. Washington was a very human sort of person with his fair share of the weakness of man. He is presented to us as possessing all of the virtues and lacking all suggestion of sin, original or acquired. As a matter of fact, he was a strong man, with all of a strong man's virtues and many of a strong man's faults, who lived in an age when it was not bad form to offer the minister a drink.

Lincoln was not a handsome man—he did not have very much on me in that respect—but he was by no means first cousin to the caveman in appearance any more than he was always slapping strangers on the back and telling them funny stories. He did have the saving grace of humor, but he was no clown. Sad, patient, mighty Abraham Lincoln was the plain man of the people, the people's president, homely, gaunt, ungainly, and this homely figure, clad in ill-fitting clothes of ugly modern type, held one of the loftiest souls that ever burned within the heart of mankind.

Jefferson Davis

An Unhung Traitor

In a public utterance of mine some eighteen or twenty years ago, I grouped together Jefferson Davis and Benedict Arnold.[1] While as a public man I expect to preserve proper reticence in what I say, yet people may as well understand that I have not the slightest apology to offer for having, as a historian, told the truth as I saw it. It is not my business now to speak of secession any more than to speak of the Alien and Sedition Acts, but when I, in my writings, touch on secession, I shall say about it what I really feel, and I shall speak of its leaders as I think they deserve.

Jefferson Davis wrote me a letter of violent protest, a rather ill-tempered and undignified letter. Instead of ignoring it I answered it with an acerbity which, being a young man, struck me at the time as clever, whereas it does not strike me as in the least so now. I have preserved both his letter and a copy of my answer thereto.

Beauvain, Miss.,
September 29, 1885
Mr. Theodore Roosevelt
New York, New York

Sir:

You have recently chosen publicly to associate the name of Benedict Arnold with that of Jefferson Davis, as the only American with whom the traitor Arnold need not fear comparison.

You must be ignorant indeed of American history if you do not know that the career of those characters might be aptly chosen for contrast, but not for similitude, and if so ignorant, the instinct of a gentleman, had you possessed it, must have caused you to make inquiry before uttering an accusation so libelous and false.

I write you directly to repel the unproved outrage, but with too low an estimate of you to expect an honorable retraction of your slander.

Yours, etc.,
(Signed) Jefferson Davis

I thought it most undignified of him to write me at all, and of course it would have been simply silly to have entered into an argument with him as to whether his conduct did or did not compare unfavorably with that of Benedict Arnold. I wrote him back that I must decline to enter into any controversy with him of any kind, sort, or description.

New York
October 8, 1885

Mr. Theodore Roosevelt is in receipt of a letter purporting to come from Mr. Jefferson Davis,[2] and denying that the character of Mr. Davis compares unfavorably with that of Benedict Arnold. Assuming the letter to be genuine Mr. Roosevelt has only to say that he would indeed be surprised to find that his views of the character of Mr. Davis did not differ radically from that apparently entertained in relation thereto by Mr. Davis himself. Mr. Roosevelt begs leave to add that he does not deem it necessary that there should be any further communication whatever between himself and Mr. Davis.

As a matter of pure morals I think I was right. Jefferson Davis was an unhung traitor. Now, this is my personal belief. I have always drawn a sharp line between the men who intrigued for secession and the men who, like Lee, when the Civil War was on went with their section. If secession was not a crime, if it was not a black offense against humanity to strive to break up this great republic in the interest of the perpetuation of slavery, then it is impossible ever to commit any political crime, and there is no difference between good men and bad men in history. Jefferson Davis for many years had intrigued for secession—had intrigued for the destruction of this republic in the interest of slavery, and the evidence is overwhelming to my mind that in this course he was largely influenced by the eager desire to gratify his own ambition.

If you will turn to Scott's *Memoirs* you will see that he championed the repudiation of the Mississippi bonds. During Van Buren's administration many States, in the rage for public improvements, had contracted debts which they refused to pay. It is a painful and shameful page in our history, and every man connected with the repudiation of the States' debt ought, if remembered at all, to be remembered only with scorn and contempt. Before Jefferson Davis took his place among the arch-traitors in our annals he had already long been known as one of the chief repudiators. It is not unnatural that to dishonesty toward the creditors of the public he should afterward add treachery toward the public itself.

He did not, like Benedict Arnold, receive money for his treachery, but he received office instead. The difference is one of degree, not of kind. The two men stand on an evil eminence of infamy in our history. They occupy the two foremost positions in the small group of Americans which also numbers the names of Aaron Burr, of Wilkinson, of Floyd.[3] As a matter of exact historic accuracy I later came to the conclusion that Jefferson Davis did not divide the first position with Benedict Arnold, but that if one were to draw degrees of infamy, he should come second; that is, taking into account his prominence and his crime, he came behind Benedict Arnold and ahead of Aaron Burr and Wilkinson on the roll of dishonor.

One of the stock arguments of Southerners in '61, and of their sympathizers in England, was that Jefferson Davis was simply doing what George Washington had done, and that the secession of the Southern States stood on an exact par with the secession of the thirteen colonies from England. Of course such a comparison was utterly absurd. The South revolted from a great free republic in which the Southerners had always had amplest justice and recognition, because they could not force from the North abject submission to their demands as regards slavery. The American colonies revolted from England because England declined to treat them as freemen with equal rights, but insisted that the American was subject to the Englishman.

Rebellion, revolution, the appeal to arms to redress grievances—these are measures that can only be justified in extreme cases. It is far better to suffer any moderate evil, or even a very serious evil, so long as there is a chance of its peaceable redress, than to plunge the country into civil war. All civil wars loosen the bands of orderly liberty, and leave in their train disorder and evil. Hence, those who cause them must rightly be held guilty of the gravest wrongdoing, unless they are not only pure of purpose, but sound of judgment, and unless the result shows their wisdom.

If there are such virtues as loyalty and patriotism, then there must exist the corresponding crime of treason. If there is any merit in practicing the first, then there must be equal demerit in committing the last. Emasculated sentimentalists may try to strike from the national dictionary the word "treason," but until that is done, Jefferson Davis must be deemed guilty thereof. The men who head or instigate armed rebellions for which there is not the most ample justification must be held as one degree worse than any but the most evil tyrants.

Under Jefferson Davis, the Southern States revolted in order to establish a slaveholding republic, and to break up the greatest experiment at successful democratic republican government which the world had ever seen. There was no adequate cause—indeed no cause whatever—for the attempted secession, and if successful, the movement would have been fraught with incalculable damage to all mankind.

In view of the extreme freedom of statement indulged in the South of this country about every Northern leader (including, if that is of any consequence, myself) during the last half century, and its folly of expecting anyone to retract or explain these, it seems hardly worthwhile for any person now to feel offended about what I said. If you will go back twenty years further you will find plenty of bitter statements by Southern leaders about the course of Benjamin F. Butler in New Orleans, about the course of Thaddeus Stevens, especially during the Reconstruction period, in the House of Representatives.

Robert E. Lee

In the Foremost Rank of the Great Captains

There is no need to dwell on General Lee's record as a soldier. The son of "Light Horse Harry" Lee of the Revolution, he came naturally by his aptitude for arms and command. His campaigns put him in the foremost rank of the great captains of all time. The world has never seen better soldiers than those who followed Lee, and their leader will undoubtedly rank as without any exception the very greatest of all the captains that the English-speaking peoples have brought forth—and this, although the last and chief of his antagonists may himself claim to stand as the full equal of Marlborough and Wellington.

The greatest general of the South was Lee, and his greatest lieutenant was Jackson. Both were Virginians, and both were strongly opposed to disunion. Lee went so far as to deny the right of secession, while Jackson insisted that the South ought to try to get its rights inside the Union. But when Virginia joined the Southern Confederacy, and the war had actually begun, both men cast their lot with the South.

I feel nothing but the most cordial and hearty goodwill and admiration for Lee,[1] Jackson, and the many brave men who fought so valiantly for the wrong, believing it was for the right, an admiration only less strong than that I feel for such Southerners as Farragut, Thomas, and Drayton,[2] who dared to stand by their famous old flag even when their own States went against it. When such an ex-Confederate as that gallant Southern general, Longstreet, shows that he is willing in good faith to accept the results of the war, the Republicans always in turn show that they are not only ready but eager to do him honor.

General Lee has left us the memory, not merely of his extraordinary skill as a general, his dauntless courage and high leadership in campaigns and battle, but also of that serene greatness of soul characteristic of those who most readily recognize the obligations of civic duty. Once the war was over he instantly undertook the task of healing and binding up the wounds of his countrymen. Immediately after the close of hostilities he announced, with a clear-sightedness which at that time few indeed of any section possessed, that the interests of the Southern States were the same as those of the United States.

Although absolutely without means, he refused all offers of pecuniary aid, and all positions of emolument, although many such, at a high salary, were offered him. He declined to go abroad, saying that he sought only "a peace to earn honest bread while engaged in some useful work." This statement brought him the offer of the presidency of Washington College, a little institution in Lexington, Virginia. It was eminently fitting that this great man should turn his attention toward educational work, toward bringing up in fit fashion the younger generation.

Stonewall Jackson

With His Bible and Sword

Stonewall Jackson was as true a type of the "General of the Lord, with his Bible and Sword," as Cromwell. No Northern general approached the Roundhead type—the type of stern, religious warriors who fought under Cromwell—so closely as Stonewall Jackson. He was a man of intense religious conviction, who carried into every thought and deed of his daily life the precepts of the faith he cherished. He proved not only a commander of genius but a fighter of iron will and temper, who joyed in the battle, and always showed at his best when the danger was greatest. The vein of fanaticism that ran through his character helped to render him a terrible opponent.

Few generals as great as Lee have ever had as great a lieutenant as Jackson. He was a master of strategy and tactics, fearless of responsibility, able to instill into his men his own intense ardor in battle, and so quick in his movements, so ready to march as well as fight, that his troops were known to the rest of the army as the "foot cavalry." In the first battle in which Jackson took part, the confused struggle at Bull Run, he gained his name Stonewall from the firmness with which he kept his men to their work and repulsed the attack of Union troops.

From that time until his death, less than two years afterward, his career was one of brilliant and almost uninterrupted success.

At Chancellorsville Jackson himself was mortally wounded. He had been leading and urging on the advance of his men, cheering them with voice and gesture, his pale face flushed with joy and excitement,[1] while from time to time as he sat on his horse he took off his hat and, looking upward, thanked Heaven for the victory it had vouchsafed him. As darkness drew near he was in the front, where friend and foe were mingled in almost inextricable confusion. He and his staff were fired at, at close range, by the Union troops, and, as they turned, were fired at again, through a mistake, by the Confederates behind him. Jackson fell, struck in several places.

For several days he lingered, hearing how Lee beat Hooker, in detail, and forced him back across the river. Then the old Puritan died. In the end his mind wandered, and he thought he was again commanding in battle, and his last words were: "Let us cross over the river and rest in the shade." Thus perished Stonewall Jackson, one of the ablest of soldiers and one of the most upright of men, in the last of his many triumphs. What a happy death Jackson's was after all! Of course, the finest of all epitaphs is "Here Lies Wolfe Victorious." And Jackson deserved just such an inscription.

Ulysses Grant

The Hammer of the North

Owen Wister's little book about Grant,[1] by reciting with entire truth certain facts of Grant's life and passing over with insufficient notice the remainder, could have drawn a picture of him as a drunken, brutal, and corrupt incapable, a picture in which almost every detail in the framework would have been true in itself, but in which the summing up and general effect would have been quite as false as if the whole had been a mere invention.[2]

In the Union armies there were generals as brilliant as Grant, but none with his iron determination. Grant's supreme virtue as a soldier was his doggedness, the quality which found expression in his famous phrases of "unconditional surrender" and "fighting it out on this line if it takes all summer." He was a master of strategy and tactics, but he was also a master of hard hitting, of that "continuous hammering" which finally broke through even Lee's guard. When an armed foe was in the field, it never occurred to Grant that any question could be so important as his overthrow. He felt nothing but impatient contempt for the weak souls who wished to hold parley with the enemy while that enemy was still capable of resistance.

The great silent soldier, the Hammer of the North, Grant did well as a boy and well as a young man. Then came a period of trouble and failure,[3] and then the Civil War and his opportunity, and he grasped it, and rose until his name is among the greatest in our history. In the Civil War men who rose to command, who were fit for the service, rose on their own merits from any position, without any aid but what their powers gave them. Grant began the war with no friends whatever. Sherman's early career in the Civil War impressed well-meaning but stodgy outsiders with the view that he was a lunatic. Farragut was an old man when the war opened who was thought well of but not regarded as of any particular note.

General Grant's Book

The greatest piece of literary work which has been done in America, or indeed anywhere, of recent years, was done by a citizen of New York—not a professed man of letters, but a great general, an ex-president of the United States, writing his memoirs on his deathbed, to save his family from want. Grant, after leaving the presidency, lost all his money at the hands of some Wall Street swindlers. General Grant's book has had an extraordinary sale among the people at large, though even yet hardly appreciated at its proper worth by the critics. And it is scarcely too high praise to say that, both because of the intrinsic worth of the matter, and because of its strength and simplicity as a piece of literary work, it almost deserves to rank with the speeches and writings of Abraham Lincoln.

Reconstruction

Reconstruction Was a Mistake

Reconstruction was a mistake as it was actually carried out, and there is very much to reprobate in what was done by Sumner and Seward and their followers. But the blame attaching to them is as nothing compared to the blame attaching to the Southerners for forty years preceding the war, and for the years immediately succeeding it. They brought their punishment absolutely on themselves, and are, in my judgment, entitled to not one particle of sympathy. The North blundered, but its blunders were in trying to do right in the impossible circumstances which the South had itself created, and for which the South was solely responsible.

The policy of "trusting the South" at that time was tried by Andrew Johnson. It produced peonage clauses in the constitutions and laws of the Southern States. If persisted in it would have produced the reintroduction of slavery, under a slightly modified form, in the South. Under the leadership of Andrew Johnson, the South rejected the Fourteenth Amendment, and therefore forced the North to back the evil folly of Sumner and Stevens in pushing the Fifteenth Amendment. The Fifteenth Amendment in the South has been a failure.

I suppose that no one now seriously contends that during the Reconstruction days the Negro majority in Mississippi and South Carolina acted wisely, or that it was possible to continue the government in the hands of that majority. On the other hand, the whites of Mississippi and South Carolina, not merely by a majority but with substantial unanimity, decided in 1861 to leave the Union, decided to plunge the country into four years of dreadful war and to ruin their own States, with the purpose of breaking up the one great free republic on the face of the earth, and of enthroning slavery in perpetuity.

For years the Republican Party has striven to build up in the Southern States a party in which the Negro should be dominant, a party consisting almost exclusively of Negroes. Those who took the lead in this experiment were actuated by high motives, and no one should now blame them because of what, with the knowledge they then had and under the then existing circumstances, they strove to do. But in actual practice the result has been lamentable from every standpoint. The solution of the impractical visionaries, who adored Sumner and still adore his memory, was perhaps the very worst, save only the solution advocated by the extreme reactionaries.

I believe the great majority of the Negroes in the South are wholly unfit for the suffrage, and that if we were able to succeed in giving them an unbought, uncoerced, and undefrauded suffrage we would reduce parts of the South to the level of Haiti. I have always felt that the passage of the Fifteenth Amendment at the time it was passed was a mistake, but to admit this is very different from admitting that it is wise, even if it were practicable, now to repeal the amendment.

A Cynical Violation of the Fifteenth Amendment

We may deplore, but we can hardly complain of, the Democratic solidity of such States as Kentucky, Arkansas, and Texas, where the majority of the people are Democratic, but when such naturally Republican States as South Carolina, Mississippi, and Louisiana are kept solidly Democratic by force and fraud, I hold it to be a gross and crying evil against which every honest man who is not a coward should protest with all his might and heart. There is no white man from a southern district in which blacks are numerous who does not tell you, either defiantly or as a joke, that any white man is allowed to vote, no matter how ignorant and degraded, and that the Negro vote is practically suppressed because it is the Negro vote.

In 1880 South Carolina had nearly a million people within its borders, somewhat less than two-thirds of whom were blacks. These blacks are almost entirely Republicans, yet in 1884 nearly seventy thousand of the ninety thousand votes cast were Democratic. Is it "waving the bloody shirt" to ask how it happens in that State that two-fifths of the voters cast four-fifths of the votes? Does any man think that such a result is brought about honestly? If so, he is indeed simple-minded.

Take John Sharp Williams, for instance.[1] He represents a district in which there are 48,000 whites and 143,000 blacks. That is, for every white man like John Sharp Williams there are three colored men. He and his fellow whites have suppressed this vote so absolutely by force, by fraud, by every species of iniquity that it is not only not worthwhile for a colored man to vote, but it is not worthwhile for a white man to vote after the Democrats have nominated their candidate. At the last election Williams did not have a single vote against him, and but 1,400 for him, and with what I feel is peculiarly repulsive hypocrisy, he whose very political existence is the negation of the Declaration of Independence declaims against our policy in the Philippines on the ground that it is a contravention of the Declaration of Independence and of the "consent of the governed" theory!

Williams is the true old-style Jeffersonian of the barbaric blatherskite variety, much such a man as Jefferson's tool, Giles,[2] was in the Second and Third Congresses. He was educated abroad. He is financially, I do not doubt, an honest man. He is an untruthful blackguard in his public attitude toward all public men who are employed in doing valuable work. John Sharp Williams's existence in Congress means a cynical violation of the Fifteenth Amendment.

Loaded Dice

I need hardly say that I regard the condition of affairs in the South as an outrage. The Negroes of the South, who are not allowed to vote, are nevertheless used to give the Southern whites (and therefore the Democratic Party), fifty electoral votes and fifty congressmen, to which they are no more entitled than the people of Kamchatka.

Until the Civil War the white votes of the South represented not only their own numerical power, but in addition to that, by a provision of the Constitution, three-fifths of the dark-skinned Americans whom they held in bondage and who had no voice in that election. We have freed the slaves, but the one effect upon a national contest of their manumission has been that the Southern white vote has swelled, not only to the extent of three-fifths, but to the extent of all the blacks in the Southern States. That has been the sole difference between the vote as it then stood and the vote as it now stands. In other words, the Democracy plays this game to rule the Union with loaded dice.

During my term as president bills have been introduced to cut down the Southern representation so as to have it based in effect only on the white vote. With absolute unanimity the Southerners have declared that to deprive them of the right to extra representation, which as white men they get by fraudulent or violent suppression of the black vote, is an outrage. With their usual absurd misuse of nomenclature they inveigh against the effort to prevent them crediting themselves with the votes of which they deprive others as "waving the bloody shirt," or being a plea for "Negro domination."

The Pitiful Chance to Have a Little Reward

On the Negro question my views are those of Abraham Lincoln[3] and not those of Wendell Phillips, Garrison, and Charles Sumner. I do not believe that the average Negro in the United States is as yet in any way as fit to take care of himself and others as the average white man, for if he were there would be no Negro problem. Neither do I believe that our treatment of him should be based upon a brutal disregard of any sense of obligation to him, and upon a determination to keep him in a state of utter debasement and of more or less modified slavery, and to frown especially upon those very members of his race who most deserve encouragement.

My own personal belief is that the talk about the Negro having become worse since the Civil War is the veriest nonsense. He has on the whole become better. Among the Negroes of the South when slavery was abolished there was not one who stood as in any shape or way comparable with Booker Washington. Incidentally, I may add that I do not know a white man of the South who is as good a man as Booker Washington today. Too many Southern people and too many Northern people repeat like parrots the statement that these "educated darkies" are "a deal worse than the old darkies." As a matter of fact almost all the Tuskegee students do well.

Are you acquainted with the case of the Indianola post office in Mississippi in connection with the Cox family?[4] I found in office there a colored woman as postmaster. She and her husband were well-to-do, and were quite heavy taxpayers. She was a very kindly, humble, and respectable colored woman. The best people in the town liked her. I reappointed her, and the Senators from Mississippi moved her confirmation. The Coxes are the new Negroes of the generation that has grown up since the war, the educated Negroes.

Afterward, the low whites in the town happened to get stirred up by the arrival of an educated colored doctor. His practice was of course exclusively among the Negroes. He was one of those men who are painfully educating themselves, and whose cases are more pitiful than the cases of any other people in our country, for they not only find it exceedingly difficult to secure a livelihood but are followed with hatred by the very whites who ought to wish them well. This particular Negro doctor took away the Negro patients from the lowest white doctors of the town. They instigated the mob which held the mass meeting and notified the Negro doctor to leave town at once, which to save his life he did that very night.

Not satisfied with this the mob then notified the colored post-mistress that she must at once resign her office. The "best citizens" of the town "deprecated" the conduct of the mob and said it was "not representative of the real Southern feeling," and then added that to save trouble the woman must go! She went. The mayor and the sheriff notified her and me that they could not protect her if she came back. I shut up the post office for the remainder of her term.

This is at present the typical Southern attitude toward the best type of colored men or colored women, and absolutely all I have been doing is to ask, not that the average Negro be allowed to vote, not that ninety-five percent of the Negroes be allowed to vote, not that there be "Negro domination" in any shape or form, but that these occasionally good, well-educated, intelligent, and honest colored men and women be given the pitiful chance to have a little reward, a little respect, a little regard, if they can by earnest useful work succeed in winning it.

My children sit in the same school with colored children. I strive my best to secure to colored men an exact equality of right with their white neighbors. I have had them eat at my table and sleep in my house. I am an ardent believer in the theory that the only way to work out our political salvation is to treat each man on his merits as a man.

PART V
Gilded Age
(1877-1900)

The Election of 1884

The Effort to Prevent Blaine's Nomination

Although I had met Cabot Lodge once or twice in the Porcellian Club, I never really knew him until the spring of 1884,[1] when we came together in connection with the effort to prevent Blaine's nomination for president. We both took the same view, namely that if possible Blaine should not be nominated, but that if nominated we would support him. About all the work in the convention that was done against him was done by Cabot Lodge and myself, who pulled together and went in for all we were worth.

I am glad to have been present at the convention, and to have taken part in its proceedings. It was a historic scene, and one of great, even if of somewhat sad, interest. Blaine was nominated by Judge West, the blind orator from Ohio. It was a most impressive scene. The speaker, a feeble old man of shrunk but gigantic frame, stood looking with his sightless eyes toward the vast throng that filled the huge hall. As he became excited his voice rang like a trumpet, and the audience became worked up to a condition of absolutely uncontrollable excitement and enthusiasm.

Of all the men presented to the convention as presidential candidates, I consider Blaine as by far the most objectionable, because his personal honesty, as well as his faithfulness as a public servant, are both open to question. Yet beyond a doubt he was opposed by many, if not most, of the politicians and was the free choice of the great majority of the Republican voters of the northern States. That such should be the fact speaks badly for the intelligence of the mass of my party, as well as for their sensitiveness to the honesty and uprightness of a public official, and bodes no good for the future of the nation, though I am far from thinking that any very serious harm can result even from either of the two evils to which our choice is now limited—a Democratic administration or four years of Blaine in the White House. The country has stood a great deal in the past and can stand a great deal more in the future.

Speaking roughly, the forces were divided as follows: Blaine 340, Arthur 280, Edmunds 95, Logan 60, Sherman 30, Hawley 15. But the second choice of all, of the Logan and Sherman and of nearly half the Arthur men, was Blaine, which made it absolutely impossible to form a combination against him. Arthur's vote was almost entirely from officeholders, coming mainly from the South, and from the great cities of the North. Except among a few of the conservative business men he had absolutely no strength at all with the people.

The very weakest candidate we could nominate, Arthur, made a very good president,[2] but the bitterness caused by his succession to power nearly tore the party in twain. I led the Edmunds men, who held the balance of power between the followers of Blaine and of Arthur. The Edmunds men represented the majority of the Republicans of New England, and a very respectable minority in New York. It included all the men of the broadest culture and highest character that there were in the convention, all those who were prominent in the professions or eminent as private citizens; and it included almost all the "plain people," the farmers and others, who were above the average, who were possessed of a keen sense of personal and official honesty, and who were accustomed to think for themselves.

Blaine adherents included the remainder. These were the men who make up the mass of the party. Their ranks included many scoundrels, adroit and clever, who intend to further their own ends by supporting the popular candidate, or who know Mr. Blaine so well that they expect under him to be able to develop their schemes to the fullest extent. But for the most part these Republicans were good, ordinary men, who do not do very much thinking, who are pretty honest themselves, but who are callous to any but very flagrant wrongdoing in others, and who are captivated by the man's force, originality, and brilliant demagoguery.

Questioning the Propriety of Bolting

Now, our brother Independents ask us to support Mr. Cleveland because they say he will do well in spite of the Democratic Party. I think Mr. Cleveland would be governed by the Democratic machine management. I think he has very good intentions, but I doubt his being able to put them in active operation. I would say that I am far from questioning the propriety of bolting in certain cases. I merely question the expediency of so doing in this particular instance.

During the convention I worked practically to prevent Mr. Blaine's nomination. Since the convention I have always intended to vote for the Republican ticket. Blaine's nomination meant to me pretty sure political death if I supported him.[3] This I realized entirely, and went in with my eyes open. Most of my friends seem surprised to find that I have not developed hoofs and horns. I have received shoals of letters, pathetic and abusive, to which I have replied with vivacity and ferocity. I get so angry with the "Mugwumps,"[4] and get to have such scorn and contempt for them.

Mr. Blaine was nominated much against the wishes of many of us, against my wishes and against my efforts. He was nominated against the wishes of the most intellectual and the most virtuous and honorable men of the great seaboard cities, but he was nominated fairly and honorably, because those who represent the bone and sinew of the Republican Party wished it, and I for one am quite content to abide by the decision of the plain people. I can oppose Cleveland with a very clear conscience. Why, look at the Democratic candidate for vice president. It is Mr. Hendricks, one of the arch-snakes from the old Copperhead nest,[5] whose presence on the ticket is an insult to every man who was loyal to the Union in the days of darkness.

Grover Cleveland

His Rugged Strength of Character

I was a member of the legislature when Mr. Cleveland became governor of the State of New York at the beginning of the year 1883,[1] and for the next twenty-five years on several different occasions I was brought into close contact with him. For two years during his second administration I served under him as Civil Service commissioner. Like all others who were thrown closely with him I was much impressed by his high standard of official conduct and his rugged strength of character.[2] Cleveland grew in office. He was bigger as president than as governor and sustained me as Civil Service commissioner better than Harrison. Harrison would never go ahead of the public sentiment of his party. Cleveland was sturdy and independent.

Not only did I become intimately and thoroughly acquainted with the manner in which he upheld and enforced the civil service law, but I also saw at close quarters his successful fight against free silver, and the courage which he, aided by men like the late Senator Cushman K. Davis of Minnesota, supported the judiciary at the time of the Chicago riot.

And, finally, I happened to be in a position in which I knew intimately how he acted and the reasons why he acted in the Venezuelan matter. This knowledge gained at first hand enables me to bear testimony, which I am more than glad to bear, to the late president's earnest purpose to serve the whole country, and the high courage with which he encountered every species of opposition and attack. My position has been consistent for a long time on the Monroe Doctrine. I supported President Cleveland in 1896 on this point. I thank Heaven that I stood straight up for his policy at that very time. When President Cleveland's Venezuela message went into the Senate I promptly applied for a command at the War Department, just as I afterward did in the war with Spain.

Owing to a peculiar combination of circumstances he went out of office assailed even more bitterly by his own party than by the opposing party, and shortsighted people thought that the great mass of American citizens had repudiated him and disbelieved him. Six years later it happened that I was at St. Louis as president when Mr. Cleveland, then a plain private citizen, arose to make an address in the great hall of the Exposition, and no one who was there will ever forget the extraordinary reception given him by the scores of thousands present.

Completely Controlled by the Corporations

Cleveland, because of his defects no less than his good qualities, represents to the Wall Street type of men almost the ideal president. Some of the big banks paid the expenses of Cleveland's campaign in 1892. There are many wealthy men who have changed parties at different elections, and supported, for instance, Cleveland first, and then McKinley.

Cleveland has never been brought into contact from the philanthropic side with wage workers, with poor people. He knows nothing of sweatshops or of the East Side. All the people around him are the big corporation people and lawyers, who, like Francis Stetson, are good fellows, but who are incapable of taking anything but the corporation attitude. The old conservative wing was uppermost when Cleveland was in power. They turned down Bryan and silver with a smash.

Mr. Cleveland, whom I like, was more completely controlled by the corporations—largely through Messrs. Whitney and Olney—than any president we have had in our time. But I do not for a moment believe that he was conscious that they were controlling him. Mr. Olney is a very good fellow and a strong man, but he is one of the most extreme pro-corporation men in the entire country, as he showed when he was attorney general.[3] He never took action of any kind such as Knox has taken against the great corporations, whom he allowed to violate the laws he was sworn to enforce.

A Good Governor for a Democrat

I think Cleveland made an excellent governor on the whole, although he yielded to political and personal considerations in a way that I have never yielded, and would never feel justified to yield. In criticizing Mr. Cleveland, it must be remembered that while in one aspect he is doubtless an entirely independent man in another aspect he is simply the most important cog in what is familiarly known as the "Manning machine." I respect him in spite of certain of the things that he has done, because like all men of good sense I judge men by the aggregate of their deeds, knowing perfectly well that they will occasionally be guilty of shortcomings.

You may perhaps know that when in the New York legislature I argued before Governor Cleveland for the Tenement House Cigar Law and (so he told me) secured his signature to it. Now, we had several bills that bore upon Tammany Hall. The governor signed those most unflinchingly—with reckless heroism. In his personal relations with me he has always been most courteous and most considerate. He has been a good governor for a Democrat. That Mr. Cleveland has done better than most other Democrats would have done, and that he has done as well as his party would let him, is probably true.

We Ought to Take Hawaii

President Cleveland was all wrong about Hawaii. I am surprised all the time to receive new proofs that every man, even every southerner, who lives outside the country has gotten to have a perfect hatred and contempt for Cleveland's administration because of its base betrayal of our interests abroad. It seems incredible that the Democratic Party, the historic party of annexation, should be inclined to go against the annexation of Hawaii. They seem willing to strike hands with the Mugwumps on this point.

I think President Cleveland's action was a colossal crime, and we should be guilty of aiding him after the fact if we do not reverse what he did. There is one thing that I personally feel very strong about, and that is about hauling down the flag at Hawaii. I am a bit of a believer in the Manifest Destiny doctrine. I believe in more ships. I believe in ultimately driving every European power off of this continent, and I don't want to see our flag hauled down where it has been hauled up.

I was much amused at my good friend, Mr. Smalley, putting in the *London Times* a wail over my supposed jingoism. I wish to heaven we were more jingo about Cuba and Hawaii! The trouble with our nation is that we incline to fall into mere animal sloth and ease, and tend to venture too little instead of too much. We ought to take Hawaii.

Hawaii is of more pressing and immediate importance than Cuba. If we don't take Hawaii it will pass into the hands of some strong nation, and the chance of our taking it will be gone forever. If we fail to take Cuba it will remain in the hands of a weak and decadent nation, and the chance to take it will be just as good as ever. If we do not take Hawaii now we may find to our bitter regret that we have let pass the golden moment forever. We did not create Hawaii. It is there. All we can do is to decide whether we shall make it an outpost of defense for the Pacific slope or allow it to be taken by the first hostile power with whom we are brought into contact, to be seized as the surest means of offense against the Pacific coast cities.

If I had my way we would annex those islands tomorrow. If that is impossible I would establish a protectorate over them. I believe we should build a Nicaraguan canal at once, and in the meantime that we should build a dozen new battleships, half of them on the Pacific coast, and these battleships should have large coal capacity and a consequent increased radius of action. I am fully alive to the danger of Japan, and I know that it is idle to rely on any sentimental goodwill toward us. My own belief is that we should act instantly. I would send the *Oregon*, and, if necessary, also the *Monterrey*, to Hawaii, and would hoist our flag over the island, leaving all details for after action.

I am a quietly rampant *"Cuba Libre"* man. I doubt whether the Cubans would do very well in the line of self-government, but anything would be better than the continuance of Spanish rule. I believe that Cleveland ought now to recognize Cuban independence and interfere, sending our fleet promptly to Havana. There would not in my opinion be very serious fighting, and what loss we encountered would be thrice over repaid by the ultimate results of our action, but the president shies off from anything except Venezuela. We ought to drive the Spaniards out of Cuba, and it would be a good thing, in more ways than one, to do it.

This Country Needs a War

Let no one pretend that the present Venezuelan case does not come within the strictest view of the Monroe Doctrine. If we permit a European nation in each case itself to decide whether or not the territory it wishes to seize is its own, then the Monroe Doctrine has no real existence. England's pretensions in this case are wholly inadmissible, and the president and secretary of state and the Senate and House deserve the highest honor for the course they have followed. Nothing will tend more to preserve peace on this continent than the resolute assertion of the Monroe Doctrine. Let us make this present case serve as an object lesson, once for all.

I am very much pleased with the president's or rather with Olney's message—he is far more of a man than the president and is the mainspring of the administration in the Venezuela matter. I do hope there will not be any back-down among our people. Let the fight come if it must. I don't care whether our seacoast cities are bombarded or not. We would take Canada. If there is a muss I shall try to have a hand in it myself! They'll have to employ a lot of men just as green as I am even for the conquest of Canada. Our regular army isn't big enough. It seems to me that if England were wise she would fight now. We couldn't get at Canada until May, and meanwhile she could play havoc with our coast cities and shipping. Personally, I rather hope the fight will come soon. The clamor of the peace faction has convinced me that this country needs a war.

The antics of the bankers, brokers, and Anglomaniacs generally are humiliating to a degree. The stock-jobbing timidity, the Baboo kind of statesmanship, which is clamored for at this moment by the men who put monetary gain before national honor, or who are still intellectually in a state of colonial dependence on England, would in the end most assuredly invite war. A temperate but resolute insistence upon our rights is the surest way to secure peace. The moneyed and semi-cultivated classes, especially of the Northeast, are doing their best to bring this country down to the Chinese level.

The Authorities Have to Put Down Mob Violence

The demagogue, in all his forms, is as characteristic an evil of a free society as the courtier is of a despotism, and the attitude of many of our public men at the time of the great strike in July 1894, was such as to call down on their heads the hearty condemnation of every American who wishes well to his country. It would be difficult to overestimate the damage done by the example and action of a man like Governor Altgeld of Illinois.[4]

The governor, who began his career by pardoning anarchists, and whose most noteworthy feat since was his bitter and undignified, but fortunately futile, campaign against the election of the upright judge who sentenced the anarchists, is the foe of every true American and is the foe particularly of every honest workingman. Had it not been for the admirable action of the Federal Government,[5] Chicago would have seen a repetition of what occurred during the Paris commune. President Cleveland and Attorney General Olney acted with equal wisdom and courage, and the danger was averted. The completeness of the victory of the federal authorities, representing law and order, has perhaps been one reason why it was so soon forgotten.

It is urgently necessary to keep before the minds of our people the great danger of permitting any growth of that unhealthy sentimentality and morbid "class-consciousness" which in their extreme form find vent in sympathy or excuse for the scoundrally utterances of Debs, which condone the action of Altgeld, which are halfhearted in condemning, or even faintly excusing, the Haymarket bomb-throwers. The authorities have to put down mob violence although the interests directly threatened may be those of a very wicked corporation.

Benjamin Harrison

Harrison Has Not Sustained His Commission

For six years, from May 1889 to May 1895, I was a member of the National Civil Service Commission. The spoils system, which can only be supplanted through the agencies which have found expression in the act creating the Civil Service Commission, has been for seventy years the most potent of all the forces tending to bring about the degradation of our politics. No republic can permanently endure when its politics is corrupt and base, and the spoils system—the application in political life of the degrading doctrine that to the victor belongs the spoils—produces corruption and degradation. Curse patronage.

After Congress enacted into a law the so-called "Pendleton Bill," to reform the Civil Service, it was really curious to hear a great many quite intelligent men speaking as if the reform was thereby made an accomplished fact, whereas, in reality, the enactment of the law was merely a single, although a lengthy, step in the right direction. It must always be remembered that the prime object of the reform under consideration is to take the Civil Service out of politics. What made the reform vitally necessary to the well-being of the nation was the fact that the public service had by degrees been turned into a vast political engine.

Altogether I am by no means pleased with what our party, at both the White House and the Capitol, has done about Civil Service reform. Frankly, I think the record pretty bad for both Cleveland and Harrison, and it is rather Walrus and Carpenter work choosing between the records of the two parties, as far as Civil Service reform is concerned. Cleveland had a much worse commission, but Harrison has not sustained his commission at all. The offices have been used for political purposes more shamefully and openly than even under the last administration.

There is much the administration has done of which I do not in the least approve. I am going to struggle "mighty hard" to stay in the Republican Party, and it is rather discouraging to see our president in the New York appointments do, on the whole, rather worse than Cleveland. He has deliberately set to work to build up a Platt machine, he has utterly ignored the progressive wing of the party, and has distinctly lowered the standard of appointments. I did not mind Pearson's being turned out[1] so much as a ward politician's being put in. Platt seems to have a ring in the president's nose as regards New York. I feel very uneasy over it.

The Little Gray Cold-Blooded Toad

I really enjoy my work as Civil Service commissioner, but I am having a hard row to hoe. Thank Heaven I have Thompson as a colleague.[2] Lyman is a good, honest, hardworking man, very familiar with the law, but he is also the most intolerably slow and pompous old muttonhead who ever adored red tape and has no more tact or manners than a cow.

This commission has been able to do effective work because we have waged war on wrongdoers. I have made this commission a living force, and in consequence the outcry among the spoilsmen has become furious. It has evidently frightened both the president and Halford[3] a little. They have shown symptoms of telling me that the law should be rigidly enforced where people will stand it, and gingerly handled elsewhere. But I answered militantly that as long as I was responsible the law should be enforced up to the handle everywhere, fearlessly and honestly. I am a great believer in practical politics, but when my duty is to enforce a law, that law is surely going to be enforced, without fear or favor. I am perfectly willing to be turned out—or legislated out—but while in I mean business. As a matter of fact I believe I have strengthened the administration by showing, in striking contrast to the facts under Cleveland, that there was no humbug in the law now.

I saw the president yesterday and had a long talk with him. The conclusion of the talk was rather colorless, as usual. Heavens, how I like positive men! His one anxiety is not to have anything to do with us or the Civil Service law. Throughout the interview he was of course as disagreeable and suspicious of manner as well might be, looking on with cold and hesitating disapproval. He is a genial little runt.[4]

The worried, halting president actually refuses to consider the changes in the rules which are necessary to enable us to do our work effectively. He has never given us one ounce of real backing. He won't consider any method of improving the service, even when it in no way touches a politician. It is horribly disheartening to work under such a chief. However, the very fact that he takes so little interest gives me a free hand to do some things, and I know well that in life one must do the best one can with the implements at hand, and not bemoan the lack of ideal ones. If the president would only act a little differently, there is a whole raft of work which we could do, and which I should very much like to do. The old fellow always wants to half-do a thing.

Wanamaker seems to be the only one of the cabinet who wants to pitch into us.[5] Wanamaker has been as outrageously disagreeable as he could possibly be, and he hinted at so much that when the president telegraphed for us yesterday we thought it looked like a row. But as a matter of fact he has, if not supported us against Wanamaker, at least not supported Wanamaker against us, and when we are guaranteed a fair field I am quite able to handle that hypocritical haberdasher by myself. We have done our best to get on smoothly with him, but he is an ill-constitutioned creature, oily, but with bristles sticking up through the oil.

The little gray man in the White House could stop this without any trouble, but true to his nature, the little gray cold-blooded toad looks on and lets me fight it without help or hindrance. He is an absolute mediocrity. He may be successful, for the turbulent political sea is often kind to mere driftwood, but I have a very positive contempt for him. Damn the president! He is a cold-blooded, narrow-minded, prejudiced, obstinate, timid old psalm-singing Indianapolis politician.

The Affair with Chile

During the administration of President Harrison, our intercourse with foreign nations has been carried on in a manner highly honorable to our government and in a way that should make all Americans proud of their country. No other administration since the Civil War has made so excellent a record in its management of our foreign relations. Of all the diplomatic incidents that have occurred the most important was the affair with Chile, an affair of the most serious character, which at one time threatened open war, and the successful settlement of which reflects the highest honor upon the administration. It is safe to state in the most sweeping terms possible that throughout the controversy with Chile the United States was absolutely in the right and Chile absolutely in the wrong.

The facts of the affair are briefly as follows: One of the revolutions so deplorably common in South America broke out in Chile and was attended by unusually bloody and desperate fighting, the Chileans being a fierce and brave race. Our minister, Mr. Egan, was forced to extend the asylum of his legation to certain members of the revolutionary party, and when the Balmacedists threatened to take these refugees away by force he promptly notified them that he would raise the American flag over his building and shoot the first man who attempted to make forcible entry into it. He thus made practical proof of his willingness to risk death rather than see the flag dishonored by surrender of the refugees who had trusted to its protection. It is hard for a man with a particle of American feeling in him to read of Mr. Egan's action in this case without feeling his veins thrill.

Soon after the complete triumph of the revolutionary party the most serious incident of all occurred. Two weeks after the final triumph of the revolutionists, when ample time in which to restore order had elapsed, and when other foreign warships in port were granting their sailors the usual liberty, a portion of the crew of the American warship *Baltimore* was similarly allowed ashore. Suddenly, they were assailed by an organized mob; several of the men were killed and others mishandled with circumstances of inhuman and revolting brutality.

The most careful investigation has shown conclusively that the American sailors committed no act of disorder, and that the attack was wanton and unprovoked, and due merely to the fact that the unfortunate victims wore the uniform of our republic. Under these circumstances our government made immediate demand for reparation. To this the Chileans at first refused to accede.

From the moment that hostilities became possible, the Navy Department had been quietly preparing a thoroughly adequate naval force. So admirably was the work done that by the time affairs in Chile came to a head the United States had made ready a force amply sufficient to insure the destruction of the Chilean navy, the bombardment of the Chilean forts, and the ruin of Chile's foreign commerce. All that was necessary was to show the Chileans that this force would be used forthwith if there was not an immediate compliance with our just demands for reparation.

Accordingly, the president sent to the Chilean government his ultimatum,[6] and four days afterward very properly sent a message to Congress explaining what he had done, and practically announcing that unless our demands were complied with immediately and fully by Chile there would be a war. This timely display of firmness produced a change of heart in our opponents. The Chilean government promptly replied to the ultimatum granting all that was asked. They voluntarily agreed to pay to our representative, Mr. Egan, the sum of seventy-five thousand dollars as indemnity for the lives of the sailors who had been slain by the Chilean mob.

It was the fact that the navy had been begun that we steered clear of our difficulties with Chile under President Harrison. If at the time of our trouble with Chile we had not already possessed the nucleus of a new navy we should almost certainly have been forced into fighting, and even as it was, trouble was only averted because of the resolute stand then taken by the president and by the officers of the navy who were on the spot.

The Election of 1896

He Is Not a Strong Man

In the larger field of politics I feel very nervous. McKinley, whose firmness I utterly distrust, will undoubtedly be nominated, and this in itself I much regret. I greatly regret the defeat of Reed, who was in every way McKinley's superior. McKinley himself is an upright and honorable man, of very considerable ability and good record as a soldier and in Congress. He is not a strong man, however, and unless he is well backed I should feel rather uneasy about him in a serious crisis, whether it took the form of a soft-money craze, a gigantic labor riot, or danger of foreign conflict.

I do hope he will take a strong stand both about Hawaii and Cuba. I do not think a war with Spain would be serious enough to cause much strain on the country, or much interruption to the revival of prosperity. There are big problems in the West Indies. Until we definitely turn Spain out of those islands (and if I had my way that would be done tomorrow), we will always be menaced by trouble there. I do feel that it would be everything for us to take firm action on behalf of the wretched Cubans. I would be a splendid thing for the navy, too.

A Witches' Sabbath

Not since the Civil War has there been a presidential election fraught with so much consequence to the country. The silver craze surpasses belief. The populists, populist-Democrats, and silver—or populist—Republicans who are behind Bryan are impelled by a wave of genuine fanaticism. Not only do they wish to repudiate their debts, but they really believe that somehow they are executing righteous justice on the moneyed oppressor. They feel the eternal and inevitable injustice of life. They do not realize, and will not realize, how that injustice is aggravated by their own extraordinary folly, and they wish, if they cannot lift themselves, at least to strike down those who are more fortunate or more prosperous.

What a witches' Sabbath they did hold at Chicago! Bryan admirably suits the platform. I can't help hoping that before November he will have talked himself out, and his utter shallowness be evident, but just at this moment I believe him to be very formidable, even in the Middle West and of course in the Far West and South. The hardest fight the Democracy could give this year was on the free silver issue. They have done wisely (if one disregards considerations of morality) in making the issue so thoroughgoing there is not a crook or criminal in the entire country who ought not to support them.

At present they are on the crest, and were the election held now they would carry the country, but I hope that before November the sober common sense of the great central Western States, the pivotal States, will assert itself. McKinley's position is very hard. The main fight must be for sound finance, but he must stand by protection also, under penalty if he does, of making his new Democratic allies lukewarm, and if he does not, of making a much larger number of his old followers hostile. Matters are very doubtful. Bryan's election would be a great calamity, though we should in the end recover from it.

The campaign is one of remarkable enthusiasm. Bryan is usually greeted by enormous crowds as he journeys to and fro. McKinley stays at home, and the people come to see him from all over the Union in such masses as seriously to disarrange the railway traffic. The hatred of the East among many westerners, and the crude ignorance of even elementary finance among such a multitude of well-meaning, but puzzleheaded, voters, give cause for serious alarm throughout this campaign.

William Jennings Bryan

The Debasement of the Currency

Mr. Bryan I regard as being a man of the Thomas Jefferson type, although of course not as able. Down at bottom Bryan is a cheap soul, the cheapest faker we have ever had proposed for president. His theories are almost as preposterous as those of Jefferson himself, and he has all of Jefferson's nervous fear of doing anything that may seem to be unpopular with the rank and file of the people, and his desire to take any side that he thinks will be popular.

Populism never prospers save where men are unprosperous, and your true Populist is especially intolerant of business success. If a man is a successful businessman he at once calls him a plutocrat. Silver is connected in his mind with scaling down debts, the partial repudiation of obligations, and other measures aimed at those odious moneyed tyrants who lend money to persons who insist upon borrowing. Now the Populists in their platform, on which Mr. Bryan stands just as squarely as he does on the Chicago platform, declared that there is not enough money in the country and demanded enough money to give each citizen fifty dollars. Mr. Bryan's Democratic platform demands free silver upon the ground (an entirely false ground, by the way) that it would double the amount of money in circulation.

The question of the free coinage of silver is not complicated at all. Very many honest men honestly advocate free coinage. Nevertheless, in its essence, the measure is one of partial repudiation, and is to be opposed because it would shake the country's credit, and would damage that reputation for honest dealings which should be as dear to a nation as to a private individual. When a man quotes, "Thou shalt not steal," and another promptly replies by asking, "Why not?" really the best answer is to repeat the commandment again. If a man cannot at the first glance see that it is as immoral and vicious to repudiate debts as it is to steal, why, it becomes quite a hopeless task to try to convince him by the most elaborate arguments.

The worst lesson that can be taught a man is to rely upon others and to whine over his sufferings. If an American is to amount to anything he must rely upon himself, and not upon the State. He must take pride in his own work, instead of sitting idle to envy the luck of others. The two greatest of all Americans were Washington, who founded the republic; and Lincoln, who saved and perpetuated it. Who cares which of them it was that trained himself while splitting rails and handling a flatboat and which one got his training while managing his inherited estate?

Beneath the Social Crust

The Bryanites do not depend and cannot depend only upon the cry for cheap money. Dishonest finance is only one of their rallying cries. They wish also a debased judiciary and an executive pledge not to interfere with violent mobs. What they appeal to is the spirit of social unrest, the spirit of discontent. It is not a nice thing to wish to pay one's debts in coins worth fifty cents on the dollar, but it is a much less nice thing to wish to plunge one's country into anarchy by providing that the law shall only protect the lawless and frown scornfully on the law-abiding.

Savages do not like an independent and upright judiciary. They want the judge to decide their way, and if he does not, they want to behead him. The Populists experience much the same emotions when they realize that the judiciary stands between them and plunder. The men who object to what they style "government by injunction" are, as regards the essential principles of government, in hearty sympathy with their remote skin-clad ancestors who lived in caves, fought one another with stone-headed axes, and ate the mammoth and woolly rhinoceros.

Bryan is a personally honest and rather attractive man, a real orator, and a born demagogue, who has every crank, fool, and putative criminal in the country behind him, and a large portion of the ignorant honest class. His utterances are as criminal as they are wildly silly. All the ugly forces that seethe beneath the social crust are behind him. The appeal for him is frankly based on class and sectional hatred. The combination of all the lunatics, all the idiots, all the knaves, all the cowards, and all the honest people who are hopelessly slow-witted is a formidable one to overcome when backed by the solid South.

William McKinley

McKinley Thought It Wicked to Expose Corruption

It was the necessity of saving the Union that called the Republican
Party into being. It accomplished that purpose, and for many years
governed the country wisely and well. Then it became fat, and soft,
and lazy. It ceased to be the party of all of the people. In 1896 and
again in 1900 we won a victory which was really a victory for ultra-
conservatism against wild radicalism. If things had been allowed to
continue in our party just as they were, we should have been upset
with a smash soon afterward. My business was to take hold of the conservative party and turn it into what it had been under Lincoln, that
is, a party of progressive conservatism, or conservative radicalism, for
of course wise radicalism and wise conservatism go hand in hand.

The "old commercial conservatism" of that Republicanism which
dominated the party for many years and culminated in Hanna was
totally unlike the Lincoln Republicanism of the party's first decade. In
the free silver campaign one most unhealthy feature of the situation
was that in their panic the conservative forces selected as their real
champion Hanna, a man of many good qualities, but who embodied in
himself, more than any other big man, all the forces of coarse corrup-

tion that had been so prominent in our industrial and political life, and the respectable people either gave to him or approved of giving to him of a colossal bribery fund. As it happens, I think that in that campaign for the most part the funds were honestly used as a means of convincing people, but the obligations Hanna incurred and the way in which the fund was raised were most unfortunate.

The man who is content to let politics go from bad to worse, jesting at the corruption of politicians, the man who is content to see the maladministration of justice without an immediate and resolute effort to reform it, is shirking his duty and preparing the way for infinite woe in the future. Remember a famous character named Mr. Podsnap in one of Dickens's works? Whenever Mr. Podsnap heard of anything disagreeable or unfortunate he always thrust it behind him with a wave of his hand, remarking that he didn't believe it was true, and that if it were true he did not wish to hear anything whatever about it. McKinley thought it wicked to expose corruption. I have never heard him denounce or assail any man or any body of men.

Satisfaction with His Policies

We have every reason to be proud of what the president and Congress have done during the five months of office, and unquestionably times are improving. Of course to prophesy about our politics is a little like prophesying about a kaleidoscope, and no human being can foretell anything with any accuracy, but it certainly seems to me as though this administration was opening, unlike every other administration of the last twenty years, with the prospects steadily brightening for its continuance during a second term. There is in the country at this time the most widespread confidence in and satisfaction with his policies.

The president has stood firm as a rock on the two great issues of honest money and an honest Civil Service, and this against very heavy pressure. He is the first president who ever, at the beginning of his administration, has taken a step so pronounced in favor of the Civil Service law as to challenge the bitter hostility of the spoilsmen. We are going to come through all right on Civil Service reform, but we have had a rocky time. Thank Heaven President McKinley takes more interest in the affair than President Harrison did.

I am very much pleased over the Hawaiian business. By concluding the treaty of annexation with Hawaii he undid, so far as it could be undone, the worst mischief of Cleveland's administration, and remedied a blunder which, if let stand, would have told against this nation for centuries to come.

The Spanish-American War

McKinley Is Bent on Peace, I Fear

Now, about the Spanish war. I would regard a war with Spain from two standpoints: First, the advisability on the grounds both of humanity and self-interest of interfering on behalf of the Cubans, and of taking one more step toward the complete freeing of America from European dominion. Second, the benefit done our people by giving them something to think of which isn't material gain, and especially the benefit done our military forces by trying both the navy and army in actual practice.

Personally, I can hardly see how we can avoid intervening in Cuba if we are to retain our self-respect as a nation. What the administration will do I know not. In some points it has followed too closely in Cleveland's footsteps to please me. In the name of humanity and of national self-interest alike, we should have interfered in Cuba two years ago. McKinley is bent on peace, I fear. From my own standpoint, however, and speaking purely privately, I believe that war will have to, or at least ought to, come sooner or later, and I think we should prepare for it well in advance. I should have the Asiatic squadron in shape to move on Manila at once. I am of course a strong advocate of immediate action against Spain. I do not think half-measures will avail anything. If there is trouble I shall go down in the New York contingent, whether it is to Cuba, or Canada, or Haiti, or Hawaii. I don't want to be in an office during war. I want to be at the front.

If I should consult purely my own feelings I should earnestly hope that we would have peace. I like life very much. I have always led a joyous life. I like thought, and I like action, and it will be very bitter to me to leave my wife and children. And while I think I could face death with dignity, I have no desire before my time has come to go out into the everlasting darkness. I don't want to be shot at any more than anyone else does, still less to die of yellow fever. It is very hard to have to act against the wishes and strongly expressed advice of all of my best friends.

Almost Crazy in Their Eagerness for Peace

It may be impossible to ever settle definitely whether or not the *Maine* was destroyed through some treachery upon the part of the Spaniards. The coincidence of her destruction with her being anchored off Havana, by an accident such as has never before happened, is unpleasant enough to seriously increase the many existing difficulties between us and Spain. Of course, I cannot pass any judgment in the matter until we hear from the court. The opinion of the other officers at Havana is nearly unanimous to the effect that there was no accident, but that the ship was destroyed by a floating mine from without. Our "yellow" newspapers have been shrieking forth the same view, but in their case wholly without any facts to back it.

We are drifting toward, and not away from, war, but the president will not make war, and will keep out of it if he possibly can. Nevertheless, with so much loose powder round, a coal may hop into it at any moment. In a week or so I believe we shall get the report. If it says the explosion was due to outside work, it will be very hard to hold the country, but the president will undoubtedly try peaceful means even then, at least at first.

The president is resolute to have peace at any price. As far as he is concerned, unless the Spaniards declare war, we will not have it. Congress, however, is in an entirely different temper. The most influential man in it, Tom Reed, is as much against war as the president, and the group of senators who stand closest to the president are ferociously against war. Nevertheless, Congress as a whole wishes either war or action that would result in war. Their most patriotic and able men take this view, and I doubt if they can be much longer restrained, although, as I am in hearty sympathy with them, my judgment may on this point be colored by my wishes.

The trend of events is for war. Congress is for war. All it needs is a big leader, but the two biggest leaders, the president and the speaker, both of whom have enormous power, are almost crazy in their eagerness for peace, and would make almost any sacrifice to get peace. Personally, I cannot understand how the bulk of our people can tolerate the hideous infamy that has attended the last two years of Spanish rule in Cuba, and still more how they can tolerate the treacherous destruction of the *Maine* and the murder of our men! I have felt that every consideration of national interest and humanity made war imperative, even before the destruction of the *Maine*.

No More Backbone Than a Chocolate Éclair

I am happy to say that I believe the administration has made up its mind that we will have to fight unless Spain makes the only amends possible for the loss of the *Maine* by at once leaving the western world. We can take no blood money for our murdered men, nor can we haggle and barter and submit to arbitration. All the atonement we can take is the independence of Cuba and the driving of the Spaniard from American soil. I have advised the president as strongly as I knew how on this line in the presence of his cabinet.

The president has taken a position from which he cannot back down without ruin to his reputation, ruin to his party, and above all, lasting dishonor to his country, and I am sure he will not back down.

What McKinley did, wanting to throw the whole matter over to Congress, was really an abandonment of duty. Imagine Washington, or Lincoln, or Andrew Jackson taking such a position! The first duty of a leader is to lead. McKinley has no more backbone than a chocolate éclair.[1]

Yesterday We Struck the Spaniards

All day we have steamed close to the Cuban coast, high barren looking mountains rising abruptly from the shore, and at this distance looking much like those of Montana. We are well within the tropics, and at night the Southern Cross shows low above the horizon. It seems strange to see it in the same sky with the friendly Dipper.

Las Guasimas, June 25th '98. Yesterday we struck the Spaniards and had a brisk fight for 2½ hours before we drove them out of their position. We lost a dozen men killed or mortally wounded, and sixty severely or slightly wounded. Brodie was wounded. Poor Capron and Ham Fish were killed. One man was killed as he stood beside a tree with me. Another bullet went through a tree behind which I stood and filled my eyes with bark. The last charge I led on the left using a rifle which I took from a wounded man. Every man behaved well. There was no flinching. The fire was very hot at one or two points where the men around me went down like ninepins. The Spaniards shot well, but they did not stand when we rushed. It was a good fight. I am in good health.

Our general is poor. He is too unwieldy to get to the front. I commanded my regiment, I think I may say, with honor. We lost a quarter of our men. For three days I have been at the extreme front of the firing line. How I have escaped I know not. I have not blanket or coat. I have not taken off my shoes even. I sleep in the drenching rain, and drink putrid water. We have won so far at a heavy cost, but the Spaniards fight very hard and charging these entrenchments against modern rifles is terrible. Well, whatever comes I feel contented with having left the Navy Department to go into the army for the war, for our regiment has been in the first fight on land, and has done well.

I Left Six Children Behind

A man's usefulness depends upon his living up to his ideals in so far as he can. Now, I have consistently preached what our opponents are pleased to call "jingo doctrines" for a good many years. One of the commonest taunts directed at men like myself is that we are armchair and parlor jingoes who wish to see others do what we only advocate doing. When the chance came for me to go to Cuba with the Rough Riders Mrs. Roosevelt was very ill and so was Teddy. It was a question if either would ultimately get well. Yet I made up my mind that I would not allow even a death to stand in my way, that it was my one chance to cut my little notch on the stick that stands as the measuring rod in every family. I know now that I would have turned from my wife's deathbed to have answered that call.

I loathe war. When I went to Cuba I left six children behind. In the night before each fight, I never dared to think of either my wife or children because it really tended to unman me. I should be ashamed of my sons if they shirked war, just as I should be ashamed of my daughters if they shirked motherhood. I have seen my wife, for whom of course I care infinitely more than for myself, nearer to death in childbirth than ever I was on the battlefield.

I Killed One of Them

I am having great fun now as governor and I had even greater fun last summer. I had a great regiment for a volunteer organization. I have always believed that with proper leadership there were no better natural soldiers in the world than those hunters, cowpunchers, and miners of the West. The Spanish were a queer lot. They possessed no initiative, and yet they stood and fought with extraordinary courage when behind cover. They did not like standing in the open much. The country was extremely difficult and on our side the battle was not delivered with very much judgment, so we lost heavily.

In the San Juan fighting I happened to get thrown into close quarters with a couple of Spaniards, both of whom shot at me and whom I shot at in return, just after they had done so. I killed one of them, and throughout the fall campaign one of the favorite cries of my opponents was that I had "shot a man in the back." As it happened he was not shot in the back, but in the left breast as he turned. Having a revolver and my two antagonists having rifles, I ran in as hard as possible, thinking to minimize the disadvantage imposed by the poor quality of my weapon.

I Am Entitled to the Medal of Honor

I feel that the Medal of Honor is the greatest distinction open to any American. I should be more proud than I can say to have earned it myself. If I didn't earn it, then no commissioned officer ever can earn it. I moved through the 9th Regiment, of my own accord, and gave the order to charge, and led in person that portion of the line on horseback, being the first man on the Hill, and killing a Spaniard with my own hand. I led in person the next charge on the second line of block-houses. I led in person the third charge, and then at the extreme front commanded the fragments of the six cavalry regiments and brigade until the next morning. This will seem very egotistical. I am entitled to the Medal of Honor, and I want it.[2]

Extraordinary Manifestations of Panic

After the *Maine* blew up, the American people began to think war probable, and there was a curious lull in the newspaper yelling about Spain. I thought this attitude of quiet and dignified waiting very good. On the other hand, as soon as the war broke out there were the most extraordinary manifestations of panic (which of course means both folly and fear) that could be imagined.

A very good fellow, a personal friend of mine, the governor of a great State, publicly announced that he would not allow the national

guard of the State to leave it, on the ground that they would be needed
to repel attacks of Spaniards on that State, these attacks being just as
likely as an invasion of Hottentots. My New York friends petitioned
me for monitors and battleships to protect their country houses on the
seacoast, to protect Jekyll Island (the Georgia congressmen joining in
this request).

Senator Hale was in a rather worse panic than anyone else. He
and Tom Reed bedeviled the Department for a warship to protect the
city of Portland until finally quieted by our sending there some naval
militia on board of one of the Civil War monitors, a vessel which would
have been unable to give protection from any foe more modern than
about the time of the Spanish armada. However, its arrival gave great
satisfaction and quieted all the panic.

England Stood by the United States

I feel a keen remembrance of England's friendly attitude during the
Spanish-American War. Every man connected with American diplomacy knows that England stood by the United States when all the
continental powers were against us. You must remember that English
friendliness for the United States is something comparatively new.
Certain Englishmen were always friendly. Other Englishmen felt a
kindliness, coupled with a firm conviction that they were kindly toward inferiors. But there was much active hostility and much indifference. In '98 there was almost for the first time an attitude of real and
practical friendliness.[3] In some men—and I was one of them—this
attitude worked an abiding change in their feeling toward England.

Admiral Dewey Performed One of the Great Feats

Our present navy was begun in 1882. At that period our navy consisted
of a collection of antiquated wooden ships, already almost as out of
place against modern war vessels as the galleys of Alcibiades and

Hamilcar. The work of upbuilding the navy went on, and ships equal to any in the world of their kind were continually added. The result was seen in the short war with Spain, which was decided with such rapidity because of the infinitely greater preparedness of our navy than of the Spanish navy.

Admiral Dewey performed one of the great feats of all time. At the very outset of the Spanish War he struck one of the two decisive blows which brought the war to a conclusion, and as his was the first fight, his success exercised an incalculable effect upon the whole conflict. He set the note of the war.

There was no delay, no hesitation. As soon as news came that he was to move, his war-steamers turned their bows toward Manila Bay. In the tropical night he steamed past the forts, and then on over the mines to where the Spanish vessels lay. Steaming in with cool steadiness, Dewey's fleet cut the Spaniards to pieces, while the Americans were practically unhurt. Then Dewey drew off to breakfast, satisfied himself that he had enough ammunition, and returned to stamp out what embers of resistance were still feebly smoldering. The victory ensured the fall of the Philippines, for Manila surrendered as soon as our land forces arrived.

The Election of 1900

Luck Favored Me in Every Way

Last year luck favored me in every way, though the year opened gloomily enough with Mrs. Roosevelt literally at death's door for months. First, to get into the war, then to get out of it, then to get elected. I had worked hard all my life, and have never been particularly lucky, but this summer I was lucky, and I am enjoying it to the full. If I hadn't happened to return from the war in a year when we had a gubernatorial election in New York, I should probably not now be governor. If, on the other hand, I had returned at the end of the second instead of the first term of the existing president, I should have had a fair show for the nomination.

I believed with all my heart in the war with Spain, and I would have been very discontented if I had not been able to practice what I preached. I had a corking good regiment, although the men were only volunteers. I am more than proud to be governor of New York, and shall not care if I never hold another office, and I am very proud of my regiment. I have just come back from a week in the West, where I went to attend my regimental reunion in Las Vegas. It would really be difficult to express my surprise at the way I was greeted. At every station at which the train stopped in Indiana, Illinois, Wisconsin, Iowa, Missouri, Kansas, Colorado, and New Mexico, I was received by dense throngs exactly as if I had been a presidential candidate.

I had a great time out West, and was received with such wild enthusiasm that I became a little uneasy lest some lunatic should believe I was fool enough to be dreaming of the presidency, so I came out in support of McKinley. Of course, I should like to be president, and I feel I could do the work well, but I have seen too many men, beginning with Tom Reed and Dewey, at close quarters when they were suffering the effects of the presidential bee ever to get it into my head. Moreover, it would be simply foolish for me to think seriously of my chances of getting the office, when the only certain feature of the situation is that my own State will be against me.

I would not know how to organize a canvass for myself. I have no Hanna. There is no person who could take hold of my canvass and put money in it and organize it, and the big corporations who supply most of the money vary in their feeling toward me from fear to tepid dislike. I have never won any office by working for it by the ordinary political methods and if I should try now I should probably merely fail and be humiliated. I don't think I can play the game that way. The result would be that my usefulness would go. I have confined myself to trying to be a middling decent governor.

A Great Growth of Economic Unrest

I received from the president a cordial invitation to go to Washington and spend a night at the White House. I accordingly went on and he received me with the utmost heartiness, being evidently very much pleased at my having coming out for him. The president jollied me to his heart's content. I do most earnestly hope he will get a definite policy and follow it out both in the Philippines and in Cuba. I wish he had more backbone.

If now he will be true to his best side and will stand up ruggedly for unflinching honesty in all our home affairs and for a thoroughly efficient administration of the War Department, without the slightest heed to political considerations, we can carry the next election with him and prevent the menace of a Bryan administration, which would mean the abandonment of our destiny abroad and treachery to all traditions of honor at home. I am trying my best to strengthen the forces around the president which tell for right.

There is a great growth of economic unrest among the laboring classes of the East, who show a strong tendency to turn to Bryan, simply because they are against the established order and feel bitterly because of wrongs which are really inherent in the nature of things, and not in the least due to any party policy. The agitation against trusts is taking an always firmer hold. It is largely unreasonable and fanned into activity by the Bryan type of demagogue.

But when there is a good deal of misery and of injustice, even though it is mainly due to the faults of the individuals themselves, or to the mere operation of nature's laws, the quack who announces he has a cure-all for it is a dangerous person. Around the State of New York I am surprised to find how many of the workingmen who were with us three years ago are now sullenly grumbling that McKinley is under Hanna's dictation, that Bryan is the only man who can control the trusts, and that the trusts are crushing the life out of the small man.

To Get Me Out of the State

I have been doing my best during my term as governor to show that the man and not the dollar was the force which I was striving to uphold. The anti-expansionists and lunatic goo-goo crowds hate me with an entire and perfect hatred, and will do all they can to beat me at the polls. I have no real community of principle or feeling with the machine. So far I have gotten along very well with them, but I never can tell when they will cut my throat. My being in politics is in a sense an accident, and it is only a question of time when I shall be forced out.

I have found out one reason why Senator Platt wants me nominated for the vice presidency. He is, I am convinced, genuinely friendly, and indeed I think I may say really fond of me, and is personally satisfied with the way I have conducted politics, but the big-moneyed men with whom he is in close touch, and whose campaign contributions have certainly been no inconsiderable factor in his strength, have been pressing him very strongly to get me put in the vice presidency, so as to get me out of the State. The big insurance companies, possessing enormous wealth, want me out.

Dewey Made a Fool of Himself

What a perfectly extraordinary affair this Dewey outburst is! As regards the man himself, while it does not diminish my regard for him because of what he has done in the past, it cannot help but alter my view of him now, for he has made a pitiable showing. Upon my word, I think Bryan would be preferable to a creature so vain and so ignorant that in his desire for the presidency he says he will take the nomination from any party, that he does not care what the policies of any party are, and that he has no principles which he desires to enunciate.

Of course, among right-thinking people there can be but one verdict upon it, and I cannot help but believe that he will be laughed out of court. Still, the unthinking may under the glamour of his naval glory support him, and the educated jacks who especially delight to call themselves "thinkers" here in the East are actually coming out in his favor, because they hate the Republican Party and do not want to go back to Bryan. What a crew they are!

As a fighting man, as a man on the bridge or in the conning tower, Dewey had no superior. He was everything the traditions demand an American sailor-man shall be. But take him off his quarterdeck and set him in a swivel chair and he was lost. Dewey made a fool of himself.

Nominated for Vice President

I was nominated for vice president. I would have preferred to have continued as governor but the nomination came unanimously and with such a demand that it was out of the question to refuse, for it was believed that I would greatly strengthen the ticket in the West, where they regard me as a fellow barbarian and like me much. I shall be glad to get a little in touch with national affairs again because I am really down at the bottom more interested in them than in State and municipal affairs. I realize the great importance of franchise taxation, tenement house reform, and the like, and while I work at them just as conscientiously as I know how, they really don't interest me as much as building up the navy, administering the Philippine policy, and studying the situation in China.

I Hope Bryanism Is Dead

I am delighted to have been on the national ticket in this great historic contest, for after McKinley and Hanna, I feel that I did as much as anyone in bringing about the result, though after all it was Bryan himself who did the most. Well, I hope Bryanism is dead. At any rate we are now reasonably safe from disgrace at home or abroad for the next few years. I was on the stump a little over nine weeks, traveling over eighteen thousand miles and speaking six hundred and eighty-one times, the speeches ranging from talks of only four or five minutes in length from the rear platform of the car to speeches of two hours' duration in huge halls containing as high as twenty thousand people. Once or twice I had rather rough experiences and there was a good deal of interrupting, occasionally by legitimate questions and more often by howls for Bryan.

The Assassination of President McKinley

A Regular Jollier

The president, who is a regular "jollier," in a cold-blooded way, has always rather liked me, or at least admired certain qualities in me. There are certain bits of work he would be delighted to have me do. But at bottom neither he nor Hanna (although I really like both) sympathize with my feelings or feel comfortable about me, because they cannot understand what it is that makes me act in certain ways at certain times, and therefore think me indiscreet and overimpulsive.

The president made up his mind that I was needed on the ticket with him last year and wanted me nominated, while Hanna did not. He is perfectly cordial and friendly to me now, but he does not intend that I shall have any influence of any kind, sort, or description in the administration from the top to the bottom. This he has made evident again and again, although always in an entirely pleasant and courteous way. I have really much less influence with the president now that I am vice president than I had even when I was governor.

Shot by an Anarchist

On the 6th of September, President McKinley was shot by an anarchist while attending the Pan-American Exposition in Buffalo, and died in that city on the 14th of the month. Of the last seven elected presidents, he is the third who has been murdered, and the bare recital of this fact is sufficient to justify grave alarm among all loyal American citizens.

Both President Lincoln and President Garfield were killed by assassins of types unfortunately not uncommon in history, President Lincoln falling victim to the terrible passions aroused by four years of Civil War, and President Garfield to the revengeful vanity of a disappointed office seeker. President McKinley was killed by an utterly depraved criminal belonging to that body of criminals who object to all governments, good and bad alike. This criminal was a professed anarchist.

The occasion chosen by the assassin was one when the President was meeting great masses of his fellow citizens in accordance with the old American idea of the relations between the president and the people. That there might be no measure of Judas-like infamy lacking, the dog approached him under pretense of shaking hands. There is no baser deed in all the annals of crime.

Of course, I feel as I always have felt, that we should war with relentless efficiency not only against anarchists, but against all active and passive sympathizers with anarchists. Moreover, every scoundrel like Hearst and his satellites who for whatever purposes appeals to and inflames evil human passion has made himself accessory before the fact to every crime of this nature, and every soft fool who extends a maudlin sympathy to criminals has done likewise. Hearst and Altgeld, and to an only lesser degree Tolstoy and the feeble apostles of Tolstoy, like Ernest Howard Crosby and William Dean Howells, who unite in petitions for pardons of anarchists, have a heavy share in the burden of responsibility for crimes of this kind.

I felt that the only course to follow was that which was natural, and that the natural thing was to come at once to Buffalo, where I might see how the president was getting on, and to stay here until he was on the high road to recovery. It is a dreadful thing to come into the presidency this way, but it would be a far worse thing to be morbid about it. Here is the task, and I have got to do it to the best of my ability, and that is all there is about it.

McKinley's Time of Tremendous Popularity

On Tuesday evening I started on my western trip—a day earlier than I had expected because of poor Mrs. McKinley's death. Poor soul, it was a mercy for her to go, and she had long been wishing it. I was very much touched this year when she sent Archie a pair of slippers which she had knit, and a little photograph of President McKinley. Root, Garfield, and Secretary Wilson went out with me to Canton and the funeral. We lunched with Judge Day, then we went around to the house and followed the funeral to the tomb in which the poor lady was laid beside her husband. They have left no children, and her death seemed to me like the final drawing of a curtain. As we sat in the house listening to the funeral service I kept thinking of the different times I had seen McKinley and had been in that house before.

I first met him when we were both of us delegates to the Republican National Convention. The next year we both spoke on the same platform at Cleveland, where I was John Hay's guest, and while I was Civil Service commissioner and he was prominent in the House I saw him a number of times and once had him to dinner. Then when he was running first against Bryan, Lodge and I stopped at his house in Canton to see him when we were on a campaigning trip.

At his home in Canton anyone could see him just as easily as anyone else could be seen. At that time the little city was jammed with visitors. I remember perfectly well one funny old couple from the country who had gravely sat down in the front yard of McKinley's house to eat their dinner, which they had brought with them. The house itself was filled to overflowing, and the people had tramped over the yard so that not a spear of grass was left, and they had taken away all the wooden pickets for mementos, so that finally an iron railing had to be put up instead. That was the beginning of McKinley's time of tremendous popularity, which lasted just five years, when it was closed by the bullet of Czolgosz.

PART VI

Twentieth Century

(1901-1918)

Theodore Roosevelt

I Have Toiled and Fought with Men

I have no right to the title of Excellency.[1] I am simply Theodore Roosevelt, President of the United States. I would rather be called Colonel than anything else. My people have been for eight generations in America. I was born in New York, October 27, 1858, my father of old Dutch Knickerbocker stock; my mother, a Georgian, descended from the Revolutionary Governor Bulloch, was an unreconstructed rebel to the day of her death. I am a descendent of slaveholders—until the day of their death I pensioned two of my southern grandfather's ex-slaves, whom I had never seen, but whom I knew intimately through the stories of my mother and her sister had told me of them.

Perhaps the very fact that I am half southern and half northern in blood, and that for many years I was brought into peculiarly close association with the life of the great West, makes it natural for me to feel with intensity the strong sense of kinship with every portion of our great common country, which should be the birthright of every true American. Since I have been president I have visited every State and territory within the borders of the Union, save such as can only be reached by sea. I have traveled from the Atlantic to the Pacific, from the Great Lakes to the Gulf.

I have literally never spent an unhappy day, unless by my own fault! I have thoroughly enjoyed it all—being president, being colonel in the Spanish War, my African trip, my ranch life in the West, my work and association with the men of our great cities who are trying to help better our civic and social and economic conditions. I have toiled and fought with men!

There is a sentence in Ruskin of which I have always been fond, wherein he points out that those marvelous Gothic cathedrals were built, not by architects whose names are handed down for all time, but by men whose names have perished, by men who were simply master masons, who worked primarily because they gloried in doing the work and whose reward was found in having done that work well. More and more it seems to me that about the best thing in life is to have a piece of work worth doing and then to do it well.

It Is the Muckers That Govern

I have known plenty of men who are only able to do their work because they have inherited means. This is absolutely true of both Cabot and myself, for instance. Cabot is quite a rich man, but I am not. But each of us has been able to do what he has done because his father left him in such shape that he did not have to earn his own living. My own children will not be so left, and of course I regret the fact.

I graduated at Harvard in 1880. In college I did fairly in my studies, taking honors in natural history and political economy, and was very fond of sparring, being champion lightweight at one time— prizefighting is brutal and degrading, but boxing tends to make men manly and courageous. While at Harvard and for a year or two afterward I moved in what might be called Mugwump circles, where the *Nation* and the *Evening Post* were treated as well-nigh final authorities, until I got out into the world of men and myself took part in the rough-and-tumble of the life where deeds are actually done. My whole career in politics is due to the simple fact that when I came out of Harvard I was firmly resolved to belong to the governing class, not to the governed.

As soon as I left college I wanted to take an interest in political life. I wanted to find out how the work of governing was really done. Quite a number of nice people in New York, along Fifth Avenue, solemnly advised me not to join any of the regular political organizations, because I would find that they were composed only of "muckers," not of "gentlemen." The answer was easy: "Then they are the ones that govern. If it is the muckers that govern, I want to see if I cannot hold my own with them. I will join with them in governing you if you are too weak to govern yourselves."

So I joined the political club in my district, went around there steadily, took part in all the work both at primaries and elections, peddled tickets myself, etc. Without my knowing it, and without my even now being able to tell exactly why or how, I gradually found myself getting so that the various opportunities that came along passed in my direction. Some I took. Some I at least partially failed to take, but I was always on hand, and I gradually acquired what may be called the "political habit," and so immediately after leaving college I went to the legislature.

I was elected to the assembly from the 21st District of New York in the autumn of 1881. I was the youngest man there, and I rose like a rocket. I was reelected next year by an enormous majority in a time when the Republican Party as a whole met with great disaster, and the Republican minority in the house, although I was the youngest member, nominated me for speaker, that is, made me leader of the minority. I immediately proceeded to lose my perspective, also. The result was that I came an awful cropper and had to pick myself up after learning by bitter experience the lesson that I was not all-important and that I had to take account of many different elements in life. It took me fully a year before I got back to the position I had lost, but I hung steadily at it and achieved my purpose.

A Cattle Ranch in Dakota

Finding the work in Albany, if conscientiously done, very harassing, I was forced to take up some out-of-doors occupation for the summer—a cattle ranch in Dakota. When I went out West I all the time had in view the possibility of using those western men, and my knowledge of them, in the event of war. Both at the time of the Chilean and of the Venezuelan troubles I put myself in touch with my western friends and made ready to organize a troop of mounted riflemen. When the Spanish-American War came I was able to move in a groove which I had roughly marked out a long time before. Many of my old friends with whom I had lived on the ranches and worked in the roundups in the early days came on to see me inaugurated.

Once I made a very successful hunting trip. It took sixteen days traveling (during which I killed a few bucks) before I reached the foot of the snowcapped Bighorn range. We then left our wagon and went into the mountains with pack ponies, and as I soon shot all the kinds of game the mountains afforded, I came out after two weeks, during which time I killed three grizzly bear, six elk (three of them have magnificent heads and look well in the "house on the hill"). My bears were killed close up, and the shots were not difficult so long as one did not get rattled.

Buffalo Bill used to hunt bear and white goat and caribou and elk with me in Montana, Idaho, and British Columbia. Buffalo Bill is really a fine fellow, a Medal of Honor man, who fought gallantly in the Civil War and the Indian wars, was one of the most remarkable scouts we ever had on the plains, and is now a good citizen, much interested in irrigation besides his Wild West show. I remember when I was running for vice president I struck a Kansas town just when the Wild West show was there. He got up on the rear platform of my car and made a brief speech on my behalf, ending with the statement that "a cyclone of the west had come, no wonder the rats hunted their cellars!" I do not mean to bore you with reminiscences.

Abolishing the Tramp Lodging Houses

In May 1895, I was made president of the newly appointed Police Board, whose duty it was to cut out the chief source of civic corruption in New York by cleansing the Police Department. One important bit of reform was abolishing the tramp lodging houses, which had originally been started in the police stations, in a spirit of unwise philanthropy. These tramp lodging houses, not being properly supervised, were mere nurseries for pauperism and crime, tramps and loafers of every shade thronging to the city every winter to enjoy their benefits. We abolished them, a municipal lodging house being substituted. Here all homeless wanderers were received, forced to bathe, given nightclothes before going to bed, and made to work next morning, and in addition they were so closely supervised that habitual tramps and vagrants were speedily detected and apprehended.

Love Is Best

I am the first vice president who became president by the death of his predecessor who has ever been nominated for the president's office. This is no small triumph in itself. As the result of my being president I at least won the unquestioned leadership in my own party, and I have to my credit a big sum of substantive achievement—the Panama Canal, the creation of the Department of Commerce and Labor with the Bureau of Corporations, the settlement of the Alaska boundary, the anthracite coal strike, the success of such suits as that against the Northern Securities Company which gave a guaranty in this country that rich man and poor man alike were held equal before the law.

I hope you will not think this egotistical. I can entirely assure that there is not a particle of genius or of any unusual talent in anything I have ever done. By a combination of accidents I am where I am. My own party machine would of course never put me up for president, and only the chance of my being in the Spanish War procured me the nomination for governor. I so firmly believe that all other success, once the means of actual subsistence have been secured, counts for nothing compared to the success of the man in winning the one woman who is all the world to him. It is, if I remember aright, the last line of Browning's "Love among the Ruins," which sums up the whole matter.[2] I have always felt an utter contempt for the sordid souls who regard themselves as practical and hardheaded because they have not the capacity to understand what love is.

I Bounced Forward with My Umbrella

Today, as I was marching to church, with Sloan some twenty-five yards behind, I suddenly saw two terriers racing to attack a kitten which was walking down the sidewalk. I bounced forward with my umbrella,[3] and after some active work put to flight the dogs while Sloan captured the kitten, which was a friendly, helpless little thing, evidently too well accustomed to being taken care of to know how to shift for itself. I inquired of all the bystanders and of people on the neighboring porches to know if they knew who owned it, but they all disclaimed, with many grins, any knowledge of it. I marched ahead with it in my arms for about half a block. Then I saw a nice colored woman and little colored girl looking out of the window of a small house with on the door a dressmaker's advertisement, and I turned and walked up the steps and asked them if they did not want the kitten. They said they did, and the little girl welcomed it lovingly.

It Is Sagamore That We Love

I am a college-bred man, belonging to a well-to-do family so that, as I was more than contented to live simply, and was fortunate enough to marry a wife with the same tastes, I have not had to make my own livelihood, though I have always had to add to my private income by work of some kind.

I do not see very much of the big-moneyed men in New York, simply because very few of them possess the traits which would make them companionable to me, or would make me feel that it was worth while dealing with them. To spend the day with them at Newport, or on one of their yachts, or even to dine with them save under exceptional circumstances, fills me with frank horror. Money is undoubtedly one form of power and I appreciate this fact in them and acknowledge it, but I would rather have had the career of Dewey or of Tom Reed, though both ended in a failure (I say "a failure" and not "failure," for the latter would not be true) than the career of Pierpont Morgan. I should selfishly prefer my old-time ranch on the Little Missouri to anything in Newport. Heaven forbid that anyone for whom I care should treat riding to hounds as the serious business of life!

Fond as I am of the White House and much though I have appreciated years in it, there isn't any place in the world like home, like Sagamore Hill, where the things are our own, with our own associations, and where it is real country. It is Sagamore that we love. It contains about a hundred acres, most of it woodland, but a considerable portion pastureland or under the plow. My father and grandfather both lived at Oyster Bay, but I cannot tell the exact time when they came. They were both summer residents merely. My father's house here was named Tranquility, which he hired and did not buy. I lived at Tranquility until I left college in 1880. The following year I purchased Sagamore Hill. We are but an hour from New York. It is a most sleepy spot.

We have a great big house which is very comfortable, although in appearance and furnishing, painfully suggestive of that kind of elegance which one sees in a swell Chicago hotel or in the boardroom of the directors of some big railway. I never feel in the least embarrassed because at Sagamore Hill, at my own house, we have a maid to wait on the table and open the door, instead of having a butler. This house has been my home for years. It is the one place where all my things are. Whenever I live anywhere else I simply rent a house.

November always seems to me one of the loveliest seasons of the year. I like the wintry sunsets, and the tang in the air, and the wood fires in the North Room and library. I hunted the game whose heads are on the wall. Personally, I only keep heads of my own shooting. Heavens and earth! I don't believe I shall ever shoot at game again. I am by no means certain I could hit it anyway, unless it stayed very still and was very close up. I should give a great deal to again hear the wind in the pine trees as I camped out in the wilderness by some little brook and to feast on trout and elk meat and blue grouse, but I rather doubt whether I shall do any of these things again.

I thoroughly believe in large families, and am always glad to hear of them. Mrs. Roosevelt and I have six children. Quentin is the only one of my boys that seems to be really bright. Then there is Archie, a boy with a wooden head and a golden heart; and my eldest son, Theodore, a plug-ugly refined by Harvard. He should have been a prize-fighter by profession. I do not believe you could drive with a club any of my children away from Sagamore Hill. They love the place.

The other night I took out the boys in rowboats for a camping-out expedition. We camped on a beach under a low bluff near the spot where a few years ago on a similar expedition we saw a red fox. This time two young foxes, evidently this year's cubs, came around the campfire half a dozen times during the night, coming up within ten yards of the fire to pick up scraps and seeming to be very little bothered by our presence. Yesterday on the tennis ground I found a mole shrew. He was near the side lines first. I picked him up in my handkerchief, as he bit my hand, and after we all looked at him I let him go.

I am interested in birds,[4] and this spring have been quite enthralled by finding a black-throated green warbler breeding near the house which I had not before known bred on Long Island at all. Yesterday John Burroughs was here for lunch and I took him out to the grove where the warbler is, and the warbler most obligingly was very much in evidence. Last year was the first time I ever saw the purple finch breeding around this place. Here at Oyster Bay my observations have gone over some thirty-one years. Around my home here on Long Island the robins, wood thrushes, catbirds, meadowlarks, song sparrows, chipping sparrows, grasshopper finches, and Baltimore orioles are as plentiful as ever. So with the barn swallows at the stable.

I Believe in Power

I have a definite philosophy about the presidency. I think it should be a very powerful office, and I think the president should be a very strong man who uses without hesitation every power that the position yields. But because of this very fact I believe that he should be sharply watched by the people, held to a strict accountability by them, and that he should not keep the office too long. In the great days of the Roman republic no harm whatever came from the dictatorship, because great though the power of the dictator was, after a comparatively short period he surrendered it back to those from whom he gained it.

While president I have been president, emphatically. I have used every ounce of power there was in the office and I have not cared a rap for the criticisms of those who spoke of my "usurpation of power," for I knew that the talk was all nonsense and that there was no usurpation. I believe that the efficiency of this government depends upon its possessing a strong central executive, and wherever I could establish a precedent for strength in the executive—as I did for instance as regards external affairs in the case of sending the fleet around the world, taking Panama, settling affairs of Santo Domingo and Cuba—why, in all these cases I have felt not merely that my action was right in itself, but that in showing the strength of, or in giving strength to, the executive, I was establishing a precedent of value. I believe in a strong executive. I believe in power, but I believe that responsibility should go with power.

I much prefer to really accomplish something good in public life, no matter at what cost of enmity from even my political friends, than to enjoy a longer term of service, fettered by endless fear, always trying to compromise, and doing nothing in the end. I had rather be a real president than a figurehead.

My Hand on the Lever

I enjoy being president, and I like to do the work and have my hand on the lever. It would be quite absurd to say that I follow public opinion and don't lead it. I do lead it. We should have never had Panama without me. Nobody else would have got Panama. Nobody else would have dared to make the move I made. Nobody in the wide world. I did that, and public sentiment responded instantly and said that I was right. Nobody but me would have sent the fleet around the globe. I led in settling the anthracite strike. Who was it proposed all these things? Who worked the country up to them? The great movement to which the country is now aroused for the preservation of our national resources— am I following or leading in that?

During my term as president I have more than doubled the navy of the United States, and at this moment our battle fleet is doing what no other similar fleet of a like size has ever done—that is, circumnavigating the globe—and is also at this moment in far more efficient battle trim. The improvement in both army and navy over things as they were at the beginning of the Spanish War is marvelous. I do not think we can afford to let the army go back, and I think we must keep building the navy up. Arbitration is an excellent thing, but ultimately those who wish to see this country at peace with foreign nations will be wise if they place reliance upon a first-class fleet of first-class battleships rather than on any arbitration treaty which the wit of man can devise. Nelson said that the British fleet was the best negotiator in Europe, and there was much truth in the saying.

Then take the Panama Canal. I do not think that any feat of quite such far-reaching importance has been to the credit of our country in recent years, and this I can say absolutely was my own work, and could not have been accomplished save by me or by some man of my temperament. I think the peace at Portsmouth was a substantial achievement. I have succeeded in getting the administration of the civil government in the Philippine Islands put upon a satisfactory basis. In dealing with the Philippines I have the jack fools who seriously think that any group of pirates and headhunters needs nothing but independence in order that it may be turned forthwith into a dark-hued New England town meeting.

I have trebled or quadrupled the forest reserves of the country; have put through the reorganization of the forest service, placing it under the Agriculture Department; and, I may add as a small incident, have created a number of reservations for preserving the wild things of nature, the beasts and birds as well as the trees. I will do everything in my power to protect not only Yosemite, which we have already protected, but other similar great natural beauties of this country.

Then take the settlement of the anthracite coal strike—I was of course not required by the Constitution to attempt this settlement, and if I had failed to attempt I should have held myself worthy of comparison with Franklin Pierce and James Buchanan among my predecessors. If the strike had not been settled there would have been within thirty days the most terrible riots that this country has ever seen. The strike certainly would not have been settled if I had not interfered.

Traveling through Europe last year I was impressed by the fact that in every nation the leading statesmen whom I met had always before their minds as the two great feats performed by the American people during the last decade these two—the voyage of the battle fleet around the world, and the digging of the Panama Canal. I do not think I need tell you that foreign nations are not in the least impressed with what we say ourselves—not in the least. All that impresses them is what we do.

I am the only American in public life whom the Europeans really understand. You see, we speak the same language. I am a gentleman and follow the code of a gentleman. I am a graduate of a great university. I commanded a crack cavalry regiment during the war with Spain. I am a big-game hunter and a sportsman. Those things the Europeans understand. But they are utterly unable to understand our politicians.

A Corrupt Pithecoid Community

I have had a most interesting time about Panama. The entire fool Mugwump crowd have fairly suffered from hysterics, and a goodly number of the senators even of my own party have shown about as much backbone as so many angleworms. On the score of morality it seems to me that nothing could be more wicked than to ask us to surrender the Panama people, who are our friends, to the Colombian people, who have shown themselves our foes, and this for no earthly reason save because we have, especially in New York City and parts of the Northeast, a small body of shrill eunuchs. I have to encounter the opposition of the vague individuals of serious mind and limited imagination, who think that a corrupt pithecoid community in which the president has obtained his position by the simple process of clapping the former president into a wooden cage and sending him on an oxcart over the mountains (this is literally what was done at Bogotá) is entitled to just the treatment that I would give, say, to Denmark or Switzerland.

To my mind this building of the canal through Panama will rank in kind, though not of course in degree, with the Louisiana Purchase and the acquisition of Texas. I can say with entire conscientiousness that if in order to get the treaty through and start building the canal it were necessary for me forthwith to retire definitely from politics, I should be only too glad to make the arrangement accordingly, for it is the amount done in office, and not length of time in office, that makes office worth having. The building of this canal has been something upon which the American people has set its mind for decades. The precedents upon which I have acted were set by Polk, by Cass, by Bayard, no less than by Grant and by Seward. We wanted Panama. I took it.

I did not foment the revolution on the Isthmus. It is idle folly to speak of there having been a conspiracy with us. The people of the Isthmus are a unit for the canal, and in favor of separation from the Colombians. Panama revolted from Colombia because Colombia, for corrupt and evil purposes or else from complete governmental incompetency, declined to permit the building of the great work which meant everything to Panama. By every law, human and divine, Panama was right in her position.

The case in a nutshell is this: the government of Colombia was solemnly pledged to give us the right to dig that canal, yet the government refused to ratify this treaty. I do not think that the Bogotá lot of jackrabbits should be allowed permanently to bar one of the future highways of civilization. We have been more than just, have been generous to a fault, in our dealings with Colombia. They have received exact justice, after I had in vain endeavored to persuade them to accept generosity. In their silly efforts to damage us they cut their own throats. They tried to hold us up, and too late they have discovered their criminal error.

To Prevent a Revolutionary Movement

One of the serious problems with which we are confronted under the conditions of modern industrial civilization is that presented by the great business combinations, which are generally known under the name of "trusts." The problem is an exceedingly difficult one. I myself believe very strongly in both the State and the Nation taking ample powers for the supervision, and if need be, of the regulation of trusts, and indeed of all corporations. But I believe even more strongly in exercising this power with the utmost caution and self-restraint.

During the past quarter of a century probably more mischief has been done, and is now being done, by our treatment of the trusts than by any other phase of our governmental activity. The Sherman Antitrust Law has, on the whole, worked very great evil. Indeed, almost the only good that has been accomplished under it has been accomplished by the Northern Securities suit, and this merely by establishing the power of the National Government to deal with corporations engaged in interstate business, a power secured by getting the Supreme Court to reverse a previous most unwise and improper decision.

Attorney General Knox has done more against trusts and for the enforcement of the antitrust law than any other man we have ever had in public life. Knox is in my judgment the best attorney general we have ever had. On the advice of Knox, I directed the bringing of the Northern Securities case, one of the great achievements of my administration.[5] I look back upon it with great pride, for through it we emphasized in signal fashion, as in no other way could be emphasized, the fact that the most powerful men in this country were held to accountability before the law. Now we must not spoil the effect of this lesson.

It is difficult for me to understand why there should be this belief in Wall Street that I am a wild-eyed revolutionist. I cannot condone wrong, but I certainly do not intend to do aught save what is beneficial to the man of means who acts squarely and fairly. Bryan has always been far more violent in his denunciation of trusts than I have been. Cleveland in what he said was at least as severe about trusts and big corporations as ever I have been. The only difference has been that I have made my words good and have always striven to be a little more decided in action than I was in speech. To me speech is of value only in so far as it represents action.

I am genuinely independent of the big-moneyed men in all matters where I think the interests of the public are concerned, and probably I am the first president of recent times of whom this could be truthfully said. I am very keenly aware that there are not a few among the men who claim to be leaders in the progressive movement who bear unpleasant resemblances to the lamented Robespierre and his fellow progressives of 1791 and '92. What I am earnestly trying, as far as my abilities permit, is to prevent this country from sinking into a condition of political oscillation between the progressive of the Robespierre type and the conservative of the Bourbon type.

My most violent critics, if they had their way, would have the government adopt a course of action which would literally precipitate a revolution. I have a real horror of Hearst. Wall Street regards me as a radical, so violent as to be almost a lunatic, but in reality my horror of the Wall Street man of the E. H. Harriman type is no greater than my horror of the demagogue of the Hearst type, of his recklessness in stirring up evil and exciting class hatred. To reform real abuses is the best way to prevent a revolutionary movement which would derive its strength from the fact that the abuses were left unreformed, and which when started would work more evil than good.[6]

A More Satisfactory Distribution of Wealth

The entire movement into which I have gone was begun by the suit that Knox, with my hearty approval, undertook against the Northern Securities Company. Our aim must be the supremacy of justice, a more satisfactory distribution of wealth—so far as this is attainable—with a view to a more real equality of opportunity, and in sum a higher social system. Much can be done by taxation.

The constitutional amendment about the income tax is all right, but an income tax must always have in it elements of gross inequality and must always be to a certain extent a tax on honesty. A heavily progressive inheritance tax would be far preferable to a national income tax. I would not apply the inheritance tax to small inheritances, but I would apply it progressively and with such heaviness to big inheritances as to completely block the transmission of enormous fortunes to the young Rockefellers, Vanderbilts, Astors, and Morgans. The really large fortunes are needless and useless, for they make no one really happy and increase no one's usefulness, and furthermore they do infinite harm and they contain the threat of far greater harm. The great bulk of my social friends violently disagree with me on this point.[7]

The question of taxation is difficult in any country. The National Government has long derived its chief revenue from a tariff on imports and from an internal or excise tax. As the law now stands it is undoubtedly difficult to devise a national income tax which shall be constitutional. But whether it is absolutely possible is another question, and if possible it is most certainly desirable. The first pure income tax law was passed by the Congress in 1861, but the most important law dealing with the subject was that of 1894. This the Court held to be unconstitutional. The question is undoubtedly very intricate, delicate, and troublesome. The decision of the Court was only reached by one majority. The hesitation evidently felt by the Court as a whole in coming to a conclusion, when considered together with the previous decisions on the subject, may perhaps indicate the possibility of devising a constitutional income tax law.

Back to the Lincoln Basis

While I have been a government officer in various positions, ranging from assemblyman in New York and Civil Service commissioner in Washington to deputy sheriff in North Dakota, I have always been more interested in the men themselves than in the institutions through and under which they worked. I have always kept a cartoon that appeared about me while I was president. This cartoon was called "His Favorite Author." It represented a barely furnished room, and before a small fire, seated in a shabby old rocking chair, shabbily dressed, was an old fellow, apparently a farmer, with furrowed chin and whiskered face. It was the picture of a man who worked hard, for whom life was not too easy, who had had no unfair advantages in life—the face of a kindly, good, hardworking man—and the "Favorite Author's" work which he was reading was one of my presidential messages. The cartoon represents very much to me. That is the man I have tried to represent.

I am, in my own way, a radical Democrat myself; that is, I am a thorough believer in the genuine democracy of Abraham Lincoln, the democracy of the plain people, which believes in these people and seeks to guide them aright and to give utterance to that which is best in them. A well-defined opinion was growing up among the people at large that the Republican Party had become unduly subservient to the so-called Wall Street men, to the men of mere wealth, the plutocracy. I thoroughly broke up this connection, so far as it existed. Personally, I think that while I was in power I got the Republican Party very well back to the Lincoln basis. The Republican Party does not belong to the corporations, either in whole or in part. The Republican Party is Lincoln's party. It is the party of the plain people, who do not desire injustice to anyone. I do not say that the people are infallible. But I do say that our whole history shows that the American people are more often sound in their decisions than is the case with any of the governmental bodies to whom, for their convenience, they have delegated portions of their power.

I'm a Mason myself. So was George Washington. I don't take their shibboleth seriously, of course, but it has its use in a democracy like ours, for it keeps the people contented. Why? I'll explain what I mean by a personal illustration. When I am staying at Oyster Bay I go horseback riding every morning. I have a fine horse and my clothes are made by a good tailor. On my rides I usually stop to chat with a neighbor of mine, a fisherman, who has to work hard for a living. I find him in old clothes and hip boots, mending his nets or painting his dory.

It would be quite natural for him to envy me. But he doesn't, because he knows that our positions will be reversed at the next lodge meeting. He is the master of our local lodge and will be sitting in the seats of the mighty, whereas I shall be down with the common herd. That is why I believe in fraternal organizations. They prevent class feeling by evening up things.

The Pure Food Law

The Pure Food Law was one of the achievements during my administration of which I felt we all had a right to be proud. We got it through in the teeth of the opposition of the multitude of men who were making fortunes by the sale of adulterated foods, and who owed much of their wealth to the fact that in the absence of the law they could sell their goods by a label which did not correspond to the contents of the package. We had to face the opposition not only of the men in that business themselves but of the newspapers and the magazines which did the advertising for that kind of business. And the opposition was so powerful that it was six years before I was able to secure the passage of a law which gave us a reasonable chance to see that, if food were bought for a baby, the food was not poisoned.

On the appearance of Mr. Sinclair's book *The Jungle* (parenthetically, I wish he had left out the ridiculous socialistic rant at the end, which merely tends to make people think his judgment is unsound and to make them question his facts) I called the attention of the Department of Agriculture to the case and directed full and thorough investigation. Sinclair, the socialist, portrays the results of the present capitalistic system in Chicago as on one uniform level of hideous horror. I have an utter contempt for him. He is hysterical, unbalanced, and untruthful. Three-fourths of the things he said were absolute falsehoods. For some of the remainder there was only a basis of truth. Nevertheless, in this particular crisis he was of service to us.

I Hoped to See the Pope

In Rome, my first experience was with the Vatican. I had anticipated trouble and had been preparing for it. My relations with Pope Leo XIII while I was president had been more than cordial, as he was a broad-minded man, with a genuine knowledge of foreign affairs and of the needs of the time. As a token of his recognition of the way I had handled the Friars' Lands question in the Philippines he had sent me a beautifully done mosaic picture of himself in his garden. His successor was a worthy, narrowly limited parish priest, completely under the control of his secretary of state, Merry del Val, who is a polished man of much ability in a very narrow line, but a furious bigoted reactionary, and in fact a good type of sixteenth-century Spanish ecclesiastic.

Merry del Val stated that the audience could only take place on the understanding that I was not intending to see the Methodists, as he phrased it. I responded that I hoped to see the pope, but that it must be distinctly understood that I would not make any stipulation in any way impairing my liberty of conduct to see anyone I chose. Merry del Val, through a servile tool of his, Kennedy,[8] the head of the so-called American College in Rome, then responded that the Holy

Father would be unable to see me. Accordingly, I was not presented at the Vatican.

The different sects of Christians instead of warring against one another should devote their attention to a rivalry to see which can do most for the uplifting of mankind, and for the endeavor to make conduct rather than dogma the test of a man's standing in any Christian church.

Booker T. Washington

I Have Had Booker T. Washington to Dine

While police commissioner of New York City, in May 1895, when Rector Alward came over here to preach an anti-Jewish crusade, after some thought I decided that the best thing to do was to have him protected by forty Jewish policemen. Of course, it was my duty to see that he was not molested, and it struck me to have him protected by the very members of the race he was denouncing was the most effective answer to that denunciation. When I went into the Rough Riders a certain number of Jews enlisted. All of them did well. One was promoted to a lieutenancy by me for gallantry. Another, being wounded, had his wounds dressed and returned immediately to the regiment, continuing to serve as before. I may add that I did not promote the one I made lieutenant because he was a Jew, any more than I promoted his four companions at the same time because they were Christians.

In my cabinet at the present moment there sit side by side Catholic and Protestant, Christian and Jew, each man chosen because in my belief he is peculiarly fit to exercise on behalf of all our people the duties of the office to which I have appointed him. Do you know Booker Washington? He is a man of whom I have the highest regard and in whose judgment I have much faith. I am sorry to say that the idiot or vicious Bourbon element of the South is crazy because I have had Booker T. Washington to dine. I shall have him to dine just as often as I please. I would not lose my self-respect by fearing to have a man like Booker T. Washington to dinner if it cost me every political friend I have got.

I have not been able to think out any solution of the terrible problem offered by the presence of the Negro on this continent, but of one thing I am sure, and that is that inasmuch as he is here and can neither be killed nor driven away, the only wise and honorable and Christian thing to do is to treat each black man and each white man strictly on his merits as a man, giving him no more and no less than he shows himself worthy to have. I say I am "sure" that this is the right solution. Of course, I know that we see through a glass dimly, and, after all, it may be that I am wrong, but if I am, then all my thoughts and beliefs are wrong, and my whole way of looking at life is wrong.

The path of the race upward will necessarily be painful (and a great deal of all life is necessarily painful as far as it goes), and we are not only bound to help the race in every way on the upward path but work for them. The problem is insoluble, in the sense of obtaining an immediate and satisfactory solution, but I do think that, taking the South as a whole, I am gradually producing a better condition, gradually preparing the way for a possible solution. The one hope of the Negro in the South is to be treated each man individually on his worth as a man, and not as a member of a race which will be judged collectively.

I have stood as valiantly for the rights of the Negro as any president since Lincoln. I am the first president that has appointed colored men to responsible positions in the North. I could not give you the exact numbers of Negro appointments that I have made in the South, but I have decreased the total number of appointees and I think I have immeasurably raised their character. As a matter of fact, in the Southern States as a whole the great majority of these appointments that I have made have been of Democrats, and not more than one or two percent have been of colored men. But I have felt that it would be a base and cowardly act not to appoint occasional colored men who showed the qualities which we should unhesitatingly reward in white men. I did not want needlessly to excite alarm and resentment. On the other hand, in the interest of both the white and the black in the Southern States, I could not afford to connive at, and thereby strengthen, a movement of retrogression, which in its essence was aimed at depriving all colored men, good and bad, intelligent and degraded, alike, of the elementary rights of citizenship.

All Men Up and Not Some Men Down

When I asked Booker T. Washington to dinner I did not devote very much thought to the matter one way or the other. I respect him greatly and believe in the work he has done. I have consulted so much with him it seemed to me that it was natural to ask him to dinner to talk over this work, and the very fact that I felt a moment's qualm on inviting him because of his color made me ashamed of myself and made me hasten to send the invitation. I did not think of its bearing one way or the other, either on my own future or on anything else. As things have turned out, I am very glad that I asked him, for the clamor aroused by the act makes me feel as if the act was necessary.

It is not hyperbole to say that Booker T. Washington was a great American, a genius such as does not arise in a generation. Eminent though his services were to the people of his own color, the white men of our republic were almost as much indebted to him, both directly and indirectly. They were indebted to him directly, because of the work he did on behalf of industrial education for the Negro, thus giving impetus to the work for the industrial education of the white man. The indirect indebtedness of the white race to Booker T. Washington is due to the simple fact that here in America we are all in the end going up or down together. Our only safe motto is "All men up" and not "Some men down." The man who makes a substantial contribution uplifting any part of the community has helped to uplift all of the community.

Henry Cabot Lodge

The Dear Old Goose

I am devoted to Senator Lodge.[1] He is probably my closest, certainly one of my two or three closest, personal and social friends. In politics, he and I sometimes differ entirely, as we do as regards certain of the policies roughly characterized as "progressive." He was in no shape or way my spokesman in the Senate. There were matters on which he and I agreed absolutely, and others where we equally emphatically did not. The qualities that make Cabot invaluable as a friend and invaluable as a public servant also make him quite unchangeable when he has determined that a certain course is right.

He has had an astonishing career, and while of course the opportunity was good, he took advantage of it only because of his remarkable energy, capacity, and persistence. I know Massachusetts politics well. I know Lodge's share of them. During the years he has been in Washington he has been on the whole the best and most useful servant of the public to be found in either house of Congress.

Lodge is a man of very strong convictions, and this means that when his convictions differ from mine I am apt to substitute the words "narrow" and "obstinate" for "strong," and he has a certain aloofness and coldness of manner that irritate people who don't live in New England. But he is an eminently fit successor of Webster and Sumner in the senatorship from Massachusetts. He is a bigger man than Sumner, but of course has not dealt with any such crisis as Sumner dealt with. He is not as big a man intellectually as Webster, but he is a far better man morally. Whatever his faults may be, Lodge is a straight-out American. He is alright in every way.

I have discussed almost every move I have made in politics with him, provided he was at hand and it was possible for me to discuss it. The most loyal friend that ever breathed, the dear old goose would do anything possible for me. During the year preceding the outbreak of the Spanish War I was assistant secretary of the navy. It was Lodge who engineered it, at the end as at the beginning, working with his usual untiring loyalty and energy. I was even more pleased than I was astonished at the appointment, for I had come to look upon it as very improbable. McKinley rather distrusted me. It was Cabot's untiring energy and devotion which put me in.

Some persons were foolish enough to think we would break because he supported Taft in 1912. There never was the remotest chance for that. I knew where Lodge stood and respected his position. There never was a chance of a personal falling-out. He is not only the staunchest friend I have ever known, but the very staunchest friend I have ever read of, and the more I see of public life, the more I realize and appreciate what he is and what he has done.

John Hay

The Tone of Satirical Cynicism

John Hay was my father's friend. I dearly loved him. Hay's death is to
me a severe loss, and no one in America can quite fill the gap he makes,
because of his extraordinary literary and personal charm as well as his
abilities as a public man. His name, his reputation, his staunch loyalty,
all made him a real asset of the administration. But in actual work I
had to do the big things myself, and the other things I always feared
would be badly done or not done at all. He had grown to hate the Kaiser so that I could not trust him in dealing with Germany.

Hay was a man of remarkable ability. I think he was the most
delightful man to talk to I ever met, for in his conversation he continually made out of hand those delightful epigrammatic remarks
which we would all like to make, and which in books many people appear to be making, but which in actual life hardly anyone ever does
more than think about when it is too late to say them. He was, moreover, I think without exception, the best letter writer of his age.

His dignity, his remarkable literary ability, his personal charm,
and the respect his high character and long service commanded

throughout the country, together with his wide acquaintance with foreign statesmen and foreign capitals, made him one of the public servants of real value to the United States. But he was not a great secretary of state. For instance, he was not to be mentioned in the same breath with Root. He was no administrator. He had a very ease-loving nature and a moral timidity which made him shrink from all that was rough in life, and therefore from practical affairs.

He was at his best at a dinner table or in a drawing room, and in neither place have I ever seen anyone's best that was better than his, but his temptation was to associate as far as possible only with men of refined and cultivated tastes, who lived apart from the world of affairs, and who, if Americans, were wholly lacking in robustness of fiber. His close intimacy with Henry James and Henry Adams—charming men, but exceedingly undesirable companions for any man not of a strong nature—and the tone of satirical cynicism which they admired, and which he always affected in writing them, marked that phase of his character which so impaired his usefulness as a public man. In public life during the time he was secretary of state under me he accomplished little.

In the Department of State his usefulness to me was almost exclusively the usefulness of a fine figurehead. He never initiated a policy or was of real assistance in carrying through a policy. As an executive he was a complete failure. I could never get him to remove a minister or consul who was a grafter or a ninny, but he would remove the very best men in the service if a Senator asked it for political reasons, and then try to square his conscience over it later by abusing the Senator to me. I could never get him to act.

I have been reading the letters of John Hay. The only ones which are of any interest, namely those connected with his son's death, ought not to have been printed and the others are all childish and inane. There is not one letter that will add to his reputation and most of them will detract from it. It is distressing to read the letters in which Hay harps on how tired he is of the "sordid wrangles" he lives among. They are not the letters of a strong or brave man. It is pathetic to read Hay's ceaseless jeremiads about the way senators forced bad appointments, and then to realize that under the same president and the same Senate all the difficulties ceased as soon as Root took charge.

It is curious also to read what Hay says about certain of the treaties. The first canal treaty was a simple atrocity as he drew it up. It prevented our fortifying the Isthmus, gave us no real control over it, and actually invited the powers of continental Europe to interfere in the matter. The Senate acted with the highest wisdom and patriotism in amending this treaty. The British government rejected the treaty on account of the amendments.

The fact was that Hay could not be trusted where England was concerned. His letter to Balfour shows this. He had been the intimate companion of Lincoln. He was at the time secretary of state, and had held that position under two presidents, yet he wrote to Balfour congratulating him upon having become prime minister in a letter in which he stated that the position of prime minister was "the most important official post known to modern history." If he really thought the position of prime minister more important than that of president, he was foolish, but to give expression to the thought in writing to the English prime minister while he was the American secretary of state was worse than foolish.

Elihu Root

The Greatest Corporation Lawyer in the Country

Some foolish people would think I was speaking hyperbolically, whereas I am speaking what I believe to be the literal truth, when I say that in my judgment Root will be regarded as the greatest and ablest man who has ever filled the position of secretary of state. Root is I think the biggest cabinet minister now in any government in the civilized world. While I do not agree with his views on trusts, I believe Root would make a most admirable president.

Root is one of the very strongest men before the people in our whole party. His advice is invaluable, not merely in reference to his department, but in reference to all branches of the service. It is because Root would not hesitate to express an opinion that he was immensely more valuable to me in the cabinet than John Hay was. Hay was a splendid character, likable and lovable, but he would never criticize. He wouldn't fight for an opinion. Root would, and he'd give persistent battle for his viewpoint. He was a most dogged fighter.

Sometimes I would accept his views. Sometimes I would allow his opinion to modify my own. More often, perhaps, I would ignore him altogether and follow my own ideas. But his frankness, his outspokenness, were of great help in making me see all sides of a question. It was his practice to analyze everything from the standpoint of the other fellow. If there was a hole in an argument, he'd point it out. If there was a place where the other fellow could kick a hole, he'd proceed to plug that point if he could. Lord, I wish you could have seen the condition in which State papers came back to me after Root had gone over them! Sometimes I would not recognize my own child.

John Hay had no such value. He would approve *en bloc* anything I put before him. Now, there was, of course a reason for this. It lay in the different lives they led. Hay, as you know, had led a quiet and rather sheltered life—he had never been in real contact with life; he'd never had to fight for anything. Root's life, you might say, was one long fight. He had to fight for everything he got. All his life he'd been doing business with big, domineering men like the elder Morgan, men in the habit of having their own way in all things. With them, Root simply had to stand up and fight to get them to do things the way he saw they ought to be done.

Root was the greatest corporation lawyer in the country, but neither he nor I ever gave this fact a thought when it came to appointing him. At the time when Root came down here to be secretary of war his personal property for taxing purposes in New York was assessed at $40,000. He had a very large practice, I suppose about $100,000 a year. He gave this up for the opportunity of taking an incredibility difficult position with a salary of $8,000 a year. He thereby abandoned the chance of leaving his children rich. No man in the country has rendered better services to the whole country than he has. If he should leave me I should feel that the loss was literally irreparable.

Root's Offense Was as Rank as Taft's

I have always said there were men to whom I owed more than to any others during the time I was president. One was Elihu Root. Another was Gifford Pinchot. These two were with me throughout my term of office, and perhaps therefore I should say I owed them the most. As soon as I left office both obeyed the centrifugal tendencies of the time and flew in opposite directions—Root in the direction of sacrificing idealism to an excessive taste and desire to be severely practical, and Gifford in the direction of sacrificing practical achievement to an excessive, and sometimes, twisted, idealism.

You must remember about Root that the leading Progressives (and I share their feeling) feel that his action in the Chicago Convention was morally exactly as bad as the actions for which very many Tammany and small Republican politicians who have committed election offenses are now serving or have served terms in Sing Sing. Elihu Root shared Taft's guilt. Indeed, if there must be a choice between them, I think that Root's offense was as rank as Taft's and more wanton. I feel very strongly against Root, because Root took part in as downright a bit of theft and swindling as ever was perpetrated by any Tammany ballot box stuffer, and I shall never forgive the men who were the leaders in that swindling.

Andrew Carnegie

I Have Tried Hard to Like Carnegie

I am continually brought in contact with very wealthy people. They are socially the friends of my family, and if not friends, at least acquaintances of mine, and they were friends of my father's. I think they mean well on the whole, but the more I see of them the more profoundly convinced I am of their entire unfitness to govern the country, and of the lasting damage they do by much of what they are inclined to think are the legitimate big business operations of the day. They are as blind to some of the tendencies of the time, as the French noblesse was before the French Revolution.

Moreover, usually entirely without meaning it, they are singularly callous to the needs, sufferings, and feelings of the great mass of people who work with their hands.[1] If Andrew Carnegie had employed his fortune and his time in doing justice to the steelworkers who gave him his fortune, he would have accomplished a thousand times what he has accomplished or ever can accomplish in connection with international peace.

I have tried hard to like Carnegie, but it is pretty difficult. There is no type of man for whom I feel a more contemptuous abhorrence than for the one who makes a god of mere moneymaking and at the same time is always yelling out that kind of utterly stupid condemnation of war which in almost every case springs from a combination of defective physical courage, of unmanly shrinking from pain and effort, and of hopelessly twisted ideals. All the suffering from the Spanish War comes far short of the suffering, preventable and non-preventable, among the operators of the Carnegie steelworks during the time that Carnegie was making his fortune.

I have no respect for the businessman who makes enormous sums of money without any regard whatever for advanced principles of doctrinaire ethics, but who applies these same principles in their advanced and least rational form to war. It is as noxious folly to denounce war per se as it is to denounce business per se. Unrighteous war is a hideous evil, but I am not at all sure that it is a worse evil than business unrighteousness.

William Randolph Hearst

The Most Potent Single Influence for Evil

It is a little difficult for me to give you an exact historic judgment about a man whom I so thoroughly dislike and despise as I do Hearst. I think that he is a man without any real principle, that though he is posing as a radical, he is in reality no more radical than he is conservative. But when I have said this, after all, I am not at all sure that I am saying much more about Hearst than could probably be said—or which would contain a large element of truth if said—about both Winston Churchill and his father, Lord Randolph.

I have been tempted at times to smash into that leprous spot upon our civilization, Hearst's *New York Journal*, by way of a heavy libel suit, criminal or civil, but it has been a question with me if they would not gain by the advertisement. Of course, all they would care for would be the pecuniary loss. Hearst and Brisbane[1] are engaged in carrying on their profession on terms which make the trades of the pimp and pander seem respectable by comparison, and there is no good in any argument that does not touch either their pockets or their hides.

Hearst's private life has been disreputable. He is now married, and as far as I know, entirely respectable. His wife is a chorus girl or something like that on the stage, and it is of course neither necessary nor advisable, in my judgment, to make any allusion to any of the reports about either of them before their marriage. It is not the kind of family which people who believe that sound home relations form the basis of national citizenship would be glad to see in the executive mansion in Albany, and still less in the White House.

Hearst has edited a large number of the very worst type of sensational, scandalmongering newspapers. They have been edited with great ability and with entire unscrupulousness. The editorials are well written, and often appeal for high morality in the abstract. Moreover, being a fearless man, and shrewd and farsighted, Hearst has often been of real use in attacking abuses which benefited great corporations, and in attacking individuals of great wealth who have done what was wrong. In these matters he has often led the way. I disapprove of the whitewash brush quite as much as of mudslinging, and it seems to me that the disapproval of one in no shape or way implies approval of the other.

He will never attack any abuse, any wickedness, any corruption, not even if it takes the most horrible form, unless he is satisfied that no votes are to be lost by doing it. He preaches the gospel of envy, hatred, and unrest. His actions so far go to show that he is entirely willing to sanction any mob violence if he thinks that for the moment votes are to be gained by so doing. He, of course, cares nothing whatever as to the results to the nation, in the long run, of embroiling it with any foreign powers, if for the moment he can gain any applause for so doing. He cares nothing for the nation, nor for any citizens in it.

If the circumstances were ripe in America, which they are not, I should think that Hearst would aspire to play the part of some of the least worthy creatures of the French Revolution. There is, I believe, literally nothing at which he would stop in the way of adding fuel to the fire of discontent, reasonable and unreasonable, innocent or fraught with destruction to the whole body politic. He is the most potent single influence for evil we have in our life. I certainly feel that neither Tweed nor Benedict Arnold began to do as much damage to this country as Hearst has done.

Oliver Wendell Holmes

One of the Most Interesting Men I Have Ever Met

Judge Gray has been one of the most valuable members of the Court. I should hold myself as guilty of an irreparable wrong to the nation if I should put in his place any man who was not absolutely sane and sound on the great national policies for which we stand in public life. I want on the bench a follower of Hamilton and Marshall and not a follower of Jefferson and Calhoun, and what is more I do not want any man who from frivolity, or disinclination to think, or ignorance, or indifference to popular moods, goes wrong on great questions.

Judge Holmes's whole mental attitude, as shown for instance by his great Phi Beta Kappa speech at Harvard,[1] is such that I should naturally expect him to be in favor of those principles in which I so earnestly believe. After much careful thought I have decided to offer the place to Chief Justice Holmes. Judge Holmes was shot three times in the Civil War. He is a great jurist and constructive statesman and one of the most interesting men I have ever met.

The labor decisions which have been criticized by some of the big railroad men and other members of large corporations constitute to my mind a strong point in Judge Holmes's favor. The ablest lawyers and greatest judges are men whose past has naturally brought them into close relationship with the wealthiest and most powerful clients, and I am glad when I can find a judge who has been able to preserve his aloofness of mind so as to keep his broad humanity of feeling and his sympathy for the class from which he has not drawn his clients. I think it eminently desirable that our Supreme Court should show in unmistakable fashion their entire sympathy with all proper effort to secure the most favorable possible consideration for the men who most need that consideration.

I appreciate as every thoughtful man must the immense importance of the part to be played by the Supreme Court in the next twenty-five years. I do not at all like the social conditions at present. The dull, purblind folly of the very rich men, their greed and arrogance, and the way in which they have unduly prospered by the help of the ablest lawyers, and too often through the weakness or shortsightedness of the judges or by their unfortunate possession of meticulous minds—these facts, and the corruption in business and politics, have tended to produce a very unhealthy condition of excitement and irritation in the popular mind, which shows itself in part in the enormous increase in the socialistic propaganda.

I Could Carve Out of a Banana

It seems to me that the head of the Supreme Court should be not merely a learned lawyer but a constructive statesman. It is the failure to understand this fact which has caused certain of the Supreme Court judges to go so lamentably wrong during the past few years. In my own time I have seen upright well-meaning judges, such as Peckham, Fuller, and Brewer, whose presence on the Supreme Court was a menace to the welfare of the nation, who ought not to have been left there a day.

Some of these judges I have myself appointed, urged thereto not merely by senators but by bar associations and lawyers and big businessmen generally. The recommendations I got for these men were often on their face so excellent that I thought I was making unusually good appointments, and yet they turned out to be men who, if not dishonest, were at least without any conception of real social justice, and any understanding or appreciation of the needs of the bulk of their countrymen. Holmes should have been an ideal man on the bench.[2] As a matter of fact he has been a bitter disappointment, not because of any one decision but because of his general attitude. I could carve out of a banana a judge with more backbone.

I am not prepared to say what, if anything, should be done as regards the federal judiciary, and I have no sympathy with sweeping general attacks upon it, but I have just as little sympathy with failure to recognize the many and grave shortcomings of the federal judiciary, including the Supreme Court, during the past three decades or so.

Eugene V. Debs

Let Us Try to Level Up

Have you ever seen Debs's paper, *The Appeal to Reason?* On its merits it should be kept out of the mails, for it is an appeal not to reason but to hatred and malice, and again and again it contains open incitement to murder, while it always justifies murder. Debs's paper and speeches are largely mere pieces of the literature of criminal violence. We have not kept it out, because to do so would I think work more mischief than the paper itself does.

To praise and champion Debs, to condone his faults, is precisely like praising and championing Tweed and condoning Tweed's faults. The well-meaning, or ill-meaning, clergymen and others who now champion Debs stand on par with the New York voters of one of the tenement house districts who after Tweed was exposed sent him to the State senate. They sent him to the senate on the ground that he had stolen from the rich men, but was the poor man's friend.

I have felt that the growth of the Socialist Party in this country was far more ominous than any Populist or similar movement of time past. The Debs type of socialist points the way to national ruin as surely as any swindling financier or corrupt politician. You may notice that the socialists and anarchists, although in theory and on academic grounds not in accord, have in practice adopted the red flag as a common symbol and cheerfully work together. An anarchist or socialist paper published the statement that as police commissioner I invented spiked clubs for policemen to use against rioters.

We can just as little afford to follow the doctrinaires of an extreme individualism as the doctrinaires of an extreme socialism. Individual initiative, so far from being discouraged, should be stimulated, and yet we should remember that, as society develops and grows more complex, we continually find that things which once it was desirable to leave to individual initiative can, under the changed conditions, be performed with better results by common effort. For instance, when people live on isolated farms or in little hamlets, each house can be left to attend to its own drainage and water supply, but the mere multiplication of families in a given area produces new problems which have to be considered from a common standpoint.

Much of the discussion about socialism and individualism is entirely pointless, because of failure to agree on terminology. It is not good to be the slave of names. I am a strong individualist by personal habit, inheritance, and conviction, but it is a mere matter of common sense to recognize the State, the community, the citizens acting together can do a number of things better than if they were left to individual action.

To say that the thriftless, the lazy, the vicious, the incapable, ought to have the reward given to those who are farsighted, capable, and upright is to say what is not true and cannot be true. Let us try to level up, but let us beware the evil of leveling down. If a man stumbles, it is a good thing to help him to his feet. Every one of us needs a helping hand now and then. But if a man lies down, it is a waste of time to try to carry him. I never will accept the ultra-socialistic doctrine that there must be equality of reward for inequality of work.

The most cruel form of injustice that can be devised would be to give a man who has not earned it the reward that ought to come only to the man who has earned it. The Roman mob, living on the bread given them by the State and clamoring for excitement and amusement to be purveyed by the State, represent for all time the very nadir to which a free and self-respecting population of workers can sink if they grow habitually to rely upon others, and especially upon the State, either to furnish them charity, or to permit them to plunder, as a means of a livelihood.

The socialism that nominates Debs is a well-nigh unmixed evil, and the ultra-socialism which has for one of its necessary tenets free love would, if applied, bring men back to the unpolished stone age and to living as scattered hordes of savages, were it not for the fact that long before this event could happen, it would have produced by simple reaction the rule of absolutism and despotism everywhere, in order to save civilization. But there are plenty of people who call themselves socialists, many of whose tenets are not only worthy of respect but represent real advances. I am a near-socialist! That is, I want to adopt many excellent things in the socialist propaganda without adopting the things that seem to me to be evil. Constructive change offers the best method of avoiding destructive change. Reform is the antidote to revolution. Social reform is not the precursor but the preventive of socialism.

Thoughts on Other Nations

The Spread of the Little Kingdom of Wessex

I am a believer in the fact that it is for the good of the world that the English-speaking race in all its branches should hold as much of the world's surface as possible. The spread of the little kingdom of Wessex into more than a country, more than an empire, into a race which has conquered half the earth and holds a quarter of it is perhaps the greatest fact in all history. Our two peoples are the only really great free peoples.

In my autobiography I did not like to speak of the various presents given me by European sovereigns. Next to Hay's gift of the ring with the hair of President Lincoln the gift I appreciated most which I received while in the White House was from King Edward. It was a very beautiful miniature of John Hampden, sent me at the time of my inauguration.[1] It seemed to me to mark King Edward's tact and genuine refinement of feeling that he should have chosen that precise gift for an American president. It is a little ungracious for me to add what I am about to add, but I cannot resist saying that the worthy Kaiser sent me on the same occasion an enormous bronze bust of himself, weighing about a ton, which was brought to the White House on a four-horse dray, and which caused me real anguish until I found an accommodating art gallery that was willing to stow it away in a basement.

Though an American with hardly a drop of English blood in my veins, I always feel more at home in England than on the Continent. I have, and I trust I shall always retain, the good old country-cousin feeling about London. I like its size, the swing and rush of the life, and the importance of the interests of which it is the center. The mere social part does not impress me so very much. The balls and parties are about like those in New York. So are the dinners, except that the married women talk better and the girls not so well. They are very pleasant, but they are too much like what we already know.

I am tempted to tell a little story, although it is rather against myself. It was at a dinner in London, and I was sitting next to a very pretty woman, who was evidently bent on saying pleasant things about America. Indeed, to some of her speeches I was obliged faintly to demur—as when she credited us with the national ownership of the River Amazon. Finally, she electrified me by observing that she liked to hear me speak, "because she was so fond of the American accent, it reminded her of a banjo!" The remark was evidently made in perfect good faith. I murmured my acknowledgments, and she continued the conversation with the vivacity naturally attendant upon the pleased consciousness of having paid a neat compliment.

To us, the charm of London lies in the fact that there we meet men who know how to have a good time and yet play their parts in the world. It is pleasant to stay at the country house of a mighty Nimrod who is also a prominent factor in politics, to meet men of note at the clubs, and to discuss art and literature at a dinner where there are leaders of Parliament in addition to leaders of fashion.

I saw the Englishman Winston Churchill here and although he is not an attractive fellow, I was interested in some of the things he said. I have been over Winston Churchill's life of his father. I dislike the father and dislike the son, so I may be prejudiced. Still, I feel that, while the biographer and his subject possess some real farsightedness, especially in their appreciation of the shortcomings of that "Society" which had so long been dominant in English politics, and which produces in this country the missionary and the Mugwump, yet they possess or possessed such levity, lack of sobriety, lack of permanent principle, and an inordinate thirst for that cheap form of admiration which is given to notoriety, as to make them poor public servants. Winston Churchill is a dreadful cad,[2] but his book was a very bright and clever one and I was amused by it, but I should most mortally hate to have any son of mine write such a book about me!

It was decades before we got over the remembrance of England's attitude during the Civil War. In 1898 England was our really effective friend, and from that day to this I have stood by England. A couple of centuries hence we may all be in one great federation. A man who has grappled, or is grappling, with Cuba, Panama, and the Philippines has a lively appreciation of the difficulties inevitably attendant upon getting into Egypt in the first place, and then upon the impossibility of getting out of it in the second. It was a good thing for Egypt and the Sudan, and for the world, when England took Egypt and the Sudan. It is a good thing for India that England should control it. And so it is a good thing, a very good thing, for Cuba and for Panama and for the world that the United States has acted as it has. I believe in the expansion of great nations. India has done an incalculable amount for the English character. If we do our work well in the Philippines and the West Indies, it will do a great deal for our character.

The South African business makes me really sad. I have a genuine admiration for the Boers, but the downfall of the British Empire I should regard as a calamity for the race, and especially to this country. I was greatly concerned over the death of poor Cecil Rhodes. His work in Matabeleland represented a great and striking conquest for civilization. I wish I could have met Rhodes. He was a very great figure.

I am an optimist, but there are grave signs of deterioration in the English-speaking peoples, here and there, not merely in the evident lack of fighting edge in the British soldier, but in the diminishing birthrate here and in English Canada, as well as Australia, in the excessive urban growth, in the love of luxury, and the turning of sport into a craze by the upper classes. I am a firm believer that the future will somehow bring things right in the end for our land. I believe that this republic will endure for many centuries.

Russia's Day Is Yet Afar Off

I think that Russia has an enormous part to play, a great destiny before her. Undoubtedly the future is hers unless she mars it from within. Sometimes I do feel inclined to believe that the Russian is the one man with enough barbarous blood in him to be the hope of a world that is growing effete. But I think that this thought only occurs when I am unreasonably dispirited. Of course, both the English and the Americans are less ruthless, and have the disadvantages of civilization.

The English-speaking race shares with the Slav the future, although the German too will play a great part in the present century. I suppose that what I am about to say is a dream, but I do wish that Russia could grow fast enough in civilization to make it possible to cooperate with her and let her have her own way in working up Slav civilization in her part of Asia, provided she did not interfere elsewhere. Russia's day is yet afar off. I think the twentieth century will still be the century of the men who speak English. The growth of the Slav is slow.

The Russians offer a very much more serious problem than the Germans, if not to our generation, at least to the generations which will succeed us. Russia and the United States are friendly, but Russians and Americans, in their individual capacity, have nothing whatever in common. The Russians strike me as corrupt, tricky, and inefficient. They think they should be looked upon as huge, powerful barbarians, cynically confident that they will in the end inherit the fruits of our civilization, firmly believing that the future belongs to them, and resolute to develop their own form of government, literature, and art, despising as effete all of Europe and especially America. I look upon them as a people to whom we can give points, and a beating, a people with a great future, as we have, but a people with poisons working in it, as other poisons, of similar character on the whole, work in us.

The Russian started far behind, yet he has traveled that path very much farther and faster since the days of Ivan the Terrible than our people have traveled it since the days of Elizabeth. He is several centuries behind us still, but he was a thousand years behind us then. All other nations of European blood, if they develop at all, seem inclined to develop on much the same lines, but Russia seems bound to develop in her own way, and on lines that run directly counter to what we are accustomed to consider as progress. If Russia chooses to develop purely on her own line and to resist the growth of liberalism, then she may put off the day of reckoning, but she cannot ultimately avert it, and instead she will sometime experience a red terror which will make the French Revolution pale.

War with Japan

I am certain that there is an immense amount we could learn from the Japanese with extreme advantage to us as a nation. Japan's growth and change during the last half century has been in many ways the most striking phenomenon of all history. Intensely proud of her past history, intensely loyal to certain of her past traditions, she has yet with a single effort wrenched herself free from all hampering ancient ties, and with a bound has taken her place among the leading civilized nations of mankind.

This strange alien civilization is a very high civilization, just as the post-Homeric Greek civilization was high, but the people who make it up have ideas as alien to ours on some points as had those depicted by Aeschylus. I suppose we are all of us wondering now what effect the extraordinary increase of industrialization in Japan will have upon the qualities which give them such an extraordinary soldierly capacity. The Japs have made a great name for themselves as fighters.

You have doubtless seen the trouble we are having in connection with the Japanese in California. Under the lead of the trade unions the San Francisco people, and apparently also the people in certain other

California cities, have been indulging in boycotts against Japanese restaurant keepers, have excluded the Japanese children from the public schools, and have in other ways threatened, sometimes by law and sometimes by the actions of mobs, the rights secured to Japanese in this country by our solemn treaty obligations with Japan. I am doing everything in my power to secure the righting of these wrongs.

They may possibly bring about war with Japan. I do not think that they will bring it about at the moment, but even as to this I am not certain, for the Japanese are proud, sensitive, warlike; are flushed with the glory of their recent triumph; and are in my opinion bent upon establishing themselves as the leading power in the Pacific. The peril is greater than our people have been permitted to know. That was why I insisted on the United States having a strong fleet. And I sent it around the world because I wanted to give Tokyo an object lesson. The fleet is our first line of defense. In case of a war with Japan it would prove our salvation. If the Japanese could sink it, as they did the Russian fleet at Port Arthur, they could land a quarter of a million men on our Pacific coast and it would take us several years and cost us an enormous sum in men and money to dislodge them. The Japs have been very cocky since the war with Russia, but they will hesitate to molest us as long as we carry a big stick.

No one dreads war as I do. The little that I have seen of it, and I have seen only a little, leaves a horrible picture on my mind. But the surest way to prevent this war with the East is to be thoroughly prepared for it. The Japanese leaders and court have lost much prestige by what they think was their failure to crush Russia, and while the terms they secured at Portsmouth were much more then they could have secured six months later, the treaty was not altogether satisfactory to the nation and sooner or later they will try to bolster up their power by another war. Unfortunately for us we have what they want most, the Philippines. The Philippines form our heel of Achilles.

The security of the throne will depend upon some sensational war, and the Japanese politician is not without daring to try one. When it comes we will win over Japan but it will be one of the most disastrous conflicts the world has ever seen. It will be rapine on their part, not war, and you will see every modern means used to crush our armament and weaken our forces.

It is very difficult to make this nation wake up. Individually the people are very different from the Chinese, of course, but nationally our policy is almost as foolish. I sometimes question whether anything but a great military disaster will ever make us feel our responsibilities and our possible dangers. The history of all wars up to and including the very latest has shown that in over half the cases one or both of the combatants endeavor to strike a crippling blow before the actual declaration of war. I have urged as strongly as I know how the immediate building of impregnable fortifications to protect Pearl Harbor and the adjacent region from any possible land attack. It seems to me that the determining factor in any war with Japan would be the control of the sea.

William Howard Taft

I Had Him in the Hollow of My Hand

Taft is president, and the tradition is very strong to give a president a second nomination, even where, as in the case of Harrison, it is unlikely that he can win. I do not believe he has been a bad president, and I am sure he has been a thoroughly well-meaning and upright president. I think he is a better president than McKinley and probably than Harrison, but the times are totally different, and he has not the qualities that are needed at the moment.

Taft in this respect has not gone wrong; he simply has stayed wrong. He has simply stayed substantially where Hanna and McKinley were a dozen years ago. I feel only a real sadness that the man who was so admirable as a lieutenant should have so totally failed as a leader. The trouble is, as far as I can make out, that he really has not one particle of understanding of, and therefore no particle of sympathy for, the great movements of our time. I have never been so bitterly disappointed in any man.

The break in our relations was due to no one thing, but to the cumulative effect of many things: the abandonment of everything my administration had stood for, and other things. Taft changed greatly between the time he was elected and the time he took office. The first friction came in the matter of his cabinet. When he was nominated I went to him and asked whom he wished to have take his place as secretary of war. I told him I considered it as much his appointment as mine, and that I would appoint no one not acceptable to him, though I had a good man in mind. I told him the man was Luke E. Wright. He said Wright was absolutely the man he would have chosen himself. Wright, he recalled, had been with him in the Philippines and was the man for the place. By inauguration time, however, Mr. Taft had changed his mind, just as I feared he would, and it made a great deal of feeling. That was the first bit of friction—the beginning.

Taft takes his color so completely from his immediate surroundings that he is continually finding himself in situations where he really has broken his word, or betrayed some former associate. I never realized at the time how much of myself I put into Taft. As was probably inevitable, he permitted his wife and brother, and a number of less disinterested advisers, to make him very jealous of me, and very anxious to emphasize the contrast between our administrations by sundering himself from my especial friends and followers, and appearing hereafter as the great, wise conservative. In consequence he has frequently taken a reactionary attitude, and the progressives and radicals in the party, being left without any progressive leadership at all, have gone every which way, and have often been both violent and foolish.

Everything I said of Taft as a member of the cabinet and governor of the Philippines was deserved. I have not reversed my position. He has reversed his. Taft was nominated solely on my assurance to the western people especially, but almost as much to the people of the East, that he would carry out my work unbroken, not (as he has done) merely working for somewhat the same objects in a totally different spirit, and with a totally different result. There is only a little harsh criticism either of my sincerity or of his, but there is a very widespread feeling that, quite unintentionally, I have deceived them.

What do I owe to Taft? It was through me and my friends that he became president. I had him in the hollow of my hand and I had merely to turn my hand and he would have dropped out. That Mr. Taft should feel grateful because I put him in the presidency is of very little consequence, but it is of great consequence that his deeds should falsify his words. In office, his militancy evaporated and he at once set about undoing all my administration had done. He is a flubdub with a streak of the second-rate and the common in him, and he has not the slightest idea of what is necessary if this country is to make social and industrial progress.

Mr. Taft Has Stolen the Nomination

It was very bitter for me to see the Republican Party, when I had put it back on the Abraham Lincoln basis, in three years turned over to a combination of big financiers and unscrupulous political bosses. In my campaign for the Republican nomination I worked for the overthrow of every boss, and my nomination would have meant putting the Republican Party definitely on an antiboss and progressive basis. This was why the bosses preferred my defeat to Republican victory.

The convention that nominated Mr. Taft is rightly called the convention of forty thieves, and any man who supports him is simply endorsing theft. I cannot consent to do anything that looks as if I was joining with him. I won't go into a friendly contest with a pickpocket as to which of us shall keep my watch which he stole. I was the choice of the rank and file and he only the choice of the swindlers on the National Committee. Mr. Taft has stolen the nomination at Chicago, and no honest man can support him for it. The Republican Party had become pretty nearly hopeless. Either it had to be radically regenerated from within, or a new party had to be made. I attempted the regeneration. By simple swindling, the party bosses defeated the attempt.

I Did Not Care a Rap for Being Shot

Just one word about the madman who shot me. He was not really a madman at all. He was a man of the same disordered brain which most criminals, and a great many noncriminals, have. I very gravely question if he has a more unsound brain than Senator La Follette or Eugene Debs. He simply represents a different stratum of life and of temperament, which if not more violent is yet more accustomed to brutal physical expression. He had quite enough sense to avoid shooting me in any Southern State, where he would have been lynched, and he waited until he got into a State where there was no death penalty. I have not the slightest feeling against him. I have a very strong feeling against the people who, by their ceaseless and intemperate abuse, excited him to the action, and against the mushy people who would excuse him and all other criminals once the crime has been committed.

I was in the automobile when this fellow shot me. He reached over the edge like, and the next thing I knew was a flash and a fearful blow. It seemed as though I had been hit with a sledgehammer. The bullet passed through the manuscript of my speech and my iron spectacle case, and only went three or four inches into the chest, breaking a rib and lodging against it. As I was standing unsteadily I half fell back for a second. As I stood up I coughed blood and at once put my hand to my lips to see if there was any blood. There was none, so that as the bullet was in the chest I felt the chances were twenty to one that it was not fatal.

There was then a perfectly obvious duty, which was to go on and make my speech. In the very unlikely event of the wound being mortal I wished to die with my boots on, so to speak. It has always seemed to me that the best way to die would be in doing something that ought to have been done, whether leading a regiment or doing anything else. I went through with my engagement to speak, but it was somewhat difficult. After the bullet I had no real pain. The wound felt hot. When I began to speak my heart beat rapidly for some ten minutes.

I did not care a rap for being shot. It is a trade risk, which every prominent public man ought to accept as a matter of course. For eleven years I have been prepared any day to be shot, and if any one of the officers of my regiment had abandoned the battle merely because he received a wound that did nothing worse than break a rib, I should never have trusted that officer again. I would have expected him to keep on in the fight as long as he could stand, and what I expect lieu-tenants to do I expect, *a fortiori*, a leader to do.

The bullet, you know, was never removed. It passed through a rib and through the outer case of the lungs. It was thought best not to try and remove it, as it did not seem to be doing any damage. I carry the Milwaukee bullet in me but it does not bother me the least bit in the world. The fellow who shot me, the doctors found him to be insane, so they put him into an insane asylum for the balance of his days. It was the best way to dispose of the case.

The Free Soil Party of Our Day

The Progressive Party today stands precisely where the Republican Party stood under Lincoln sixty years ago, where the Democratic Party stood in the early days of Jefferson and Jackson. It is the party of the people them-selves, and it is organized to promote social and industrial justice.

Personally, I feel that what we did was worthwhile.[1] Our move-ment in 1912 was the loftiest and sanest movement in our politics since the days of Lincoln, and the platform we issued was the only great constructive platform for social and economic justice that has been brought forth since the days of the Civil War. When a sufficient time has passed by for some of the bitterness to subside, this platform will have to be adopted explicitly or implicitly in our governmental system if our democracy is really to amount to very much.

Of course I feel badly over the result. As soon as the returns came in 1912 and it became evident that, although my vote was greater than Taft's, the Republicans had done three or four times as well as the Pro-gressives as regards congressmen, senators, State officers, and the like, I made up my mind that there was practically no hope for the Progressive Party to establish itself. The average American is deeply wedded to the two-party system. He wishes to vote with his own party and the name has an enormous influence over him. When he goes with a third party it is for temporary and usually for local reasons.

This was not the young Republican Party born over. It was the

Free Soil Party of our day, and there has always been a very real question as to whether the men who followed Sumner into the Free Soil Party movement were wiser than the men who stayed under Webster and Winthrop and Everett in the Whig Party until the Republican Party had been established. My own private judgment is that nothing whatever more can be done with the Progressive Party.

Thank the Lord poor Taft is out of the presidency. He made a poor showing, from the public standpoint a wretched showing. Even his private good nature was not compatible with great vindictiveness and malevolence toward weak and obscure men whom he could persecute with impunity. Taft showed himself a plain fool, and Wilson is not a fool. Wilson has a very difficult party situation, but a difficulty is also always an opportunity. If he is big enough to master his party he may make a great record and rivet the attention of the country upon him. My own view is that if Wilson behaves himself, the Democrats will continue in power for some time.

Woodrow Wilson

He Is Not a Nationalist

Wilson is a good man who has in no way shown that he possesses any special fitness for the presidency. Until he was fifty years old, as college professor and college president he advocated with skill, intelligence, and good breeding the outworn doctrines which were responsible for four-fifths of the political troubles in the United States. He poses as, and believed himself to be, a strong conservative, and was being groomed by a section of Wall Street as the special conservative champion against me and my ideas. Then he ran as governor of New Jersey, and during the last eighteen months discovered that he could get nowhere advocating the doctrines he had advocated, and instantly turned an absolute somersault so far as at least half of these doctrines concerned. He still clings to the other half, and he has shown not the slightest understanding of the really great problems of our present industrial situation.

He is an able man, and I have no doubt could speedily acquaint himself with these problems, and would not show Taft's muddleheaded inability to try to understand them when left by himself. But he is not a nationalist, he has no real and deep-seated convictions on the things that I regard as most vital, and he is in the position where he can only win by standing on a platform which he must afterward repudiate under penalty of himself becoming a grotesque disaster to the community, and furthermore, he can win only by the help of the worst bosses in this country, and by perpetuating their control of their several States in return for their aid.

Wilson was from their standpoint the best man they could have nominated, an adroit man, a good speaker and writer, with a certain amount of ability of just the kind requisite to his party under present conditions. He showed his adroitness during the campaign, and he may well be able to show similar adroitness during the next four years in the presidency, and with the same result. In the campaign he talked ardent but diffuse progressivism. It was from the outset exceedingly unfortunate that so many of our people kept talking as if Wilson and Bryan were themselves progressives. This is not true in any real sense. Wilson is a wonderful dialectician, with a remarkable command of language. But his language is admirably and intentionally designed not to reveal the truth but either to conceal his real purpose or else to conceal the fact that he has no definite purpose at all.

World War I

Our Most Probable Serious Opponent

I have always regarded Germany while the Kaiser lives as our most probable serious opponent. There is much that I admire about the Kaiser and there is more that I admire about the German people. But the German people are too completely under his rule for me to be able to disassociate them from him, and he himself is altogether too jumpy, too volatile in his policies, too lacking in the power of continuous and sustained thought and action for me to feel that he is in any way such a man as for instance Taft or Root.

I don't know that I should be sorry to see a bit of a spar with Germany. The burning of New York and a few other seacoast cities would be a good object lesson on the need of an adequate system of coast defenses. And I think it would have a good effect on our large German population to force them to an ostentatiously patriotic display of anger against Germany. Besides, while we would have to take some awful blows at first, I think in the end we would worry the Kaiser a little.

A Human Trombone

The whole question of peace and war in Europe trembles in the balance, and at the very moment when this is the case, and when that great black tornado trembles on the edge of Europe, our own special prize idiot, Mr. Bryan, and his ridiculous chief, Mr. Wilson, are prattling pleasantly about the steps they are taking to procure universal peace by little arbitration treaties which promise impossibilities, and which would not be worth the paper on which they are written in any serious crisis. It is not a good thing for a country to have a professional yodeler, a human trombone like Mr. Bryan as secretary of state, nor a college professor with an astute and shifty mind, a hypocritical ability to deceive plain people, unscrupulousness in handling machine leaders, and no real knowledge or wisdom concerning internal and international affairs as head of the nation.

Bryan is, I really believe, the most contemptible figure we have ever had as secretary of state, and of course Wilson must accept full responsibility for him. I regard Wilson with contemptuous dislike. He has the nerve that his type so often shows in civil and domestic affairs where there is no danger of physical violence. He will jump up and down on cheap politicians, and bully and cajole men in public life who are anxious not to part company with their political chief. But he is a ridiculous creature in international matters. He is a narrow and bitter partisan, and he is intellectually thoroughly dishonest.

I regard the Wilson-Bryan attitude of trusting to fantastic peace treaties, to impossible promises, to all kinds of scraps of paper without any backing in efficient force, as abhorrent. It is infinitely better for a nation and for the world to have the Frederick the Great and Bismarck tradition as regards foreign policy than to have the Bryan or Bryan-Wilson attitude as a permanent national attitude, for the Bryan-Wilson attitude is one that would Chinafy the country and would reduce us to the impotence of Spain. A milk-and-water righteousness unbacked by force is to the full as wicked as and even more mischievous than force divorced from righteousness. The Germans have believed in force without righteousness. Our own feeble folk of the Bryan type have believed in righteousness, or at least a very diluted milk-and-water brand of righteousness, without force.

Neutrality Does Not Serve Righteousness

More and more I come to the view that in a really tremendous world struggle, with a great moral issue involved, neutrality does not serve righteousness, for to be neutral between right and wrong is to serve wrong. I am utterly sick of the spiritless "neutrality" of the administration. The most depressing feature of the present situation is that the great majority of Americans strongly approve Wilson's stand.

To me the crux of the situation has been Belgium. If I had been president I should have acted as head of a signatory power of the Hague treaties, calling attention to the guaranty of Belgium's neutrality and saying that I accepted the treaties as imposing a serious obligation which I expected not only the United States, but all other neutral nations, to join in enforcing. Of course, I would not have made such a statement unless I was willing to back it up. I believe that if I had been president the American people would have followed me. But whether I am mistaken or not as regards this, I am certain that the majority are now following Wilson. They tend, and ought to tend, to support the president in such a crisis.

In its essence the attitude of Wilson and Bryan has been: First, that it is our duty as a nation to be neutral between right and wrong, to practice a neutrality as complete as that of Pontius Pilate, and not by word or even by thought to side with a little nation like Belgium, which has been so terribly wronged, or against the wrongdoer. Second, that the signature of the Hague Conventions by us was a mere platonic action and that these Conventions are not even to be alluded to once that war has come. It is not merely ridiculous, it is wicked hypocrisy for us ever to talk of entering into another Hague Convention unless we in good faith strive to secure the carrying out of the Hague Conventions into which we have already entered.

I do not believe that this administration can be kicked into war. An army officer tells me that recently he was at a bullfight in a Mexican city. One bull would not fight. Thereupon the audience began to call "He is a Woodrow Wilson, he is an American bull. Take him out. Take out Woodrow Wilson and bring in a Mexican bull that will fight." This exactly expresses the German attitude toward us no less than the Mexican attitude toward us.

He Has Dulled the National Conscience

As for the *Lusitania* matter, failure to act within twenty-four hours following her sinking was an offense that is literally inexcusable and inexplicable. The hideous thing is that I believe that Wilson largely achieved his purpose. He intended to talk about the *Lusitania* and consume time so that people might forget, and I believe they have now forgotten. They are cold. They have been educated by this infernal peace propaganda of the last ten years into an attitude of sluggishness and timidity.

When the *Lusitania* was sunk, our people would have fought at least as readily as in the actual event two years later. The result of this ocean of praise for Wilson was that during the first nine months of the war he felt absolutely secure that he could do anything, and accordingly, as regards the war itself, he did almost nothing. Instead, he indulged in rhetorical fireworks. Leaders went into hysterics of applause over all of them and praised him as a great idealist—a term to which he is about as entitled as Machiavelli was. For Heaven's sake never allude to Wilson as an idealist. He hasn't a touch of idealism in him. His advocacy of the League of Nations no more represents idealism on his part than his advocacy of peace without victory, or his second statement that we had no concern with the origin or cause of the European war, or with his profoundly unethical refusal for two and a half years to express a particle of sympathy for poor Belgium.

President Wilson has rendered to this people the most evil service that can be rendered to a great democracy by its chosen leader. He has dulled the national conscience and relaxed the spring of lofty, national motives by teaching our people to accept high-sounding words as the offset and atonement for shabby deeds and to use words which mean nothing in order to draw all meaning from those which have a meaning. It will be no easy task to arouse the austere self-respect which has been lulled to slumber by those means. Nothing is more sickening than the continual praise of Wilson's English, of Wilson's style. He is a true logothete, a real sophist, and he firmly believes, and has no inconsiderable effect in making our people believe, that elocution is an admirable substitute for and improvement on action. If anyone kicks him, he brushes his clothes, and utters some lofty sentence.

Like Maggots in a Cheese

There were ten or twelve years when I played a considerable part in American life and exercised a certain influence on American thought, as well as directly upon our governmental action. The kaleidoscope has been shaken. My influence has very nearly gone, and the battle I am still waging is not made with the hope of success but because I feel it my duty to make it. I am in fundamental sympathy with my countrymen on many things, but I am fundamentally out of sympathy with all the American analogues of the unhung traitor Keir Hardie,[1] the blue-rumped ape Bernard Shaw, and the assemblage of clever and venomous but essentially foolish and physically timid creatures of the type of the editors of the *Nation*. They swarm like maggots in a cheese. At the moment I think the ideas I hold are only shared by a minority and perhaps only by a small minority of our people.

I think the American people feel a little tired of me. I have spoken out as strongly and as clearly as possible, and I do not think it has had any effect beyond making people think that I am a truculent and bloodthirsty person, endeavoring futilely to thwart able, dignified, humane Mr. Wilson in his noble plan to bring peace everywhere by excellently written letters sent to persons who care nothing whatever for any letter that is not backed up by force! Wilson and Bryan are cordially supported by all the hyphenated Americans, by the solid flubdub and pacifist vote. Every soft creature, every coward and weakling, every man who can't look more than six inches ahead, every man whose god is money, or pleasure, or ease, and every man who has not got in him both the sterner virtues and the power of seeking after an ideal, is enthusiastically in favor of Wilson.

The antics of the peace people here pass belief. President Wilson's delightful statement about the nation being "too proud to fight" seemed to me to reach the nadir of cowardly infamy. But as a whole our people did not especially resent it. Taft, Nicholas Murray Butler, Andrew Carnegie, and the rest of the crowd are at the moment engaged in holding a grand Peace Conference to insist that everything shall be arbitrated everywhere. This country has behaved very badly because there has been no popular revolt against what Wilson has done. I am of course utterly heartsick about my own country.

Mr. Wilson's conduct in international matters has been precisely that of a man whose wife's face is slapped by another man, who thinks it over and writes a note telling the other man he must not do it again, and when the other man repeats the insult and slaps the wife's face again, writes him another note of protest, and then another and another and another, and lets it go on for a year. Technically that man may have "kept the peace" and avoided trouble, but I cannot imagine any human being willing to be in his place.

As a nation we have thought very little about foreign affairs. We don't realize that the murder of the thousand men, women, and children on the *Lusitania* is due, solely, to Wilson's abject cowardice and weakness in failing to take energetic action when the *Gulflight* was sunk but a few days previously. He and Bryan are morally responsible for the loss of the lives of those American women and children. The proper thing to do is to protest against wrongdoing at the moment instead of talking with inconclusive vagueness about possible right-doing in the future.

Wilson is the heir of Jefferson and Buchanan. To leave Wilson alone in the face of a foreign crisis is like leaving Pierce or Buchanan or Tyler alone in the presence of secession. I think that Wilson has been the very worst president we have had since Buchanan, and I say this though I think that Taft was a very poor man indeed. Wilson's attitude in foreign affairs and as regards our national defense is utterly scandalous. The old proverb applies: there are no bad regiments but there are plenty of bad colonels. The United States would stand like a unit if we had in the presidency a man of the stamp of Andrew Jackson. Think of Old Hickory letting our citizens be constantly murdered on the high seas by the Germans and in Mexico by the Greasers! But men are easily puzzled, and it is easy to mislead them, if one chooses to give them high-sounding names to excuse ignoble deeds. This is an evil service that President Wilson has rendered and is now rendering the American nation.

How I wish I were president at this moment! This is one of those rare times which come along at long intervals in a nation's history, when the action taken determines the basis of the life of the generations that follow. Such times were those from 1776 to 1789, in the days of Washington; and from 1858 to 1865, in the days of Lincoln.

His Soul Is Rotten Through and Through

Wilson carried Kansas and California last year on the issue of "He kept us out of war," and he put us into war within a month. How any human being can fail to detect such hypocrisy, I fail to understand. I have upheld him and refused to assail him since the war broke out because I wished to give him every chance, but he is exceedingly base. His soul is rotten through and through. He hasn't a thought for the welfare of this country, or for our honor, or for anything except his own mean personal advancement. Wilson did not come into this war for democracy. For two and a half years he announced again and again and again that he was neutral and that we should all be neutral in the war, and he didn't know what the different peoples were fighting about, that he didn't side with one party more than the other, that we had no concern with the purpose of the war, and finally, that we ought to strive for a peace that did not bring victory.

What is perfectly impossible, what represents really nauseous hypocrisy, is to say that we have gone to war to make "the world safe for democracy," in April, when sixty days previously we have been announcing that we wished a "peace without victory," and had no concern with the "causes or objects" of the war. If we are all fighting for democracy what did he mean by saying that he hoped there wouldn't be a victory for democracy? He is a treacherous hypocrite, and to praise him is to praise moral obliquity.

He believes that whatever sense of injury the British may like to show they won't show it, that when the time comes they will turn to him for help and that he will then gain great glory as the righteous peacemaker. I think this is very probably a correct estimate of the future on his part. I think it is very probable that he will profit by his wrongdoing, and that the fact that he has declined to do his duty as regards the Belgians and has his share in the guilt of those who are responsible for the present dreadful tragedy will be completely covered by the further fact that England and France will find that his own misconduct has made him available for action as a mediator between them and Germany. The woodenheaded fools have been taken in by Wilson much as he has taken in our own people, and they are inclined to play his game.

He Was Not Even a Valorous Barbarian

When the war first broke out I did not think the Kaiser was really to blame. I thought he was simply the tool. Gradually I was forced to realize that he was one of the leading conspirators, plotters, and wrongdoers. The last fortnight has shown that he was not even a valorous barbarian. He was unwilling to pay with his body when his hopes were wrecked. Think of the Kaiser and his six sons saving their own worthless carcasses at the end, leaving their women, like their honor, behind them.

Quentin Has Been Killed

I have been inexpressibly saddened by this war. Of my four boys, Quentin has been killed. There is no use of my writing about Quentin, as I should break down if I tried. His death is heartbreaking, but it would have been far worse if he had lived at the cost of the slightest failure to perform his duty. To feel that one has inspired a boy to conduct that has resulted in his death has a pretty serious side for a father, and at the same time I would not have cared for my boys and they would not have cared for me if our relations had not been just along that line.

We are profoundly moved and profoundly pleased by the way in which Quentin's comrades have marked his grave and treated it, in a certain sense, as almost a place of pilgrimage. It is a very sad thing to see the young die when the old who are doing nothing, as I am doing nothing, are left alive. Therefore it is very bitter to me that I was not allowed to face the danger with my sons. But whatever may be their fate, I am glad and proud that my sons have done their part in this mighty war against despotism and barbarism.

ACKNOWLEDGMENTS

This book represents the end of a journey that began with a simple idea: create a book that looked at American history from a new angle, from the perspective of Theodore Roosevelt—a major historian, whose historical opinions were, oddly enough, largely ignored despite his colorful views of the past and his own prominent place in American history. While the idea was simple, I quickly realized that I needed help to transform it into an actual book, and help was forthcoming. I extend a blanket thank-you to all those who made contributions to this project, but I would be remiss if I did not specifically acknowledge and thank the following people by name:

The late John Gable, longtime head of the Theodore Roosevelt Association, was the first person I approached with my idea. About six months before John's death we had dinner in Oyster Bay, fittingly only a few miles from Sagamore Hill. John immediately embraced the idea because, as he told me, a book devoted to TR's thoughts on American history did not exist. He encouraged me to push forward with the project, recommending that I expand the scope of the book so that it included the years of TR's adult life (i.e., 1876 and after)—advice I followed. Without John's support, this book would have remained nothing more than an idea.

After his green light, I began to research the book in earnest. Many archivists helped in this effort, especially Wallace Dailey, the curator of the Theodore Roosevelt Collection at Harvard College. Once my research was finished, I drafted an early version of the manuscript in Randsburg, California—an old gold-mining town in the Mojave Desert. This unique place, reminiscent in so many ways of TR's old stomping grounds, the Dakota Badlands, was the perfect place to work on a TR book. Many thanks to my friend Bruce Blair for letting me use the historic Rose Cottage in Randsburg as a quiet work sanctuary, and for the austere beauty and productive solitude of the high desert that came with it.

A group of others made important contributions. My sister Marianne Ruddy-Pinto and my brother, Chris Ruddy, helped in ways too numerous to list here; and my sister Lainie Ruddy-Davanzo added intangible support of great value. Putting their PhDs to good use, my friends Tom Lawton and Kevin Michaels provided valuable feedback on the manuscript. My editors, Elisabeth Dyssegaard and Bill Strachan, with the able assistance of Kate Whitenight, shepherded the book through the production process and pushed it across the finish line. Along the way, Theron Raines—the Nestor of literary agents— gave me invaluable counsel that I came to rely on because it was invariably sound.

Finally, my sincere thanks go out to Thomas Fleming and Edmund Morris—two generous and open-minded historians who went out of their way to help an unknown add something new and different to the mountain of scholarship that has been built on the life, ideas, and personality of Theodore Roosevelt. To everyone who helped me and to that mysterious spiritual agency that is essential to any creative process (it certainly helped mine), I am deeply grateful.

WORKS CITED
AND OTHER SOURCES

I. PRINCIPAL SOURCES

Most of Roosevelt's words included in this book come from four main sources and will be cited as Works, Letters, Papers, and Collection.

Works: *The Works of Theodore Roosevelt*, ed. Herman Hagedorn, National Edition, 20 vols., Scribner, 1926. Includes all of TR's books, and most of his essays and speeches.

Letters: *The Letters of Theodore Roosevelt*, ed. Elting Morison and John Blum, 8 vols., Harvard University Press, 1951–1954. The most interesting of TR's letters (including those in the Theodore Roosevelt Papers held in the Library of Congress) are published in these eight volumes.

Papers: *Theodore Roosevelt Papers*, Library of Congress, Washington, D.C. 485 reels of microfilm containing letters to and from TR, mostly after 1897. Nearly all of these letters of TR's were dictated to a stenographer, and are copies of originals sent to recipients.

Collection: *Theodore Roosevelt Collection*, Harvard College Library, Cambridge, Massachusetts. Main manuscript source of pre-1897 material, and main repository for family letters before and after this year. This collection also includes a very large amount of other material related to TR.

II. OTHER SOURCES

Arnold, Matthew. *Civilization in the United States: First and Last Impressions of America*, Cupples and Hurd, 1888.

Bishop, Joseph Bucklin. *Theodore Roosevelt and His Time*, 2 vols., Scribner, 1920. Extensive excerpts from TR's letters, many of which can also be found in Letters, Papers, and Collection.

Butt, Archie. *The Letters of Archie Butt: Personal Aide to President Roosevelt*, ed. Lawrence Abbott, Doubleday, 1924.

———. *Archibald Butt Papers*, Georgia Archives, Morrow, Georgia. Contains the complete, unedited versions of the Butt Letters published in 1924.

Clowes, William Laird. *The Royal Navy*, Vol. 6, Sampson Low, 1901. Contains "The War with the United States, 1812–1815," by Theodore Roosevelt (pp. 1–180).

Decopett, André. *André Decoppett Collection*, Manuscripts Division, Department of Rare Books and Special Collections, Princeton University Library. A manuscript collection that includes a handful of TR's letters.

Donald, David Herbert. *Lincoln*, Simon and Schuster, 1995.

Garland, Hamlin. *Companions on the Trail: A Literary Chronicle*, Macmillan, 1931.

Hale, William Bayard. *A Week in the White House with Theodore Roosevelt*, Putnam, 1908.

Harbaugh, William. *Power and Responsibility: The Life and Times of Theodore Roosevelt*, Farrar Straus and Cudahy, 1961.

Heckscher, August. *Woodrow Wilson*. Scribner, 1991.

Jay Family Papers, Columbia University. A manuscript collection that includes TR's letters to John Jay, a grandson of the Founding Father John Jay and a friend of TR's father.

Leary, John J., Jr. *Talks with T.R.*, Houghton Mifflin, 1920.

Matthews, Brander. *An Introduction to the Study of American Literature*, American Book Company, 1896.

Powell, E. Alexander. *Yonder Lies Adventure!* Macmillan, 1933.

Presidential Addresses and State Papers of Theodore Roosevelt, 4 vols., Collier, 1970.

Selections from the Correspondence of Theodore Roosevelt and Henry Cabot Lodge. Scribner, 1925. (Cited as Lodge Letters. The unedited letters between Lodge and TR are cited as Lodge Papers, which are found in the Massachusetts Historical Society.)

Truman, Harry S. *Where the Buck Stops: The Personal and Private Writings of Harry S. Truman*, ed. Margaret Truman, Warner Books, 1989.

III. HISTORIANS THEODORE ROOSEVELT ADMIRED

To shed further light on Roosevelt's historical views, I have supplemented them in the Explanatory Notes with selected opinions of historians whom he admired and who were his friends. The most important of these historians was Henry Cabot Lodge, Roosevelt's closest friend and political mentor. Roosevelt's and Lodge's perspectives on American history are remarkably aligned. Other historians who can give us a better sense of Roosevelt's historical views include John Torrey Morse (Lodge's cousin and editor of TR's biographies of Gouverneur Morris and Thomas Hart Benton), James Ford Rhodes (TR considered his history of the Civil War the best written), William E. Dodd (his biography of Jefferson Davis influenced TR's opinion of Davis), Frederick Scott Oliver (TR instantly fell in love with his biography of Alexander Hamilton), Thomas Babington Macaulay (his ideas helped TR extract valuable practical lessons from history and shaped general philosophy about history more than any other historian), and George Otto Trevelyan (TR wrote some of his best letters to Trevelyan, one of the great British historians of the day and a worthy successor to Macaulay, who was Trevelyan's uncle). Although Winfield Scott was a general and not a historian, I have included him as a source for additional perspective, as he had a significant impact on TR's historical thinking, especially as regards Thomas Jefferson and Jefferson Davis.

The list that follows is intentionally limited to those historians who could be linked directly to TR in the sense that he knew them or commented on their work. He was, of course, influenced by other historians and, indeed, in all likelihood read most of the major works about American history written up to and during his life.

Dodd, William E. *Dodd Papers*, Library of Congress.

———. *Jefferson Davis*, Jacobs, 1907.

Lodge, Henry Cabot. *Lodge Papers*, Massachusetts Historical Society, Boston.

———. *Alexander Hamilton*, Houghton Mifflin, 1882.

———. *Daniel Webster*, Houghton Mifflin, 1883.

———. *George Washington*, Houghton Mifflin, 1889.

———. *Historical* Essays, Houghton Mifflin, 1892.

Macaulay, Thomas Babington. *Selections from the Writings of Lord Macaulay*, ed. G. O. Trevelyan. Longmans Green, 1876.

Morse, John Torrey. *Morse Papers*, Massachusetts Historical Society, Boston.

Oliver, Frederick Scott. *Alexander Hamilton: An Essay on American Union*, Constable, London, 1906.

Rhodes, James Ford. *Rhodes Papers*, Massachusetts Historical Society, Boston.

———. *The McKinley and Roosevelt Administrations, 1897–1909*, Macmillan, 1923.

———. *The History of the United States from the Compromise of 1850 to the McKinley-Bryan Campaign of 1896*, 8 vols., Macmillan, 1920.

———. *Historical Essays*, Macmillan, 1909.

Scott, Winfield. *Memoirs of Lieut.-General Scott*, Sheldon, 1864.

Trevelyan, George Otto. *The American Revolution*, Longmans Green, 1880–1914.

EXPLANATORY NOTES

INTRODUCTION

[1] *These "pearls of thought"* ... TR's habit of throwing verbal bombs critical of historical figures into his books (especially the books he wrote before he achieved national fame) did not go unnoticed. One reviewer wrote that with a little practice he might be the "hanging judge" of American history, that "his black cap is always on" (Collection, TR Scrapbooks, *The Nation*, March 29, 1888).

[2] *"no one has a right to grade"* ... President Kennedy is quoted in Donald's *Lincoln*, p. 13.

[3] *Wilson's historical works are remembered* ... The quoted comments given here are those of Wilson's biographer August Heckscher. For the full context of these observations and more comments on Wilson's deficiencies as a historian see his book *Woodrow Wilson*, pp. 119–21. Heckscher chided Wilson for "lazy scholarship" and a "cloying style," and called his biography of George Washington "an embarrassment." He noted that Wilson believed that the historian "must not be in haste to judge"—the exact opposite of TR's belief that a historian must take sides.

[4] *he speaks to us with a unique authority* ... This point is consistent with TR's own view. He detested "parlor critics" and placed great value on viewpoints rooted in personal experience. In this respect, he saw himself at an advantage compared with scholars whose ideas were based on book learning alone. "I think the best critic is the doer who also possesses the power of criticism," he wrote during his second term in the White House. "*The Federalist*, one of the greatest political books ever written, owes its greatness to the fact that Hamilton, Madison and Jay were great doers as well as great thinkers, and that they did not write in the closet and the study from

experience gained only in the closet and study, but wrote as men who had taken, were taking, and were to continue to take, an active part in the turbulent world of the management of men and measures" (Papers, TR to W. Thayer, Mar. 1, 1907).

[5] *"a party that tried to destroy the Union"* . . . The Civil War significantly influenced historians of TR's generation and shaped their view of the past, elevating and emphasizing fidelity to the Union as one of the main criteria by which they judged American historical figures. TR's opinion of the Democratic Party should be viewed in this context.

[6] *Roosevelt's practical use of historical knowledge* . . . TR's letters reveal many instances where his historical insights influenced his actions. In 1909, for example, he presciently urged that Pearl Harbor be fortified because "the history of all wars up to and including the very latest has shown in over half the cases one or both of the combatants endeavor to strike a crippling blow before the actual declaration of war" (Letters, TR to G. Foss, Feb. 18, 1909). He also personally used his historical learning on the battlefield. Writing to the author of *The Study of the Battle of Fredericksburg*, he said: "It struck me at the time as being perhaps, in the proper sense of the word, the most scientific effort—that is, the most intelligent and truth-desiring effort, to get at the facts and learn the lessons of a given battle, that I had seen in the literature of the Civil War. It may possibly interest you to know that I strove to apply some of the lessons it taught in dealing with my own regiment in the late Spanish War" (Letters, TR to G. Henderson, Feb. 14, 1899).

[7] *a campaign formula that Jackson had tested* . . . TR was well acquainted with Andrew Jackson's decision to veto the recharter of the Bank of the United States, having written about it extensively for his 1887 biography of Thomas Hart Benton. The words he used in that book to describe Jackson's action could have been used almost verbatim to describe his own action in 1902 against the "money power" of his day. TR wrote: "Jackson's attack upon the Bank was a move undertaken mainly on his own responsibility, and one which, at first, most of his prominent friends were alarmed to see him undertake. . . . An assault upon what Benton called 'the money power' is apt to be popular in a Democratic republic, partly on account of the vague fear with which the poorer and more ignorant voters regard a powerful institution whose workings they do not understand and partly on account of the jealousy they feel toward those who are better off than themselves. When these feelings are appealed to by men who are intensely in earnest, and who are themselves convinced of the justice and wisdom of their course, they become very formidable factors in any political contest" (Works, Vol. 7, pp. 75–76).

[8] *to increase the public perception* . . . One of TR's successors in the White House, Harry Truman, believed that TR made a "great publicity stunt of being a trustbuster," that he "wanted, in a very cynical way, to appear to be backing certain attractive or popular things in order to get a lot of space and admiration in the newspapers," adding that, "he finally got to be called a trustbuster, but he didn't bust very many of them" (Truman, pp. 14–15, 100). Truman's judgment of

TR is not completely wrong, but it lacks a full understanding of TR's motives, for it is clear that something more than personal vanity and political gain made him act as he did. After leaving the White House, TR said, "I have never cared in the least for the kind of popularity which Lafayette so thoroughly enjoyed, and which Jefferson enjoyed . . . without reference to transmuting it into any positive achievement. I want to accomplish things" (Letters, TR to HCL, May 5, 1910). TR probably enjoyed popularity more than he cared to admit, but there can be no doubt that he was interested in real achievements. Most of all he wanted to create a healthy balance between stability and reform so that the United States could progress forward without severe economic and societal dislocations. With this in mind, he chose one big case (his Northern Securities antitrust suit) to use as an object lesson, to add needed reform "without paralyzing the energies of the business community" (Letters, TR to G. Trevelyan, Mar. 9, 1905) as a whole. This was not a cynical publicity stunt. It was a well-thought-out strategic plan that carefully weighed and balanced competing factors, and it had the interests of the United States very much in mind.

[9] *a phrase of TR's that is imprinted . . .* The full quote inside the current U.S. passport is as follows: "This is a new nation, based on a mighty continent, of boundless possibilities."

[10] *not always original . . .* TR's friend James Bryce, the scholar who wrote the classic treatise *The American Commonwealth* and was later British ambassador to the United States, said about TR after his death: "much as I admired his energy and immense variety of interests . . . his mind seemed to me to lack originality" (Rhodes Papers, J. Bryce to JF Rhodes, Jun. 6, 1919). There is some truth in Lord Bryce's observation. TR's immense knowledge of history helped guide his decision making, but at times it also kept him from "thinking outside the box." In international affairs, it was Woodrow Wilson who embraced a new effort to improve the old global system based on "balance of power" politics—not TR, who remained firmly entrenched in historical patterns of *realpolitik*, in what he called "the Bismarck tradition as regards foreign policy." Wilson's system, though in many ways utopian and unworkable, represented a real step forward and a turning of the page. None of TR's achievements rise to this level of originality, to the level of what today would be called a "discontinuous innovation." His achievements tended to involve harking back to lessons learned from the past: for example, bringing the Republican Party "back to the Lincoln basis," setting off a new wave of Jacksonian economic populism, and pulling off a heavy-handed land grab in Panama (not the first time an American president had seized territory using questionable methods).

[11] *This, and other evidence . . .* TR could joke with Henry Cabot Lodge about Andrew Jackson's "financial antics being like those of a monkey with a watch" (Letters, TR to HCL, Jun. 7, 1886), but his own knowledge of finance and economics was not much better. He admitted this when he told Lodge that there is "a tinge of economic agnosticism in me" (Letters, TR to HCL, Oct. 27, 1894), adding on

another occasion, "I get very much puzzled at times on questions of finance and the tariff" (Lodge Letters, Vol. 2, p. 121). TR took heart from the fact that his great hero had the same shortcoming, writing, "Abraham Lincoln knew mighty little about currency or the tariff, and he would have made a fool of himself if he had tried to take the lead as regards them. His service had to be along other lines, and it is the same way with a great many very humble followers of his" (Letters, TR to E. Garrison, Mar. 3, 1911).

[12] *none have relied on it more . . .* It was outside the scope of this book to investigate how much other presidents used historical knowledge to guide their decision making, but I think it is safe to say that none used it "more than" TR. This is, of course, a question that lends itself to interpretation, and thus is difficult to answer. It is also hard to prove whether historical knowledge helps presidential decision making, but anecdotal evidence supports that idea. The two professional historians who became president (TR and Woodrow Wilson) rank among the stronger presidents, as does Harry Truman (who could fairly be called an amateur historian), if the consensus of today's historians is believed. In contrast, the two engineers who became president (Herbert Hoover and Jimmy Carter) rank among the weaker presidents, and presidents from other professional backgrounds (e.g., lawyer, military leader, business owner) offer a mixed bag of low to high in presidential rankings.

HISTORY AS LITERATURE

[1] *as I pass down the river . . .* I thought it appropriate to begin this book with TR in motion, on a riverboat going down the Mississippi River through the heart of the United States. One journey naturally leads into another as TR travels, in the pages of this book, through the heart of American history. TR himself was always moving forward toward some goal, and he admired this trait in other humans and in nations. He was deeply proud of the rapid progress the United States had made from the time of the first settlers and was determined to see that the nation's progress continued at a rapid pace by promoting policies that achieved this end. He was also deeply impressed by the rapid growth of Japan during the nineteenth century, saying that Japan "with a single effort wrenched herself free from all hampering ancient ties," calling this impressive leap forward "in many ways the most striking phenomenon of all history."

TR's perspective on the development of nations, races, and individuals contained many elements of social Darwinism, an intellectual movement that began some years after the publication of Charles Darwin's *On the Origin of Species* (1859) and was popularized by such thinkers as Herbert Spencer, who coined the now famous phrase "survival of the fittest." Followers of Darwin and Spencer saw life as a never-ending struggle for survival, in which the strong won and pushed forward, supplanting the weak. TR had great respect for Darwin and put his achievement on the same level as that of Copernicus, in "effecting a complete revolution in the thought of the age, a revolution as great as that caused by the discovery of the truth about the solar system" (Works, Vol. 12, p. 8).

While TR accepted the main tenets of social Darwinism popular during the "gilded age," he grafted a moral component onto them, transforming what was otherwise a base contest for human supremacy into something nobler. He declared: "Normally the individual rises to greatness only through labor and strife. As we all know this is invariably the case with the species. In the great majority of cases it is also true of the nation. . . . It is only through strife—righteous strife—righteously conducted, but still strife, that we can expect to win to the higher levels where the victors in the struggle are crowned" (Letters, TR to G. Becker, Sep. 9, 1899).

To TR, history was the story of peoples and nations progressing forward in time at different speeds in a Darwinian race toward civilization and power. Absorbing that lesson, he became an ardent reformer, realizing that without frequent self-correction the development of the United States could grind to a halt. This is one reason why he admired Abraham Lincoln. Lincoln, of course, removed the ball and chain of slavery from the nation's ankle, allowing the United States to sprint forward at a rapid pace in the post–Civil War period.

[2] *has been one of expansion* . . . TR identified national territorial growth with presidents Washington, Adams, Monroe, and, grudgingly, Jefferson (he believed that Louisiana had been "thrust upon" Jefferson), but did not mention the names of James Polk and Andrew Johnson in connection with the significant territorial expansion that occurred during their respective administrations. This was intentional. TR did not like either of these presidents.

[3] *No merchant, no banker* . . . Although TR diminished the importance of merchants, it must be remembered that he himself was part of a family (on his father's side) of wealthy merchants. TR's inherited wealth and upper-class lifestyle came directly from that merchant activity. His preference for warriors over merchants is an implicit repudiation of his own roots, at least in a relative sense, and suggests that he may have felt some level of guilt about the privileged life he was born into.

[4] *the barbarian virtues* . . . When TR told Governor James Cox of Ohio that Andrew Jackson was a "barbarian," this was taken by Cox as a disparagement of Old Hickory. In truth, it was praise. In TR's lexicon the descriptor "barbarian" suggested hardy, manly virtues. TR sometimes referred to himself as a barbarian, as when he wrote to his English friend Cecil Spring-Rice: "Oh, Springie, Springie! I fear you are forgetting your barbarian friends on this side of the water" (Letters, TR to C. Spring-Rice, Apr. 28, 1897). As a passionate reformer, TR was eager to push the United States forward in its Darwinian race into modernity, but he was just as eager to see it retain the rugged frontier strength of the nation's formative years, embodied in the "half-civilized" Andrew Jackson. He wanted the United States to keep up with Japan, which had shown remarkable fighting prowess on the battlefield, indicating that it had retained the samurai warrior's spirit as it entered the twentieth century. Japan, in a sense, had become in his eyes a nation of civilized barbarians, and he felt that oxymoronic combination was desirable for the United States as well.

[5] *one shall be able to read it* . . . TR's thoughts about historians were heavily influenced by the English historian Thomas Babington Macaulay. TR took Macaulay's complete works with him on his 1909 hunting trip to Africa, writing: "I always take in my saddle pocket some volume . . . and among the most worn are the

volumes of Macaulay. Upon my word, the more often I read him, whether the *History* or the *Essays*, the greater my admiration becomes. . . . Of all the authors I know I believe I should first choose him as the man whose writings will most help a man of action who desires to be both efficient and decent" (TR to G. Trevelyan, Sep. 10, 1909). One of Lord Macaulay's essays, *The Historian*, which stresses the importance of imagination and readability in historical work, describes the ideal historian in terms very similar to those used by TR. Many of the ideas TR laid out in his address "History as Literature" (see next note) appear to be lifted out of Macaulay's essay.

[6] *and turn it into literature* . . . TR communicated these ideas in one of his greatest speeches: "History as Literature," an address he gave to the American Historical Association in 1912, while he was serving as its president. In the audience was a friend, the historian James Ford Rhodes, who observed: "Mr. Roosevelt took for his subject 'History as Literature.' . . . It was excellent and interesting, delivered in a dignified and scholarly manner. Mr. Roosevelt has been thinking about this subject for many years. . . . He had an audience of about 2,000, especially limited to the members of the different learned associations meeting here. Of course, it was impossible to have the hall open to the public . . . Concerning Mr. Roosevelt's audience of 2,000 Mr. Charles Francis Adams said to me, 'If you or I had given an address we should have had an audience of about 150.' It is remarkable the fascination Mr. Roosevelt exerts on so many educated men. His hold on the mass is indisputable" (Rhodes Papers, J. F. Rhodes to G. Trevelyan, Jan. 19, 1913).

[7] *the unbroken continuity of the nation's history* . . . TR's appreciation of American history can be seen in his actions as well as in his words. He went out of his way to appoint the descendants of historical figures to government jobs. He put Fitzhugh Lee, the nephew of Robert E. Lee, on his White House staff, along with the grandson of Ulysses Grant. He insisted that the grandson of Stonewall Jackson be appointed to West Point. He made appointments like these not only to help reunify the nation after the Civil War, but also to recognize the historical importance of men like Lee, Grant, and Jackson to the nation's story. He did not stop with the Civil War. Appreciating the importance of the Old West, he gave Bat Masterson (the sheriff of Dodge City), Pat Garrett (the lawman who killed Billy the Kid), and Seth Bullock (the sheriff who cleaned up Deadwood) government jobs, declaring that they "correspond to those Vikings, like Hastings and Rollo, who finally served the cause of civilization" (Papers, TR to W. Hunter, Feb. 9, 1905). In this telling comment we see more evidence for TR's admiration for civilized barbarians, that is, men who had adapted themselves to modern times without losing their innate toughness.

[8] *I claim to be a historian*... Writing before TR gained national fame in the Spanish-American War, the southern historian William Peterfield Trent declared publicly that TR would have been one of the greatest historians of his generation had he been able to devote his full time to the profession. Trent wrote: "The author of the Lives of Benton and Gouverneur Morris might in 1888 have essayed such tasks as

Mr. Schouler, Prof. McMaster, Mr. Henry Adams, and Mr. Rhodes have set themselves, and he would have won laurels in the competition. . . . We have had few abler or more conscientious historians than Mr. Roosevelt. I know of none who has had a broader or firmer grasp upon the main threads of our history" (W. P. Trent, "Theodore Roosevelt the Historian," *Forum*, July 1896).

[9] *expressed my opinions* . . . TR's publicly expressed historical opinions generated controversy, which grew in intensity as he grew in fame. He continually had to answer questions about his attacks on Thomas Paine, Jefferson Davis, and others. During his presidential campaign in 1904, his historical opinions were used against him politically. He wrote to his campaign manager: "The Democrats are just about putting out a long series of extracts from my writings to show my attacks upon Jefferson, Madison, Jackson, etc. My own view is that it is not worth while answering these statements. Often they are twisted. Generally they are taken out of their context. Sometimes they represent the exact truth, by which I will stand" (Letters, TR to G. Cortelyou, Sep. 23, 1904).

[10] *The man who becomes Europeanized* . . . TR felt contempt for Americans who left their country and lived permanently abroad. He refused to meet William Waldorf Astor (who, like Henry James, eventually became a British subject), explaining: "The other day I was asked to dinner to meet 'Mr. Astor.' At first I thought it was Jack Astor and accepted, for Jack Astor, with all his faults, is an American, but when I found it was William Waldorf Astor, I wrote again refusing, pleading inability to attend. I am not going to join in any way in greeting Willie Astor" (Letters, TR to HCL, Apr. 11, 1896).

[11] *Have you seen that London* Yellow Book . . . The *Yellow Book* was a short-lived illustrated quarterly magazine published in book form, featuring writers who were moving away from the literary conventions of the Victorian age.

[12] *No earthly reason that he should not call New York a pig trough* . . . In a travel essay published in the *Times* of London in 1892, Rudyard Kipling had called New York City a "long, narrow pig-trough" with primitive streets in such horrible condition that they were the "first cousins to a Zanzibar foreshore, or kin to the approaches of a Zulu kraal." The term "pig-trough" rankled TR (he knew it was an accurate description of his hometown, with its lack of a modern sanitation system), and he must have felt a sting of displeasure with another sentence from Kipling's essay, which attacked the United States as a whole: "Behind her stands the ghost of the most bloody war of the century caused in a peaceful land by long temporizing with lawlessness, by letting things slide, by shiftlessness and blind disregard for all save the material need of the hour, till the hour long conceived and let alone stood up full-armed, and men said, 'Here is an unforeseen crisis,' and killed each other in the name of God for four years." TR would not have disagreed with Kipling's verdict on America's past. The lesson of the Civil War sank deeply into his soul. His loud voice, always urging reform, would not allow the nation to "let things slide" again.

[13] *A careful reading of* Martin Chuzzlewit . . . Charles Dickens visited the United States in 1842, and the observations he made during his trip were the basis of his

critical comments about American life. Here again we see TR's focus on the rapidity of national growth, on how far the nation had come since Dickens's visit. Also on display: his hypersensitivity to criticism of the United States by foreigners.

[14] *fishing a poet, Arlington Robinson, out of a Boston millinery store*... TR also wrote a review of Edwin Arlington Robinson's book of poetry *The Children of the Night* and helped get it republished. In his review TR wrote: "To a man with the poetic temperament it is inevitable that life should often appear clothed with a certain sad mysticism. . . . I am not sure I understand 'Luke Havergal,' but I am entirely sure that I like it." TR was keenly interested in promoting the growth of the United States, not only in terms of territory and military power, but also by encouraging the development of a distinct American culture through active support for worthy American writers and artists.

[15] *Here Lies Wolfe Victorious*... TR did not get his wish to die in battle. Instead, he died in his bed at Sagamore Hill during an otherwise quiet night. His favorite epitaph belongs to James Wolfe, the British general who died in battle while successfully capturing Quebec during the French and Indian War. TR's admiration for men who died in battle—from John Hampden to James Wolfe to Stonewall Jackson—represents a distinct pattern of thought. He must have felt immense pride when his son Quentin died in battle during World War I, although there is little evidence to suggest that this pride lessened his profound grief, made worse by his knowledge of the uncomfortable fact that he had pushed all his sons to volunteer to fight in the war.

THE REVOLUTIONARY WAR

[1] *The wise negligence of Walpole* . . . Robert Walpole, British prime minister from 1721 to 1742, supported the unofficial policy of "salutary neglect," which placed limited restrictions on the American colonies and gave them a reasonable amount of autonomy.

[2] *A constantly increasing measure of liberty*... TR drew an important lesson from history when he saw how the British government had failed to manage political change and, as a consequence, lost its American colonies. He did not want to make the same mistake when it came to the great changes occurring in the United States during his own lifetime. As his praise for Walpole's "wise negligence" shows, he believed that wise statesmanship could prevent a revolution.

[3] *The war brought forth*... As one who had seen multiple labor riots disturb the tranquility of the United States during his life, TR naturally disliked mobs and mob leaders, so he had mixed feelings about the street agitators of the American Revolution, men like Samuel Adams and John Hancock. He felt they did a service to the nation in triggering the Revolution, but otherwise believed that their "violence better fitted them to raise mobs than to carry through a great revolution." To TR they were "hot-headed men of small capacity and much energy, part patriot and part demagogue," not completely removed from the criminal labor agitators

of his own time. He believed that Washington and his fellow warriors, "not the leaders of the liberty mobs," deserved most of the credit for winning the Revolution (Works, Vol. 10, pp. 457–59; Letters, TR to R. Baker, Nov. 28, 1905).

THE TREATY OF PEACE

[1] *The chief credit for* . . . TR's high estimate of John Jay's role in the Paris peace negotiations of 1783 was perhaps artificially inflated, as it was directly influenced by Jay's grandson—also named John Jay—who was a friend of TR's father. Using this family connection, TR gained access to the Jay family papers for his biography of Gouverneur Morris. Later, Jay sent TR his own interpretation of his grandfather's role in the peace negotiations, which TR accepted and used in his book, possibly in part as a way of returning the favor the Jay family had shown him in allowing access to their private property (Jay Papers, TR to J. Jay, Jul. 10, 1887; TR to J. Jay, Aug. 21, 1887).

[2] *Mr. Brander Matthews's volume on American literature* . . . A reference to *An Introduction to the Study of American Literature*, published in 1896.

[3] *Franklin's character wherein the philosopher fell short* . . . TR undoubtedly considered Benjamin Franklin a great American, especially for his contributions to American literature and science, and for his diplomatic skill in bringing France into the Revolutionary War as an ally of the United States. (TR called Franklin "the second greatest Revolutionary figure" and on another occasion grouped him with Washington and Lincoln in the pantheon of American worthies.) Still, TR had a noticeable lack of enthusiasm toward him, probably for the reasons Brander Matthews mentions, as well as for what TR described as Franklin's "weak government" views, expressed during the Constitutional Convention in 1787. In one cryptic comment, TR said that Franklin "embodied just precisely the faults which are most distrusted in the average American of the North today." This was probably a criticism of Franklin's decadent lifestyle, implying that he was soft, over-civilized, and lacked the fighting spirit of someone like the Virginian George Washington, who had grown to maturity fighting Indians on the frontier.

THOMAS PAINE

[1] *Huxley as an agnostic* . . . Thomas Henry Huxley, the English biologist, helped promote Darwin's theory of evolution during the nineteenth century. He is credited with coining the terms "agnostic" and "agnosticism." Here again we see evidence of Darwin's influence on TR.

[2] *That is my religion, my faith* . . . TR's religious beliefs are hard to nail down. He valued the Bible as an important instruction manual on how to lead a moral life, but there is no evidence that he accepted it as literal fact. We would expect a Christian to speak of death as "going home to the Lord," but TR was not so certain about a heavenly afterlife, frequently referring to death as a great unknown, as our turn to "go out into the blackness." He declared that "the essence of religion"

was "to do justly and to love mercy and to walk humbly with thy God," leaving out the core Christian belief in the promise of resurrection and life after death. TR's words about the "everlasting blackness," and about religion have the feel of someone who was an agnostic or a deist, not a Christian by a strict definition of the word. His personal beliefs aside, he obviously believed that Christianity and religion, as he broadly defined them, were great forces for good in human affairs. Still, his mind was scientific in its workings and always, as a reflex action, returned to facts, not faith. In this sense, Charles Darwin exerted a greater influence on his worldview than did Jesus Christ.

GEORGE WASHINGTON

[1] *I should like to have continued as President* . . . TR's decision not to seek the presidency in 1908 shows how his appreciation for American history affected his decision making. He believed that Washington and Lincoln were the two greatest Americans, not only because of their achievements but also because they were willing to give up power. TR wanted to follow their example in both respects. He could have easily won another term in office in 1908 had he chosen to run again, as the easy victory of his weaker lieutenant, Taft, proves.

[2] *Of the Fabian order* . . . TR admired the cautious Fabian strategy Washington used to win the Revolutionary War. He praised the historian George Otto Trevelyan's comparison of Washington to the famous Roman general Fabius, when Trevelyan wrote: "The Roman Republic could show an almost interminable list of celebrated captains who had won brilliant triumphs, and added rich provinces to the empire. But the Roman people reserved their highest esteem, and their warmest regard, for the great citizen who, under a cloud of obloquy, had steadfastly and resolutely opposed his own policy of caution to the daring genius of Hannibal. The poet Ennius . . . told how the glory of Fabius increased as the years went on because, when his country was in mortal danger, he paid no attention to the talk of men, and looked only to the safety of the state" (Trevelyan, *The American Revolution*).

[3] *Lord Wolseley speaks a good deal of General Washington* . . . Garnet Wolseley, a British general and veteran of the Crimean War, visited the South in 1862 without the consent of Lincoln's government. His pronounced sympathy for the Confederacy and fulsome praise of Robert E. Lee triggered a fierce reaction from TR, who felt compelled to publish a sarcastic rebuttal. "If that flatulent conqueror of half armed savages chances to read it, it will just make his hair curl," TR wrote to Lodge with glee (Letters, TR to HCL, Jun. 11, 1887). The words of Wolseley that angered TR most were those that put Lee in a place of greatness that TR had reserved for Lincoln. Wolseley wrote, "I believe all will admit that General Lee towered far above all men on either side in that struggle: I believe he will be regarded not only as the most prominent figure of the Confederacy, but as the great American of the nineteenth century, whose statue is well worthy to stand on an equal pedestal with that of Washington" ("General Lee," *Macmillan's Magazine*, March 1887).

ALEXANDER HAMILTON

[1] *the man of most brilliant mind* ... When TR used the word "brilliant" to describe Alexander Hamilton, he meant Hamilton's extraordinary brain, with its high-powered intelligence and vast storehouse of knowledge. He also respected Thomas Jefferson in this regard, believing him to be, despite many faults, "the most brilliant President we have ever had" (Butt Papers, Letter to his mother, Jul. 24, 1908).

[2] *the touch of the gallant, the dashing* ... When TR looked at Alexander Hamilton, he saw a fellow romantic warrior. TR's favorite biography of Hamilton, by Frederick Scott Oliver, described him this way: "There are occasions in Hamilton's career when we are puzzled whether to laugh or to cry out with admiration at the boyish confidence undaunted by the grimmest difficulties. There is a heroic quality even in his longest letters on taxation. Their passionate sincerity, their joyful audacity, bridge the gulf of years and create an intimacy such as we have felt with our heroes of romance—with Quentin Durward and with d'Artagnan, a confusion of wonder with personal affection." Anyone who reads a representative sample of TR's letters is struck by the same "boyish confidence" and "joyful audacity."

[3] *He possessed an austere purity and poise of character* ... This appears to be an indirect reference to Hamilton's extramarital affair with Maria Reynolds. A Victorian moralist, TR considered marital infidelity a gross sin similar in kind, though not degree, to treason.

[4] *Adams, in his efforts to keep peace* ... In 1798, Alexander Hamilton wished to declare war on France because of its misconduct toward American ships on the seas, but President John Adams refused to take this step. Exactly a century later, TR stood in Hamilton's shoes and wished to go to war with Spain, but President William McKinley, like Adams, was reluctant to fight. McKinley did so only when pushed into it. TR felt McKinley had failed to lead, a feeling he may have had toward Adams, too, though the historical record is silent on this point. Curiously, TR made no direct judgments about John Adams—at least none that research for this book revealed. We can only speculate as to why, but one reason might have been that TR moved in the same social circles as the descendents of Adams. He was a friend of Henry and Brooks Adams, and he may not have wanted to make waves by criticizing their great-grandfather. This is one explanation for TR's silence; another is that he did not think Adams important enough to discuss. But knowing TR and his preference for warriors, it is unlikely that he could have had anything more than guarded respect for the portly, intellectual Adams, who never came close to physical combat, either personally or in war.

[5] *actually proposed to Jay* ... Henry Cabot Lodge considered this action of Hamillton's in asking John Jay to negate the election of Jefferson in New York state, and by doing so defeat Jefferson's effort to win the White House, "the one dark blot upon the public career of Hamilton" (HCL, *Alexander Hamilton*).

[6] *The great Federalist Party fell from power* ... TR fought against the conservative wing of the Republican Party (the faction in the party that resembled the old

Federalists) and ran against their nominee (President Taft) in 1912 to bring the G.O.P. "back to the Lincoln basis." In the end, he failed not only to win the White House, but also in his effort to transform the Republican Party, which remained in exile until Warren Harding was elected president in 1920 on a "return to normalcy" platform, a conservative message far removed from TR's progressive activism.

NORTHWEST ORDINANCE OF 1787

[1] *among the Foremost of American State papers . . .* It is noteworthy that TR included Washington's Farewell Address among this select group of state papers. This was no accident. Many of us have read the Declaration of Independence and Lincoln's Second Inaugural, but how many of us have read Washington's Farewell Address? TR did read it and took its words to heart. Washington urged his fellow Americans to preserve the Union and said that "many artifices" would be employed to weaken the belief of the American people in the importance of the "unity of Government, which constitutes you one people." In TR's mind, Washington's prophesy about "many artifices" was proved true by the separatist actions of Thomas Jefferson, John C. Calhoun, Jefferson Davis, and others. This prophecy helped form his belief that the Civil War was a product of ambitious politicians who were willing to sacrifice the Union to further their own selfish ends.

THE CONSTITUTION

[1] *Pinckney was a thoroughgoing nationalist . . .* Charles Cotesworth Pinckney is one of the most overlooked of the Founding Fathers, but it is not surprising that TR singled him out for praise, given Pinckney's desire to give the central government more power. Pinckney was a stand-up guy. As a diplomat abroad during Adams's administration, he refused to accept a bribe from revolutionary France during the XYZ Affair and is credited with the famous response, "Millions for defense, but not one cent for tribute," words that warmed TR's heart. TR put Pinckney in an exclusive group of great American diplomats that included Benjamin Franklin, Charles Francis Adams, and Gouverneur Morris (Papers, TR to A. White, Sep. 15, 1902) and lamented that the South failed to produce nationalist leaders like him after the Revolutionary War era had ended.

[2] *Oliver Ellsworth, of Connecticut, whose name should be branded with infamy . . .* Ellsworth committed other offenses against TR's value system at the Constitutional Convention. He was responsible for removing the words "national government" from the Constitution, replacing them with the words "government of the United States," thereby suggesting a confederacy of states rather than a single sovereign power.

[3] *the strongest opponent of the adoption of the Constitution . . .* As TR's biographer Carleton Putnam has pointed out, TR was mistaken in stating that Jefferson opposed the Constitution: Jefferson did support the Constitution once the Bill of Rights was added. But TR was nonetheless right in a larger sense. Jefferson may

have, in the end, officially supported the ratification of the Constitution, but he continued to resist activating much of its potential power after it became the supreme law of the land. Those who opposed the Constitution prior to ratification formed the core of the Jeffersonian party, and it was Jefferson who led them into power on a party platform that sought to limit the power of the Constitution by a strict interpretation of its text.

GOUVERNEUR MORRIS

[1] *Gouverneur Morris was too unstable* . . . It was hard for TR to forgive Morris's "treason" during the War of 1812, but when given the chance to write about John Jay instead of Morris, he balked, telling Henry Cabot Lodge: "Gracious Heavens, Cabot, do you really think I want to change that entertaining scamp Morris for dear, dull, respectable Jay? Not much. I think the latter had a good deal more influence on the country, but the other is twice as good a character to write about" (Letters, TR to HCL, Jun. 28, 1887).

THE FRENCH REVOLUTION

[1] *The French Revolution* . . . At first glance, a chapter about TR's perspective on the French Revolution may seem out of place in a book about American history. It is not. The French Revolution is one of three Rosetta stones that help us decipher TR the historian and statesman (the others are Charles Darwin and the Civil War). Much of TR's historical worldview and governing philosophy was rooted in the lessons he learned from his study of the French Revolution. In his own time he saw the wealthy elite who resisted sensible political and economic change as reactionary analogues to the woodenheaded French noblesse. At the other extreme, he saw William Randolph Hearst and Eugene Debs as new versions of the radicals Robespierre and Danton. He saw himself as the moderating force in the middle holding both extremes back by instituting necessary reforms to release revolutionary steam from the societal pressure cooker that, he believed, threatened to explode into a bloody revolution of class antagonism.

JOHN MARSHALL

[1] *The leader in giving a broad construction* . . . One wonders how TR would have felt about today's use of his "broad construction" philosophy to justify social policies like legal abortion. Given his Victorian sensibilities, it is doubtful he would have agreed with the use of "broad construction" in this way. That being the case, it shows an inherent weakness in his view of the Constitution. He advocated "broad construction" of the Constitution by Supreme Court justices who were "constructive statesmen," but he never said at what point they should stop being "constructive." TR liked and admired John Marshall because Marshall made "the Constitution march," but TR never spoke of the danger that came with these marching orders, of the risk that once the Constitution was in motion it could march off a cliff. It is true that during his 1912 presidential campaign he did advocate the popular recall

of judicial decisions by State courts when their decisions were wildly unpopular, but he did not think a similar limitation should be placed on the Supreme Court.

[2] *The Dartmouth College case* . . . In this famous case the Supreme Court under Marshall ruled in favor of the trustees of Dartmouth College and against the New Hampshire legislature, which was attempting to make the college a state institution. TR did not like the Court's limiting the power of government to act on behalf of the people or, as he put it, siding with the forces of "privilege."

THOMAS JEFFERSON

[1] *as a whole was very distinctly evil* . . . To our ears, this judgment of Thomas Jefferson seems very harsh, but by the standards of TR's day such an opinion was in the mainstream of historical thinking, at least in the North. In the period after the Civil War the study of American history was dominated by historians concentrated in New England, who naturally looked on Jefferson with disfavor, blaming him for weakening the Union at its birth. TR's negative views of Jefferson aligned nicely with those of his friends and fellow historians Henry Cabot Lodge and John Torrey Morse, who also despised Jefferson. During the "Gilded Age" Alexander Hamilton, not Jefferson, was the hero of historians in the North.

[2] *Jomini has left on record* . . . This is a reference to Baron Henri de Jomini, who, like his more famous counterpart Carl von Clausewitz, was a European military scholar of the Napoleonic era and wrote extensively on the nature of war. TR strengthened his case against Jefferson by citing this expert opinion.

[3] *Jefferson was not a fighting man* . . . It is interesting that in all of TR's criticism of Jefferson there are no comments about his questionable conduct as "war governor" of Virginia during the Revolutionary War, when Jefferson failed to repel the British invasion of Virginia, led by Benedict Arnold, and was forced to flee from Monticello. TR ascended to the national pantheon by charging up a hill in Cuba. Jefferson, in contrast, hurt his historical reputation when he charged down a hill in Virginia to escape approaching British troops. The source of TR's intense hatred for Jefferson remains something of a mystery, but what is clear is that Jefferson represented in TR's mind the personification of national weakness caused by too much civilization, loss of the "barbarian virtues," and overreliance on soft ideas untested in the real world of Darwinian strife among men and nations.

[4] *Jefferson was the father of nullification, and therefore of secession* . . . TR was not the first to blame Jefferson for nullification and secession. Winfield Scott wrote in 1864: "nullification, almost identical with rebellion, both in part the posthumous works of Mr. Jefferson" (Scott, *Memoirs*, p. 182). TR read Scott's *Memoirs* for the first time in his early twenties and appears to have been influenced by Scott's critique of Jefferson. TR's charge was more direct and forceful than Scott's, but both expressed the same judgment: that Jefferson was partly responsible for the Civil War. TR's charge against Jefferson might also be traced back to the diaries of John Quincy Adams, which TR is known to have read, though when he did so

for the first time is uncertain. Adams wrote: "Every school-boy is taught to execrate the Alien and Sedition laws, and John Adams bears the odium of them, but no responsibility worth speaking of for nullification attaches to Jefferson. He was the father of it and the sponsor of it."

[5] *Jefferson's course in the matter*... The historian Frederick Jackson Turner felt that TR was unfair in his criticism of Jefferson as regards Michaux and Genet. In his review of TR's book *The Winning of the West,* Turner said: "This is a serious charge, one of the most serious ones that has ever been brought against Jefferson." Turner pointed out that Jefferson had expressed a distinctly anti-French sentiment when he declared only a few years before Michaux and Genet arrived in the United States "that there is on the globe one single spot, the possessor of which is our natural and habitual enemy. It is New Orleans." TR was aware of all this when he made his charge, but he believed Jefferson made statements like this for political reasons to maintain his popularity in regions of the country that wanted the United States to control the Mississippi River. He refused to retract his charge against Jefferson, despite the weak foundation it stood on.

[6] *This first exploring expedition* . . . TR was enthusiastic about scientific exploration—as shown, for example, in his own expedition in 1913 to explore the "River of Doubt," an unchartered tributary of the Amazon River in Brazil. He also closely followed the efforts of Admiral Robert Peary to reach the North Pole.

AARON BURR

[1] *Wilkinson, the double traitor, the bribe taker* . . . This is a reference to General James Wilkinson, who historians later learned was in the pay of Spain. Wilkinson is most remembered for his treason and his role in the Burr conspiracy, but he also fought during the War of 1812, albeit with no distinction. Winfield Scott believed that Wilkinson was an "unprincipled imbecile." TR agreed with that judgment and believed something worse, that Wilkinson deserved to be grouped in infamy with Benedict Arnold, Aaron Burr, and Jefferson Davis.

THE WAR OF 1812

[1] *Scott records in his autobiography that* . . . Winfield Scott's *Memoirs,* published during the Civil War, had an important influence on TR's thinking about American history. TR read Scott's book when he was in his early twenties, as part of the research he conducted for his own book *The Naval War of 1812.* His disdain for Thomas Jefferson began around the time he read Scott's words pointing out Jefferson's "contempt for military character" and Jefferson's role in causing the Civil War (Scott, *Memoirs,* pp. 35, 182).

JAMES MADISON

[1] *A ridiculously incompetent leader*... TR felt James Madison was a bad president, but nonetheless thought enough of him to take his family to Madison's home on Thanksgiving Day, 1907. A newspaper account described the visit this way:

"President Roosevelt spent today at the old home of President Madison near Montpelier, Virginia. . . .The President was particularly interested in visiting the tomb of President Madison and remained near it for some time" (*New York Times*, Nov. 29, 1907). Contrast this show of respect with TR's visit to Jefferson's home during an official visit to the University of Virginia, when he did not get off his horse to pay his respects when he passed Jefferson's grave: "The President . . . started on the three-mile ride to Monticello. . . .The party halted at the tomb of Jefferson on the mountain side, but did not dismount" (*Richmond Times-Dispatch*, Jul. 17, 1903).

JAMES MONROE

[1] *Whose greatness is thrust upon them* . . . TR told the historian John Torrey Morse that John Jay was "certainly a far greater man than John Randolph or James Monroe" (Letters, TR to J. T. Morse, Jun. 22, 1887), giving us more evidence that he felt Monroe was an empty suit.

JOHN QUINCY ADAMS

[1] *"the Blackleg and the Puritan"* . . . When John Randolph used the word "blackleg" he meant that Clay was prone to cheat when he gambled. Referring to Clay's reputation for "loose living," TR did not disagree. He nonetheless seemed to admire Clay's willingness to confront Randolph in a duel. TR criticized dueling, but it was perfunctory criticism. He showed willingness to participate in a duel himself when he was a rancher in North Dakota in the 1880s. He could never completely condemn an activity that placed a premium on honor and courage even if it was, on the whole, disreputable.

ANDREW JACKSON

[1] *Buell's* Life of Andrew Jackson *dedicated to me* . . . TR did not usually give official permission for book dedications, and did not in this case either, but he nonetheless went out of his way to state that he was "very pleased" with Buell's dedication: "To the embodiment in our times of the Jacksonian spirit, Theodore Roosevelt, the author respectfully dedicates these volumes" (Augustus C. Buell, *Andrew Jackson: Pioneer, Patriot, Soldier, Politician, President*, Scribner, 1904). TR's tacit approval of this dedication is a tangible sign of his increased admiration for Jackson and his attachment to the "Jacksonian spirit."

[2] *my admiration has grown steadily* . . . TR's visit to Jackson's home was described in a newspaper account this way: "After a walk through the spacious apartments of the Hermitage, the ladies of the Hermitage Association invited him to tea. . . .'From Lafayette's cup I drink in Jackson's home,' he said, and then remarked, 'This tastes mighty good after hunting bears in Louisiana.' . . . He took lunch with the granddaughter of Old Hickory . . . then asked to be shown the way to Jackson's tomb in the yard. . . . Uncovering his head he placed a wreath on the tomb and whispered to Jackson's granddaughter, 'What a privilege' " (*New Orleans Times-*

Democrat, Oct. 23, 1907). "As the President spoke to the crowd a mockingbird mounted a magnolia branch just over the grave of Old Hickory and poured forth a flood of melody. The bird seemed to fairly try and vie with the President in giving forth his message to the great and happy throng. . . . Wasn't that a good omen?" wrote the *Nashville American*. Four months later TR still remembered this birdsong: "Yes, I heard that mockingbird while I was visiting the Hermitage, both when I stood out on the porch and again when I was at the tomb. It was beautiful" (Papers, TR to H. Miller, Feb. 13, 1908).

[3] *From the outbreak of the Revolution* . . . The time frame TR gives here indicates that he believed Andrew Jackson was a better general than George Washington, but not as great a general as Robert E. Lee.

[4] *Some claim it as being mainly the work of Jackson, others as that of Livingston* . . . This is a reference to Edward Livingston, Jackson's secretary of state, and suggests that TR did not believe that the "half-civilized" Jackson could have written such a fine document entirely on his own. That judgment would not have been inaccurate. Jackson is known to have used learned ghostwriters throughout his life.

[5] *An assault upon "the money power"* . . . TR always said that Abraham Lincoln was his "great hero," but Andrew Jackson's career is more similar to his own. Like Jackson, TR was catapulted into high political office by feats on the battlefield. TR's "trust busting" is analogous to Jackson's war on the Bank of the United States. Both were popular assaults on institutions controlled by the wealthy, and both assaults endeared the president who launched them to the common man. TR's presidency in many ways represented a mixture of Jackson's economic populism and Lincoln's political skill, and that was not an accident. He had thoroughly studied the political careers of both Jackson and Lincoln.

[6] *a central bank would be a very good thing* . . . Sometimes TR's knowledge of American history acted as a brake that stopped him from going forward with a particular reform that he favored. He wanted to create a national bank, for instance, but did not make the attempt, because he felt that there would be a popular reaction against such an institution similar to what had happened when Nicholas Biddle was head of the Bank of the United States in the early 1830s. Some of TR's contemporaries thought he was impulsive. In truth, he could be very cautious about initiating policies that he believed could generate more harm than good for the nation as a whole and for himself politically. The central bank TR feared to create came into being only four years after he left office in the form of the Federal Reserve System, created during Woodrow Wilson's administration in 1913.

JAMES POLK

[1] *The Liberty Party, in running Birney, simply committed a political crime* . . . TR's condemnation of Birney and the Abolitionists who made up the Liberty Party for causing the defeat of Henry Clay in 1844 is noteworthy because one could argue that he committed the same "political crime" himself in 1912. Like Birney, TR ran as the head of a long-shot third party and threw the election to the candidate

(Woodrow Wilson) he opposed the most. TR never ceased to attack idealistic politicians who hurt the cause of "righteousness" by refusing to be practical, and yet this is the path he went down in 1912. In doing so, he violated a core principle that he had preached throughout his political career.

[2] *These three men—Calhoun, Birney, and Isaiah Rynders* . . . Isaiah Rynders was a Tammany Hall political operative in New York City during the 1840s and 1850s. He worked with Irish street gangs to create voting blocs of immigrants to help Democrat candidates such as James Polk, Franklin Pierce, and James Buchanan.

[3] *unrighteous war with Mexico* . . . TR wrote extensively about every American war except one—the Mexican War. There is a good reason for this omission. In the North during TR's time the consensus was that the Mexican War had been engineered by the slave power of the South, through its tool, President James Polk, to acquire more slave territory. TR was a self-proclaimed expansionist, and thus one would expect him to celebrate Polk's acquisition of California and a vast tract of territory in the Southwest—the fruits of the Mexican War—but he could not speak favorably about what he believed was an immoral war that Abraham Lincoln himself had vigorously opposed. Other statements made by TR (e.g., those concerning the Louisiana Purchase) suggest that he believed the West would have been eventually conquered and settled without the benefit of the "unrighteous war" with Mexico that opened the door to the Civil War.

ZACHARY TAYLOR

[1] *one of the great presidents* . . . TR saw Zachary Taylor as a Whig version of Andrew Jackson. Both possessed the "barbarian virtues," both were victorious generals (though TR knew Taylor lacked Jackson's military genius), both were Southern slaveholders who strongly believed in preserving the Union, and both proved it by their actions confronting the slave power of the South, Jackson during the Nullification crisis in the early 1830's and Taylor during the crisis caused by California's desire to join the Union in 1850. Today, historians have little regard for Taylor, and that appears unfair in light of TR's observations. Taylor may not have been, as TR believed, a "great president," but his actions with regard to the most important issue of his time—the slave question—were certainly more robust than those of any other president between Jackson and Lincoln.

THOMAS HART BENTON

[1] *the position of Webster at the time of his famous 7th of March speech* . . . TR admired Daniel Webster's intellect and speaking ability, but thought less of him for his moral failings in dealing with slavery. Henry Cabot Lodge described Webster's 7th of March speech this way: "Mr. Webster's strong argument in favor of the Fugitive Slave Law pleased the South, of course, but it irritated and angered the North . . . The trouble was that he had no word to say against the cruelty and barbarity of the system. . . . Instead of denouncing and deploring it, and striking at it whenever the Constitution permitted, he apologized for its existence, and urged the enforcement of its most obnoxious laws. This was not his attitude in

1820. This was not what the people of the North expected of him in 1850" (HCL, *Daniel Webster*). Webster falls into a grout that might include Benjamin Franklin, John Adams, and James Madison, that is, among notable Americans who were intellectuals, not warriors. TR could respect such men, but they never rose to a lofty height in his mind. Abraham Lincoln was no warrior, but as commander in chief he won a horrific Civil War and died a tragic hero, and this does not fit the Webster group.

ABRAHAM LINCOLN

[1] *Mr. Matthew Arnold grants us that Washington is distinguished* . . . Arnold had written that "Alexander Hamilton is indeed a man of rare distinction" and Washington "has true distinction and character," but that "these men belong to the pre-American age." In other words, they were born as subjects of the British king and were thus colonial Englishmen, and not "typical Americans." Arnold then added that Lincoln "is a man with qualities deserving the most sincere esteem and praise, but he has not distinction" (Arnold, p. 176). We can see now, of course, that TR was right and Arnold wrong. No one today disputes that Lincoln had "distinction."

[2] *The only weakness in the great war president* . . . Blinded by hero-worship, TR was reluctant to admit other weaknesses of Lincoln. "My father loved Lincoln, I didn't," said TR's daughter Alice in 1967. "I could always make him angry about Lincoln. I'd say, 'How do you account for Lincoln writing that letter to Grant in which he said that his son had just finished Harvard when the Civil War was still on, but he thought it would be very nice of General Grant to take him on his staff?'" (*New York Times*, Aug. 6, 1967). Contrast TR's silence about Lincoln protecting his son from combat with his scathing criticism of the Kaiser for doing the same with his sons during World War I, and we can see Alice's point.

[3] *his failure to catch up with the great corruptionists* . . . TR seems to have shared Henry Cabot Lodge's view that the pervasive corruption of the Gilded Age began in the Civil War, when, out of necessity, corruption was winked at. Lodge wrote: "After the war there was a very great demoralization such as is sure to follow any period of civil strife. Such a war as ours was necessarily demoralizing to the moral standard both in business and in politics. Out of that demoralization came the scandals of Grant's time. . . . These were the natural outcome of the Civil War when the only question asked in regard to any man was whether he was loyal" (Rhodes Papers, HCL to J. F. Rhodes, May 28, 1900).

[4] *to portray Lincoln as rude and uncouth* . . . TR was not blind to Lincoln's "uncouth" personality. Concerning Lincoln's reported fondness for "smutty stories," TR told Hamlin Garland, "That has always grieved me sorely. Grant's refusal to have such stories told in his presence is greatly to his honor" (Garland, p. 205).

JEFFERSON DAVIS

[1] *In a public utterance of mine some* . . . Prior to 1908 TR considered Jefferson Davis another Benedict Arnold, and excoriated him regularly. In early 1908, however, TR read William E. Dodd's biography of Davis, and thereafter he began to praise

Davis—a startling reversal of judgment. Dodd was invited to the White House, where, according to Dodd, TR "said he had a good many things to take back referring to an article he had written years ago in *The Century* in which Davis was sharply criticized, but that he could not do so until his term expired" (Dodd Papers, "Memorandum," Mar. 5, 1908).

Five years later, in 1913, TR showered Jefferson Davis with glowing public praise that is almost unbelievable to read, given his history of verbal assaults on Davis's character: "Tom Benton of Missouri and Jefferson Davis of Mississippi were opposed to each other. . . . Each possessed an iron will and undaunted courage, physical and moral. Each led a life of varied interest and danger. . . . One, the champion of the Union, fought for the principles as unyieldingly as the other fought for what he deemed right in trying to break up the Union. Each was a colossal figure. Each, when the forces against which he fought overcame him, . . . fronted an adverse fate with the frowning defiance, the high heart, and the stubborn will which Dante has commemorated for all time in his hero who 'held hell in great scorn'" (Works, Vol. 12, pp. 101–2).

It appears that Dodd's book played a key role in TR's remarkable change of heart. TR had made a significant mistake when he accused Jefferson Davis of repudiating the Mississippi debt in the years prior to the Civil War—a serious sin in TR's eyes, as he considered debt repudiation equivalent to outright theft. Dodd's book showed that Davis was not one of the repudiators. To make his charge against Davis, TR had relied on Winfield Scott's *Memoirs*, which mentioned the "Mississippi bonds, repudiated, mainly by Mr. Jefferson Davis" (Scott, *Memoirs*, p. 148).

Putting the historical judgment about Davis to the side, TR's reversal of opinion shows his willingness to change a strongly held view if confronted with new facts—in short, to admit that he was wrong.

[2] *Mr. Theodore Roosevelt is in receipt...* TR's annoyance at Davis's letter can be seen in the fact that he wrote his pompous response in the third person, mimicking the puffed-up third-person style of Davis's letter of protest. TR never wrote letters in the third person (this is the only one I discovered in researching this book).

[3] *the names of Aaron Burr, of Wilkinson, of Floyd...* This last name refers to John B. Floyd, a Virginian who served as President James Buchanan's secretary of war. In that capacity he was indicted for fraud in connection with helping corrupt army contractors. In the days leading up to the Civil War, he was accused of sending arms to federal arsenals in the South, knowing that these arms would eventually be seized by rebel forces. After the war broke out, he served as a general in the Confederate army and surrendered to Ulysses Grant at Fort Donelson.

ROBERT E. LEE

[1] *hearty goodwill and admiration for Lee...* Henry Cabot Lodge did not share TR's admiration of Lee. Lodge wrote to John Torrey Morse: "I am aware of the Lee worship. He was a great soldier and a man of fine character, but he did not save the Union by refusing to enter on guerrilla warfare after Appomattox. The South was fought out absolutely. . . . Lee did more than any other one man to destroy the

Union, and failed. That the South should make a hero of him is all right, but I revolt at the claim that he is a national hero" (Morse Papers, HCL to JT Morse, Mar. 2, 1914).

[2] *Southerners as Farragut, Thomas, and Drayton...* The last name refers to Percival Drayton, who was a native of South Carolina yet served in the Union navy. He fought alongside Admiral David Farragut at the Battle of Mobile Bay.

STONEWALL JACKSON

[1] *His pale face flushed with joy and excitement* . . . It is easy to see why TR liked Stonewall Jackson, the Cromwellian general "with his Bible and Sword." Like TR, Jackson was the embodiment of a leader who believed in righteous war. If we ever wonder why TR acted as he did in Cuba during the Spanish-American War, the simple answer is that he wanted to be another Stonewall Jackson, heroically leading men in a battle for a cause he fervently believed in, even if this meant he had to die to accomplish the feat.

ULYSSES GRANT

[1] *Owen Wister's little book about Grant* . . . A reference to Wister's biography of Grant, published in 1900. TR forgave, or at least chose to not harp on, the manifold faults of the Grant administration; and this is noteworthy, since TR's entire career was built on opposing corruption in all its forms, and government corruption reached its zenith during Grant's time in the White House. TR's silence is out of character in this respect, but his praise of Wister's book offers us a probable explanation: TR believed that Grant's achievement in winning the Civil War outweighed all his faults, and that disproportionate criticism of Grant would, in the words of Wister, "hurt the general American soul" (Rhodes Papers, O. Wister to J. F. Rhodes, Nov. 19, 1906).

[2] *Had been a mere invention...* Here again we see the influence of one of TR's favorite historians, Thomas Babington Macaulay, who warned in his essay "The Historian": "A history in which every particular incident may be true may on the whole be false" (Macaulay, p. 355). It appears that TR took Macaulay's idea to heart and used it to divert attention from Grant's failures before and after the Civil War.

[3] *Then came a period of trouble and failure* . . . TR was largely silent about Grant's life before the Civil War, which presented a picture as unpleasant to view as the corruption of Grant's White House years. James Ford Rhodes wrote: "James Rood told me Grant was a drunken loafer in Galena. People when they saw him coming would cross the street to avoid being asked to loan him $5. Schurz intimated he used to strike people for loans of 25 cents" (Rhodes Papers, Index Rerum).

RECONSTRUCTION

[1] *Take John Sharp Williams, for instance* . . . Williams served as a Mississippi congressman and senator from 1894 to 1923. A segregationist leader, he had no qualms about suppressing the voting rights of blacks in the South. While running for the Senate in 1907 he said that the candidates running for the Senate seat were

"paying no more attention to Negroes in Mississippi than they are to the mules tied up by those Negroes." A harsh critic of TR, he fired a broadside on the floor of the Senate in 1912 branding TR a hypocrite: "Colonel Roosevelt never attacked anyone so bitterly as he did the old Populists, although his new Progressive Party has stolen every one of its planks from the old Populist platform" (*Washington Post*, Aug. 22, 1912).

[2] *Jefferson's tool, Giles* . . . This refers to William Giles, a highly partisan ally of Thomas Jefferson during the politically turbulent 1790s. As a prominent member of the House of Representatives from Virginia, Giles criticized Alexander Hamilton's conduct as secretary of the treasury and Federalist policies in general. It is widely believed that he did so at least in part at the behest of Jefferson.

[3] *On the Negro question* . . . By the standards of his generation, TR was ahead of his time on race issues, embracing Abraham Lincoln's progressive, albeit imperfect, views on the subject. But TR's generally positive record on race is marred by his controversial decision to discharge Negro soldiers from the army in 1906 for their alleged involvement in shooting white citizens in Brownsville, Texas. The one-sided perspective of this book does not lend itself to fair treatment of this complicated incident, and thus discussion of it has been omitted.

[4] *the case of the Indianola post office in Mississippi* . . . Minnie Geddings Cox, the first black postmistress in the United States, was appointed at age twenty-two by President Benjamin Harrison, in 1891. Facing death threats, Cox submitted her resignation to TR, who, to his credit, refused to accept it. Rather than yield to the demands of a mob that insisted he put a white person in Cox's job, he chose instead to close the Indianola post office and reroute the mail through another facility. He insisted that Cox continue to receive her salary, even if she could not work in Indianola out of fear for her life. Honoring her sacrifice, Congress officially renamed the building she worked in the "Minnie Cox Post Office" in 2008.

THE ELECTION OF 1884

[1] *Until the spring of 1884* . . . TR's first step into national politics began in 1884, when he attended the Republican convention with Henry Cabot Lodge. Before this, there is a large gap in the historical record concerning his thoughts on the administrations of three Republican presidents: Grant, Hayes, and Garfield. TR has left us a few indirect comments about Grant's presidency, but nothing at all concerning that of Rutherford Hayes. We do know that President Hayes nominated TR's father to head the New York Customs House, and that the senior Roosevelt died soon thereafter. If there was some link, psychological or other, between TR's silence and Hayes's association with his father's death, we do not know what it was. TR's silence about Hayes is a little odd because Hayes made the first important steps toward civil service reform and, in addition, served gallantly in the Civil War and was an honest, decent man. TR usually praised leaders such as Hayes.

TR had a little more to say about President James Garfield, the successor to Hayes. He told his aide Archie Butt that Garfield's "great fault lay in the fact that he had no horror of corruption. He cared nothing about it while a perfectly honest man himself. Just as McKinley thought it wicked to expose corruption so Garfield thought it necessary to condone it as a matter of policy. But next to Jefferson, Garfield was the most brilliant President we have ever had" (Butt Papers, letter to his mother, July 24, 1908). President Garfield's son, James R. Garfield, was a member of TR's "Tennis Cabinet" and a close friend of the Roosevelt family. TR's silence about the Republican presidents between 1873 and 1888 was probably driven, at least in part, by a sense of shame about the party's failures during this period, when it governed the nation in a manner that fell far short of his high standards.

[2] *Arthur made a very good president* . . . TR opposed the nomination of Chester Arthur as the Republican nominee in 1884, but he had a generally favorable view of Arthur's presidency. Defying expectations, Arthur ran a clean administration after Garfield's assassination unexpectedly put him in the presidential chair. It was during his term that the modern American navy began to be built with ships made of steel; in TR's opinion, this was the first step that ultimately led to victory in the Spanish-American War, a war won by the American navy. Arthur also signed into law the Pendleton Act, the first legislative action taken to remove the "spoils system" from politics. This act created the need for federal Civil Service commissioners, and TR was lifted onto the national stage when he secured one of the new jobs.

[3] *sure political death if I supported him* . . . TR was wrong about this. His support of James Blaine in 1884, and his refusal to bolt the Republican Party that year with the independents he was ideologically sympathetic to, was a hardheaded political decision that laid a granite foundation for his entire political career. Had he bolted the G.O.P. in 1884 it is unlikely that he would have been able to secure the political appointments in the Harrison and McKinley administrations that pushed his career forward. Without these appointments, it is doubtful he could have reached the presidency, at least in the way he did. The years 1884 and 1912 are bookends that bracket TR's political career. In 1884 he chose to be a practical politician who was willing to accept the best possible, not the ideal. In 1912 he made the opposite choice, choosing idealism instead of expediency, and committed what was arguably the biggest mistake of his career.

[4] *I get so angry with the "Mugwumps"* . . . "Mugwump" was a word of derision used to describe the idealistic Republicans who bolted their party in 1884 after it nominated James Blaine as its candidate for president. These reform-minded progressives could not stomach Blaine, whose reputation was marred by charges of corruption, and instead supported the Democrat candidate, Grover Cleveland. Their action helped Cleveland win the presidency and angered many loyal Republicans, even those like TR who were sympathetic to their reform-minded agenda.

[5] *Mr. Hendricks, one of the arch-snakes* . . . Thomas Hendricks was a Democratic United States senator from Indiana during the Civil War. He became vice president when Grover Cleveland was elected in 1884.

GROVER CLEVELAND

[1] *I was a member of the legislature*... TR the Republican and Grover Cleveland the Democrat respected each other. Richard Olney, Cleveland's secretary of state, told this anecdote. "In 1893, when the question of choosing a President of the Civil Service Commission was presented to the Cabinet—every member of which was in favor of the promotion of Mr. Roosevelt, then a member of that body—President Cleveland was strongly opposed to this action, and said: 'I want to tell you gentleman now that you are making a mistake. I have known this young man Roosevelt since 1883, and I tell you that, without exception, he is the most ambitious man and the most consummate politician I have ever seen. However, as you all favor this nomination I will not oppose it. I only want you to bear my words in mind. The time will come when you will see that I am right'" (Collection, "Cleveland's Opinion of Men," *McClure's Magazine*, April 1909).

[2] *his rugged strength of character*... Henry Cabot Lodge also had a high opinion of Cleveland. He told James Ford Rhodes: "Cleveland... shines more than ever now that we have his Democratic successor [Woodrow Wilson] before us. Cleveland was a thoroughly patriotic man, honest and fearless. He was not a man, I think, of extraordinary abilities, but he was a real man, and his first thought was of his country when any great question arose" (Rhodes Papers, HCL to J. F. Rhodes, Feb. 5, 1920).

[3] *Mr. Olney is a very good fellow and a strong man*... Richard Olney was the strongest member of the cabinet during Cleveland's second term. As attorney general, Olney secured "writs of injunction" from federal courts to help put down the Pullman strike in 1894; and as secretary of state in 1895, he helped craft Cleveland's hawkish policy toward Britain during the Venezuelan crisis.

[4] *a man like Governor Altgeld of Illinois*... John Altgeld pardoned three anarchists convicted in the Haymarket bombing that occurred in Chicago in 1886. The bombing, which set off a riot and gunfire that cost the lives of police officers, occurred during a labor protest. Eight years later, in 1894, Governor Altgeld refused to allow federal troops into Illinois to put down riots that occurred during the Pullman Strike. The Haymarket bombing and the Pullman strike confirmed in TR's mind the existence of violent forces seething "beneath the social crust" and showed that what had happened in France after 1789 could occur in the United States during his own lifetime. He condemned leaders like Altgeld, seeing them as irresponsible radicals whose actions could recklessly provoke a revolution. He was at his cattle ranch in North Dakota during the Haymarket bombing. After he heard the news, he vented his fury in a letter to his sister: "My men here are hardworking, laboring men, who work longer hours for no greater wage than many of the strikers, but they are Americans through and through. I believe nothing would give them greater pleasure than a chance with their rifles at one of the mobs" (Letters, TR to ARC, May 15, 1886).

[5] *the admirable action of the Federal Government*...James Ford Rhodes's description of Cleveland's action in breaking the Pullman strike helps explain TR's praise.

Rhodes wrote: "In the railroad strikes of 1894 Cleveland . . . made a precedent in the way of interference for the supremacy of law and the maintenance of order. The Governor of Illinois would not preserve order, and the President determined that at all hazards riotous acts must be suppressed and law must resume its sway. In ordering United States troops to the scene of the disturbance without an application of the Legislature or Governor of Illinois he accomplished a fresh extension of executive power without an infraction of the Constitution" (*Historical Essays*, p. 225). Cleveland's willingness to act in the interests of big business was undoubtedly one reason TR felt Cleveland was to Wall Street "almost the ideal president."

BENJAMIN HARRISON

[1] *I did not mind Pearson's being turned out* . . . This refers to Henry Pearson, the postmaster of New York, turned out of office by President Harrison. Pearson was replaced by Cornelius Van Cott, whom TR described as the "ward politician being put in" Pearson's place.

[2] *I have Thompson as a colleague* . . . TR was one of three members of President Harrison's Civil Service Commission. His colleagues were Hugh Thomson and Charles Lyman.

[3] *both the President and Halford a little* . . . Elijah Halford was President Harrison's private secretary.

[4] *He is a genial little runt* . . . Henry Cabot Lodge's assessment of Benjamin Harrison was more generous. Lodge wrote to James Ford Rhodes: "In the case of Harrison, again you have done justice to a man who I think has been much underrated. His repellant manners led to a very unjust attitude toward the President himself. Harrison was a very able man. I remember Henry Adams saying to me at the time, that he was one of the ablest men who had been in the Presidency for many years, that is, excepting Lincoln, but that his manners had injured him" (Rhodes Papers, HCL to J. F. Rhodes, Feb. 5, 1920).

[5] *Wanamaker seems to be the only one of the cabinet* . . . John Wanamaker was a multimillionaire department store owner who became Harrison's postmaster general. In this role, Wanamaker fired thousands of postmasters in the federal service and replaced them with loyal Republicans, drawing the wrath of Civil Service reformers like TR.

[6] *The president sent to the Chilean government his ultimatum* . . . An independent Harrison acted boldly against the wishes of his more cautious secretary of state, James Blaine. Henry Cabot Lodge wrote to James Ford Rhodes: "As to Blaine's attitude in regard to Chile. He sent for me one Sunday morning. . . . I remember that morning very well. Blaine was greatly worked up over the whole thing. He thought the warlike attitude was a mistake, and I shall never forget the energy and vigor with which he spoke about it. At the time I was very much inclined to great sympathy with Harrison's attitude, but I was deeply impressed by Blaine's opposition to the extremities to which it had been carried" (Rhodes Papers, HCL to J. F. Rhodes, Feb. 5, 1920).

THE SPANISH-AMERICAN WAR

[1] *McKinley has no more backbone than a chocolate éclair* ... TR's anger at McKinley's vacillation after Americans were killed when the *Maine* blew up contrasts with the praise he showered on President Harrison for "his timely display of firmness" when dealing with Chile after American sailors had been killed by a mob. Although a U.S. Navy court of inquiry at the time determined that the *Maine* had been destroyed by a mine, it could not determine whether this was an aggressive act of Spain. Without the presence of a clear *casus belli*, McKinley's caution was in some sense justified, but this mattered little to TR, who wanted to go to war with Spain even before the *Maine* blew up. The cause of the explosion that sank the *Maine* remains shrouded in mystery to this day. The most recent investigation by the U.S. Navy, in 1976, concluded that an internal coal dust fire, not a mine, caused the explosion, but this finding is not accepted by all.

[2] *I am entitled to the Medal of Honor* ... TR's criticism of the War Department's handling of the Spanish-American War may have blocked the award of this medal, which he eventually received in 2001. Bestowing the posthumous Medal of Honor, President Clinton said on the occasion: "This is the thirty-seventh Medal of Honor I have presented, but the first I presented in the recipient's old office—(laughter)—in front of a portrait of him in full battle gear. It is a tradition in the Roosevelt Room that when a Democrat is in the White House, a portrait of Franklin Roosevelt hangs above the mantle, and when a Republican is here, Teddy Roosevelt occupies the hallowed spot. I chose to break with tradition these last eight years because I figured if we could have even half the luck and skill leading America into the twenty-first century that Theodore Roosevelt did in leading America into the twentieth century, our nation would do just fine."

[3] *In '98 there was almost for the first time an attitude of real and practical friendliness* ... Britain's support of the United States in the Spanish-American War is an important, and usually forgotten, turning point in American history. It marks the beginning of the so-called "special relationship" between the two nations. The change in TR's attitude toward Britain is a microcosm of this birth of mutual good feeling after more than a century of friction between the two great English-speaking nations. It is easy to forget that in 1895, only three years before the Spanish-American War, the United States and Britain nearly went to war themselves over a dispute in Venezuela. At that time, TR was eager to get to the front and join in the fight. He felt an affinity for Britain and had English friends, but he was not an Anglophile. After the Spanish-American War in 1898 his generally friendly attitude toward Britain increased dramatically, and it went to an even higher level when World War I began in 1914.

THEODORE ROOSEVELT

[1] *I have no right to the title of Excellency* ... These were not empty words. The sister of the historian James Ford Rhodes (Mark Hanna's wife) told her brother this story about TR's humility soon after he became president in 1901: "I wish I could

give you an adequate description while it is fresh in my mind of the dinner at the White House. . . . The guests, about fifty in number, assembled in the East Room, suddenly the band began to play, the doors opened, and in blew the President, with Mrs. Roosevelt trotting behind. The President, greeting everybody in the most cordial, hearty way, which is certainly very taking. . . . He turned to me saying . . .'you know, I am as nervous as a witch.' . . . Wasn't that refreshing? The very honesty, and candor, of the man, was delightful. It was so different from the old days [McKinley's administration] that I had been accustomed to it fairly took my breath away" (Rhodes Papers, Mrs. M. Hanna to J. F. Rhodes, 1901).

[2] *Browning's "Love among the Ruins"* . . . The last line of the poem is "Love is best."

[3] *I bounced forward with my umbrella* . . . This book would not be complete without this amusing Don Quixote–like moment where the sitting president of the United States saves a helpless kitten from two menacing dogs, and gives it as a gift to a young girl. He shared this funny little story in a letter he wrote to his daughter Ethel in June 1906.

[4] *I am interested in birds* . . . A passionate bird-watcher, TR always became excited when he saw rare birds. During a hunting trip to Louisiana in 1907, he wrote to the naturalist John Burroughs to tell him that "in a grove of giant cypress I saw two magnificent ivory-billed woodpeckers. I should be sorry to have missed them" (Papers, TR to J. Burroughs, Oct. 13, 1907). Only months before this sighting he wrote to Burroughs: "On May 18th near Keene, Albemarle County, Virginia, I saw a flock of a dozen passenger pigeons. I have not seen any for twenty-five years and never dreamed I should see any again, but I could not have been mistaken" (Papers, TR to J. Burroughs, May 23, 1907). Today, passenger pigeons are extinct. Ivory-billed woodpeckers were believed to have suffered the same fate, but during the last decade there have been credible sightings of this elusive bird, notably along the White and Cache rivers in Arkansas.

[5] *the Northern Securities case, one of the great achievements* . . . TR's decision to bring this antitrust lawsuit marks the birth of an activist federal government willing to proactively interfere in the economy to, in TR's words, "promote social and industrial justice." Andrew Jackson had taken a similar bold step in the 1830s, when he used executive power to dismantle the Bank of the United States, but Jackson's action decentralized economic power outward to the States, whereas TR's did exactly the reverse, increasing the power of the federal government over economic activity. In this sense, it is not a stretch to call TR the "father of big government."

[6] *would work more evil than good* . . . TR's fear of revolution and his desire to act before it occurred may have been influenced by Thomas Babington Macaulay, who wrote: "Revolutions are almost always the consequences of moral changes, which have gradually passed on the mass of the community, and which ordinarily proceed far before their progress is indicated by any public measure. An intimate knowledge of the domestic history of nations is therefore absolutely necessary to the prognosis of political events" (Macaulay, pp. 360–61). In these lines we see TR's own philosophy, namely, that the greatest statesmen were those who discerned the trend of events and acted accordingly.

[7] *The great bulk of my social friends*... A generation before Franklin Roosevelt was accused of being "a traitor to his class" for advocating progressive economic policies, TR was drawing similar ire from the members of the same privileged class.

[8] *a servile tool of his, Kennedy*... This is a reference to Archbishop Thomas Kennedy, rector of the American College in Rome. When TR's meeting with Pope Pius X failed to materialize and became a public controversy, Kennedy issued a statement to the press. He said that the Vatican had requested as a matter of "common courtesy" that TR not meet with the most objectionable Protestants in Rome during his visit to the city. The Holy See, Kennedy said, did not object to TR's meeting with Protestants; it objected just to those "anti-Papal elements" that had behaved in a "most aggressive and insulting manner" (*New York Times*, Apr. 7, 1910).

HENRY CABOT LODGE

[1] *I am devoted to Senator Lodge*... Ability and ambition fueled TR's career, but so did inherited wealth and personal connections. His great friend Henry Cabot Lodge, the consummate wire-puller, could always be counted on to intervene on TR's behalf to get him plum government jobs (notably as Civil Service commissioner in 1889 and assistant secretary of the Navy in 1897), and when TR was struggling financially in 1887, Lodge got him a book deal. John Torrey Morse recounts that story this way: "One summer forenoon I was sitting on my piazza at Prides Crossing when Cabot Lodge and Theodore Roosevelt appeared, and in due time suggested that if luncheon was soon to be ready they would be also. As we moved to the table, Lodge managed to pull me aside, and said: 'John, won't you give Theodore the life of Gouverneur Morris for the [American Statesmen] Series?' Astonished, I replied: 'But, Cabot, you surely don't expect Morris to be in the Series! He doesn't belong there.' Lodge shrugged his shoulders in something like assent, but said: 'You see, the fact is that just now Theodore has nothing to do—in a word, he needs the money.' A moment later we were engaged in our chairs, and before we left them Roosevelt was engaged to write the Morris" (*Proceedings of the Massachusetts Historical Society*, November 1931).

ANDREW CARNEGIE

[1] *they are singularly callous to the needs, sufferings, and feelings*... TR's efforts to promote the interests of "the plain people" (to use one of his favorite expressions) have been viewed by some as politically motivated, and by his harshest critics as outright demagoguery. TR unquestionably saw the electoral advantages of Jacksonian-style economic populism, but his feelings for the common man went beyond political considerations, as is shown in his thoughts before he became a national political figure. Newly married and only twenty-two years old, he made the following observation during his honeymoon in Europe in a private letter to his sister: "The Age of Chivalry was lovely for the knights, but it must have at times been inexpressibly gloomy for the gentlemen who had to occasionally act in the capacity of daily bread for their betters" (Letters, TR to ARC, Aug. 21, 1881).

WILLIAM RANDOLPH HEARST

[1] *Hearst and Brisbane are engaged in* ... Arthur Brisbane was the editor of the New York *Evening Journal*, owned by Hearst.

OLIVER WENDELL HOLMES

[1] *his great Phi Beta Kappa speech at Harvard* ... Oliver Wendell Holmes's speech given at Harvard on May 30, 1895, was called "A Soldier's Faith," and expressed ideas about the nobility of struggle and sacrifice that were similar to TR's own philosophy. A week after it was given TR declared his approval: "By Jove, that speech of Holmes' was fine" (Letters, TR to HCL, Jun. 5, 1895). Seeming to endorse the notion that it was noble to blindly sacrifice one's life as cannon fodder in battle, Holmes said: "I do not know what is true. I do not know the meaning of the universe. But in the midst of doubt, in the collapse of creeds, there is one thing I do not doubt, that no man who lives in the same world with most of us can doubt, and that is that the faith is true and adorable which leads a soldier to throw away his life in obedience to a blindly accepted duty, in a cause which he little understands, in a plan of campaign of which he has little notion, under tactics of which he does not see the use."

[2] *Holmes should have been an ideal man* ... The "bitter disappointment" TR refers to here was triggered by Holmes's dissent in the Northern Securities case, decided by a close 5-to-4 vote of the Supreme Court in the government's favor. TR and Holmes, on friendly terms before the decision of the court, grew distant afterward.

THOUGHTS ON OTHER NATIONS

[1] *a very beautiful miniature of John Hampden* ... The principle behind the war cry "No taxation without representation" did not originate in the American colonies; its antecedents could be found in the history of the mother country, in the life of John Hampden. TR admired Hampden, and often compared this English patriot of the seventeenth century to George Washington, because Hampden resisted King Charles I when Charles tried to impose taxes without the consent of Parliament. Hampden died in battle during the English Civil War, fighting, like Washington, for freedom from the arbitrary rule of an unelected ruler. For his efforts, he is remembered in English history as "Patriae Pater": "Father of the People."

[2] *Winston Churchill is a dreadful cad* ... Why did TR dislike Churchill? TR's daughter Alice said it was because of Churchill's bad manners when the two men met in December 1900, while TR was governor of New York and Churchill was on a lecture tour of the United States. Alice said Churchill refused to get up when older men or women came into the room as "he puffed on a cigar and was generally obnoxious." Alice hinted at a deeper competitive reason for her father's disdain, adding: "I always felt that if Winston and my father had been the same age, there would have been a terrific encounter between them, or a great friendship. One or the other. Both were Kiplingesque, both—what is now a bad word—jingoes" (*New York Times*, Aug. 6, 1967; *Saturday Evening Post*, Dec. 4, 1965). TR was forty-two

years old in 1900 when he met Churchill, who was only twenty-six. At that time, both men had recently achieved great celebrity status for warfare heroics—TR for charging up a hill in Cuba (July 1898) and Churchill for a daring escape when he was a prisoner of war in South Africa (December 1899). It is easy to understand how TR might have seen Churchill as a brash young intruder on his own glory.

WILLIAM HOWARD TAFT

[1] *Personally, I feel that what we did was worthwhile* . . . James Ford Rhodes gave a different verdict about TR's failed run for the presidency in 1912, writing: "What a pity that Roosevelt shall have broken up a great party on what seem now very trifling issues. Had he not done so, he would have been triumphantly elected President in 1916, taken the country into the European war at once and administered it much better than it was administered. He should not have gone to Brazil on a futile errand and got the disease which finally killed him" (Rhodes Papers, J. F. Rhodes to G. Trevelyan, Sep. 18, 1920). When we look back almost a century later at the presidential election of 1912, Rhodes's judgment appears sound. TR had little justification beyond a sense of personal injury to bolt from his party in 1912. Taft and party bosses may have stolen the nomination from him, but this did not mean that the nation was therefore in such grave danger that it desperately needed TR in the White House. As late as September 1911, TR declared to his son Ted that we "must not be blind to the fact that [Taft] is a better President than either Harrison or McKinley," two Republican presidents TR had heartily supported for reelection. Less than a year later TR forgot that Taft was not so bad, proclaiming: "We stand at Armageddon, and we battle for the Lord." In truth, it was not Armageddon. There was no crisis. Both Taft and Wilson accepted many parts of TR's progressive agenda, and Wilson, once elected, governed in many respects as a progressive. In this context, TR's actions in 1912 seem hysterical and self-serving. It was not his finest hour and, in a way, canceled out his praiseworthy decision to voluntarily relinquish presidential power in 1909. When he did that he acted in the spirit of Washington and Lincoln, but when he sought to regain power in 1912 he forfeited comparison to his heroes.

WORLD WAR I

[1] *The unhung traitor Keir Hardie* . . . Hardie was a Scottish version of Eugene Debs and one of the founding members of the Labour Party in Britain. A pacifist, he tried to organize a general strike of workers to end World War I. George Bernard Shaw also protested against the war, explaining why in his pamphlet *Common Sense about the War*, published in 1914. TR did not always condemn antiwar protesters, as is shown by his praise of Abraham Lincoln for protesting against the Mexican War. He reserved his condemnation for those who protested against what he believed were righteous wars, and to his mind World War I fell in that category.

SOURCE NOTES

How to Read the Source Notes: As described in the Introduction, the text of this book was, in some instances, created by splicing sentences or fragments of sentences together. A semicolon used within a source note indicates the point in my text where the splice was made. Put another way, each semicolon indicates that the words preceding it stand alone in the original source from which they were extracted. When an ellipsis appears, it means that there are more words in a stand-alone extract. When *no* ellipsis appears, there are no additional words in the extract. So, for example, in the following source note: There is no hold . . . ; It is; Pleasant going down the river . . . (Papers, TR to A. Roosevelt, Oct. 1, 1907), the words "It is" stand alone in the original source, in this case a letter TR wrote to his son Archie. The other references, "There is no hold . . . " and "Pleasant going down the river . . . " are separate extracts from the same letter that continue with additional words. To emphasize each stand-alone extract, I have capitalized the first word even if it is not capitalized in my own text within this book. So, in the example above, "Pleasant" is capitalized in the source note, but in my text it is lowercase as part of the sentence "It is pleasant going down the Mississippi."

Abbreviations: In the notes that follow, HCL refers to TR's friend Henry Cabot Lodge, and ARC refers to TR's sister Anna Roosevelt Cowles. In terms of research for this book, they were his most important correspondents. He wrote to them more often than anyone else, and what he wrote displayed a candor that is unmatched in letters he wrote to others.

ON WRITING HISTORY

3   How completely the old life . . . (Lodge Letters, TR to HCL, Dec. 26, 1912).

3   It is melancholy to . . . ; How the antelope . . . ; That on the Little Missouri . . . (Letters, TR to F. Selous, Nov. 23, 1900).

3   It was a pretty wild . . . ; The buffalo not yet . . . (Papers, TR to O. Wister, Mar. 16, 1899).

3   For a number of years I spent . . . (Works, Vol. 8, p. xliv).

3   My ranch was in North Dakota . . . (Letters, TR to F. Selous, May 18, 1897).

3   I was just in time to see . . . (Letters, TR to F. Selous, Nov. 30, 1897).

3   We guarded our herds . . .: In the valley of the . . . (Works, Vol. 8, p. xliv).

4   I think of it all . . . ; It is my first trip . . . ; After speaking at Keokuk . . . ; I of course felt . . . (Letters, TR to K. Roosevelt, Oct. 1, 1907).

4   There is no hold to . . . ; It is; Pleasant going down the . . . (Papers, TR to A. Roosevelt, Oct. 1, 1907).

4   The river is beautiful at least . . . (Letters, TR to E. Roosevelt, Oct. 1, 1907).

4   How wonderful in its rapidity . . . ; For a century its effects . . . ; Then the change came with a . . . (Letters, TR to K. Roosevelt, Oct. 1, 1907).

4   Of course our whole national history . . . (Works, Vol. 13, p. 337).

4   This expansion is not a matter of . . . (Works, Vol. 13, p. 476).

5   Under Washington and Adams we . . . (Works, Vol. 13, p. 338).

5   Andrew Jackson being the most . . . (Letters, TR to E. Wolcott, Sep. 15, 1900).

5   And then into Texas and California . . . (Works, Vol. 13, p. 338).

5   We have a magnificent empire west . . . (Papers, TR to G. Chamberlain, May 7, 1907).

5   I only wish one of my forefathers . . . ; in 1808 (Papers, TR to A. Weir, Mar. 28, 1899).

5   Gouverneur Morris (Works, Vol. 7, p. 237).

5   Thoroughly appreciated the marvelous . . . (Works, Vol. 7, p. 456).

5   United States (Works, Vol. 12, p. 244).

5   Writing in 1801 he says . . . (Works, Vol. 7, p. 456).

5   In all the history of mankind . . . ; Save only the preservation . . . (Works, Vol. 13, p. 454).

5   Our greatest statesmen have always been . . . (Works, Vol. 13, pp. 452-53).

5   I have been part of all that . . . (Letters, TR to R. Gilder, Jul. 19, 1888).

5   I heartily enjoy this life . . .: Limitless prairies rifle . . . (Letters, TR to HCL, Aug. 24, 1884) .

5   You would be amused to see . . . (Letters, TR to HCL, Aug. 12, 1884).

6   Every now and then . . . ; I used to hunt . . . (Letters, TR to E. Martin, Jul. 30, 1903).

6   Glory and honor give what . . . ; It is better for a nation . . . (Works, Vol. 12, pp. 283–84).

6   One of the prime dangers of civilization . . . (Works, Vol. 12, p. 76).

6   Unless we keep the barbarian . . . ; Oversentimentality, oversoftness; Washiness and mushiness . . . (Letters, TR to G.S. Hall, Nov. 29, 1899).

7   We believe in waging relentless war . . . (Works, Vol. 13, p. 18).

7   The man who does nothing . . . ; It is war-worn Hotspur spent . . . (Works, Vol. 13, p. 511).

7   Every public servant no matter how valuable . . . (Works, Vol. 17, p. 138).

7   Peace is not the end . . . (Works, Vol. 18, p. 206).

7   I do not want to see Christianity . . . (Presidential Addresses, Vol. 1, p. 460).

7   The non-resistance of the . . . ; Made me so angry . . . (Letters, TR to J.A. Riis, Sep. 2, 1897).

7   Christianity was saved in . . . ; From the hammer of . . . (Works, Vol. 18, pp. 314–15).

7   A politician who really serves his country . . . (Works, Vol. 13, p. 33).

8   Far better it is to dare mighty . . . (Works, Vol. 13, p. 321).

8   I feel we cannot too strongly insist . . . (Letters, TR to G. S. Hall, Nov. 29, 1899).

8   Peace is a goddess only when . . . (Works, Vol. 13, p. 183).

8   I do wish people would . . . ("The Gospel of Intelligent Work," The Chautauquan, Oct., 1899).

8   A number of women . . . ; Any teachers in . . . ; True teachers of . . . (Works, Vol. 18, pp. 62–63).

8   To learn anything from the past . . . (Works, Vol. 6, p. xxiv).

8   It is an absolute . . . ; Next to truth-telling . . . (Letters, TR to J. McCarthy, Mar. 15, 1900).

8   Many learned people seem to feel that . . . (Works, Vol. 12, p. 8).

8   In a very small way I have been . . . (Letters, TR to G. Trevelyan, Jan. 25, 1904).

9   The great historian; Has vision and imagination . . . (Works, Vol. 12, p. 11).

9   Not merely a huge string of . . . (Letters, TR to B. Wheeler, Feb. 27, 1900).

9   In any great work of literature . . . ; No quantity of photographs . . . (Works, Vol. 12, pp. 6–7).

9   If great events lack a great historian . . . (Works, Vol. 12, pp. 17–18).

9   History is not a panegyric (Works, Vol. 6, p. 229).

9   There are always men who consider it unpatriotic . . . (Works, Vol. 6, p. 226).

10   The greatest historian should also be a great. . . . (Works, Vol. 12, p. 13).

10   It is a wicked thing to be neutral between . . . (Works, Vol. 18, p. 206).

10   The best historian must of . . . ; All that is necessary . . . (Works, Vol. 12, p. 250).

10   I do not think partisanship should . . . (Letters, TR to M. Roosevelt, Sep 14, 1881).

10   It is sometimes the habit . . . (Collection, TR speech to Hamilton Club, Jan. 20, 1893).

10   Since I have been a boy and first studied the history . . . (Works, Vol. 11, p. 176).

10   The conquest of this . . . ; The establishment of national . . . (Works, Vol. 12, p. 247).

10   To me the history of the United States in . . . (*New York Times*, Dec. 3, 1893).

10   It is an excellent thing to study the history . . . (Works, Vol. 11, p. 205).

10   There are few things more important . . . (Papers, TR to S. Corwart, Jun. 22, 1903).

10   History taught for a directly and immediately . . . (Works, Vol. 12, p. 7).

10   I have now been in politics for a . . . (Papers, TR to F. Whitridge, Feb. 27, 1904).

10   I have had on occasion . . . ; In particular I have . . . (Papers, TR to G. Lorimer, May 12, 1906).

11   I claim to be a historian and I speak simply . . . (Works, Vol. 16, p. 227).

11   My literary work occupies a good . . . (Letters, TR to J. S. Van Duzer, Jan. 15, 1888).

11   My books so far . . . ; The Naval History of . . . (Letters, TR to F. Kruse, Apr. 6, 1891).

11   If I had time for literary work I would . . . (*Chicago Daily Tribune*, Jul. 19, 1900).

11   Do you know what I should really . . . ; I should like to get . . . ; Although a Republican politician . . . (Papers, TR to H. Thompson, May 16, 1901).

11   I think I have learned to be . . . (DeCoppet Collection, TR to M. Long, Dec. 14, 1887).

11   As regards most historical . . . (Papers, TR to W. Van Der Weyde, Aug. 21, 1918).

11   When I think of the . . . ; Years ago there are . . . (Letters, TR to A. White, Dec. 3, 1900).

11   As I grow older and less . . . (DeCoppet Collection, TR to M. Long, Dec. 14, 1887).

11   I wish I could persuade the general . . . (Letters, TR to G.H. Putnam, Sep. 11, 1896).

11   I am by inheritance and education a . . . (Works, Vol. 14, p. 40).

11   A gentleman told me recently that he . . . (Works, Vol. 14, p. 43).

11   Speaking quite dispassionately and . . . Letters, TR to HCL, Jul. 19, 1908.

11   The Democrats can be trusted to . . . (Letters, TR to W. Hubbell, Aug. 14, 1884).

12   I do congratulate myself that my father . . . (Letters, TR to J. Hay, Jul. 22, 1902).

12   Certainly I would prefer to go . . . ; We know that it is . . . (Works, Vol. 14, pp. 56–57).

12   As long as the history of our nation has lasted . . . (Works, Vol. 14, p. 13).

12   From Polk the mendacious through Pierce . . . (Works, Vol. 14, p. 19).

12   We have always had to . . . ; I do not propose to apologize . . . (Works, Vol. 14, pp. 20–21).

12   We are the party of . . . ; I think we can . . . ; It is the party . . . (Works, Vol. 14, pp. 13–14).

12   The Republican Party stands for; The national idea (HCL Letters, Vol. 1, p. 64).

12   In speaking to my own countrymen there is . . . (Works, Vol. 10, p. 360).

13   I believe and I feel most people . . . (Letters, TR to O. Howes, May 5, 1892).

13   The man in whom intense love of country . . . (Works, Vol. 12, p. 313).

13   The men who actually do . . . ; Yet there are small groups . . . ; To whom all this does . . . ; We produce some educated . . . (Works, Vol. 12, pp. 301–2).

13   Thank Heaven Henry James is now . . . (Lodge Papers, TR to HCL, Feb. 17, 1887).

13   The Americans who make their . . . (Collection, *Market World*, May 1908, pp. 11–12).

13   The acquisition of a species of . . . (Collection, *Market World*, May 1908, p. 13).

13   The man who becomes Europeanized . . . (Works, Vol. 13, p. 17).

13   These permanent exiles are too feeble a folk . . . (Works, Vol. 12, p. 302).

14   I am constitutionally incapable of . . . (Collection, *Market World*, April 1908, p. 5).

14   Being a healthy man with a brain . . . (Letters, TR to ARC, Jan. 30, 1887).

14   Books are the greatest of all . . . (Letters, TR to C. D. Willard, Oct. 28, 1911).

14   Ah I like books. . . . (*Chicago Daily Tribune*, Jul. 19, 1900).

14   I like to read better than anything else . . . (*New York Times*, Oct. 9, 1898).

14   I admit a liking for novels where . . . (Works, Vol. 3, p. 345).

14 I want ghosts who do things . . . (Butt, p. 88).

14 "The Turn of the Screw" (Papers, TR to G. Lodge, Apr. 30, 1906).

14 Kind of ghosts I want real sepulchral ghosts . . . (Butt, p. 88).

14 I am old-fashioned or sentimental . . . (Letters, TR to A. Rice, Feb. 4, 1904).

14 It is only the very exceptional . . . ; Of course I know . . . (Works, Vol. 3, pp. 345–46).

14 Have you seen that London . . . ; The book is simply . . . (Letters, TR to J.B. Matthews, Jun. 29, 1894).

14 There is a good deal of Browning . . . ; I don't care a rap . . . ; Love Among the Ruins . . . (Letters, TR to M. Dunn, Sep. 6, 1902).

15 The two great fiction . . . ; There are parts . . . (Letters, TR to C. Spring-Rice, Aug. 11, 1899).

15 A sexual degenerate (Letters, TR to L. Abbott, Jun. 17, 1908).

15 The man has a diseased mind . . . (Letters, TR to R. Grant, Sep. 1, 1904).

15 Kreutzer Sonata is a fit supplement . . . (Letters, TR to L. Abbott, Jun. 17, 1908).

15 When he again and again spends pages . . . (Letters, TR to ARC, Jun. 19, 1886).

15 Rudyard Kipling; Is a pleasant little man . . . (Letters, TR to ARC, Mar. 10, 1895).

15 An underbred little fellow with a tendency . . . (Letters, TR to ARC, Feb. 11, 1894).

15 I hope it is true that Kipling is not . . . (Letters, TR to J. Matthews, May 31, 1892).

15 It always interests me about Dickens . . . (Letters, TR to K. Roosevelt, Feb. 23, 1908).

16 Dickens was an ill-natured selfish . . . (Papers, TR to K. Roosevelt, Feb. 29, 1908).

16 I commend a careful reading of Martin Chuzzlewit . . . (Works, Vol. 16, p. 11).

16 Dickens; Remarked with hearty geniality . . . (Collection, *Market World*, April 1908, p. 8).

16 You will find it a real comfort . . . ; See what a well-meaning pessimist . . . ; But it is rank folly . . . (Works, Vol. 16, p. 11).

16 Unquestionably and very . . . ; After all taming . . . (Collection, *Market World*, May 1908, p. 12).

16 Edgar Allan Poe (Letters, TR to G. Trevelyan, Jan. 22, 1906).

16 Is our one super eminent genius . . . ; Even as sane a man as . . . (Butt, p. 124).

17 I have steadfastly . . . ; Where I have authority . . . (Papers, TR to J. La Farge, Jun. 9, 1907).

17 When I was President . . . ; Poet; Arlington Robinson out . . . (Letters, TR to A. Cochran, Feb. 4, 1915).

17 It was my son . . . ; I hunted him . . . ; I am free to say . . . (Letters, TR to J. Canfield, Aug. 16, 1905).

17 Just as Walt Whitman and . . . (Papers, TR to R. Gilder, Mar. 21, 1905).

17 A poet may do far more for a country . . . (Works, Vol. 13, p. 10).

17 It is a very great disadvantage . . . (DeCoppet Collection, TR to H. Scudder, Feb. 6, 1894).

17 Tolstoy wrote for mankind . . . (Works, Vol. 12, p. 318).

17   It is always better to be an original . . . (Works, Vol. 13, p. 18).

17   We must strike out for ourselves . . . (Letters, TR to J. B. Matthews, Jun. 29, 1894).

17   When that day comes . . . ; We shall use statues . . . (Works, Vol. 12, p. 318).

18   The answer the Neo-Greek or Roman . . . (Papers, TR to G. Wetmore, Feb. 22, 1912).

18   The names of many of our cities . . . (Collection, *Market World*, May 1908, p. 13).

18   As is natural we have won our greatest success . . . (Works, Vol. 11, pp. 282–83).

18   I know nothing at all . . . ; Perhaps the pictures . . . ; They; Interest me far . . . ; I have really . . . ; Rembrandt is by . . . (Letters, TR to C. Roosevelt, Aug. 24, 1881).

19   Life is a long campaign where every . . . (Letters, TR to G. Trevelyan, Mar. 9, 1905).

19   For the last six years . . . ; I have grown . . . (Letters, TR to F. Selous, Nov. 23, 1900).

19   I am feeling like a worn-out . . . (Papers, TR to W. Chanler, Jun. 23, 1906).

19   I am not in the least concerned . . . (Letters, TR to W. White, Nov. 28, 1906).

19   The life that is worth living . . . (Works, Vol. 13, p. 556).

19   What does the fact amount . . . ; That queer creature (Letters, TR to O. W. Holmes, Dec. 5, 1904).

19   Eugene Ware (Letters, TR to T. Roosevelt Jr., Mar. 1, 1903.)

19   Once wrote the following (Letters, TR to O. W. Holmes, Dec. 5, 1904.)

20   Be this as it may our duty is the . . . (Letters, TR to C. Spring-Rice, Mar. 12, 1900).

20   It is a good thing to die in the . . . (Letters, TR to C. Spring-Rice, Jul. 24, 1905).

20   When it comes our turn to go out . . . (Letters, TR to HCL, July 18, 1905).

20   There are many worse ways of ending . . . (Letters, TR to W. Chanler, Mar. 12, 1915).

20   Of course the finest of all epitaphs . . . (Letters, TR to G. F. R. Henderson, Feb. 14, 1899).

REVOLUTIONARY ERA (1776–1824)

23   I do not want to be misled by . . . (Letters, TR to G. O. Trevelyan, Nov. 11, 1907).

23   The American colonies revolted from . . . (Letters, TR to O. Gresham, Nov. 30, 1903).

23   The European theory of a colony . . . ; The colony was held . . . (Works, Vol. 10, p. 450).

23   The English and the Americans . . . ; England's treatment of . . . (Works, Vol. 7. pp. 243–244).

24   However admitting all that can be urged . . . (Works, Vol. 10, pp. 451–52).

24   Yet for all this . . . ; It is perfectly . . . ; But the chance . . . ; He fairly rivaled . . . (Works, Vol. 7. pp. 244–246).

24   Had England's King and . . . ; Wise statesmanship and . . . (Works, Vol. 10, p. 453).

24   English writers are fond . . . ; When the French court . . . (Works, Vol. 7. pp. 269–70).

25   I have studied history . . . ; Beyond all question . . . ; My forefathers Northerners . . . ; So I am not prejudiced . . . (Letters, TR to O. Wister, Apr. 27, 1906).

25 The Revolutionary leaders can never be too . . . (Works, Vol. 7. p. 270).

25 In the Civil War our people . . . (Letters, TR to O. Wister, Apr. 27, 1906).

25 If the Americans . . . ; And the outcome . . . ; As for the other . . . (Works, Vol. 7. p. 292).

26 It has been so habitual . . . ; We certainly have . . . ; A very slight . . . ; No Revolutionary regiment . . . ; None of the . . . ; The Light Brigade . . . (Works, Vol. 8, pp. 532–34).

26 Had the Americans of 1776 . . . ; The truth is that in . . . (Works, Vol. 7. pp. 270–71).

27 The war brought forth many hard fighters . . . (Works, Vol. 7. p. 314).

27 I have never felt that Cornwallis . . . (Letters, TR to G. O. Trevelyan, Nov. 11, 1907).

27 His being hemmed in and . . . (Letters, TR to HCL, Aug. 24, 1884).

27 Tarleton was a most dashing . . . (Letters, TR to G. O. Trevelyan, Nov. 11, 1907).

27 My admiration for that; Somewhat ruthless cavalryman . . . ; Men are apt to consider as cruel . . . (Letters, TR to G. O. Trevelyan, Jan. 1, 1908).

27 If a man is not decent then the abler . . . (*Atlanta Constitution*, Sep. 9, 1902).

28 What a base web was shot through the . . . (Letters, TR to G. Trevelyan, Jan. 1, 1908).

28 Now about (Letters, TR to W. Kimball, Nov. 19, 1897).

28 These; Bunker Hill; Cannon; We have Bunker Hill . . . ; To ask outright . . . ; I had not the . . . ; I suppose somewhere . . . ; I should think . . . (Papers, TR to W. Gompf, Jun. 4, 1908).

29 Great Britain had begun the struggle . . . ; Toward the close . . . ; In America; The day had gone conclusively . . . (Works, Vol. 7. pp. 312–13).

29 We had waged war against Britain . . . ; To conduct the negotiations . . . ; Congress in appointing . . . ; Jay promptly persuaded . . . ; Have been in the dust . . . ; There was much generous . . . ; The peace negotiations brought all this . . . (Works, Vol. 7. pp. 315–16).

30 He wished to establish the . . . ; America then was determined . . . ; Our true policy was admirably . . . ; Our statesmen won . . . (Works, Vol. 7. pp. 316–18).

31 The chief credit for the resulting diplomatic triumph . . . (Works, Vol. 9, p. 106).

31 Mr. Brander Matthews's volume on . . . ; No better little sketch . . . ("An Introduction To American Literature," *Bookman*, February 1896).

31 Benjamin Franklin (DeCoppet Collection, TR to H. Scudder, Feb. 6, 1894).

31 Has ever appeared . . . ("An Introduction to American Literature," *Bookman*, February 1896).

31 He wrote (Works, Vol. 12, p. 318).

31 "Humor indeed he had so abundantly" . . . (Matthews, p. 36).

32 I have written various historical . . . (Letters, TR to W. M. Van Der Weyde, Apr. 19, 1918).

32 When I wrote of Tom Paine . . . (Papers, TR to W. M. Van Der Weyde, Aug. 21, 1918).

32 The Life of Gouverneur (Letters, TR to F. Kruse, Apr. 6, 1891).

32 Over thirty years ago contains . . . (Papers, TR to W. M. Van Der Weyde, Aug. 21, 1918).

32   I was a very young man when I . . . (Papers, TR to M. M. Mangasarian, Apr. 11, 1918).

32   I wrote (Papers, TR to W. M. Van Der Weyde, Aug. 21, 1918).

32   One man had a very narrow escape . . . (Works, Vol. 7, p. 422).

33   Permit me to say that the word "atheist" . . . (Letters, TR to W. E. Warner, Feb. 1, 1900).

33   The only alteration I would . . . (Papers, TR to W. M. Van Der Weyde, Aug. 21, 1918).

33   "Atheist would have been" . . . (Letters, TR to W. M. Van Der Weyde, Apr. 19, 1918).

33   I think the kind of . . . ; From the standpoint . . . (Papers, TR to W. M. Van Der Weyde, Jul. 1, 1918).

33   I should myself of course . . . (Papers, TR to W. M. Van Der Weyde, Aug. 21, 1918).

33   I have no patience with those who attack . . . (Leary, pp. 66–67).

34   I am mighty weak on the Lutheran . . . (Letters, TR to W. H. Taft, Aug. 28, 1908).

34   I wonder if you recall one verse . . . (Leary, pp. 64–65).

34   The word; Filthy described with . . . (Letters, TR to W. E. Warner, Feb. 1, 1900).

34   The expression referred; To a visit Gouverneur Morris . . . ; The language of Morris . . . (Papers, TR to H. T. Bray, Feb. 4, 1916).

34   The quotation appears in . . . (Papers, TR to W. M. Van Der Weyde, Apr. 4, 1918).

34   If you will turn to Volume I . . . (Letters, TR to W. M. Van Der Weyde, Apr. 19, 1918).

34   The statement quoted . . . (Papers, TR to M. M. Mangasarian, Apr. 11, 1918).

35   A swine in a sty was physically . . . (Wister Papers, TR to O. Wister, Sep. 25, 1901).

35   I haven't the time to write . . . (Papers, TR to W. M. Van Der Weyde, Jul. 1, 1918).

35   I think Paine was a man who . . . (Papers, TR to M. M. Mangasarian, Apr. 11, 1918).

36   As a nation we have had our full share . . . (Works, Vol. 13, p. 500).

36   Washington alike statesman . . . ; Of Americans Lincoln . . . (Works, Vol. 7, p. 271).

36   I think you will find that the fundamental difference . . . (Works, Vol. 11, p. 333).

36   Washington created the Rebublic . . . (Works, Vol. 11, p. 331).

36   Washington was the Revolution (Letters, TR to S. Eaton, Jun. 29, 1901).

36   Without Washington we should probably never . . . (Works, Vol. 13, p. 3).

37   After the American Revolution Washington's . . . (Works, Vol. 10, p. 249).

37   If when that most imbecile of Congresses . . . (Butt Letters, pp. 124–26).

37   I should like to have continued as . . . (Letters, TR to William II, Dec. 26, 1908).

37   In my own case . . . ; Nine-tenths of my reasoning . . . ; There was every justification . . . ; Of course there are those . . . (Butt Letters, pp. 124–26).

38   Only a very limited amount of the success . . . (Works, Vol. 13, p. 574).

38   Washington was not a genius . . . (Butt Letters, pp. 124–26).

38   He was just the average man . . . ; It isn't genius that does big . . . (Hale, pp. 148–49).

38   Washington was not even excepting Lincoln . . . (Letters, TR to HCL, Aug. 24, 1884).

38   Many of us read with a . . . ; In Macmillan's Magazine for . . . ; Lord Wolseley speaks a good deal . . . (Collection, *Market World*, April 1908, pp. 5–6).

39   As a mere military man Washington himself . . . (Works, Vol. 7, p. 271).

39   It may interest his lordship . . . ; To compare; Lee; To Washington who was . . . ; Absurd; Washington's main difficulties . . . (Collection, *Market World*, April 1908, p. 6).

39   With the short-sighted and sour jealousies . . . (Works, Vol. 10, pp. 478–79).

39   If Washington had been backed . . . (Collection, *Market World*, April 1908, p. 6).

39   Washington would not let his officers try . . . (Works, Vol. 10, p. 250).

40   A strong nation can only be saved by itself . . . (Works, Vol. 10, pp. 334–35).

40   Washington's Farewell Address . . . ; No American should . . . (Works, Vol. 19, p. 49).

40   In this fortunate country of ours liberty . . . (Papers, TR to J. Ireland, Jun. 1, 1907).

40   Washington; Demanded a national morality based . . . ; In his Farewell Address . . . ; Washington lacked Lincoln's gift of words . . . (Works, Vol. 19, p. 133).

41   It is impossible to estimate too highly . . . (Works, Vol. 8, pp. 532–33).

42   Alexander Hamilton stands in the very first class . . . (Works, Vol. 7, p. 246).

42   Hamilton's extraordinary career of usefulness . . . (Works, Vol. 11, p. 189).

42   I have recently been reading a book (Letters, TR to E. Root, Aug. 18, 1906).

42   The best life of Alexander Hamilton . . . (Papers, TR to K. Grahame, Jun. 20, 1907).

42   By an Englishman named Oliver . . . (Letters, TR to E. Root, Aug. 18, 1906).

42   It is little short of a scandal . . . (Papers, TR to F. Collins, Feb. 7, 1908).

42   The man of most brilliant mind . . . ; Whom we have ever . . . (Works, Vol. 19, p. 473).

42   As great a cabinet officer as we have . . . (Letters, TR to A. Carnegie, Feb. 18, 1910).

43   Hamilton; Had about him that "touch of the purple" . . . (Works, Vol. 7, p. 237).

43   The touch of the heroic; The touch of the gallant . . . (Letters, TR to G. Morris, Nov. 23, 1910).

43   That mighty leader of thought . . . ; Was not even born in this country . . . (Collection, Hamilton Club Speech, Jan. 20, 1893).

43   Do you know how . . . ; Refused to support . . . (Letters, TR to P. Tucker, Oct. 22, 1895).

43   The biggest and most beneficial . . . ; When Alexander Hamilton made a deal . . . (Letters, TR to T. Roosevelt Jr., Aug. 23, 1910).

43   Hamilton; Was a struggling man of moderate . . . ; Marshall; Neither had in him one touch of the demagogue . . . (Works, Vol. 11, p. 191).

44   Hamilton embodied what was best in the . . . (Letters, TR to G. Morris, Nov. 23, 1910).

44   Hamilton the most brilliant American statesmen . . . (Works, Vol. 10, pp. 485–86).

44   They were men of singularly noble . . . ; Hamilton born out of New York . . . ; Jay lacked Hamilton's brilliant audacity . . . (Works, Vol. 10, p. 489).

44   As soon as the project . . . ; He was the greatest man . . . ; The cold suspicious

temper . . . ; Nevertheless Hamilton won . . . ; Finally he crowned . . . (Works, Vol. 10, pp. 486–87).

45   It needed all of Hamilton's wonderful genius . . . (Works, Vol. 7, p. 344).

45   After Washington the greatest . . . ; Throughout the country . . . (Works, Vol. 10, p. 498).

45   Hamilton of course was the leader of his party . . . (Works, Vol. 10, p. 489).

45   Four-fifths of the talent and ability . . . (Works, Vol. 7, p. 443).

45   The Federalists upheld the honor and interest . . . (Works, Vol. 11, p. 195).

46   The Federalists were split into two factions . . . (Works, Vol. 7, p. 444).

46   In spite of the jarring . . . ; It was in New York . . . ; Actually proposed to Jay . . . (Works, Vol. 7, pp. 447–48).

46   In the electoral college Jefferson and Burr . . . (Works, Vol. 10, p. 493).

46   In a government such as ours . . . (Works, Vol. 7, p. 443).

47   The great Federalist Party fell from power . . . (Works, Vol. 10, p. 492).

47   I have not much sympathy with . . . ; That the highly cultivated . . . ; And the moneyed classes . . . (Letters, TR to Frederick Scott Oliver, Aug. 9, 1906).

47   Hamilton was a statesman rather than a politician (Works, Vol. 10, p. 492).

47   Hamilton's admirers are apt to speak . . . ; This is a very rough-and-tumble . . . ; Unconsciously carried out . . . (Letters, TR to Frederick Scott Oliver, Aug. 9, 1906).

48   Over a century ago in the days of . . . (Letters, TR to P. Girouard, Jul. 21, 1910).

48   We never have accomplished anything . . . ; The Hamiltonians and Jeffersonian . . . (Papers, TR to F. E. McGovern, Aug. 4, 1911).

49   The far Northwest; Was won; By the arms and . . . ; by the victory . . . (Works, Vol. 9, p. 209).

49   The lands became part of the Federal domain . . . (Works, Vol. 9, p. 212).

49   It remained for Congress to determine . . . (Works, Vol. 9, p. 214).

49   The Ordinance of 1787 was so . . . ; The sixth and most . . . (Works, Vol. 9, pp. 218–19).

50   Like so many other great . . . ; The slave question was . . . (Works, Vol. 9, pp. 221–22).

51   The national convention to form . . . ; Among the delegates . . . (Works, Vol. 7, pp. 323–24).

51   The statesmen who met in 1787 . . . ; They were emphatically good men . . . ; They were resolute to free themselves . . . (Works, Vol. 7, p. 325).

51   All our great men saw the absolute need . . . (Works, Vol. 7, p. 320).

51   It was all-important that there should be a Union . . . (Works, Vol. 7, p. 342).

51   The Revolution had left behind . . . ; The task of building up . . . (Works, Vol. 9, p. 94).

51   Long before the Revolutionary War . . . ; The best and wisest men . . . ; The outbreak of armed rebellion . . . (Works, Vol. 10, pp. 484–85).

54   No sooner was peace declared . . . (Works, Vol. 7, p. 319).

54   Their leaders were; Designing politicians who feared that . . . (Works, Vol. 7, p. 321).

54   Henry himself made one slip when he opposed . . . (Works, Vol. 9, p. 103).

54   But the usefulness of each of the other two . . . (Works, Vol. 7, p. 321).

54   The difficulties for the convention to surmount . . . (Works, Vol. 7, p. 329).

54   Morris believed in letting the United States . . . (Works, Vol. 7, p. 331).

55   The fierce little Palmetto State . . . ; The brilliant little group . . . (Works, Vol. 7, p. 445).

55   Serious struggle took place . . . ; Recognized it as a terrible . . . (Works, Vol. 7, p. 339).

55   Some of the high-minded Virginian statesmen . . . ; Vigorous; In their denunciation . . . ; The Virginians were opposed to the . . . (Works, Vol. 7, pp. 340–41).

56   It was better to limit . . . ; No man who supported . . . ; The crazy talk . . . (Works, Vol. 7, pp. 342–43).

56   Had the slavery interest been in the least . . . (Works, Vol. 7, pp. 343–44).

56   If the Constitution of . . . ; Had declared for . . . ; It would never have . . . (Works, Vol. 10, p. 307).

56   The fierceness of the opposition to the adoption . . . (Works, Vol. 7, p. 343).

56   The men who opposed the adoption of the . . . (Works, Vol. 10, p. 485).

56   Recollect that the strongest . . . ; We got our Constitution . . . (Works, Vol. 14, p. 35).

57   The Jeffersonian or anti-national opponents . . . (Works, Vol. 11, p. 193).

57   The doctrinaires to the contrary notwithstanding . . . (Works, Vol. 7, p. 331).

57   Hamilton; Said a government ought to contain in itself . . . (Works, Vol. 17, p. 87).

58   Gouverneur Morris; Was too unstable and erratic to leave . . . (Works, Vol. 7, p. 237).

58   Imperious light-hearted . . . ; Occasionally he showed . . . (Works, Vol. 7, p. 309).

59   It is a painful thing to have to record . . . (Works, Vol. 7, p. 459).

59   In fact throughout the War of 1812 . . . (Works, Vol. 7, p. 464).

59   The men who opposed the War of 1812 . . . (Works, Vol. 13, p. 187).

59   The utter weakness and folly of Jefferson's second term . . . (Works, Vol. 7, p. 457).

59   Though one of the founders of the Constitution . . . (Works, Vol. 7, p. 459).

59   He sneered at . . . ; Morris's opposition to . . . ; Singularly forgetful of his . . . ; He found space . . . ; He actually advocated . . . ; He thus advanced . . . (Works, Vol. 7, pp. 462–63).

60   He was an exceptionally able man . . . (Works, Vol. 7, p. 464).

60   We have never had a foreign minister who deserved . . . (Works, Vol. 7, p. 425).

60   As minister to France he successfully performed . . . (Works, Vol. 7, pp. 469–70).

60   His two years' history as minister forms . . . (Works, Vol. 7, p. 402).

60   Morris was the only foreign minister who remained . . . (Works, Vol. 7, pp. 415–16).

60   He stayed at the risk of his life . . . (Works, Vol. 7, p. 402).

60   Once or twice in the popular tumults . . . (Works, Vol. 7, pp. 415–16).

60   Few foreign ministers have faced such difficulties . . . (Works, Vol. 7, pp. 402–3).

61   Writing to a friend who was especially hostile to . . . (Works, Vol. 7, p. 423).

61   His horror of the base mob . . . (Works, Vol. 7, pp. 404–5).

61   The shelter of Morris's house . . . ; An American gentleman who was in . . . ; As his visitor was leaving . . . ; Whether my house will be a . . . (Works, Vol. 7, pp. 406–7).

62   As an American statesman he has many rivals ... (Works, Vol. 7, p. 346).

62   No other American of note has left us writings ... (Works, Vol. 7, p. 350).

62   Like most men of strong character ... (Works, Vol. 7, p. 361).

62   He enjoyed the life of . . . ; The authors philosophers . . . (Works, Vol. 7, pp. 364–65).

64   The French Revolution was ... ; In all really free ... ; The then existing ... (Works, Vol. 7, p. 347).

64   With a people who made up in fickle ferocity ... (Works, Vol. 7, p. 392).

64   There was never another great struggle ... (Works, Vol. 7, p. 349).

65   The days of Danton and Robespierre are not days ... (Works, Vol. 7, p. 410).

65   Before the Bastille fell; The people who had most at stake . . . (Works, Vol. 7, p. 373).

65   In writing to Washington (Works, Vol. 7, p. 357).

65   Gouverneur Morris (Works, Vol. 7, p. 237).

65   Painted the outlook in colors ... ; Everybody agrees that there ... ; It is however from such crumbling . . . ; The great mass of the common . . . (Works, Vol. 7, pp. 357–58).

65   Looking at the maddening mob ... (Works, Vol. 7, p. 404).

66   Said Morris: "Since I have been in this country" ... (Works, Vol. 7, p. 407).

66   The people who five years ... ; A kind of opera ... ; Those individuals of ... (Works, Vol. 7, pp. 422–23).

66   The popular party in France composed ... (Works, Vol. 7, p. 347).

66   The sentimental humanitarians who always form ... (Works, Vol. 7, p. 352).

66   The wild friends of the French Revolution ... (Works, Vol. 7, p. 347).

66   The scenes that passed were literally beyond ... (Works, Vol. 7, pp. 408–9).

67   Most of the men of our little world . . . ; The abuses of the old . . . ; The Second Republic ... ; In the end ... ; When it fell ... (Papers, TR to G. Cushing, Feb. 27, 1908).

67   If we put in power mere ... ; To let wealthy men ... (Papers, TR to G. Davis, Oct. 29, 1906).

68   There are plenty of ... ; It is well for the men ... (Letters, TR to W. Dodd, Jan. 31, 1907).

69   The three men to whom throughout our national ... (Works, Vol. 17, p. 80).

69   John Marshall (Works, Vol. 11, p. 190).

69   Marshall is the one man whose services to the nation ... (Works, Vol. 17, p. 80).

69   He is distinctly among the greatest of ... (Papers, TR to A. Moses, May 16, 1900).

69   Marshall's permanent greatness was not ... (Papers, TR to A. Spring, Jul. 9, 1906).

69   Marshall was in a real sense ... ; The greatest of the ... (Works, Vol. 11, pp. 260–61).

69   I should put the name of Marshall ... (Papers, TR to A. Moses, May 16, 1900).

69   Marshall's career of greatness and usefulness ... (Works, Vol. 11, p. 189).

70   The office of Chief Justice is under some ... (Works, Vol. 17, p. 80).

70   Under Marshall the Supreme Court of the ... (Works, Vol. 17, p. 86).

70   The Court in his time and while it responded . . . (Works, Vol. 11, pp. 260–61).

70   Marshall performed a great and needed service . . . (Works, Vol. 17, p. 375).

70   There is no need of discussing the question . . . (Works, Vol. 17, p. 84).

70   The American judges who have left their mark . . . (Works, Vol. 11, p. 191).

70   When Marshall was appointed; It was usually assumed . . . ; No one at the time . . . ; For the first fourteen years . . . ; But Marshall in his first . . . ; Held that the Supreme Court . . . ; No such power was expressly . . . ; It was not the adoption . . . (Works, Vol. 17, pp. 85–86).

71   The reason why Marshall was so great . . . (Works, Vol. 17, pp. 86–87).

71   He stands among the men who actually . . . (Works, Vol. 11, p. 189).

71   Marshall the champion of the Constitution . . . (Works, Vol. 11, p. 193).

71   A wise court will recognize that . . . (Letters, TR to W. H. Moody, Sep. 21, 1907).

72   If we interpret the Constitution . . . ; And Hamilton we as a . . . (Works, Vol. 16, p. 71).

72   Both law and life are to be considered . . . (Works, Vol. 17, p. 137).

72   We are now entering on a period when . . . (Works, Vol. 11, p. 262).

72   John Marshall came of the . . . ; Marshall himself was in . . . (Works, Vol. 11, p. 190).

72   The majority of the men who had done the real . . . (Works, Vol. 11, p. 194).

72   Marshall was an entirely democratic man . . . (Works, Vol. 11, p. 191).

73   He earned his living . . . ; As a lawyer he . . . ; He relied on his . . . (Works, Vol. 11, p. 190).

73   This is an admirable . . . ; Marshall practiced law . . . ; Served a term . . . (Works, Vol. 11, pp. 191–92).

73   With most of our great statesmen . . . (Letters, TR to W. E. Dodd, Feb. 13, 1912).

73   Marshall; Did not work for the great . . . (Letters, TR to W. H. Moody, May 18, 1916).

75   Thank Heaven I have never . . . (Letters, TR to Frederick Scott Oliver, Aug. 9, 1906).

75   I feel that while one should . . . (Letters, TR to Frederick Jackson Turner, Nov. 4, 1896).

75   I am a strong anti-Jeffersonian (TR to George Haven Putnam, Aug. 9, 1906).

75   The more I study Jefferson . . . (Letters, TR to Henry Cabot Lodge, Sep. 21, 1907).

75   Many who get discouraged by the attitude of . . . (Clowes, p. 7).

75   Of course I am simply . . . ; Tolerated Jefferson and Madison . . . (Lodge Letters, Vol. 2, p. 489).

75   I think Thomas Jefferson's election . . . (Letters, TR to J. Strachey, Oct. 25, 1906).

76   The country suffered for at least two generations . . . (Lodge Letters, Vol. 2, p. 224).

76   The people that do harm in the end are not the . . . (Works, Vol. 14, p. 6).

76   We are naturally prone . . . ; Jefferson has been . . . (Letters, TR to Albert Bushnell Hart, Jun. 1, 1915).

76   I think Jefferson on the whole . . . ; In the second place . . . (Letters, TR to F. Oliver, Aug. 9, 1906).

76   In 1803 under President Jefferson . . . (Letters, TR to E. Wolcott, Sep. 15, 1900).

76   While I am a Jeffersonian in my genuine . . . (Letters, TR to W. Potter, Apr. 23, 1906).

77   What I chiefly object to in Jefferson is his . . . (Letters, TR to W. Trent, Apr. 20, 1897).

77   History has not yet done justice to the . . . (Works, Vol. 6, p. xxxvii).

77   We suffered disgrace after disgrace while the losses . . . (Works, Vol. 6, p. 8).

77   Jomini has left on record the contemptuous surprise . . . (Clowes, p. 147).

77   The small British army marched at will through . . . (Works, Vol. 6, p. xxxvii).

77   American historians; Usually condemn; Without stint; The army of Ross and Cockburn; But by right they should keep . . . (Works, Vol. 9, p. 346).

77   We dislike reprobate and if possible punish the . . . (Works, Vol. 12, p. 279).

77   Ever since the Federalist Party had gone out . . . (Works, Vol. 6, p. 373).

78   Jefferson who never understood . . . ; Belonged to the visionary . . . (Works, Vol. 9, p. 232).

78   Jefferson though a man whose . . . ; Without the prudence to avoid . . . (Works, Vol. 6, p. 373).

78   A class of professional non-combatants . . . ; In the long run a Quaker . . . (Works, Vol. 7, p. 26).

78   Jefferson was not a fighting man (Works, Vol. 18, p. 141).

78   But unfortunately the nation lacked the wisdom . . . (Clowes, p. 6).

78   Had Jefferson and the other leaders of popular opinion . . . (Clowes, p. 23).

78   Though he led the people . . . ; The President the Congress and . . . (Clowes, pp. 19–20).

79   The wrongs inflicted on our . . . ; Any innocent merchant . . . ; If a captain . . . (Works, Vol. 6, p. 4).

79   Instead of declaring war . . . ; Jefferson could not . . . ; The temper of Jefferson's . . . (Clowes, p. 20).

79   A preposterous system of what may be called . . . (Clowes, p. 7).

80   For a variety of reasons . . . ; It does not seem that they . . . (Works, Vol. 6, p. 165).

80   The failure of the gunboats ought to have taught . . . (Works, Vol. 6, p. 182).

80   The separatist feeling has at times . . . ; Calhoun and Pickering . . . ; Nevertheless they warred against the . . . ; Even when their motives . . . (Works, Vol. 9, pp. 95–96).

81   It is well indeed for our land that we of this . . . (Works, Vol. 7, p. 458).

81   Virginia stands easily first . . . ; Washington and Marshall to the . . . (Works, Vol. 7, p. 445).

81   When in 1798 Virginia was preparing . . . (Collection, *Market World*, April 1908, p. 6).

81   The famous Alien and Sedition law were exciting . . . (Works, Vol. 7, p. 444).

81   Patrick Henry opposed the motion . . . (Letters, TR to Oscar Hallam, May 2, 1911).

81   The State's greatest orator; Henry halted beside the grave . . . (Works, Vol. 7, p. 445).

81   A generation later (Letters, TR to E. Grey, Nov. 15, 1912).

81   During; Jackson's presidential terms (Works, Vol. 7, p. 58).

81   Old Hickory (Papers, TR to O. Read, Aug. 13, 1906).

81   And his adherents were engaged . . . ; Struggles with the Nullifiers . . . (Works, Vol. 7, p. 58).

81   At this time it is not necessary to discuss nullification . . . (Works, Vol. 7, pp. 62–63).

82   The nullification movement in South . . . ; Had nothing to do . . . (Works, Vol. 7, p. 58).

82   The South Carolinian statesmen; Proclaimed the doctrine of nullification . . . ; Jefferson was quoted as the father . . . ; The Nullifiers were correct . . . ; He used the word nullify . . . (Works, Vol. 7, p. 62).

82   The authors of the Kentucky and Virginia Resolutions . . . (Works, Vol. 9, p. 137).

82   Heaven knows how cordially I despise Jefferson . . . (Letters, TR to W. Moody, Sep. 21, 1907).

82   Hamilton and the Federalists fell from power . . . (Works, Vol. 7, p. 327).

83   I have always regarded Jefferson in spite of . . . (Letters, TR to A. Hart, Jun. 1, 1915).

83   The extreme doctrinaires who are fiercest in . . . (Works, Vol. 7, pp. 322–23).

83   It is a mistake to suppose that there was a . . . (Letters, TR to C. Older, Jun. 12, 1911).

83   I believe that the French revolutionists . . . (Letters, TR to C. Willard, Apr. 28, 1911).

83   We are naturally democratic as a people . . . (Letters, TR to A. Hart, Jun. 1, 1915).

83   The one great reason for our having succeeded . . . (Works, Vol. 7, p. 323).

83   The absolute terror with which even moderate . . . (Works, Vol. 7, pp. 450–51).

83   The Jeffersonians with all their unwisdom and . . . (Works, Vol. 9, p. 435).

84   Had embodied principles so wholly absurd in . . . (Works, Vol. 7, pp. 451–52).

84   I have no use for the Hamiltonian who . . . (Letters, TR to W. White, Feb. 19, 1909).

84   I have never cared in the least for the . . . (Letters, TR to J. Belford, Apr. 30, 1910).

84   That slippery demagogue (Letters, TR to T. Roosevelt Jr., Aug. 23, 1910).

84   That popular idol (Papers, TR to K. Roosevelt, Dec. 2, 1914).

84   Jefferson had behind him the mass of the people . . . (Works, Vol. 7, p. 47).

84   Was less fit to conduct the country . . . (Papers, TR to K. Roosevelt, Dec. 2, 1914).

84   The scholarly timid and shifty doctrinaire who supplanted . . . (Works, Vol. 7, p. 48).

84   Was politically very successful . . . ; But this will not . . . (Letters, TR to A. Hart, Jun. 1, 1915).

84   The twelve years' history of Washington's and Adams's . . . (Works, Vol. 10, p. 488).

84   The men who favored the adoption of the Constitution . . . (Works, Vol. 18, p. 312).

84   Opposed it and wished to construe it as narrowly . . . (Works, Vol. 10, p. 488).

84   The Jeffersonians; Believed in a government so weak . . . (Works, Vol. 9, p. 418).

85   The various bodies of men who afterward . . . ; Republican Party were frantically . . . ; At this period Genet was . . . ; Kentucky was ripe for . . . (Works, Vol. 9, pp. 403–4).

85   Genet immediately commissioned Clark . . . ; They got some supplies . . . ; Jefferson's course in the matter . . . (Works, Vol. 9, pp. 405–6).

85   I cannot imagine it possible for Jefferson . . . (Letters, TR to F. Turner, Nov. 4, 1896).

86   The mass of the Jeffersonians put the . . . (Letters, TR to F. Moore, Feb. 9, 1898).

86   Jefferson; Was the underhanded but malignantly bitter . . . (Works, Vol. 11, pp. 191–92).

86   The campaign he carried on against Washington . . . (Letters, TR to W. Dodd, Feb. 13, 1912).

86   Partly owing to the adroit and successful demagogy . . . (Works, Vol. 11, p. 192).

86   Isn't it humiliating to realize that . . . ; Should have been as President . . . ; Should have petitioned him to serve . . . (Letters, TR to W. Moody, Sep. 21, 1907).

86   Jefferson led the people wrong and . . . (Letters, TR to F. Oliver, Aug. 9, 1906).

86   It was the work of Washington and Hamilton . . . (Letters, TR to C. Eliot, Sep. 13, 1906).

86   The Jeffersonian Republican Party . . . ; But on the vital question . . . (Works, Vol. 9, pp. 434–35).

87   So it was with the acquisition of Louisiana (Works, Vol. 9, p. 467).

87   This purchase was the greatest instance of expansion . . . (Works, Vol. 15, p. 131).

87   Jefferson Livingston and their fellow statesmen . . . ; No American settlers were thronging into . . . ; The winning of Louisiana was due to . . . (Works, Vol. 9, pp. 466–67).

88   We were bound to have Louisiana . . . (Works, Vol. 7, p. 453).

88   The vast region that was then known as . . . (Works, Vol. 9, p. 469).

88   The Spanish rulers realized fully . . . ; It was at this time . . . ; The need of the Spaniards . . . (Works, Vol. 9, pp. 472–73).

88   Jefferson was President and Madison . . . ; It was these two timid . . . ; Jefferson was the least warlike . . . ; Jefferson was forced to tell his French . . . (Works, Vol. 9, pp. 474–75).

89   Jefferson took various means official . . . ; It was no argument of Jefferson's . . . ; Napoleon could not afford to hamper himself . . . (Works, Vol. 9, pp. 479–80).

89   The ratification of the treaty brought on sharp . . . (Works, Vol. 9, p. 483).

90   The earliest and most important . . . ; The explorers were . . . (Works, Vol. 9, pp. 503–4).

90   Beyond the Mississippi all that was . . . ; The headwaters of the Missouri . . . ; What lay beyond them and . . . (Works, Vol. 9, pp. 502–3).

90   The two officers chosen to carry through the work . . . (Works, Vol. 9, p. 504).

90   These two hardy and daring . . . ; Opened the door . . . ; A great deed (Works, Vol. 9, p. 516).

90   No man had ever crossed or . . . ; They pointed the way . . . ; (Works, Vol. 9, p. 509).

90   Later on (Works, Vol. 7, p. 466).

90   Lewis was made governor of Louisiana Territory . . . (Works, Vol. 9, pp. 516–17).

91   Jefferson stood for many ideas which in their actual . . . (Works, Vol. 9, pp. 108).

92   We have never had in the presidential chair . . . (Works, Vol. 13, pp. 309–10).

92   Have you ever read Burr's journal . . . (Letters, TR to S. Harper, Sep. 12, 1906).

92   In New York Aaron Burr; Led a political career as . . . ; His career had been . . . ; As friend or as enemy . . . ; He had shown himself as adroit . . . ; Then his open enemies . . . (Works, Vol. 9, p. 488).

92   The Clintonians and Livingstons; Reduced Burr's influence in the Democratic . . . ; Receiving the hearty support of . . . ; He was not renominated . . . ; Morgan Lewis was nominated . . . (Works, Vol. 10, p. 496).

93   Hamilton grew to regard him with especial dislike . . . (Works, Vol. 10, p. 490).

93   Burr was now a ruined . . . ; In 1804 after his defeat . . . (Works, Vol. 10, pp. 496–97).

94   Shifty and fertile in expedients; His local prestige; Ruined; Aaron Burr; Turned his restless eyes . . . ; He had already been . . . ; A particularly spectacular adventurer (Works, Vol. 9, pp. 488–89).

94   Burr; Was ready to go into either the . . . (Letters, TR to S. Harper, Sep. 12, 1906).

94   Such events as Burr's conspiracy; Cannot be properly . . . (Works, Vol. 9, p. 401).

94   There have always been plenty who took part in or . . . (Works, Vol. 7, p. 467).

94   Burr had been Vice President . . . ; His conspiracy was merely . . . (Works, Vol. 9, pp. 401–2).

94   In 1803 Aaron Burr of . . . ; There are; Very few of our statesmen . . . (Works, Vol. 7, pp. 467–68).

94   The moral difference between Benedict Arnold on the . . . (Works, Vol. 7, p. 106).

95   At present treason like adultery ranks as one of the . . . (Works, Vol. 13, p. 17).

95   In spite of Burr's personal courage . . . ; His wild schemes had . . . (Works, Vol. 9, p. 490).

95   Burr; Was put on trial for high treason with Wilkinson . . . (Works, Vol. 9, p. 501).

95   In the matter of the treason I do not . . . (Letters, TR to S. Harper, Sep. 12, 1906).

95   Wilkinson the double traitor . . . ; Thus ended ingloriously . . . (Works, Vol. 9, pp. 500–501).

96   My criticism of the United States in 1812 . . . (Letters, TR to H. Munsterberg, Oct. 3, 1914).

96   There was but one possible way by which to gain . . . (Clowes, p. 6).

96   During the early years of this . . . ; Since the year 1792 . . . ; The descendents of the Vikings . . . ; A few years before 1812 . . . ; Such was Great Britain's naval power . . . (Works, Vol. 6, pp. 20–21).

97   It must be but a poor-spirited American whose veins . . . (Works, Vol. 6, p. 367).

97   On land and water the contest took the form . . . (Works, Vol. 6, p. 8).

97   In June 1812 Madison sent in his declaration of war . . . (Clowes, p. 23).

97   War was declared and as a contest for the rights . . . (Works, Vol. 6, p. 8).

97   The material results were not very great at least . . . (Works, Vol. 6, p. 363).

98   Our victorious sea-fights; Were magnified absurdly by most . . . (Works, Vol. 6, p. 115).

98   The British navy numbering at the outset . . . ; Of the twelve single ship . . . ;

Undoubtedly redounded most to . . . ; The honors were nearly even . . . (Works, Vol. 6, p. 365).

98   For a hundred and thirty years England had . . . (Works, Vol. 6, p. 115).

98   The events of the war on land teach very little . . . (Works, Vol. 6, p. xxviii).

98   While our navy had been successful the war on land . . . (Works, Vol. 6, p. 373).

98   The battles though marked by . . . ; Our defeats were exactly . . . (Works, Vol. 6, pp. xxviii–xxix).

99   After two years of warfare Scott records in his . . . (Works, Vol. 6, p. 374).

99   British troops trained in many wars thrashed the raw . . . (Works, Vol. 6, p. xxviii).

99   All through the war the seacoasts . . . ; In August 1814 a more . . . (Works, Vol. 6, p. xxxvi).

99   Ross and Cockburn moved against . . . ; Encountered a huddle . . . (Clowes, p. 144).

99   As Ross and Cockburn led . . . ; Having completed their work . . . (Clowes, p. 146).

100   The War of 1812 was; A thoroughly discreditable war from . . . (Works, Vol. 18, p. 313).

100   And yet (Bradley Johnson Papers, TR to B. Johnson, Mar. 21, 1900).

100   In 1912 (Papers, TR to L. Abbott, Nov. 7, 1914).

100   The British and American peace enthusiasts . . . ; Were filled with a plan . . . ; John Paul Jones in front of . . . ; A more preposterous body than the American . . . (Letters, TR to A. Lee, Jul. 7, 1913).

101   The victory of Lake Erie was . . . ; But the glory acquired by . . . (Works, Vol. 6, p. 223).

101   When Great Britain seriously turned her attention to her . . . (Works, Vol. 6, p. 9).

101   Sir George Prevost with an army of; Veteran troops marched south along the . . . ; But the British fleet was captured . . . (Works, Vol. 6, p. xxxvi).

102   The effects of the victory were immediate . . . (Works, Vol. 6, p. 328).

102   It will always be a source of . . . ; Lake Erie teaches us the . . . (Works, Vol. 6, p. 226).

102   The British sailors on the lakes were as good . . . (Works, Vol. 6, p. 231).

102   Macdonough in this battle won . . . ; It was solely owing to his foresight . . . ; His skill seamanship quick eye . . . (Works, Vol. 6, p. 328).

102   I do not mean in any way or shape . . . (Papers, TR to T. Becker, Feb. 13, 1911).

102   Macdonough; To (Works, Vol. 6, p. 328).

102   Nelson (Works, Vol. 13, p. 183).

102   The greatest sea-fighter of all time (Works, Vol. 6, p. 20).

102   Trafalgar and the Nile were . . . ; The English navy at that great . . . ; Won its tremendous victories . . . ; The Spanish warships were such . . . ; The Dutch navy suffered from . . . ; The French navy the chief . . . ; Manned in a fashion . . . ; Contrast all this with the feats . . . (Letters, TR to F. Chadwick, Jul. 8, 1908).

104   In the Constitutional Convention . . . (Works, Vol. 7, pp. 327–28.)

104   Showing sheep-like submission to . . . ; At the time of the . . . (Works, Vol. 11, p. 192).

104   Men like Madison . . . ; Did the nation . . . ; At some one . . . (Works, Vol. 7, p. 468).

104   He did not believe that the . . . ; Thinking the freeholders the safest . . . ; On the suffrage his views . . . ; It is simply idle folly to talk . . . ; (Works, Vol. 7, pp. 333–35).

105   Excepting Jefferson we have never . . . (Works, Vol. 7, pp. 459–60.)

105   The nerveless administration at Washington did not even . . . (Clowes, p. 66).

105   He was entirely too timid to have embarked on . . . (Works, Vol. 7, pp. 459–60).

105   The South and West brought on the War of 1812 . . . (Works, Vol. 7, p. 333).

105   The bulk of our people and the politicians . . . (Works, Vol. 18, pp. 313–14).

105   The blame that attaches to Madison and the elder . . . (Works, Vol. 7, pp. 461–62).

106   The administration; Drifted into a war . . . ; During the first . . . ; It must be . . . (Works, Vol. 7, pp. 460–61).

106   The federal government throughout the campaign did . . . (Works, Vol. 6, p. 378).

106   The administration of the War Department . . . ; Monroe's biographer see . . . (Works, Vol. 6, p. 374).

106   Although nominally the peace . . . ; Above all the contest gave an . . . (Works, Vol. 7, p. 461).

107   James Monroe (Letters, TR to K. Roosevelt, Oct. 27, 1906).

107   The last President of the great . . . ; Was a courteous high bred . . . (Works, Vol. 7, p. 32).

107   He; Was; A very amiable gentleman but distinctly one . . . (Works, Vol. 7, p. 424).

107   As minister to France (Works, Vol. 7, p. 399).

107   Monroe; Stayed long enough to get . . . ; His appointment was an . . . (Works, Vol. 7, p. 429).

107   The United States having requested the French . . . (Works, Vol. 7, p. 424).

107   Monroe as Morris's successor entered . . . ; However the fault was really less . . . ; To appoint Monroe an extreme Democrate . . . ; While one minister was formally . . . (Works, Vol. 7, pp. 429–30).

JACKSONIAN ERA (1825–1850)

111   The year 1824 saw the complete break-up . . . (Works, Vol. 11, pp. 201–2).

111   With the close of Monroe's . . . ; Adams after his election . . . (Works, Vol. 7, pp. 40–41).

111   Jackson furiously denounced this as a corrupt . . . (Works, Vol. 11, pp. 201–2).

111   The assault was directed with . . . ; Randolph of Roanoke the privileged . . . ; Two tolerably well-defined parties now . . . ; Adams's inaugural address and first message . . . (Works, Vol. 7, pp. 41–42).

112   Adams certainly went too far in his non-partisanship . . . (Works, Vol. 7, pp. 53–54).

113   John Quincy Adams after leaving the presidency . . . (Works, Vol. 13, p. 314).

113   Adams rendered a real service when . . . (Letters, TR to E. Root, Sep. 14, 1905).

113   Adams did much to earn the gratitude of . . . (TR to *Harvard Crimson*, Jan. 2, 1896).

113   In 1812–1814 the Federalist Party when . . . (Letters, TR to J. Palmer, Aug. 9, 1900).

113   There were many other Federalist leaders in the same . . . (Works, Vol. 7, p. 464).

113   The Monroe Doctrine may be briefly defined as . . . (Works, Vol. 13, p. 168).

113   I believe with all my heart in the Monroe Doctrine (Works, Vol. 13, p. 193).

113   If the Monroe Doctrine did not already exist . . . (Works, Vol. 13, p. 168).

113   An American may of course announce his opposition . . . (Works, Vol. 13, p. 170).

114   The Monroe Doctrine had for . . . ; John Quincy Adams (Letters, TR to *Harvard Crimson*, Jan. 2, 1896).

114   Who during the presidency of Monroe first clearly . . . (Works, Vol. 13, pp. 169–170).

114   The Monroe Doctrine is not international law but there . . . (Works, Vol. 13, p. 475).

114   Lawyers as lawyers have absolutely nothing whatever . . . (Works, Vol. 13, p. 169).

114   We speak of international law but international law . . . (Works, Vol. 13, pp. 527–28).

114   The Monroe Doctrine was in danger of failing not . . . (Works, Vol. 16, pp. 252–53).

115   A good many of you are . . . ; As regards the Monroe Doctrine . . . (Works, Vol. 13, pp. 474–75).

115   The Monroe Doctrine is as strong as the United States . . . (Works, Vol. 18, p. 225).

116   Andrew Jackson did some awful things . . . (Papers, TR to W. Chandler, Aug. 2, 1897).

116   There has never been a more genuine . . . (Papers, TR to C. Sniffen, Sep. 14, 1907).

116   There was one point where Jackson did so well . . . (Works, Vol. 11, pp. 202–3).

116   I was very deeply pleased . . . ; Buell's Life of . . . ; Dedicated to me (Letters, TR to J. Walsh, Feb. 23, 1909).

116   I am pleased when I have my name . . . (Papers, TR to O. Read, Aug. 13, 1906).

116   Great admiration for Andrew Jackson and . . . (Papers, TR to S. Lake, Oct. 23, 1907).

117   Jackson was an American; one of the three or four greatest Presidents; one of the three or four greatest public men (*Nashville American*, Oct. 23, 1907).

117   A man who made mistakes but a man of iron will . . . (Works, Vol. 16, p. 11).

117   I draw a sharp distinction between . . . (*Nashville American*, Oct. 23, 1907).

117   Different Presidents have construed and have . . . (Works, Vol. 17, p. 85).

117   The power wielded by Andrew . . . ; This is merely stating . . . (Works, Vol. 13, p. 306).

117   The Jacksonian Democracy nominally the party of the . . . (Works, Vol. 7, p. 84).

117   After leaving the presidency . . . ; With the exception of . . . (Works, Vol. 11, p. 203).

117   Andrew Jackson one of the men . . . ; Jackson himself was too . . . ; Young Andrew was struck . . . ; When twenty-one years . . . ; When Tennessee was . . . ; In the backwoods . . . (Works, Vol. 11, pp. 196–98).

118   When Andrew Jackson was in Congress he voted . . . (Works, Vol. 13, pp. 502–3).

119   Andrew Jackson a real military genius (Works, Vol. 18, p. 313).

119   Stands out in history as the ablest general the . . . (Works, Vol. 6, p. 404).

119 No true American can think of his deeds at New Orleans . . . (Works, Vol. 6, p. 378).

119 Jackson showed military talent of a very high order (Works, Vol. 11, p. 200).

119 A very charming . . . ; Wellington's military successes . . . ; As a statesman . . . (Works, Vol. 7, p. 49).

119 Andrew Jackson had the instinct for . . . (Letters, TR to C. Spring-Rice, Aug. 13, 1897).

119 The War of 1812 brought him at once into national . . . (Works, Vol. 11, p. 199).

119 The crowning event of the war was the Battle of . . . (Works, Vol. 6, p. xxxvii).

119 It was a perfectly useless shedding of blood . . . (Works, Vol. 6, p. 10).

119 Nevertheless it was not only glorious . . . ; Jackson is certainly by all . . . (Works, Vol. 6, pp. 400–401).

120 There is hardly a contest of modern times where the . . . (Works, Vol. 6, p. 10).

120 According to their official returns the British loss . . . (Works, Vol. 6, p. 396).

120 The Americans; Lost but 70 men (Works, Vol. 6, p. 398).

120 Jackson's success was achieved against the best . . . (Works, Vol. 11, p. 201).

120 The Tennessee backwoodsmen and Louisiana . . . (Works, Vol. 18, p. 98).

120 The Battle of New Orleans at once made Jackson . . . (Works, Vol. 11, p. 201).

120 Jackson even thus early loomed up as the greatest . . . (Works, Vol. 7, p. 23).

120 In the presidential election of . . . ; Until 1828 all the Presidents . . . ; The Jacksonian Democracy stood for the . . . ; The change was a great one . . . ; That the change was the . . . (Works, Vol. 7, pp. 46–49).

121 The Jacksonian Democracy was already completely . . . (Works, Vol. 7, pp. 119–20).

122 The two great reasons for Jackson's success . . . (Works, Vol. 7, p. 76).

122 Jackson's administration derives a most unenviable . . . (Works, Vol. 7, p. 52).

122 The old spoils system was (and is) . . . (Collection, TR to J. Russell, Jun. 15, 1891).

122 It was during Monroe's last term that Henry Clay . . . (Works, Vol. 7, p. 39).

122 Slavery was doubtless remotely one of the irritating . . . (Works, Vol. 7, p. 33).

123 In Washington the current at . . . ; He declared himself in . . . ; When it came to Jackson's turn . . . ; The issue between the President . . . ; Rang throughout the . . . (Works, Vol. 7, pp. 63–64).

123 Jackson promptly issued a proclamation . . . ; The intensely national and anti-separatist . . . ; Was very repugnant to many . . . ; (Works, Vol. 7, pp. 66–67).

124 He had openly avowed his intention . . . ; Some historians have treated this . . . ; Had a collision occurred neither Calhoun . . . ; The feeling in Congress as a whole . . . (Works, Vol. 7, pp. 67–68).

124 His signing the compromise bill . . . ; Benton wrote; A compromise made with a state in arms . . . ; His criticisms on the wisdom . . . ; In Jackson's case it must be . . . (Works, Vol. 7, pp. 70–71).

125 During both Jackson's presidential terms he and his . . . (Works, Vol. 7, p. 58).

125 Jackson's attack upon the Bank was a move undertaken . . . (Works, Vol. 7, p. 75).

125 He was ultimately successful; He had much justice on . . . (Works, Vol. 11, p. 202).

125 Jackson's ruinous policy of making deposits in . . . (Works, Vol. 7, pp. 89–90).

125 An assault upon; "The money power" is apt . . . ; The Bank itself beyond . . . (Works, Vol. 7, pp. 75–76).

126 Today (Papers, TR to S. Corwart, Jun. 22, 1903).

126 Our fiscal system is not good . . . ; That the inevitable popular distrust . . . ; Sooner or later there would . . . ; That sentence is as long . . . ; As yet our people do not . . . (Letters, TR to H. White, Nov. 27, 1907).

127 I took peculiar pride in the fact that so . . . (Papers, TR to J. Taylor, Dec. 26, 1906).

127 During the war with Spain (Powell, p. 319).

127 And that they did so well . . . (Papers, TR to J. Taylor, Dec. 26, 1906).

127 It is greatly to be wished that some competent person . . . (Works, Vol. 8, p. 79).

127 I saw recently in one of our prominent . . . ; Sitting Bull was shot while resisting arrest; The killing was not only a most righteous . . . (*Century Illustrated Magazine*, May 1893).

128 The most righteous of all . . . ; It is primeval warfare . . . ; A sad and evil . . . (Works, Vol. 9, pp. 57–58).

128 Odd things happen in a battle and the . . . (Letters, TR to E. Curtis, Apr. 8, 1908).

128 The excesses so often . . . ; One attack simple enough . . . ; In 1784 a family . . . (Works, Vol. 8, p. 75).

128 The hideous unnamable unthinkable . . . ; Any one who has ever been . . . (Works, Vol. 8, pp. 68–69).

129 The expression "too horrible to . . . " ; Impalement on charred sticks . . . (Works, Vol. 8, p. 75).

129 Much maudlin nonsense has . . . ; The simple truth is that they . . . (Works, Vol. 7, p. 38).

129 It cannot be too often insisted . . . ; To recognize the Indian ownership . . . (Works, Vol. 8, p. 79).

129 From the very nature of things it was wholly . . . (Works, Vol. 7, p. 38).

130 The dealings of the government with the Indian . . . (Works, Vol. 7, p. 112).

130 The Cherokees had advanced far on the road . . . (Works, Vol. 7, p. 38).

131 Van Buren faithfully served the mammon of . . . ; Jackson liked Van Buren because the latter . . . ; Van Buren was the first product of what . . . (Works, Vol. 7, pp. 119–20).

131 Van Buren; Was the last true Jacksonian Democrat . . . (Works, Vol. 7, p. 121).

132 Until Van Buren's overthrow the nationalists had held . . . (Works, Vol. 7, p. 150).

132 As far as slavery was concerned . . . ; The withdrawals of the United States (Works, Vol. 7, p. 122).

132 The Jacksonians during the period of Van Buren's . . . (Works, Vol. 7, p. 133).

132 Van Buren cool skillful and farsighted politician . . . ; No effort was made to stave off even . . . ; A few days after Van Buren's inauguration (Works, Vol. 7, pp. 124–25).

133 He had no reason to blame his own conduct for . . . (Works, Vol. 7, p. 121).

134 The defeat of Van Buren marks . . . ; The presidential election of 1840 . . . (Works, Vol. 7, pp. 150–51).

134 There was much poetic justice in the fact . . . (Works, Vol. 7, pp. 149–50).

135　The principles of the Whigs were . . . ; Its leaders however they might quarrel . . . ; Harrison was a true Whig . . . (Works, Vol. 7, pp. 153–54).

135　General Harrison had already shown . . . ; Tippecanoe proved quite . . . (Works, Vol. 7, pp. 149–50).

135　The Whigs in 1840 completely overthrew the Democrats . . . (Works, Vol. 7, p. 153).

135　A chance stroke of death put the . . . ; The smallest element in the coalition . . . ; Tyler; Was properly nothing but a . . . ; Tyler; Could hardly be called a Whig at all . . . (Works, Vol. 7, p. 153).

136　Tyler of Virginia whose disunion attitude was almost . . . (Works, Vol. 7, p. 68).

136　Went into opposition to his . . . ; Tyler however had little . . . ; His chief mental . . . (Works, Vol. 7, p. 154).

137　Tyler's first message to Congress read . . . ; Outlining what legislation he deemed . . . ; However the ink with which the message . . . ; The leaven had already begun working . . . (Works, Vol. 7, pp. 157–58).

137　The Whigs especially in the Senate under Henry Clay . . . (Works, Vol. 7, p. 154).

137　Clay who was their real and very positive chief . . . (Works, Vol. 7, p. 158).

137　Among the political theories to which Clay clung . . . (Works, Vol. 7, p. 163).

137　At last he stood at the head of the party controlling . . . (Works, Vol. 7, p. 157).

137　Tyler could not at first make up . . . ; But though his mind oscillated like a . . . (Works, Vol. 7, p. 163).

138　He said that his conscience . . . ; He objected to the name . . . ; And proposed to . . . ; Such preposterous folly . . . ; Clay could not . . . ; After a while . . . ; The President vetoed . . . (Works, Vol. 7, p. 164).

138　An intrigue was going on . . . ; He had given the Whigs . . . ; So when his veto . . . (Works, Vol. 7, p. 165).

138　Clay could not resist reading Tyler a lecture on his . . . (Works, Vol. 7, p. 164).

138　The Democrats looked on . . . ; But nevertheless they . . . ; Left without any . . . (Works, Vol. 7, p. 165).

139　In 1844 the Whig candidate for the presidency . . . (Works, Vol. 7, p. 186).

139　From this time the slavery question dwarfed . . . (Works, Vol. 7, p. 204).

139　Van Buren was the last Democratic . . . ; With the defeat of Van Buren . . . (Works, Vol. 7, pp. 150–51).

139　The separatist and annexationist Democrats . . . (Works, Vol. 7, pp. 198–99).

140　Hardly was Polk elected . . . ; That the separatist and . . . ; Polk's chances of . . . (Works, Vol. 7, p. 203).

140　Almost every good element . . . ; These Abolitionists had formed . . . (Works, Vol. 7, pp. 186–87).

141　Owing to a variety of causes . . . ; The Liberty Party in running Birney . . . ; With the purpose of advancing . . . ; These three men—Calhoun . . . (Works, Vol. 7, pp. 187–88).

141　Abraham Lincoln was in Congress . . . ; On pages 100 to 146 of . . . ; Lincoln justifies himself in voting . . . ; That part of the message . . . (Works, Vol. 19, p. 291).

141　He continues that he . . . ; And ends by saying . . . ; Remember that this is . . . (Works, Vol. 19, p. 292).

142 Patriotism means to stand . . . ; It is patriotic to . . . ; Lincoln had to deal . . . (Works, Vol. 19, pp. 291–92).

143 It is difficult to exaggerate the importance of the treaties . . . (Works, Vol. 7, p. 169).

143 Throughout a large part of our national career our . . . (Works, Vol. 13, p. 476).

143 No foot of soil to which we had any title in the . . . (Works, Vol. 7, p. 172).

143 Not only the Columbia but also the Red River . . . (Works, Vol. 7, pp. 170–71).

143 As long as the Canadian remains a colonist . . . (Works, Vol. 13, p. 173).

144 The territory along the Pacific coast lying between . . . (Works, Vol. 7, p. 180).

144 The whole region was still entirely unsettled and . . . (Works, Vol. 7, p. 34).

144 The British had trading posts at the . . . ; This treaty of joint occupation had . . . ; The aspect of affairs was totally . . . ; When American settlers were once in actual . . . (Works, Vol. 7, pp. 180–81).

145 Calhoun; Advocated a policy by masterly . . . ; We should have allowed . . . (Works, Vol. 7, pp. 182–83).

145 In 1844 the Democrats made their . . . ; Polk's administration was neither capable . . . ; The English; Accepted the offer of compromise; In its immediate effects the . . . (Works, Vol. 7, pp. 184–85).

147 My admiration of Texas and Texans is no new . . . (Works, Vol. 11, p. 176).

147 The conquest of Texas should . . . ; The great Texan hero . . . ; And his queerly . . . (Works, Vol. 7, pp. 115–16).

147 Houston; Was thoroughly Jacksonian in type . . . (Works, Vol. 7, p. 209).

148 The Texan struggle for independence . . . (Works, Vol. 7, p. 116).

148 Jackson (Works, Vol. 16, p. 11).

148 Administration remained nominally . . . ; The victory of San Jacinto . . . (Works, Vol. 7, p. 116).

148 The Americans at last succeeded in wresting . . . (Letters, TR to F. Selous, Mar. 19, 1900).

148 The Southerners desirous of increasing . . . ; The intrigue for the . . . (Works, Vol. 7, pp. 190–91).

148 The separatists chiefs were intriguing . . . ; Jackson himself whose name was still . . . ; The great champion of the old-style . . . ; Jackson though a Southerner warmly . . . (Works, Vol. 7, p. 191).

149 Polk's election gave an enormous impulse to the . . . (Works, Vol. 7, p. 199).

149 Texas was admitted and the foundation for our war . . . (Works, Vol. 7, p. 201).

149 Recent historians; Always speak as if our grasping after . . . (Works, Vol. 7, p. 28).

149 The Western people grew up . . . ; The pioneer; stood where he was; This belligerent or (Works, Vol. 7, pp. 12–13).

150 Which reduced to its simplest terms was that . . . (Works, Vol. 7, pp. 27–28).

151 Henry Clay was a first-class man and I (Papers, TR to W. Chandler, Aug. 2, 1897).

151 At times a man must . . . ; People are apt to . . . ; These two attitudes . . . (Works, Vol. 13, pp. 343–44).

152 Naturally there are certain subjects . . . ; No decent politician need . . . (Works, Vol. 13, p. 397).

152 Occasionally one hears some well-meaning . . . (Works, Vol. 13, p. 45–46).

152 When we cannot do the best then as . . . (Papers, TR to J. Garfield, Jul. 19, 1910).

152 During; the nullification movement in South Carolina (Works, Vol. 7, p. 58).

152 Clay was prepared to shift his stand somewhat . . . (Works, Vol. 7, p. 69).

153 A compromise which results in a half-step . . . (Works, Vol. 13, p. 343).

153 Accordingly Clay and Calhoun met . . . ; It gave South Carolina much . . . ; Unfortunately Congress as a whole . . . ; It was passed by a great majority (Works, Vol. 7, pp. 69–70).

153 A certain number of Whigs followed Webster and . . . (Works, Vol. 7, p. 68).

153 Silas Wright of New York; extreme desire which he had to remove; would vote for what; the battle did not result in (Works, Vol. 7, pp. 70–71).

153 Gained most of that for which . . . ; Without doubt the honors of the . . . (Works, Vol. 7, p. 72).

154 Henry Clay (Works, Vol. 7, p. 30).

154 Was always much bolder in opening a campaign than . . . (Works, Vol. 7, p. 162).

154 During the War of 1812 (Works, Vol. 7, p. 7).

154 The younger Democratic-Republican leaders men like . . . (Clowes, p. 23).

155 John C. Calhoun; Played a large part in the leadership . . . ; And succeeded in clothing wrong conclusions . . . (*Charlottesville Daily Progress*, Jun. 16, 1903).

155 Few criminals have worked as much harm to their country . . . (Works, Vol. 7, p. 72).

155 Doubtless in private life or as regards any financial . . . (Works, Vol. 7, p. 109).

155 Some of Calhoun's recent biographers have credited . . . (Works, Vol. 7, p. 209).

155 Calhoun's hair-splitting and metaphysical disquisitions . . . (Works, Vol. 7, p. 63).

156 Much of the opposition he was continually making . . . (Works, Vol. 7, p. 109).

156 Thomas Hart Benton (Letters, TR to G. Harvey, Sep. 19, 1904).

156 Evidently thought that this was the case and in reading . . . (Works, Vol. 7, p. 109).

156 Certain Southern extremists under . . . ; A perfectly proper and respectful . . . ; Praying for the abolition of . . . ; The District was solely under . . . ; If the right of petition meant . . . (Works, Vol. 7, pp. 106–7).

156 Calhoun (Works, Vol. 7, p. 178).

156 Wished to refuse to receive the petitions . . . ; He was still smarting from the . . . (Works, Vol. 7, p. 108).

157 Benton characterizes his system of slavery agitation . . . (Works, Vol. 7, p. 209).

157 Calhoun was also greatly exercised . . . ; The bill subjected to penalties . . . (Works, Vol. 7, p. 109).

157 A dozen Southern Senators; Joined with the bulk of the Northerners . . . (Works, Vol. 7, p. 110).

157 South Carolina and Mississippi were . . . ; The Charleston aristocrats offer as . . . ; Have never made good their . . . ; They were no more to blame than . . . ; In the Revolutionary War; The South Carolinians made as against . . . (Letters, TR to O. Wister, Apr. 27, 1906).

159 In 1848 the Democrats nominated Cass a Northern . . . (Works, Vol. 7, p. 210).

159 Webster's famous sneer at . . . ; Taylor was aimed at . . . (Works, Vol. 7, p. 9).

159 The Whigs carried; The election and once more held the . . . ; Nothing whatever was known of his political . . . ; In his first and only annual . . . (Works, Vol. 7, p. 211).

160 Declared the Union to be the greatest . . . ; Naturally it was bitterly . . . ; This is not the place to . . . ; It consisted of five . . . ; Benton opposed it; As being a concession or . . . (Works, Vol. 7, p. 212).

160 Before California was admitted into the Union old . . . (Works, Vol. 7, p. 216).

160 Taylor turned out admirably (Letters, TR to HCL, Apr. 9, 1900).

161 I don't believe in judging people . . . ; I can understand Taylor when he . . . (Butt, pp. 253–54).

162 Thomas Hart Benton (Works, Vol. 7, p. 17).

162 Had all the tenacity of a snapping . . . ; It would have been fortunate . . . (Works, Vol. 7, p. 145).

162 In point of moral character . . . ; It has always seemed to me that . . . ; I always felt it was a privilege to . . . (Papers, TR to W. Chandler, Aug. 2, 1897).

162 In my Life of Thomas Hart Benton (Letters, TR to G. Harvey, Sep. 19, 1904).

162 In 1832; Benton threw himself in heart and soul . . . (Works, Vol. 7, p. 65).

163 During his career the United States . . . ; Such Senators as Benton . . . (Works, Vol. 7, p. 205–6).

163 Benton's long political career can never be thoroughly . . . (Works, Vol. 7, p. 10).

163 Like every other hot spirit of the West . . . (Works, Vol. 7, p. 22).

163 Like Jackson Benton killed his man . . . ; Benton (Works, Vol. 7, p. 20).

163 Had his faults and lots of them but he . . . (Papers, TR to W. Chandler, Aug. 2, 1897).

163 The contrast between the conduct toward slavery . . . (Works, Vol. 7, p. 205).

163 Compare his stand against the slavery extremists . . . (Works, Vol. 7, p. 217).

163 Both he and Jackson deserve great credit for . . . (Works, Vol. 7, p. 89).

163 Benton was such a firm believer in hard money . . . (Works, Vol. 7, p. 218).

164 To be sure Benton's knowledge . . . ; A very serious disadvantage to . . . (Works, Vol. 7, p. 75).

164 A metallic currency is always surer . . . ; A craze for soft or dishonest . . . (Works, Vol. 7, p. 89).

164 Benton was one of those who . . . ; Tyler who was also on board . . . (Works, Vol. 7, pp. 230–31).

CIVIL WAR ERA (1851–1876)

167 In 1852 (Works, Vol. 7, p. 220).

167 The Whig candidate for the presidency (Works, Vol. 7, p. 204).

167 Winfield Scott (Collection, "Great Men and Famous Women," 1894, p. 338).

167 A good general but otherwise a wholly absurd and . . . (Works, Vol. 7, p. 220).

167 Was defeated by (Works, Vol. 7, p. 186).

167 Franklin Pierce (Works, Vol. 7, p. 108).

167 The nominee of the Democracy (Works, Vol. 7, p. 186).

167 One of the most subservient allies the South ever had . . . (Works, Vol. 7, p. 108).

167 Pierce the Copperhead (Works, Vol. 14, p. 19).

167 Was completely under the control of the secession wing . . . (Works, Vol. 7, p. 220).

167 We cannot but admire at least the courage and gallant (Works, Vol. 14, p. 43).

167 I can respect an ex-Confederate who fought us openly . . . (Works, Vol. 14, p. 65).

167 Thomas Hart Benton (Works, Vol. 7, p. 17).

167 Treated (Works, Vol. 7, p. 220).

167 Franklin Pierce (Works, Vol. 7, p. 108).

167 With contemptuous hostility despising him and seeing . . . (Works, Vol. 7, p. 220).

168 On the history of the pro-slavery agitation (Works, Vol. 7, p. 228).

168 Benton (Works, Vol. 7, p. 17).

168 Wrote (Works, Vol. 7, p. 70).

168 Up to Mr. Pierce's administration . . . ; The death of Harrison and the . . . (Works, Vol. 7, pp. 228–29).

168 The Missouri Compromise of 1820 had expressly . . . ; This compromise was to be repealed . . . ; It was an outrage to propose . . . (Works, Vol. 7, pp. 223–24).

168 The squatter-sovereignty theories of Douglas; Deserved ridicule; The Gadsden Treaty was also opposed . . . (Works, Vol. 7, pp. 224–25).

171 After 1840 the professed Abolitionists formed but a . . . (Works, Vol. 7, pp. 187–88).

171 The anti-slavery cause was eminently just; But the more one reads of . . . ; The more one feels that they were . . . ; I do not mean men like Birney . . . (Letters, TR to K. Johnson, Jan. 10, 1899).

171 The disunion movement among the Northern . . . ; Absolutely senseless; For its success meant the immediate abandonment . . . (Works, Vol. 7, p. 466).

172 The only hope of ultimately . . . ; The men who took a great and . . . (Works, Vol. 7, pp. 188–89).

172 The cause of the Abolitionists . . . ; Their tendency toward . . . (Works, Vol. 7, pp. 103–4).

172 The plea that slavery was a question . . . ; There are now laws on the . . . ; The same laws that in one . . . (Works, Vol. 7, pp. 189–90).

172 Many of their leaders possessed no good . . . (Works, Vol. 7, pp. 103–4).

173 The extreme advocates of any cause . . . (Letters, TR to H. Johnson, Jan. 10, 1899).

173 Wendell Phillips may be taken as a very good type . . . (Works, Vol. 7, p. 104).

173 When Wendell Phillips denounced Abraham Lincoln . . . (Works, Vol. 13, p. 346).

173 Many people in speaking of the Abolitionists . . . (Works, Vol. 7, p. 189).

174 Abraham Lincoln said that he believed the Dred Scott . . . (Works, Vol. 17, p. 372).

174 Justice Taney and the majority of the Supreme Court . . . (Works, Vol. 17, p. 370).

174 Chief Justice Taney; Belonged to those who were the . . . (Lodge Letters, Vol. 1, p. 23).

174 I do not believe we have ever had a . . . (Papers, TR to H. Stimson, Feb. 5, 1912).

174 Taney was a curse to our national life because . . . (Letters, TR to HCL, Jul. 10, 1902).

175   It was the decision of the Court at this time . . . (Works, Vol. 11, p. 261).

175   It was Buchanan who treated . . . ; It was Lincoln . . . ; Lincoln mind you . . . (Works, Vol. 17, p. 121).

175   Lincoln was always against slavery but until the . . . (Works, Vol. 19, p. 51).

176   The Civil War was a great war for righteousness (Works, Vol. 11, p. 324).

176   I most earnestly believe in . . . ; After the firing . . . (Letters, TR to J. Jusserand, Feb. 23, 1917).

176   Of course had I been old enough . . . (Letters, TR to M. Roosevelt, Sep 14, 1881).

176   The rebellion was a crime against the Nation (Letters, TR to A. Hart, Jan. 13, 1896).

176   My own belief is that there never . . . (Letters, TR to G. Henderson, Feb. 14, 1899).

176   In the end the slave was freed the Union restored . . . (Works, Vol. 13, p. 321).

176   Half a century before the . . . ; The truth is that it is nonsense to . . . (Works, Vol. 7, pp. 465–66).

177   The separatist feeling is ingrained in . . . ; Slavery was partly the cause . . . (Works, Vol. 7, p. 33).

177   Its growth was furthered and hastened by the actions . . . (Works, Vol. 7, p. 105).

177   In 1860 a majority of . . . ; The secession movement of 1860 . . . (Works, Vol. 7, pp. 465–66).

177   I am half a southerner myself . . . (Letters, TR to O. Wister, Apr. 27, 1906).

177   The decline in the militant spirit . . . ; The Southerners by their whole . . . (Works, Vol. 7, p. 26).

178   My mother was a Georgian . . . (Letters, TR to G. Henderson, Feb. 14, 1899).

178   Slavery is ethically abhorrent to all right-minded men . . . (Works, Vol. 9, p. 45).

178   The more I study the Civil War . . . (Letters, TR to J. Rhodes, Nov. 29, 1904).

178   Franklin Hamilton Jefferson Adams and their fellows . . . (Works, Vol. 7, pp. 271–72).

179   My view of John Brown is that he was . . . (Letters, TR to L. Draper, Dec. 28, 1910).

180   I do not have to tell you that my great hero . . . (Papers, TR to W. Sewell, Jun. 13, 1906).

180   Lincoln has always meant more to me than . . . (Letters, TR to L. Abbott, Jul. 3, 1905).

180   Lincoln was an average man . . . (Hale, pp. 147–48).

180   The old-school Jeffersonian theorists believed in . . . (Works, Vol. 7, p. 327).

181   Lincoln had an almost miraculous understanding of . . . (Hale, pp. 147–48).

181   One of the greatest men . . . ; One of the two or three greatest . . . (Works, Vol. 11, p. 210).

181   Lincoln saw into the future . . . (Collection, TR speech at Lincoln's birth site, Feb. 12, 1909).

181   Lincoln the uncouth farmer's . . . ; Made his way . . . (Collection, TR speech to Masons, Nov. 5, 1902).

181 Lincoln's name will always stand coupled . . . (Papers, TR to N. Ramsey, Jan. 16, 1899).

181 While I do not believe in comparisons among . . . (Papers, TR to S. McBee, Feb. 13, 1904).

181 Mr. Matthew Arnold (Collection, *Market World*, April 1908, p. 8).

181 Grants us that Washington . . . ; I cannot help . . . (Collection, *Market World*, May 1908, p. 13).

181 I think of Lincoln shambling . . . ; I wish to Heaven . . . (Papers, TR to H. Pritchett, Dec. 26, 1904).

182 In my office in the White House there is . . . (Leary, p. viii).

182 It is a reproduction of the photograph of . . . (Letters, TR to E. Wells, Oct. 5, 1903).

182 How I wish Lincoln had shaved his . . . (Papers, TR to E. Tuckerman, Dec. 4, 1905).

182 Oftentimes when I had some . . . ; Yes to me Lincoln has ever been . . . (Leary, pp. viii–ix).

182 John Hay's house was almost the only . . . (Letters, TR to L. Abbott, Jul. 3, 1905).

182 Hay was Lincoln's private secretary . . . ; And I wore the ring when I took . . . (Letters, TR to G. Trevelyan, Mar. 9, 1905).

182 Surely no other President on the eve of . . . (Letters, TR to J. Hay, Mar. 3, 1905).

182 Have you ever read Hay and Nicolay's . . . (Letters, TR to R. Bacon, Oct. 7, 1902).

182 How he does loom up as one studies and . . . (Letters, TR to J. Hay, Jul. 22, 1902).

183 Abraham Lincoln was a genius who . . . (Letters, TR to W. White, Jan. 22, 1912).

183 Washington though in some ways an even . . . (Works, Vol. 13, pp. 500–501).

183 Parenthetically I would say . . . ("The President's Policy," *North American Review*, Oct. 1885).

183 Aside from being prophets what . . . (Papers, TR to C. Lee, Mar. 23, 1899).

183 In all history I do not believe there is . . . (Works, Vol. 11, pp. 208–9).

183 He possessed that marvelous . . . (Papers, TR to *Review of Reviews*, Jan. 1, 1909).

183 There is nothing in Demosthenes . . . (Letters, TR to R. Gilder, Apr. 1, 1893).

183 There is one of his letters which . . . ; No President who has ever sat . . . ; It is a touching thing that the . . . (TR to *Review of Reviews*, Jan. 1, 1909).

184 Nobody but one of . . . ; Met as Lincoln met . . . (Letters, TR to H. Needham, Jul. 19, 1905).

184 In reading his works and addresses one is struck . . . (Works, Vol. 11, p. 216).

184 I remember John Hay telling me that . . . (Papers, TR to J. Duzer, Mar. 13, 1900).

185 It is impossible to conceive . . . ; Which makes a man . . . (Works, Vol. 11, p. 206).

185 Contrast Cromwell's conduct with that of Lincoln . . . (Works, Vol. 10, p. 316).

185 Abraham Lincoln the rail-splitter the Western country . . . (Works, Vol. 11, p. 207).

185 Every great and wise statesman has . . . (Papers, TR to G. Perkins, Feb. 26, 1917).

186 Lincoln was radical . . . ; Compared to Wendell . . . (Letters, TR to W. White, Dec. 12, 1910).

186 Let anybody study Lincoln's history . . . (Papers, TR to F. Heney, Dec. 13, 1912).

186 Such a study of Lincoln's . . . ; The fanatic the well-meaning . . . (Works, Vol. 11, p. 205).

186 I believe his success was due . . . ; Lincoln was not half-hearted . . . ; When a very young man in the Illinois . . . (Letters, TR to C. Williard, Apr. 28, 1911).

187 Lincoln had tremendous influence with . . . (Papers, TR to S. Brooks, Oct. 17, 1910).

187 He had continually to check those who wished . . . (Works, Vol. 11, pp. 212–13).

187 His great effort was to prevent the . . . (Letters, TR to G. Hoar, Jun. 16, 1902).

187 Lincoln lived in such . . . ; This was because the . . . (Letters, TR to N. Butler, Jun. 3, 1904).

187 I did not think it necessary to go as . . . (Letters, TR to C. Bonaparte, Jan. 22, 1915).

187 There were undoubtedly corrupt contractors . . . (Letters, TR to H. Garland, Dec. 14, 1915).

187 The only weakness; In the great war President . . . (Dodd Papers, Memorandum, Mar. 5, 1908).

187 It would have been difficult . . . ; It certainly was a mistake . . . (Papers, TR to J. Lowell, Feb. 20, 1900).

188 I do not understand why some persons . . . ; Lincoln was not a handsome . . . (Leary, pp. vii–viii).

188 Sad patient mighty Abraham Lincoln (Works, Vol. 13, p. 277).

188 Was the plain man of the people . . . (Works, Vol. 11, pp. 286–87).

189 In a public utterance of mine some . . . ; While as a public man I expect to . . . ; Jefferson Davis wrote me a letter . . . (Letters, TR to G. Harvey, Sep. 19, 1904).

189 A rather ill-tempered and undignified letter; Instead of ignoring it I answered . . . (Papers, TR to C. Howell, Jun. 12, 1905).

189 I; Have preserved both his letter and . . . (Letters, TR to G. Harvey, Sep. 19, 1904).

190 Beauvain, Miss. September 29 . . . (Bishop, Vol. 1, p. 41).

190 I thought it most undignified . . . ; I wrote him back . . . (Letters, TR to G. Harvey, Sep. 19, 1904).

190 New York October 8 . . . (Bishop, Vol. 1, p. 42).

191 As a matter of pure morals . . . ; Now this is my personal . . . ; I have always drawn a sharp . . . ; If you will turn to Scott's Memoirs . . . (Letters, TR to G. Harvey, Sep. 19, 1904).

191 During Van Buren's administration; Many States in the rage for . . . ; Refused to pay; It is a painful and shameful . . . ; Before Jefferson Davis took his place . . . (Works, Vol. 7, pp. 141–42).

192 He did not like Benedict Arnold receive . . . (Letters, TR to G. Harvey, Sep. 19, 1904).

192 One of the stock arguments . . . ; The South revolted . . . (Letters, TR to O. Gresham, Nov. 30, 1903).

192 Rebellion Revolution the appeal to arms to . . . (Works, Vol. 10, p. 209).

192 All civil wars loosen the bands of orderly liberty . . . (Works, Vol. 9, p. 94).

192 If there are such virtues as loyalty and patriotism . . . (Works, Vol. 7, p. 467).

193 The men who head or instigate armed rebellions . . . (Works, Vol. 10, p. 209).

193 Under Jefferson Davis the Southern . . . (Letters, TR to D. Thompson, Dec. 22, 1903).

193 In view of the extreme . . . ; If you will go . . . (Papers, TR to C. Howell, Jun. 12, 1905).

194 There is no need to dwell on General Lee's . . . (Works, Vol. 11, p. 218).

194 The world has never seen better soldiers than . . . (Works, Vol. 7, p. 26).

194 The greatest general of the South was Lee and his . . . (Works, Vol. 10, p. 104).

194 I feel nothing but the most cordial and hearty goodwill . . . (Works, Vol. 14, p. 64).

195 General Lee has left us the memory . . . (Letters, TR to H. Herbert, Jan. 16, 1907).

195 Immediately after the close . . . ; Although absolutely without . . . (Works, Vol. 11, p. 218–19).

195 It was eminently fitting . . . ; Should turn his attention . . . (Letters, TR to H. Herbert, Jan. 16, 1907).

196 Stonewall Jackson was as true a type of the . . . (Works, Vol. 10, p. 190).

196 No Northern general approached the . . . ; He proved not only a . . . ; Few generals as great as Lee . . . ; In the first battle in which . . . ; At Chancellorsville (Works, Vol. 10, pp. 104–5).

197 Jackson himself was mortally wounded . . . (Works, Vol. 10, pp. 107–8).

197 For several days he lingered hearing how . . . (Works, Vol. 10, p. 110).

197 What a happy death Jackson's was . . . (Letters, TR to G. Henderson, Feb. 14, 1899).

198 Owen Wister's little book about Grant (Papers, TR to R. Sturgis, Jun. 3, 1911).

198 By reciting with entire . . . ; Could have drawn . . . (Letters, TR to O. Wister, Apr. 27, 1906).

198 In the Union armies there were generals as brilliant . . . (Works, Vol. 13, p. 433).

198 Grant's supreme virtue as a soldier was his . . . (Works, Vol. 13, pp. 435–36).

199 The great silent soldier the Hammer of the North (Works, Vol. 13, p. 432).

199 Grant did well as a boy and as a young man . . . (Works, Vol. 13, p. 385).

199 In the Civil War men who rose . . . ; Grant began the war with . . . (Works, Vol. 16, p. 91).

199 The greatest piece of literary work which has been . . . (Works, Vol. 10, p. 537).

199 Grant after leaving the presidency . . . (Letters, TR to G. Trevelyan, Dec. 1, 1908).

199 General Grant's book has had an extraordinary . . . (Works, Vol. 10, p. 537).

200 Reconstruction was a mistake . . . ; They brought their . . . (Letters, TR to O. Wister, Apr. 27, 1906).

200 The policy of "trusting the South" . . . ; Was tried by Andrew Johnson; If persisted in it would have . . . (Letters, TR to H. Higginson, Feb. 11, 1907).

200 Under the leadership of . . . ; The Fifteenth Amendment . . . (Letters, TR to HCL, Dec. 4, 1916).

201 I suppose that no one now seriously . . . (Letters, TR to C. Willard, Apr. 28, 1911).

201 For; Years the Republican . . . ; A party in which . . . (Letters, TR to J. Harris, Aug. 1, 1912).

201 The solution of impractical visionaries . . . (Papers, TR to O. Wister, May 3, 1906).

201 I believe the great majority of the . . . (Letters, TR to HCL, Dec. 4, 1916).

201 I have always felt the passage of . . . (Letters, TR to H. Pritchett, Dec. 14, 1904).

201 We may deplore but we can hardly complain . . . (Works, Vol. 14, p. 65).

202 There is no white man from a southern . . . (Letters, TR to H. Pritchett, Dec. 14, 1904).

202 In 1880 South Carolina had nearly a million people . . . (Works, Vol. 14, p. 65).

202 Take John Sharp Williams for instance . . . ; That it is not only not worthwhile . . . ; Declaims against our policy in the Philippines . . . (Letters, TR to L. Abbott, Jul. 26, 1904).

202 Williams is the true old-style Jeffersonian . . . (Letters, TR to W. Reid, Aug. 7, 1906).

202 John Sharp Williams' existence in Congress . . . (Letters, TR to L. Abbott, Jul. 26, 1904).

203 I need hardly say that . . . ; The Negroes of the South . . . (Letters, TR to HCL, Dec. 4, 1916).

203 Until the Civil War (Works, Vol. 19, p. 51).

203 The white votes of the South; Represented not only their own numerical . . . ; We have freed the slaves but . . . (Works, Vol. 14, p. 46).

203 During my term as President bills have . . . (Letters, TR to O. Wister, Apr. 27, 1906).

203 On the Negro question my views are . . . (Papers, TR to J. Strachey, Sep. 18, 1904).

204 My own personal belief is that the . . . ; Too many southern people and too many . . . ; Are you acquainted with the case of . . . (Letters, TR to O. Wister, Apr. 27, 1906).

204 In connection with the Cox family? (Papers, TR to O. Wister, Jun. 21,1906).

204 I found in office there a colored . . . ; I reappointed her . . . (Letters, TR to O. Wister, Apr. 27, 1906).

204 The Coxes are the new Negroes of the . . . (Papers, TR to O. Wister, Jun. 21,1906).

204 Afterwards the low whites in . . . ; This particular Negro doctor . . . ; Not satisfied with . . . ; The best citizens . . . ; "Deprecated" the conduct . . . ; This is at present . . . (Letters, TR to O. Wister, Apr. 27, 1906).

205 My children sit in the same . . . ; I am an ardent . . . (Letters, TR to R. Fleming, May 21, 1900).

GILDED AGE (1877–1900)

209 Although I had met Cabot Lodge once or twice . . . (Lodge Letters, Vol. 1, p. 25).

209 About all the work in the convention . . . ; I am glad to have been present . . . ; Blaine was nominated by Judge West . . . ; Of all the men presented . . . ; That such should

be the fact . . . ; A Democratic administration or four . . . ; Speaking roughly the forces . . . (Letters, TR to ARC, Jun. 8, 1884).

210   The very weakest candidate we could . . . (Letters, TR to HCL, May 26, 1884).

210   Arthur made a very good President but the bitterness . . . (Works, Vol. 13, p. 142).

210   I led the Edmunds men who held . . . (Letters, TR to [unidentified person], May 1, 1884).

210   The Edmunds men represented the . . . ; It included all the men of the . . . ; Blaine adherents included the remainder; These were the men who make up the . . . ; But for the most part these . . . ; And who are captivated by the man's force . . . (Letters, TR to ARC, Jun. 8, 1884).

211   Now our brother Independents ask us to support . . . (Works, Vol. 14, p. 55).

211   I would say that I am . . . "The President's Policy," (*North American Review*, Oct. 1885).

211   During the convention I; Worked practically to prevent . . . (Letters, TR to R. Bowker, Oct. 31, 1884).

211   Blaine's nomination meant to me pretty sure . . . (Letters, TR to HCL, Nov. 11, 1884).

211   Most of my friends seem . . . ; I have received shoals . . . (Letters, TR to HCL, Jun. 28, 1884).

211   I get so angry with the "Mugwumps" and . . . (Letters, TR to HCL, Aug. 24, 1884).

211   Mr. Blaine was nominated much . . . ; He was nominated against the wishes . . . ; Wished it and I for one . . . (Lodge Letters, Vol. 1, p. 15).

212   I can oppose Cleveland with a very clear . . . (Letters, TR to HCL, Aug. 24, 1884).

212   Why look at the Democratic candidate for Vice President . . . (Works, Vol. 14, p. 43).

213   I was a member of the legislature . . . (Letters, TR to F. Stetson, Nov. 16, 1908).

213   Cleveland grew in office . . . (Rhodes Papers, Index Rerum, Dec. 4, 1910).

213   Not only did I become . . . ; And finally I happened . . . (Letters, TR to F. Stetson, Nov. 16, 1908).

214   My position has been consistent for a . . . (Letters, TR to A. Shaw, Dec. 26, 1902).

214   I thank Heaven that I stood straight . . . (Letters, TR to C. Fairchild, Jun. 28, 1901).

214   When President Cleveland's Venezuela . . . (Letters, TR to F. Selous, Feb. 7, 1900).

214   Owing to a peculiar combination of . . . (Letters, TR to F. Stetson, Nov. 16, 1908).

214   Cleveland because of his defects no less . . . (Letters, TR to W. White, Jul. 30, 1907).

214   Some of the big banks paid the . . . (Papers, TR to E. Baldwin, Sep. 30, 1905).

214   There are many wealthy men who . . . (Papers, TR to G. Lorimer, May 12, 1906).

214   Cleveland (Papers, TR to G. Lorimer, May 12, 1906).

214   Has never been brought into contact from . . . (Letters, TR to L. Abbott, Nov. 5, 1903).

215   The old conservative wing; Was uppermost when Cleveland was in . . . ; They turned down Bryan and silver . . . (Letters, TR to W. Taft, Jul. 15, 1901).

215 Mr. Cleveland whom I like was more . . . (Letters, TR to L. Abbott, Oct. 29, 1903).

215 Mr. Olney is a very good fellow and a . . . (Papers, TR to J. Allison, Oct. 10, 1905).

215 He; Never took action of any kind such . . . (Papers, TR to C. Guild, Oct. 20, 1903).

215 I think Cleveland made an excellent . . . (Letters, TR to J. Lowell, Feb. 20, 1900).

215 In criticizing Mr. Cleveland . . . ("The President's Policy," *North American Review*, Oct. 1885).

215 I respect him in spite of certain of the . . . (Letters, TR to J. Lowell, Feb. 20, 1900).

215 You may perhaps know that when in . . . (Letters, TR to G. Alger, Mar. 20, 1906).

215 Now we had several bills . . . ; In his personal relations with me . . . (Lodge Letters, Vol. 1, pp. 16–17).

215 That Mr. Cleveland has done . . . ("The President's Policy," *North American Review*, Oct. 1885).

216 President Cleveland; Was all wrong about Hawaii (Collection, TR to C. Evans, Dec. 31, 1897).

216 I am surprised all the time to receive new . . . (Letters, TR to HCL, Oct. 27, 1894).

216 It seems incredible that the Democratic . . . (Letters, TR to W. Chanler, Dec. 18, 1897).

216 I think President Cleveland's action was . . . (Letters, TR to A. Mahan, May 3, 1897).

216 There is one thing that I personally . . . (Letters, TR to J. Clarkson, Apr. 22, 1893).

216 I was much amused at (Letters, TR to H. White, Apr. 30, 1897).

216 My good friend Mr. Smalley (Papers, TR to P. Knox, May 6, 1902).

216 Putting in the *London Times* a wail over . . . (Letters, TR to H. White, Apr. 30, 1897).

216 We ought to take Hawaii (Letters, TR to J. Bryce, Sep. 10, 1897).

216 Hawaii is of more pressing . . . ; If we don't take . . . (Letters, TR to W. Chanler, Dec. 23, 1897).

216 We did not create Hawaii . . . (Collection, TR speech to Republican Club, February, 1898).

216 If I had my way we would annex . . . ; My own belief is that we should . . . ; I would send the Oregon and if . . . ; To Hawaii and would hoist our flag . . . (Letters, TR to A. Mahan, May 3, 1897).

217 I am a quietly rampant "Cuba Libre" man . . . (Letters, TR to ARC, Jan. 8, 1897).

217 But the President; Shies off from anything . . . (Letters, TR to ARC, Mar. 30, 1896).

217 Let no one pretend . . . ; England's pretensions in . . . (Letters, TR to *Harvard Crimson*, Jan. 2, 1896).

217 I am very much pleased with the President's . . . (Letters, TR to HCL, Dec. 20, 1895).

217 He is far more of a man than the President . . . (Letters, TR to ARC, Jan. 26, 1896).

217   I do hope there will not be any back-down . . . (Letters, TR to HCL, Dec. 20, 1895).

218   If there is a muss I shall try to have . . . (Letters, TR to W. Cowles, Dec. 22, 1895).

218   Personally I rather hope . . . ; The antics of the bankers . . . (Letters, TR to HCL, Dec. 27, 1895).

218   The stock-jobbing timidity the Baboo . . . (Letters, TR to *Harvard Crimson*, Jan. 2, 1896).

218   The moneyed and semi-cultivated classes . . . (Lodge Letters, Vol. 1, p. 218).

218   The demagogue in all his forms is . . . ; The Governor who began his career by . . . ; Had it not been for the admirable action of . . . (Works, Vol. 13, pp. 7–8).

219   President Cleveland (Letters, TR to C. Fairchild, Jun. 28, 1901).

219   And Attorney General Olney acted with equal wisdom . . . (Works, Vol. 13, p. 8).

219   It is urgently necessary to keep before . . . (Letters, TR to L. Abbott, Apr. 23, 1906).

219   The authorities have to put down mob . . . (Letters, TR to L. Abbott, Jul. 1, 1906).

220   For six years from May 1889 . . . ; The spoils system which can . . . (Works, Vol. 13, pp. 99–100).

220   Curse patronage (Letters, TR to HCL, Mar. 30, 1889).

220   After Congress enacted into law . . . ; It must always be remembered . . . ; What made the reform vitally . . . ("The Present Position of Civil Service Reform," *New Princeton Review*, 1886.)

221   Altogether I am by no means pleased . . . ; Frankly I think the record pretty bad . . . ; Cleveland had a much worse Commission . . . ; The offices have been used . . . (Letters, TR to HCL, Jul. 27, 1892).

221   There is much the Administration has done . . . (Letters, TR to HCL, Oct. 8, 1889).

221   I am going to struggle mighty hard to . . . (Letters, TR to W. Foulke, Apr. 17, 1889).

221   Platt seems to have a ring in the . . . (Letters, TR to HCL, Mar. 30, 1889).

221   I really enjoy my work as Civil . . . (Letters, TR to G. Carow, Oct. 18, 1890).

221   I am having a hard row to hoe (Letters, TR to HCL, Jun. 29, 1889).

221   Thank Heaven I have Thompson as . . . (Lodge Papers, TR to HCL, Sep. 27, 1889).

221   This Commission has been able to do effective . . . (Letters, TR to HCL, May 9, 1890).

221   I have made this Commision . . . ; I am a great believer . . . (Letters, TR to HCL, Jun. 29, 1889).

222   I saw the President yesterday . . . ; The conclusion of the . . . (Letters, TR to HCL, May 9, 1890).

222   His one anxiety is not to have anything . . . (Letters, TR to HCL, Oct. 22, 1890).

222   Throughout the interview he was of . . . (Lodge Papers, TR to HCL, Jul. 1, 1891).

222   Looking on with cold and hesitating disapproval (Letters, TR to ARC, Feb. 1, 1891).

222   He is a genial little runt (Lodge Papers, TR to HCL, Jul. 1, 1891).

222   The worried halting President (Collection, TR to ARC, 1892 [no date on letter].)

222   Actually refuses to consider . . . ; Consider any method . . . (Lodge Papers, TR to HCL, Jul. 22, 1891).

222   If the President would only act a little differently . . . (Letters, TR to HCL, Jul. 22, 1891).

222   The old fellow always wants to half-do a thing (Letters, TR to HCL, Aug. 1, 1889).

222   Wanamaker; Seems to be the only one of the . . . ; Wanamaker has been outrageously disagreeable . . . (Lodge Papers, TR to HCL, Jul. 11, 1889).

223   The little gray man in the White House (Letters, TR to ARC, Feb. 1, 1891).

223   Could stop this without any trouble but . . . (Lodge Papers, TR to HCL, Oct. 31, 1890).

223   Damn the President! He is a cold-blooded . . . (Lodge Papers, TR to HCL, Oct. 4, 1890).

223   During; The administration of . . . ; No other administration . . . (Works, Vol. 14, pp. 140–41).

223   Of all the diplomatic incidents . . . ; The most important was the . . . ; It is safe to state in . . . ; The facts of the . . . ; Our minister Mr. Egan; Was forced to extend the . . . (Works, Vol. 14, pp. 144–46).

224   Soon after the complete . . . ; The most careful investigation . . . (Works, Vol. 14, pp. 147–48).

224   From the moment that hostilities . . . ; So admirably was the work done . . . ; The United States had made ready . . . ; All that was necessary was to . . . ; Accordingly the President sent to . . . ; This timely display of firmness; Produced a change of heart . . . ; They voluntarily agreed . . . (Works, Vol. 14, pp. 149–50).

225   It was the fact that the navy . . . (Collection, TR speech to Republican Club, Feb., 1898).

225   If at the time of our trouble . . . ; We had not already . . . (Works, Vol. 13, p. 196).

226   In the larger field of politics I feel very nervous . . . (Letters, TR to ARC, Jun. 14, 1896).

226   I greatly regret the defeat . . . ; McKinley himself is . . . (Letters, TR to ARC, Jul. 20, 1896).

226   I do hope he will take a strong stand both . . . (Letters, TR to HCL, Dec. 4, 1896).

226   There are big problems . . . ; Until we definitely . . . (Letters, TR to A. Mahan, May 3, 1897).

226   I do feel that it would be everything for us . . . (Letters, TR to HCL, Aug. 3, 1897).

227   Not since the Civil War has there been . . . (Letters, TR to ARC, Jul. 26, 1896).

227   What a Witches' Sabbath they . . . ; The hardest fight the . . . (Letters, TR to HCL, Jul. 14, 1896).

227   At present they are on the crest and were . . . (Letters, TR to ARC, Jul. 26, 1896).

227   The campaign is one of remarkable . . . (Letters, TR to ARC, Sep. 20, 1896).

228   The hatred of the East among many . . . (Letters, TR to HCL, Aug. 19, 1896).

229 Mr. Bryan I regard as being a man of . . . (Letters, TR to J. Strachey, Oct. 25, 1906).

229 Down at bottom Bryan is a cheap soul (Letters, TR to HCL, Sep. 4, 1906).

229 The cheapest faker we have ever proposed . . . (Letters, TR to W. Kent, Sep. 28, 1908).

229 His theories are almost as preposterous . . . (Papers, TR to W. Taft, Sep. 4, 1906).

229 Populism never prospers save . . . ; Silver is connected in his . . . (Works, Vol. 13, p. 148).

229 Now the Populists in their platform on which Mr. Bryan . . . (Works, Vol. 14, p. 252).

230 The question of the free coinage of silver is not . . . (Works, Vol. 14, p. 245).

230 When a man quotes Thou Shalt Not Steal . . . (Works, Vol. 14, p. 251).

230 The worst lesson that can be taught a man is to . . . (Works, Vol. 13, p. 165).

230 The two greatest of all . . . ; Were Washington who . . . ; Who cares which . . . (Works, Vol. 14, p. 262).

230 The Bryanites do not depend and cannot depend only . . . (Works, Vol. 14, p. 264).

230 It is not a nice thing to wish to pay . . . ; Savages do not like an Independent . . . ; The men who object to what they style "government by injunction" . . . (Works, Vol. 13, pp. 150–51).

231 Bryan is a personally honest and rather attractive . . . (Collection, TR to ARC, Jul. 19, 1896).

231 His utterances are as criminal as they are . . . (Collection, TR to ARC, Sep. 27, 1896).

231 The combination of all the lunatics all the . . . (Letters, TR to ARC, Aug. 18, 1900).

232 It was the necessity of saving the Union that called . . . (Leary, p. 4).

232 In 1896 and again in 1900 we won a . . . (Letters, TR to S. Brooks, Nov. 20, 1908).

232 The "old commercial conservatism" of that Republicanism . . . ; Was totally unlike the Lincoln Republicanism . . . (Letters, TR to B. Wheeler, Jun. 17, 1908).

232 In the free silver campaign one most . . . (Letters, TR to W. Taft, Mar. 15, 1906).

232 The man who is content to let politics go from bad to worse . . . (Works, Vol. 13, p. 9).

233 Remember a famous character named Mr. Podsnap . . . (Works, Vol. 14, p. 64).

233 McKinley thought it wicked to . . . (Butt Papers, letter to his mother, Jul. 24, 1908).

233 I have never heard him denounce or assail . . . (Letters, TR to HCL, Sep. 9, 1901).

233 We have every reason to be proud of what . . . (Letters, TR to HCL, Aug. 3, 1897).

233 There is in the country at this time the most . . . (Letters, TR to HCL, Sep. 9, 1901).

233 The President has stood firm as a rock . . . (Letters, TR to P. Sherman, Nov. 15, 1897).

233 We are going to come through all . . . (Collection, TR to C. Bonaparte, Jan. 12, 1898).

234 I am very much pleased over the Hawaiian . . . (Letters, TR to HCL, Jun. 17, 1897).

234 By concluding the treaty of annexation . . . (Letters, TR to P. Sherman, Nov. 15, 1897).

235 Now about the Spanish war . . . ; I would regard . . . (Letters, TR to W. Kimball, Nov. 19, 1897).

235 Personally I can hardly see how we can . . . (Letters, TR to A. Mahan, Mar. 21, 1898).

235 What the administration will do . . . ; In the name of . . . (Letters, TR to B. Adams, Mar. 21, 1898).

235 McKinley is bent on peace I fear (Collection, TR to ARC, Mar. 16, 1898).

235 From my own standpoint however . . . (Letters, TR to W. Kimball, Nov. 19, 1897).

235 I am of course a strong advocate . . . (Letters, TR to H. White, Mar. 30, 1898).

236 If there is trouble I shall . . . ; I don't want to . . . (Letters, TR to C. Tillinghast, Dec. 24, 1897).

236 If I should consult purely my own . . . (Letters, TR to W. Bigelow, Mar. 29, 1898).

236 I don't want to be shot . . . ; It is very hard to . . . (Letters, TR to A. Lambert, Apr. 1, 1898).

236 It may be impossible to ever settle . . . (Letters, TR to J. Long, Feb. 16, 1898).

236 Of course I cannot pass any . . . (Letters, TR to W. Clowes, Mar. 4, 1898).

236 We are drifting towards and not away . . . (Letters, TR to D. Robinson, Mar. 6, 1898).

237 The President is resolute . . . ; The trend of events . . . (Letters, TR to D. Robinson, Mar. 30, 1898).

237 Personally I cannot understand how . . . (Letters, TR to W. Cowles, Mar. 29, 1898).

237 I have felt that every consideration of national . . . (Letters, TR to B. Tracy, Apr. 4, 1898).

237 I am happy to say that I believe . . . (Letters, TR to R. Bacon, Apr. 5, 1898).

237 The President has taken a position from . . . (Letters, TR to E. Root, Apr. 5, 1898).

238 What McKinley did; Wanting to throw the whole matter over to . . . ; Was really an abandonment of duty; Imagine Washington or Lincoln . . . (Letters, TR to J. Garfield, Apr. 28, 1911).

238 McKinley has no more backbone . . . (Rhodes, *The McKinley and Roosevelt Administrations*, p. 57).

238 All day we have steamed close . . . ; Las Guasimas June 25th 98 . . . ; One man was killed . . . ; Every man behaved well . . . ; The Spaniards shot well but . . . (Letters, TR to C. Roosevelt, Jun. 15, 1898).

238 Our General is poor . . . (Letters, TR to HCL, Jul. 3, 1898).

238 We have won so far at . . . ; Well whatever comes I feel . . . (Letters, TR to HCL, Jun. 27, 1898).

239 A man's usefulness depends upon his living up to . . . (Bishop, Vol. 1, p. 103).

239 When the chance came for me to go . . . ; Yet I made up my mind that . . . (Butt Letters, p. 146).

239 I loathe war . . . ; I left six children behind . . . ; I should be ashamed of my sons . . . ; I have seen my wife for whom . . . (Letters, TR to J. Graham, Mar. 5, 1915).

239 I am having great fun now (Papers, TR to H. Haig, Mar. 30, 1899).

239   As Governor (Letters, TR to F. Cunz, Oct. 30, 1899).

239   And I had even greater fun last summer . . . ; I have always believed that with . . . ;
       The Spanish were a queer lot . . . (Papers, TR to H. Haig, Mar. 30, 1899).

240   In the San Juan fighting I happened to get . . . (Letters, TR to W. Brown, Mar. 12,
       1901).

240   Having a revolver and my two antagonists . . . (Letters, TR to H. Turner, Aug. 19,
       1900).

240   I feel that the Medal of Honor is the greatest . . . (Letters, TR to A. Scott, Jun. 26, 1907).

240   If I didn't earn it then no . . . ; I moved through the 9th . . . (Letters, TR to HCL,
       Dec. 6, 1898).

240   This will seem; Very egotistical (Letters, TR to HCL, Dec. 27, 1898).

240   I am entitled to the Medal of Honor and I want it (Letters, TR to HCL, Dec. 6,
       1898).

240   After the *Maine* blew up . . . ; I thought this attitude of quiet and dignified . . . ; A
       very good fellow a personal . . . ; Senator Hale was in a rather worse . . . (Letters,
       TR to C. Bonaparte, Aug. 1, 1905).

241   I feel a keen remembrance of England's . . . (Letters, TR to J. Strachey, Jan. 27,
       1900).

241   Every man connected with . . . ; England stood by . . . (Papers, TR to T. Gaffney,
       Mar. 10, 1899).

241   You must remember that English friendliness for the . . . (Letters, TR to A. Lee,
       Mar. 18, 1901).

241   Our present navy was begun in 1882 . . . ; The work of upbuilding the navy went
       on . . . ; The result was seen in the short war . . . (Works, Vol. 15, p. 119).

242   Admiral Dewey performed one of the great . . . ; There was no delay no hesitation . . . ;
       In the tropical night he steamed past . . . ; Steaming in with cool steadiness . . .
       (Works, Vol. 13, pp. 428–29).

243   Last year luck favored me in every way . . . (Letters, TR to M. Selmes, Jan. 17,
       1899).

243   First to get into the war then to . . . (Letters, TR to C. Spring-Rice, Nov. 25, 1898).

243   If I hadn't happened to return from the war . . . (Letters, TR to C. Wood, Oct. 23,
       1899).

243   I believed with all my heart in the war with Spain . . . (Letters, TR to J. Bryce,
       Nov. 25, 1898).

243   I am more than proud to be Governor . . . (Letters, TR to C. Spring-Rice, Nov. 25,
       1898).

243   I have just come back from a week in the West . . . (Letters, TR to HCL, Jul. 1, 1899).

244   I had a great time out West and was received . . . (Letters, TR to ARC, Jul. 6,
       1899).

244   Of course I should like to be . . . ; I have seen too many . . . (Letters, TR to W. Taft,
       Jul. 15, 1901).

244   I would not know how to organize . . . ; I have no Hanna . . . ; I have confined myself
       to trying . . . (Letters, TR to C. Wood, Oct. 23, 1899).

244   I received from the President a cordial . . . (Letters, TR to HCL, Jul. 21, 1899).

244 The President jollied me to his heart's content . . . (Letters, TR to ARC, Jul. 12, 1899).

244 I wish he had more backbone (Letters, TR to ARC, Jul. 6, 1899).

245 If now he will be true to his best side . . . (Letters, TR to F. Funston, Jul. 22, 1899).

245 There is a great growth of economic . . . (Letters, TR to C. Spring-Rice, Aug. 12, 1899).

245 The agitation against trusts . . . ; But when there . . . (Letters, TR to HCL, Aug. 10, 1899).

245 I have been doing my best during my term . . . (Letters, TR to F. Cunz, Oct. 30, 1899).

245 The anti-expansionists and lunatic goo-goo . . . (Letters, TR to HCL, Apr. 9, 1900).

245 I have no real community of principle or . . . (Letters, TR to M. Storer, Dec. 2, 1899).

246 My being in politics is in a sense an accident . . . (Letters, TR to ARC, Dec. 17, 1899).

246 I have found out one reason why Senator Platt . . . ; The big insurance companies . . . ; Want me out (Letters, TR to HCL, Feb. 3, 1900).

246 What a perfectly extraordinary . . . ; Of course among . . . (Letters, TR to HCL, Apr. 9, 1900).

246 As a fighting man as a man on the bridge . . . (Leary, p. 13).

246 Dewey made a fool of himself (Letters, TR to HCL, Apr. 9, 1900).

247 I was nominated for Vice President . . . (Letters, TR to C. Spring-Rice, Jul. 20, 1900).

247 I shall be glad to get a little in touch . . . (Letters, TR to W. Chanler, Jul. 26, 1900).

247 I am delighted to have been on the national . . . (Letters, TR to HCL, Nov. 9, 1900).

247 Well I hope Bryanism is dead . . . (Letters, TR to H. Von Sternberg, Nov. 19, 1900).

247 I was on the stump a little over nine . . . (Letters, TR to J. Curtin, Nov. 19, 1900).

248 The President who is a regular "jollier" . . . (Collection, TR to ARC, Sep. 27, 1897).

248 In a cold-blooded way has always rather . . . ; The President made up his mind that I was . . . ; I have really much less influence . . . (Letters, TR to B. Storer, Apr. 17, 1901).

249 On the 6th of September . . . ; Both President Lincoln and President . . . (Works, Vol. 15, p. 81).

249 This criminal was a professed anarchist (Works, Vol. 15, pp. 83–84).

249 The occasion chosen by the assassin . . . (Letters, TR to HCL, Sep. 9, 1901).

249 There is no baser deed in the annals of crime (Works, Vol. 15, p. 83).

249 Of course I feel as I always . . . ; I felt that the only course . . . (Letters, TR to HCL, Sep. 9, 1901).

250 It is a dreadful thing to come into the Presidency . . . (Letters, TR to HCL, Sep. 23, 1901).

250 On Tuesday evening I started on my western . . . ; I first met him when . . . ; The next year we both spoke . . . ; When he was running first against Bryan . . . (Letters, TR to K. Roosevelt, Jun. 1, 1907).

250 At his home in Canton anyone could see him . . . (Letters, TR to HCL, Sep. 9, 1901).

250 At that time the little city was jammed . . . (Letters, TR to K. Roosevelt, Jun. 1, 1907).

TWENTIETH CENTURY (1901–1918)

255 I have no right to the title of Excellency . . . (Papers, TR to F. Podmore, Mar. 4, 1904).

255 I would rather be called Colonel than . . . (Papers, TR to E. Knapp, Feb. 10, 1899).

255 My people have been for eight generations in America (Works, Vol. 12, p. 25).

255 I was born in New York . . . ; A Georgian descended . . . (Letters, TR to [unknown], May 1, 1884).

255 Was an unreconstructed rebel to . . . (Letters, TR to H. Munsterberg, Feb. 8, 1916).

255 I am a descendent of slaveholders . . . (Works, Vol. 12, p. 215).

255 Perhaps the very fact that I am half Southern and . . . (Works, Vol. 16, p. 173).

256 I have literally never spent an . . . (Letters, TR to M. Roosevelt, Oct. 29, 1876).

256 I have thoroughly enjoyed it all . . . (Letters, TR to C. Spring-Rice, Aug. 22, 1911).

256 There is a sentence in Ruskin of which . . . ; Were built not by architects whose . . . ; Who worked primarily because they gloried in . . . ("The Gospel of Intelligent Work," *Chautauquan*, October 1899).

256 More and more it seems to me that . . . (Letters, TR to W. Taft, Mar. 12, 1901).

256 I have known plenty of men who . . . (Letters, TR to C. Spring-Rice, Jul. 3, 1901).

256 I graduated at Harvard in 1880 . . . (Letters, TR to [unknown], May 1, 1884).

256 Prize fighting is brutal and degrading . . . (Papers, TR to A. Benedict, Mar. 28, 1899).

256 While at Harvard and for a year or two . . . (Letters, TR to W. Foulke, Jan. 4, 1907).

257 My whole career in politics is due to . . . (Letters, TR to E. Kinnicutt, Jun. 28, 1901).

257 As soon as I left college I wanted . . . ; So I joined the political club . . . (Works, Vol. 13, p. 564).

257 Went around there steadily took part . . . (Letters, TR to E. Kinnicutt, Jun. 28, 1901).

257 Immediately after leaving college . . . (Letters, TR to T. Roosevelt, Jr., Oct. 20, 1903).

257 I was elected to the Assembly from the . . . (Letters, TR to [unknown], May 1, 1884).

257 I was the youngest man . . . ; The result was that . . . (Letters, TR to T. Roosevelt Jr., Oct. 20, 1903).

258 Finding the work in Albany . . . ; A cattle ranch . . . (Letters, TR to J. Duzer, Nov. 20, 1883).

258 When I went out West I all the time . . . (Letters, TR to E. Kinnicutt, Jun. 28, 1901).

258 Many of my old friends with whom I . . . (Letters, TR to G. Trevelyan, Mar. 9, 1905).

258 Once I made a very successful hunting trip; It took sixteen days traveling . . . ; Look well in the "house on the hill" . . . (Letters, TR to ARC, Sep. 20, 1884).

258 My bears; Were killed close up and the . . . (Letters, TR to H. Needham, Jul. 19, 1905).

258 Buffalo Bill; Used to hunt bear and white . . . (Papers, TR to K. Roosevelt, Feb. 19, 1904).

258 I remember when I was running for . . . (Papers, TR to T. Roosevelt, Feb. 19, 1904).

258 I do not mean to bore you with; reminiscences (Letters, TR to F. Ranlett, Jun. 24, 1907).

259 In May 1895 I was made President of the newly . . . (Works, Vol. 13, p. 119).

259 One important bit of reform was abolishing the . . . (Works, Vol. 13, pp. 136–37).

259 I am the first Vice President . . . ; The Anthracite Coal . . . (Letters, TR to K. Roosevelt, Oct. 26, 1904).

259 I hope you will not think; Egotistical I can . . . (Letters, TR to E. Kinnicutt, Jun. 28, 1901).

259 By a combination of accidents . . . ; My own party machine would . . . (DeCoppet Collection, TR to B. Johnston, Nov. 6, 1899).

260 I so firmly believe that all other success . . . ; It is if I remember aright the last line . . . ; I have always felt an utter contempt . . . (Letters, TR to G. Lorimer, May 12, 1906).

260 Today as I was marching to church . . . (Letters, TR to E. Roosevelt, Jun. 24, 1906).

260 I am a college bred man belonging . . . (Letters, TR to G. Trevelyan, Mar. 9, 1905).

261 I do not see very much of the big-moneyed . . . (Letters, TR to C. Spring-Rice, Jul. 3, 1901).

261 I should selfishly prefer . . . ; Heaven forbid that . . . (Letters, TR to C. Spring-Rice, Apr. 11, 1908).

261 Fond as I am of the . . . ; Years in it there . . . (Papers, TR to E. Roosevelt, Jun. 11, 1906).

261 It is Sagamore that we love (Papers, TR to K. Roosevelt, Oct. 14, 1906).

261 It contains about a hundred acres . . . (Letters, TR to H. Whittemore, Jul. 6, 1901).

261 We are but an hour . . . ; It is a most sleepy . . . (Letters, TR to W. Foulke, Apr. 17, 1889).

261 We have a great big house . . . (Letters, TR to C. Spring-Rice, Feb. 14, 1899).

261 I never feel in the least embarrassed . . . (Papers, TR to W. Reid, Nov. 13, 1905).

261 This house has been my home for; Years it is the one . . . (*New York Times*, Oct. 9, 1898).

261 November; Always seems to me one . . . (Letters, TR to E. Roosevelt, Nov. 4, 1914).

262 I hunted the game whose heads are . . . (Letters, TR to G. Carow, Oct. 3, 1892).

262 Personally I only keep heads of my own shooting (Papers, TR to J. Albro, Mar. 1, 1899).

262 Heavens and Earth! I don't believe I shall . . . (Papers, TR to H. Haig, Mar. 30, 1899).

262 I should give a great deal to again . . . (Papers, TR to A. Weir, Mar. 28, 1899).

262 I thoroughly believe in large families . . . (Papers, TR to E. Ligon, Jun. 6, 1903).

262 Mrs. Roosevelt and I have six children (Papers, TR to C. Wagner, Jun. 13, 1904).

262 Quentin; Is the only one of my boys . . . (Papers, TR to E. Peabody, Sep. 24, 1906).

262 Then there is (Lodge Letters, Vol. 1, p. 23).

262 Archie a boy with a wooden . . . ; And; My eldest son Theodore . . . (Powell, p. 310).

262 I do not believe you . . . ; They love the . . . (Papers, TR to P. Selmes, Jun. 10, 1902).

262 The other night I took out . . . ; Yesterday on the . . . (Papers, TR to J. Burroughs, Jul. 19, 1907).

262 I am interested in birds and this spring . . . (Papers, TR to G. Trevelyan, Jun. 20, 1907).

262 Black-throated green warbler (Papers, TR to W. Miller, Jun. 21, 1907).

262 Breeding near the house which I (Papers, TR to G. Trevelyan, Jun. 20, 1907).

262 Last year was the first time I ever saw . . . (Papers, TR to W. Miller, Jun. 21, 1907).

262 Here at Oyster Bay my observations . . . ; Around my home here on Long Island; The robins wood thrushes catbirds meadowlarks . . . (Papers, TR to E. Forbush, Jul. 21, 1904).

263 I have a definite policy about the Presidency . . . (Lodge Letters, TR to HCL, Jul. 19, 1908).

263 In the great days of the Roman Republic . . . ; While President I have been President . . . ; Why in all these cases I have felt not . . . (Letters, TR to G. Trevelyan, Jun. 19, 1908).

263 I much prefer to really accomplish . . . (Letters, TR to F. Parkman, Jul. 13, 1889).

263 I had rather be a real . . . ; Than a figurehead (Letters, TR to G. Trevelyan, May 28, 1904).

264 I enjoy being President and I like . . . (Papers, TR to K. Roosevelt, Oct. 2, 1903).

264 It would be quite absurd . . . ; We should have never . . . ; Nobody but me . . . (Hale, pp. 143–44).

264 During my term as President I have . . . (Letters, TR to S. Brooks, Dec. 28, 1908).

264 The improvement in both army and navy . . . (Letters, TR to E. Hale, Oct. 27, 1906).

264 Arbitration is an excellent thing but ultimately . . . (Works, Vol. 13, p. 183).

264 Then take the Panama Canal . . . ; I think the peace at Portsmouth was a . . . ; I have succeeded in getting the . . . (Letters, TR to S. Brooks, Dec. 28, 1908).

264   In dealing with the . . . ; The jack fools who . . . (Papers, TR to R. Kipling, Nov. 1, 1904).

265   I have trebled or quadrupled the . . . (Letters, TR to S. Brooks, Dec. 28, 1908).

265   I will do everything in my power to protect . . . (Letters, TR to J. Muir, Sep. 16, 1907).

265   Then take the (Letters, TR to S. Brooks, Dec. 28, 1908).

265   Settlement of the Anthracite Coal Strike . . . ; If the strike had not been settled . . . ; The strike certainly would not have been . . . (Letters, TR to L. Abbott, Sep. 5, 1903).

265   Traveling through Europe last year I was impressed . . . (Works, Vol. 13, p. 600).

265   I am the only man in public life whom the Europeans . . . (Powell, p. 319).

266   I have had a most . . . ; The entire fool . . . (Letters, TR to T. Roosevelt Jr., Nov. 15, 1903).

266   On the score of morality it seems . . . (Letters, TR to O. Gresham, Nov. 30, 1903).

266   I have to encounter the opposition of the . . . (Papers, TR to R. Kipling, Nov. 1, 1904).

266   To my mind this building of the canal . . . (Letters, TR to S. Small, Dec. 29, 1903).

266   The building of this canal has been . . . (Letters, TR to G. Harvey, Dec. 19, 1903).

266   We wanted Panama I took it (Rhodes Papers, Dinner Book, Dec. 1, 1911).

266   I did not foment the . . . ; It is idle folly . . . (Letters, TR to A. Shaw, Nov. 6, 1903).

266   Panama revolted from Colombia because . . . ; The case in a nutshell is this . . . ; Yet; The government refused to ratify this treaty (Letters, TR to O. Gresham, Nov. 30, 1903).

267   I do not think that the Bogota lot of jack rabbits . . . (Letters, TR to J. Hay, Aug. 19, 1903).

267   We have been more . . . ; They have received . . . (Letters, TR to O. Gresham, Nov. 30, 1903).

267   One of the serious problems with which . . . (Letters, TR to E. Wolcott, Sep. 15, 1900).

267   I myself believe very strongly in both the State . . . (Letters, TR to W. Taft, Jul. 15, 1901).

267   During the past quarter of . . . ; The Sherman Anti-trust . . . (Works, Vol. 12, p. 236).

268   Attorney General Knox . . . ; Knox is in my . . . (Letters, TR to F. Goddard, Aug. 14, 1902).

268   On the advice of Knox I directed the . . . (Letters, TR to L. Abbott, Sep. 5, 1903).

268   One of the great achievements of . . . (Letters, TR to G. Cortelyou, Aug. 11, 1904).

268   It is difficult for me . . . ; Why there should . . . (Letters, TR to J. Schiff, Mar. 25, 1907).

268   Bryan has always been far more violent . . . (Letters, TR to L. Abbott, Jul. 1, 1906).

268   To me speech is of value only in so . . . (Papers, TR to A. Thurman, Dec. 8, 1906).

268   I am genuinely independent of the big-moneyed . . . (Letters, TR to HCL, Sep. 27, 1902).

268   I am very keenly aware that there . . . (Letters, TR to H. Stimson, Feb. 5, 1912).

268   My most violent critics if they had . . . (Papers, TR to L. Whitney, Aug. 17, 1907).

268   I have a real horror of Hearst . . . (Papers, TR to E. McGaffey, Apr. 17, 1907).

269   To reform real abuses is the best way . . . (Letters, TR to T. Roosevelt, Jr., Nov. 20, 1908).

269   The entire movement into which I . . . (Papers, TR to S. Church, Aug. 14, 1907).

269   Our aim must be the supremacy of justice . . . (Papers, TR to G. Cushing, Feb. 27, 1908).

269   Much can be done by taxation (Letters, TR to E. Wolcott, Sep. 15, 1900).

269   The Constitutional Amendment about the income . . . ; Would be far preferable to a . . . (Letters, TR to HCL, Sep. 10, 1909).

269   I would not apply the Inheritance Tax . . . (Letters, TR to R. Robins, Aug. 12, 1914).

269   The really large fortunes; Are needless and . . . (Papers, TR to J. Riis, Apr. 18, 1906).

269   The great bulk of my social friends . . . (Letters, TR to M. Stimson, Oct. 27, 1911).

269   The question of taxation . . . ; The National Government . . . (Works, Vol. 15, p. 368).

270   As the law now . . . ; The question is . . . ; The hesitation evidently . . . (Works, Vol. 15, p. 371).

270   While I have been a government officer . . . (Letters, TR to F. Turner, Apr. 10, 1895).

270   I have always kept a cartoon that . . . (Letters, TR to C. Willard, Apr. 28, 1911).

270   I am in my own way a radical Democrat . . . ; A well-defined opinion was growing up . . . ; I thoroughly broke up this connection so far . . . (Letters, TR to C. Spring-Rice, Dec. 27, 1904).

270   Personally I think that while I was in . . . (Letters, TR to W. Dodd, Feb. 13, 1912).

270   The Republican Party does not belong . . . (Papers, TR to J. Sleicher, Feb. 28, 1906).

271   I do not say that the people are infallible . . . (Works, Vol. 17, p. 142).

271   I'm a Mason myself . . . ; It would be quite natural for him . . . (Powell, p. 318).

271   The Pure Food Law; Was one of the achievements . . . (Works, Vol. 13, p. 670).

272   On the appearance of Mr. Sinclair's . . . (Papers, TR to F. Doubleday, Mar. 22, 1906).

272   Sinclair the socialist; Portrays the results . . . (Letters, TR to O. Wister, Apr. 27, 1906).

272   I have an utter contempt for him . . . (Letters, TR to W. White, Jul. 31, 1906).

272   In Rome my first experience . . . ; And had been preparing . . . ; Merry Del Val stated . . . ; I responded that . . . ; Then responded that . . . ; Accordingly I was not . . . (Letters, TR to G. Trevelyan, Oct. 1, 1911).

273   The different sects of Christians instead . . . (Papers, TR to E. O'Brien, Jun. 7, 1907).

274   While Police Commissioner of New York . . . (Letters, TR to M. Smith, Mar. 24, 1915).

274   In May 1895 (Works, Vol. 13, p. 119).

274   When Rector Alward came over here to . . . (Letters, TR to G. Aiton, May 15, 1901).

274   In my Cabinet at the present moment there . . . (Letters, TR to J. Martin, Nov. 6, 1908).

274   Do you know Booker Washington? . . . (Letters, TR to W. Lewis, Jul. 26, 1900).

274   I am sorry to say that the idiot or vicious . . . (Letters, TR to C. Guild, Oct. 28, 1901).

274   I would not lose my self-respect by . . . (Letters, TR to L. Littauer, Oct. 24, 1901).

275   I have not been able to think out any . . . (Letters, TR to A. Tourgee, Nov. 8, 1901).

275   The path of the race upward will . . . (Letters, TR to W. Lewis, Jul. 26, 1900).

275   The problem is insoluble in the sense . . . (Letters, TR to N. Butler, Feb. 4, 1902).

275   The one hope of . . . ; I have stood as . . . (Letters, TR to L. Abbott, May 10, 1908).

275   I am the first President . . . ; I could not give . . . (Letters, TR to L. Abbott, Oct. 6, 1908).

275   As a matter of fact in the Southern . . . (Letters, TR to C. Schurz, Dec. 24, 1903).

275   When I asked Booker T. Washington . . . (Letters, TR to A. Tourgee, Nov. 8, 1901).

276   It is not hyperbole to say that Booker T. Washington . . . (Works, Vol. 11, p. 273).

276   A genius such as does not arise . . . (Letters, TR to J. Rosenwald, Dec. 15, 1915).

276   Eminent though his services . . . ; The indirect indebtedness . . . (Works, Vol. 11, p. 273).

276   Our only safe motto is "All men up" . . . (Letters, TR to J. Harris, Aug. 1, 1912).

276   The man who makes a substantial contribution . . . (Works, Vol. 11, pp. 273–74).

277   I am devoted to Senator . . . ; There were matters . . . (Letters, TR to M. Hinsdale, Nov. 27, 1911).

277   The qualities that make Cabot invaluable . . . (Letters, TR to ARC, Apr. 30, 1900).

277   He has had an astonishing career and (Letters, TR to ARC, Jun. 28, 1896).

277   I know Massachusetts politics well . . . ; During the; Years he has been in Washington . . . ; Lodge is a man of very strong convictions . . . (Letters, TR to L. Abbott, Feb. 23, 1906).

278   Whatever his faults may . . . ; He is alright . . . (Collection, TR to B. Johnson, Mar. 14, 1894).

278   I have discussed almost every move I have . . . (Lodge Letters, Vol. 1, p. 25).

278   The most loyal friend that ever breathed (Letters, TR to HCL, Mar. 25, 1889).

278   The dear old goose (Letters, TR to ARC, Apr. 30, 1900).

278   Would do anything possible for me (Letters, TR to C. Wood, Oct. 23, 1899).

278   During the year preceding the outbreak of the . . . (Works, Vol. 11, p. 3).

278   It was Lodge who engineered it . . . (Letters, TR to H. White, Apr. 16, 1897).

278   I was even more pleased . . . ; It was Cabot's . . . (Letters, TR to ARC, Apr. 11, 1897).

278   Some persons were foolish enough to think we would . . . (Leary, p. 91).

278 He is not only the staunchest friend . . . (Collection, TR to ARC, Jan. 23, 1899).

279 John Hay (Letters, TR to HCL, Jan. 28, 1909).

279 Was my father's friend I dearly loved him (Letters, TR to C. Hay, Jul. 1, 1905).

279 Hay's death is to me a severe loss . . . (Letters, TR to G. Meyer, Jul. 7, 1905).

279 His name his reputation his staunch loyalty . . . (Letters, TR to HCL, Jul. 11, 1905).

279 Hay was a man of remarkable ability . . . ; His dignity his remarkable literary . . . ; He was at his best at a dinner table . . . ; In the Department of State . . . (Letters, TR to HCL, Jan. 28, 1909).

280 As an Executive he was a . . . (Butt Papers, letter to Clara Butt, Jan. 23, 1909).

280 I have been reading the letters of John Hay . . . (Letters, TR to HCL, Jan. 28, 1909).

280 The only ones which are of . . . (Butt Papers, letter to Clara Butt, Jan. 23, 1909).

280 It is distressing to read the letters . . . ; It is pathetic to read Hay's . . . ; It is curious also to read what Hay . . . ; The fact was that Hay . . . : Shows this he had . . . (Letters, TR to HCL, Jan. 28, 1909).

282 Some foolish people would think I was . . . (Letters, TR to E. Root, Jan. 26, 1909).

282 Root (Letters, TR to M. Storer, Oct. 4, 1901).

282 Will be regarded as the greatest and . . . (Letters, TR to E. Root, Jan. 26, 1909).

282 Root is I think the biggest cabinet . . . (Letters, TR to T. Roosevelt, Jr., Mar. 1, 1903).

282 While I do not agree with his views on . . . (Letters, TR to F. Goddard, Aug. 14, 1902).

282 I believe Root would make a most . . . (Letters, TR to W. Taft, Jul. 15, 1901).

282 Root is one of the . . . ; His advice is . . . (Letters, TR to M. Storer, Oct. 4, 1901).

282 It is because Root . . . ; Sometimes I would . . . ; John Hay had no . . . (Leary, pp. 217–18).

283 Root was the greatest corporation lawyer . . . (Letters, TR to W. Taft, Aug. 7, 1908).

283 At the time when Root came down here . . . (Letters, TR to S. Low, Jan. 13, 1903).

283 I have always said there were; Men to whom I owed more than to any; Others during the time I was President . . . (Letters, TR to W. Moody, May 18, 1916).

284 You must remember about Root that the . . . (Letters, TR to HCL, Dec. 7, 1915).

284 Elihu Root; Shared Taft's guilt; Indeed if there must be . . . (Letters, TR to H. Stoddard, Sep. 28, 1916).

284 I feel very strongly against Root . . . (Letters, TR to W. Chanler, Apr. 1, 1913).

285 I am continually . . . ; Moreover usually entirely . . . (Letters, TR to W. Moody, Sep. 21, 1907).

285 If Andrew Carnegie had employed . . . (Letters, TR to C. Spring-Rice, Aug. 22, 1911).

285 I have tried hard to like Carnegie . . . ; During the time that Carnegie . . . ; I have no respect for the business man . . . ; It is as noxious folly . . . (Papers, TR to W. Reid, Nov. 13, 1905).

287 It is a little difficult for me to give you . . . (Letters, TR to J. Strachey, Oct. 25, 1906).

287 I have been tempted at times . . . (Papers, TR to W. McCloy, Mar. 22, 1899).

287 That leprous spot upon our civilization (Papers, TR to H. Otis, Aug. 5, 1903).

287 Hearst's (Papers, TR to R. Gilder, Feb. 7, 1903).

287 *New York Journal* (Papers, TR to H. Otis, Aug. 5, 1903).

287 By way of a heavy libel suit . . . (Papers, TR to W. McCloy, Mar. 22, 1899).

287 Hearst's private life . . . ; Hearst has edited . . . (Letters, TR to J. Strachey, Oct. 25, 1906).

288 I disapprove of the whitewash . . . (Papers, TR to R. Baker, Apr. 9, 1906).

288 He will never attack . . . ; If the circumstances . . . (Letters, TR to J. Strachey, Oct. 25, 1906).

288 There is, I believe, literally nothing at which . . . (Letters, TR to E. Root, Sep. 4, 1906).

288 He is the most potent single influence . . . (Letters, TR to J. Strachey, Oct. 25, 1906).

288 I certainly feel that neither Tweed . . . (Papers, TR to R. Gilder, Oct. 31, 1906).

289 Judge Gray has been one of the most . . . (Letters, TR to HCL, Jul. 10, 1902).

289 I want on the bench a follower of Hamilton . . . (Letters, TR to HCL, Sep. 12, 1906).

289 Judge Holmes' whole mental attitude . . . (Letters, TR to HCL, Jul. 10, 1902).

289 After much careful thought I have . . . (Letters, TR to G. Hoar, Jul. 25, 1902).

289 Judge Holmes; Was shot three . . . (Letters, TR to T. Roosevelt, Jr., Mar. 1, 1903).

289 The labor decisions . . . ; I think it eminently . . . (Letters, TR to HCL, Jul. 10, 1902).

290 I appreciate as every thoughtful man must . . . (Letters, TR to W. Taft, Mar. 15, 1906).

290 It seems to me that the head of . . . (Letters, TR to B. Wheeler, Dec. 12, 1901).

290 In my own time . . . ; Some of these . . . (Letters, TR to H. Stimson, Feb. 5, 1912).

290 Holmes should have been an ideal man . . . (Letters, TR to HCL, Sep. 4, 1906).

291 I could carve out of a banana a judge with . . . (Harbaugh, p. 162).

291 I am not prepared to say what if anything . . . (Letters, TR to H. Stimson, Feb. 5, 1912).

292 Have you ever seen Debs' paper . . . ; Debs' paper and speeches . . . ; We have not kept it out . . . ; To praise and champion . . . ; The well-meaning or . . . (Letters, TR to L. Abbott, Jun. 17, 1908).

292 I have felt that the growth of the . . . (Papers, TR to C. Gettemy, Feb. 1, 1905).

292 The Debs type of socialist points the way . . . ; You may notice; That the socialists and anarchists although . . . (Letters, TR to L. Abbott, Jun. 17, 1908).

293 An anarchist or socialist paper; Published; The statement; That as Police Commissioner I invented spiked . . . (Papers, TR to H. Brown, Jun. 3, 1904).

293 We can just as little afford . . . ; For instance when people live . . . ; Have to be considered from a common . . . ; Much of the discussion about . . . (Works, Vol. 13, p. 520).

293   To say that the thriftless the lazy the vicious . . . (Works, Vol. 13, p. 522).

293   I never will accept the ultra-socialistic . . . (Letters, TR to R. Robins, Aug. 12, 1914).

293   The most cruel form of injustice that can be devised . . . (Works, Vol. 16, p. 91).

293   The Roman mob living on the bread . . . ("Socialism," *Outlook*, Mar. 20, 1909).

294   The socialism that nominated Debs is . . . (Letters, TR to M. Egan, Aug. 5, 1908).

294   I am a near-socialist! that is I want . . . (Letters, TR to R. Kauffman, Aug. 26, 1915).

294   Constructive change offers . . . ; Reform is the . . . ; Social reform is . . . (Works, Vol. 16, p. 17).

295   I am; A believer in the fact that it is for . . . (Letters, TR to F. Selous, Feb. 7, 1900).

295   The spread of the little . . . ; It is perhaps the greatest . . . (Letters, TR to E. Capen, Jul. 3, 1901).

295   Our two peoples are the only really great . . . (Letters, TR to A. Lee, Jul. 25, 1900).

295   In my autobiography . . . ; The gift I . . . ; It seemed to . . . (Letters, TR to T. H. Warren, Jun. 7, 1916).

296   Though an American with . . . (Collection, *Market World*, April 1908, p. 5).

296   I am tempted to tell a little story . . . (Collection, *Market World*, April 1908, p. 10).

296   To us the charm of London lies . . . (Collection, *Market World*, April 1908, p. 7).

296   I saw the Englishman Winston Churchill . . . (Letters, TR to H. Sternberg, Jul. 12, 1901).

296   I have been over Winston Churchill's life . . . (Letters, TR to HCL, Sep. 12, 1906).

297   Winston Churchill is a . . . ; But his book . . . (Papers, TR to W. Reid, Oct. 19, 1906).

297   It was decades before we got over . . . (Letters, TR to A. Lee, Aug. 22, 1914).

297   In 1898 England was our really effective . . . (Letters, TR to R. Kipling, Nov. 30, 1918).

297   A couple of centuries hence we may all . . . (Letters, TR to J. Matthews, Dec. 6, 1895).

297   A man who has grappled or is grappling . . . (Letters, TR to J. Morley, Jan. 17, 1904).

297   It was a good thing for Egypt and . . . (Letters, TR to C. Spring-Rice, Jan. 18, 1904).

297   I believe in the expansion of great . . . (Letters, TR to C. Spring-Rice, Dec. 2, 1899).

297   The South African business makes me . . . (Letters, TR to ARC, Dec. 17, 1899).

297   I was greatly concerned over the death of . . . (Papers, TR to E. Grey, Apr. 1, 1902).

297   I wish I could have met Rhodes . . . (Papers, TR to E. Grey, Apr. 7, 1902).

297   I am an optimist but there are a grave signs . . . (Letters, TR to ARC, Dec. 17, 1899).

297 I am a firm believer that the future . . . (Letters, TR to F. Parkman, May 22, 1892).

298 I believe that this Republic will endure . . . (Letters, TR to J. Martin, Nov. 6, 1908).

298 I think that Russia has an enormous . . . (Letters, TR to C. Spring-Rice, Mar. 16, 1901).

298 Undoubtedly the future is hers unless she . . . (Letters, TR to G. Becker, Jul. 8, 1901).

298 Sometimes I do feel . . . ; Of course both . . . (Letters, TR to C. Spring-Rice, Aug. 13, 1897).

298 The English-speaking race shares with the . . . (Letters, TR to G. Becker, Jul. 8, 1901).

298 I suppose that what I am about . . . (Letters, TR to C. Spring-Rice, Jan. 2, 1900).

298 Russia's day is . . . ; The growth of . . . (Letters, TR to C. Spring-Rice, Mar. 16, 1901).

298 The Russians offer a very much . . . ; the Russians (Letters, TR to C. Spring-Rice, Aug. 13, 1897).

298 Strike me as corrupt tricky and . . . (Papers, TR to L. Grissom, Jul. 17, 1905).

298 They think they should be looked upon; As huge powerful barbarians . . . ; The Russian started far behind . . . (Letters, TR to C. Spring-Rice, Aug. 13, 1897).

299 All other nations of European blood . . . (Letters, TR to J. Hay, Aug. 9, 1903).

299 If Russia chooses . . . ; She will sometime . . . (Letters, TR to C. Spring-Rice, Aug. 13, 1897).

299 I am certain that there is an immense . . . (Letters, TR to C. Spring-Rice, Jan. 18, 1904).

299 Japan's growth and change during the last half . . . (Works, Vol. 12, p. 70).

299 This strange alien civilization; Is a very high civilization just as . . . ; Depicted by Aeschylus (Papers, TR to G. La Farge, Feb. 11, 1905).

299 I suppose we are all of us wondering . . . (Papers, TR to I. Hamilton, May 8, 1908).

299 The Japs have made a great name for . . . (Papers, TR to R. Davis, Jun. 29, 1904).

299 You have doubtless seen the trouble . . . ; Under the lead of the trade unions . . . ; They may possibly bring about war . . . (Letters, TR to E. Hale, Oct. 27, 1906).

300 The peril is greater than our people have been permitted . . . (Powell, p. 318).

300 No one dreads . . . ; The little that I have . . . (Butt Papers, letter to his mother, Jul. 29, 1908).

300 The Philippines form our heel of Achilles (Letters, TR to W. Taft, Aug. 21, 1907).

300 The security of the throne will depend upon . . . ; When it comes we will win over Japan but . . . (Butt Papers, letter to his mother, Jul. 29, 1908).

301 It is very difficult to make this . . . (Letters, TR to H. Von Sternberg, Jan. 17, 1898).

301 The history of all wars up to and including . . . ; I have urged as strongly as I know . . . (Letters, TR to G. Foss, Feb. 18, 1909).

301 It seems to me that the determining . . . (Letters, TR to C. Goodrich, Jun. 16, 1897).

302 Taft is President and the tradition . . . (Letters, TR to T. Roosevelt, Jr., Nov. 11, 1910).

302 I do not believe he has been a bad . . . (Letters, TR to A. Lee, Sep. 16, 1910).

302 Taft in this respect has not gone wrong . . . (Letters, TR to H. Johnson, Oct. 27, 1911).

302 I feel only a real sadness that the man . . . (Letters, TR to A. Wilson, Feb. 14, 1912).

302 I have never been so bitterly . . . (Letters, TR to A. Carnegie, Mar. 5, 1912).

302 The break in our relations was due . . . ; By inauguration time however Mr. Taft . . . ; That was the first bit of friction . . . (Leary, pp. 25–26).

303 Taft; Takes his color so completely from . . . (Letters, TR to A. Lee, Sep. 16, 1910).

303 I never realized at the time . . . (Rhodes Papers, R. Grant to J. Rhodes, Feb. 12, 1919).

303 As was probably inevitable . . . (Letters, TR to C. Spring-Rice, Aug. 22, 1911).

303 Everything I said of Taft as a member . . . (Letters, TR to A. Carnegie, Mar. 5, 1912).

303 Taft was nominated solely . . . ; There is only a . . . (Letters, TR to HCL, Apr. 11, 1910).

303 What do I owe to Taft? . . . (Rhodes Papers, R. Grant to J. Rhodes, Mar. 22, 1912).

303 That Mr. Taft should . . . ; Is of very little . . . (Letters, TR to A. Carnegie, Mar. 5, 1912).

304 In office his militancy evaporated and he at once . . . (Leary, p. 26).

304 He is a flubdub with a streak . . . (Letters, TR to T. Roosevelt, Jr., Aug. 22, 1911).

304 It was very bitter for me to see the . . . (Papers, TR to H. Lucy, Dec. 18, 1912).

304 In my campaign for the Republican . . . (Papers, TR to E. Thuring, Jul. 16, 1912).

304 The convention that nominated Mr. Taft . . . (Papers, TR to L. Keller, Jun. 26, 1912).

304 I cannot consent . . . ; I was the choice of . . . (Letters, TR to E. Valkenburg, Jul. 16, 1912).

304 Mr. Taft has stolen the nomination at Chicago . . . (Papers, TR to L. Keller, Jun. 26, 1912).

304 The Republican Party had become . . . ; Defeated the attempt (Letters, TR to A. Lee, Aug. 14, 1912).

304 Just one word about . . . ; He had quite enough . . . (Letters, TR to J. Strachey, Dec. 16, 1912).

305 I was in the automobile when this fellow shot me . . . (Leary, p. 31).

305 The bullet passed through the manuscript . . . ; As I was standing unsteadily I half fell . . . ; There was then a perfectly . . . (Letters, TR to E. Grey, Nov. 15, 1912).

305 I went through with my . . . ; But it was somewhat difficult (Leary, p. 31).

305 After the bullet I had no real pain . . . (Letters, TR to W. Bigelow, Feb. 5, 1913).

305 I did not care a rap for being shot . . . (Letters, TR to C. Spring-Rice, Dec. 31, 1912).

306 The bullet you know was never removed . . . (Leary, p. 31).

306 I carry the Milwaukee bullet in me . . . (Papers, TR to B. Daniels, Nov. 30, 1914).

306 The fellow who shot me; The doctors found him to be insane . . . (Leary, p. 30).

306 The Progressive Party today stands precisely . . . (Papers, TR to A. Tracy, Jan. 23, 1913).

306 Personally I feel that what we did was . . . (Papers, TR to W. White, Nov. 7, 1914).

306 Of course I feel badly . . . ; As soon as the . . . (Papers, TR to A. Hill, Nov. 9, 1914).

306 The average American . . . ; When he goes with . . . (Papers, TR to W. White, Nov. 7, 1914).

307 This was not the young Republican Party . . . (Papers, TR to A. Hill, Nov. 9, 1914).

307 Thank the Lord poor Taft is out of the . . . (Collection, TR to J. Bishop, Mar. 11, 1913).

307 Taft showed himself a plain fool . . . (Collection, TR to J. Bishop, Feb. 10, 1913).

308 My own view is that if Wilson behaves . . . (Letters, TR to H. White, Nov. 12, 1912).

308 Wilson is a good man who has . . . ; Then he ran as Governor of New Jersey . . . ; He is an able man and I have no doubt . . . (Letters, TR to H. Plunkett, Aug. 3, 1912).

309 Wilson was from their . . . ; An adroit man . . . (Letters, TR to H. Johnson, Jan. 28, 1913).

309 It was from the outset exceedingly . . . (Letters, TR to W. White, Nov. 7, 1914).

310 I have always regarded Germany . . . (Letters, TR to C. Spring-Rice, Jan. 2, 1900).

310 There is much that I admire about . . . (Letters, TR to C. Spring-Rice, May 13, 1905).

310 I don't know that I should be sorry . . . (Letters, TR to C. Spring-Rice, Apr. 14, 1889).

311 The whole question of peace and war . . . (Letters, TR to A. Lee, Aug. 1, 1914).

311 Bryan is I really believe . . . ; He has the nerve . . . (Letters, TR to HCL, Sep. 9, 1913).

311 I regard the Wilson-Bryan . . . ; A milk-and-water . . . (Letters, TR to H. Munsterberg, Oct. 3, 1914).

312 The Germans have believed in force . . . (Papers, TR to R. Newton, Oct. 2, 1914).

312 More and more I come to the view . . . (Letters, TR to J. Strachey, Feb. 22, 1915).

312 I am utterly sick of the spiritless "neutrality" . . . (Letters, TR to E. Derby, Nov. 4, 1914).

312 The most depressing feature of the present . . . (Papers, TR to A. Baird, Sep. 1, 1915).

312 To me the crux of the situation has been . . . (Letters, TR to E. Grey, Jan. 22, 1915).

312 If I had been President I should . . . ; As head of a signatory . . . ; I believe that if I had been . . . ; They tend and ought to tend . . . (Letters, TR to C. Spring-Rice, Oct. 3, 1914).

312 In its essence . . . ; Are not even to be . . . (Letters, TR to J. Bryce, Mar. 31, 1915).

312 It is not merely ridiculous it is wicked . . . (Letters, TR to A. White, Nov. 2, 1914).

313 I do not believe that this Administration . . . (Letters, TR to L. Warner, Jul. 2, 1915).

313 As for the Lusitania matter failure to act . . . (Bishop, Vol. 2, p. 390).

313 The hideous thing . . . ; Largely achieved his . . . (Lodge Letters, TR to HCL, Jun. 15, 1915).

313 When the *Lusitania* . . . ; Leaders went into . . . (Letters, TR to R. Kipling, Nov. 30, 1918).

313 For Heaven's sake . . . ; He hasn't a touch . . . (Letters, TR to O. Reid, Jan. 1, 1919).

314 President Wilson; Has rendered to this . . . (Letters, TR to W. Jackson, Jun. 8, 1916).

314 Nothing is more sickening than the continual praise . . . (Bishop, Vol. 2, p. 386).

314 If anyone kicks him he brushes his . . . (Letters, TR to H. Johnson, Feb. 17, 1917).

314 There were ten or twelve years . . . ; The kaleidoscope has been shaken . . . ; I am in fundamental sympathy with . . . (Papers, TR to R. Kipling, Oct. 3, 1914).

314 The unhung traitor Keir Hardie. . . . (Letters, TR to A.H. Lee, Sep. 4, 1914).

314 They swarm like maggots . . . (Papers, TR to R. Kipling, Oct. 3, 1914).

314 I think the American people feel a little . . . (Letters, TR to W. White, Dec. 12, 1910).

314 I have spoken out as strongly and . . . (Letters, TR to A. Lee, Jun. 17, 1915).

315 Wilson and Bryan are cordially supported . . . (Letters, TR to A. Roosevelt, May 19, 1915).

315 The antics of the . . . ; This country has . . . (Letters, TR to A. Lee, Jun. 17, 1915).

315 I am of course utterly heartsick . . . (Letters, TR to F. Oliver, Jul. 22, 1915).

315 Mr. Wilson's conduct in international . . . (Letters, TR to G. Perkins, Apr. 6, 1916).

315 As a nation we have thought very little . . . (Letters, TR to A. Roosevelt, May 19, 1915).

315 The proper thing to do is to protest . . . (Letters, TR to A. White, Nov. 2, 1914).

315 Wilson is the heir of Jefferson and Buchanan (Letters, TR to F. Oliver, Jul. 22, 1915).

315 To leave Wilson alone in the face of . . . (Lodge Letters, TR to HCL, Feb. 28, 1917).

316 I think that Wilson has been the very worst . . . (Papers, TR to H. Doe, Dec. 12, 1914).

316 The old proverb applies: there are (Letters, TR to K. Roosevelt, Aug. 28, 1915).

316 How I wish I were President at this moment! (Bishop, Vol. 2, p. 392).

316 This is one of those rare times which come along . . . (Bishop, Vol. 2, p. 405).

316 Wilson (Letters, TR to F. Oliver, Jul. 22, 1915).

316 Carried Kansas and . . . ; Wilson did not come . . . (Letters, TR to W. White, May 28, 1917).

317 What is perfectly impossible what represents . . . (Letters, TR to W. White, Aug. 3, 1917).

317 If we are all fighting for Democracy . . . (Letters, TR to W. White, May 28, 1917).

317   He believes that whatever . . . (Letters, TR to C. Spring-Rice, Nov. 11, 1914).

317   The wooden-headed fools have been . . . (Letters, TR to R. Bass, Jul. 28, 1916).

317   When the war first broke out I did not . . . (Letters, TR to A. Lee, Nov. 19, 1918).

318   I have been inexpressibly saddened . . . (Letters, TR to A. Apponyi, Sep. 17, 1914).

318   Of my four boys Quentin; Has been killed (Letters, TR to G. Clemenceau, Jul. 25, 1918).

318   There is no use of my writing about Quentin . . . (Bishop, Vol. 2, p. 455).

318   To feel that one has inspired a boy . . . (Letters, TR to M. Brown, Jul. 26, 1918).

318   We are profoundly moved . . . ; Have marked his grave . . . (Bishop, Vol. 2, p. 457).

318   It is a very sad thing to see the . . . (Letters, TR to G. Clemenceau, Jul. 25, 1918).

INDEX